"At present ~~a~~
general rela~~tio~~...
between the ~~...~~
species and the whole of the electromagnetic phenomenon that engages the Sun, other stars and the
galaxies." Dr. Robert Becker, State
University of New York, from a report at an MIT conference on magnetism in 1961.

Astrology is the most ancient of sciences, present from
the beginning of man's recorded history. With the dawn
of modern science it fell into disrepute; now the
scientists of the space age have rediscovered it, under
such names as "solaristics," "lunaristics," "electromagnetism."

This remarkable book offers convincing proof of the
validity of astrology. The author records authentic
testimony of scientists, economists, astronomists—of
people who have plotted their way to wealth by the use
of horoscopes, of the prediction of major historical
events such as the death of John F. Kennedy, of the
astonishing but proven phenomenon of the astral twin.

But most importantly, this leading astrological authority gives *you* all the information you need to write your
own specific horoscope, to read the message that is
clearly written in the stars about your character, talents,
potentials, and future.

Other SIGNET Mystics You Will Enjoy Reading

JOSEPH F. GOODAVAGE

WRITE YOUR OWN HOROSCOPE

A SIGNET MYSTIC BOOK from
NEW AMERICAN LIBRARY
TIMES MIRROR

Library of Congress Catalog Card Number: 68-18255

This is a reprint of a hardcover edition published by
The New American Library, Inc.
The hardcover edition was published simultaneously in Canada by
General Publishing Company, Ltd.

Sixth Printing

SIGNET TRADEMARK REG. U.S. PAT. OFF AND FOREIGN COUNTRIES
REGISTERED TRADEMARK—MARCA REGISTRADA
HECHO EN CHICAGO, U.S.A.

SIGNET MYSTIC BOOKS are published by
The New American Library, Inc.,
1301 Avenue of the Americas, New York, New York 10019

First Printing, November, 1968

PRINTED IN THE UNITED STATES OF AMERICA

For Maria and Danny

Acknowledgments

A book of this kind is a link in a long chain of discovery and knowledge that dates to dimmest antiquity. I owe a nod of thanks to all my colleagues, literary, astrological, and otherwise, for their generous contributions of time and help with research.

I wish to thank the editors of *True* magazine and Fawcett Publications for their kind permission to reprint large portions of my article in that magazine as the Introduction to this book. I also thank the editors of *Science & Mechanics* for their permission to use "How the Stars Influence Your Health" and "Interview with an Astro-Economist" as the basis for Chapters 14 and 15.

For their help and cooperation in the preparation of the manuscript, my thanks to my wife, Evelyn, and to Frances Jacoby.

To the American Federation of Astrologers and to Paul R. Grell, its executive director, I am grateful for the cooperation I have received each time I asked for it.

FOREWORD

"Astrology interested us, for it tied men to the system. Instead of an isolated beggar, the farthest star felt him and he felt the star. However rash and however falsified by pretenders and traders in it, the hint was true and divine, the soul's avowal of its large relations, and that climate, century, remote natures as well as near, are part of its biography. . . ."
                    Essay on Beauty—Ralph Waldo Emerson

Everything I have ever written on the subject of astrology has resulted in countless requests for personal horoscopes—or at least for the name and address of a competent, ethical (and usually inexpensive) astrologer. This book, hopefully, will answer every one of these needs and also provide a newly discovered scientific rationale for the oldest belief in history—that the planets and stars affect mankind: cycles of drought, famine, abundance, political supremacy, military dominance, earthquakes, hurricanes and volcanic eruptions.

Although we will touch on these important matters, the total, known effect of the surrounding cosmos on you, personally, is my chief concern in these pages. I have tried to make it as simple a process as humanly possible to set up a reasonably accurate horoscope and then to read it. In fact, you will be able to interpret almost any celestial chart with a fair degree of competence and confidence once you learn the symbols (and their meanings) of the planets and the zodiacal Signs. (A "Sign" is one of the 12 thirty-degree segments of the Zodiac in which the Sun, Moon and planets were located at your birth.) Essentially, this is almost all there is to astrology, although you'll be surprised at the subtlety of the variations as you go along. Take Venus, for example. If you were born with Venus in Sagittarius, you love variety; your freedom and independence are extremely important in your scheme of things, and yet you are somewhat ambiguous in

your affections. With Mars in the same freedom-loving, independent Sign, you are highly adventurous, often carefree
and bluntly candid in your sexual impulses. You are probably
also inclined toward sports and all kinds of outdoor activity.

Although there are only twelve Signs and ten (known)
planets in each horoscope—including the Sun and Moon,
which, for the sake of simplicity in calculations, astrologers
refer to as "planets" too—the differences in each chart are
so varied that very few horoscopes are exactly alike. In fact,
many identical twins do not have identical horoscopes. Twenty
minutes' difference in the time of birth can result in very
noticeable differences in character and personality. This applies chiefly to the Ascendant (i.e., the constellation that was
rising on the Eastern horizon at the time of your birth) and
the position of the Moon.

Still . . . most people, even when they're "sure" of the time
of their birth, are often mistaken by as much as four or five
hours. Astrologers continually make minor errors of interpretation and even prediction because a client says he was born
"at about three o'clock in the morning," when in fact it was
2:26 A.M. or even 3:30 A.M.

If the Ascendant is off by one Sign or even ten degrees of
celestial arc, it throws the entire chart off and you get a wrong
reading. However, I've taken this possibility into consideration;
the directions for setting up your chart here are broad enough
to give you a horoscope guaranteed to be *at least* 75 percent
accurate.

Those who are already familiar with the standard procedure
for setting up a horoscope will notice that I have omitted three
elements. This was done intentionally.

Most astrologers include the outermost planet, Pluto, in their
charts. Considering the fact that it takes Pluto about twenty-
five years to transit just one Sign, it stands to reason that *if*
this orbitally eccentric planet were close enough to have some
small effect on the Earth and its inhabitants, it would affect
an entire generation in exactly the same way.

Moreover, Pluto at perihelion (when closest to the Sun)
is 2,761,000,000 miles from our central star. At its most distant point from the Sun (aphelion), Pluto moves out to a
distance of 4,589,000,000 miles! Considering what is now
known of celestial dynamics, the solar wind, radiation, and
electromagnetic fields in outer space, it is highly unlikely that
Pluto has more than a negligible effect in our affairs. But again,
even if it does, astrologers and astronomers alike have known
of its existence for less than 40 years—not nearly long enough
to reach any definite conclusions about its influence.

Another element I've eliminated here is the North and South lunar nodes; that is, the points at which the Moon crosses the ecliptic each time the Moon revolves around the Earth. Since the ecliptic is simply the apparent path of the Earth around the Sun, the points of lunar intersection are the *nodes* of the Moon's orbit. Some astrologers claim that the house—also one of the 12 segments of the horoscope wheel—in which the North node falls is "fortunate," and therefore the *opposite* house unfortunate (i.e., the point of the South lunar node). Ten years of horoscopic study and (I hope) impartial evaluation have convinced me that the nodes of the Moon have no more effect on a human being than the nodes of any other planet (*all* of which cross the ecliptic and therefore have North and South nodes).

But astrologers do *not* use the nodes of any of the planets other than our Moon. I have copies of horoscopes dating back to the early Fifteenth Century; every one uses the North and South lunar nodes, and I think it is a serious error that has been copied right up to modern times. Every ephemeris (book of planetary tables) carries the Sign, degree and minute of celestial arc of every planet for every year, month and date. These planetary tables used by astrologers also carry the position of the Moon's North node. Every textbook I've ever read simply states that the South node is *exactly opposite* the North node, *which is a mistake*. The nodes move slowly westward around the Moon's orbit, i.e., backward to the Moon's own motion, so that each preceding node is 1½° West of the previous node.

Yet the rules state that if the North node is 15 degrees and 32 minutes in Gemini, the South node *must* be at 15 degrees and 32 minutes in the opposite Sign, Sagittarius. A difference of a degree and a half *could* place the South node in a different house, thus giving an entirely different reading, *if* the nodes actually had any influence.

It is vaguely possible that the recently discovered huge cloud of invisible cosmic dust or rubble, following 60 degrees behind the Moon in its orbit, might have a magnetic or gravitational effect on the Earth. But a constant 60 degrees is entirely different from the slowly changing nodes.

The third element I've omitted in an effort to clarify and modernize the horoscope is the mythical Part of Fortune, an ancient Arabic "part" which is roughly analogous to the "fortunate" North lunar node. The Part of Fortune is measured by adding the longitudinal distance between the Ascendant and the Sun and then subtracting the longitude of the Moon. I wrestled with this apparent superstition for about five years

before giving it up, and found that the elimination of the
Part of Fortune increased the accuracy of my horoscope interpretation.

Because many new facts are now being discovered about
our celestial environment and its effect on human beings, I
have also omitted some of the more advanced and complex
rules of astrology. One of these is the calculation of the parallels of declination of each planet as well as their right ascension (or celestial longitude). Every object in the heavens
can be located if its two coordinates of right ascension and
declination are known. Although it is not necessary for our
purposes here to have a thorough knowledge of exact astrological terms and their astronomical equivalents, a very helpful
book for every beginning astrologer is *1001 Questions An-
swered About Astronomy*, by James S. Pickering, former astronomer at the Hayden Planetarium (Grosset & Dunlap,
1958). I recommend it most highly.

You will find a few references here to "house cusps," i.e.,
the lines dividing the twelve segments of the horoscope. Although we're allowing a margin for error and therefore only
loosely using the cusps, the *Sign* on each cusp should be the
correct one even though we are not dealing with the exact
degree of each Sign. When an astronomer uses the term "cusp"
he is referring to the points at the ends of the lunar crescent;
these always point away from the Sun.

For the fair-minded skeptic, all I can suggest is some unbiased testing of the rules and statements made in the following pages. The scientific case for solar, lunar and planetary
influence is being rediscovered through numerous studies now
being carried on by the men and women largely responsible
for putting Earthmen on the Moon and planets. Each planet
not only has a completely different physical environment,
gravity, temperature, atmosphere, ecology, etc., it also must
have its own peculiar *astrology*. If you lived on Venus, the
influence of the Sun, Mercury and Earth would be radically
different than, say, on Mars.

It stands to reason, then, that astrology books of the future
will be entirely different from those of the past. New facts
and new knowledge will force the refinement and sharpening
of human understanding and ability to predict future events
with ever-increasing accuracy. To the best of my ability, I have
tried to make this a different kind of book on astrology—hopefully, one of the new, scientifically oriented kind of astrological
studies toward which our age seems to be heading. I have included this kind of information in appropriate places throughout the book.

At this writing, the most direct and uninvolved method of putting the whole question of astrology's validity into its proper scientific focus is the study of what I have called Time Twins or Astro Twins. These are unrelated people who share the same horoscope. According to the initial research I've done in this field, such people live parallel lives; they have illnesses, accidents and injuries at the same times. They also tend to marry at the same time, to have the same number of children of the same age and same sex. They purchase property at the same time and often live in similar locations; many times their wives' and husbands' first names are the same, and they are engaged in the same kind of work.

To me, this similarity was a startling discovery, and it has proved to be a subject of gripping interest to large numbers of people, including psychologists, and to universities and other institutions. Many students have written me for further information for their theme papers, and I've cooperated to the best of my ability. However, what is really needed is a large-scale coordinated study of the phenomenon.

An unprecedented astronomical event occurred on February 4th and 5th, 1962, when all the planets (except Uranus, Neptune and Pluto) moved into almost perfect alignment in the Sign of Aquarius. A handful of fanatical Hindu astrologers catapulted into the headlines of the world by predicting a global catastrophe. However, the more conservative, scientific astrologers in America and Europe predicted enormous scientific advancement and huge social upheavals. Inasmuch as the world is still reverberating with social protest and scientific discoveries, they've been proven right. The astrological press of that time will bear me out on this.

The least noticed of all the predictions concerned the children who were born at the time of the great conjunction-eclipse. I'm watching with keen interest the development of these bright and talented children. If you have such a child or know the parents of a boy or girl born between February 3rd and 6th, 1962, I'd be grateful to hear from you. (See *Astrology: The Space-Age Science,* Chapter One, Signet Books, The New American Library.)

Joseph F. Goodavage
New York, 1968

CONTENTS

WRITE YOUR OWN HOROSCOPE

INTRODUCTION

Surprising Revelations
from a Suspect Science

Most scientists still call astrology a fake, and charlatans still use it to gull the credible. But evidence from space indicates the stars do affect our weather and may guide our fortunes and our lives.

—*True* Magazine

Not so many years ago, any claim that forces from without our universe could affect human beings and their environment would have thrown astronomers and other scientists into an uproar. To accept such a thesis would have been to acknowledge a belief in astrology—and to orthodox science, believing in astrology was like believing in witchcraft.

Now, however, the climate of scientific opinion is changing and evidence is emerging which suggests that what goes on in the heavens may well have some cause and effect connection with all of us here on Earth. An increasing number of scientists are studying the relationship of stars and planets to man; they are seriously probing the claim that astrologers have knowledge with which to make accurate predictions of future events.

Many scientists are still reluctant to acknowledge their interest. One astronomer at a well-known observatory admits he knows how to read astrological tables and cast horoscopes, but he wants the fact kept quiet. "My professional life is at stake," he says. Yet despite such fears, more and more scientists are willing to speak out on the subject of astrology.

Dr. Ellsworth Huntington, a Yale University historian, has traced the correlation between movements of the planets and the recorded fates of several civilizations of the past.

Dr. Bryant Tuckerman, while at the Institute for Advanced Study at Princeton, New Jersey, made a study of early Babylonian astrological computations, checking them closely against history. Since the Babylonian astrologers included a variety of information in their tablets, including commodity prices, Doctor Tuckerman's study points out a basis for new research. Glenn T. Seaborg, chairman of the Atomic Energy Commission, has stated that the Tuckerman data could reveal vital information about modern economic cycles.

Dr. Harlan T. Stetson of the Massachusetts Institute of Technology told the New York Electrical Society some years ago, "If these (celestial-terrestrial) relationships are not pure coincidence . . . they may prove the beginning of two new sciences—solaristics and lunaristics—scientific versions of medieval astrology. By means of these it may be possible to predict the flux of business cycles and the coming of earthquakes, as well as other phenomena."

Whether astrology will evolve into a fully respectable science remains to be seen. At present it is a calling which attracts both charlatans and sincere practitioners. The latter carefully undertake to study the meaning of heavenly bodies and their movements in relation to man and his world. To cast a horoscope, the serious astrologer must know the *exact* time and place of the subject's birth, reconstructing from these facts the positions of the Sun and Moon and various constellations at that time. He then broods about his calculations for a time, computing, he would say, "the interrelationships of celestial forces." He ends up with a horoscope that "is as individual as a fingerprint," in the words of Paul R. Grell, executive secretary of the American Federation of Astrologers. Grell is a brisk, straightforward man who hates astrological fakery and theatrics. He believes that astrology is a reputable vocation.

Superstitious nonsense?

It has been "smart" to call astrology nonsense ever since the Industrial Revolution. "The stars and planets," snorts the noted astronomer, Harlow Shapley, "are too far away to have any effect upon living organisms, and that includes man."

But now, with the new look science is turning toward

astrology, experts are starting to consider some extensions of facts that have been known for ages. For example, among our celestial neighbors, the Sun influences us in ways we can see every day. The Moon's gravitational effects show up in the ocean's tides. Planets in their orbits pull us off course in our own journey around the Sun. Light reaching us from stars is a form of radiation—and not all of it is visible. (Several billion particles of energy from the cosmos have shot through your body since you started reading this.) All these influences can be detected either with the naked eye or with simple scientific instruments.

Genuine astrologers believe that these and other celestial influences must affect individual human lives; they just can't say how. But it isn't necessary to know a full cause-and-effect relationship in order to make an accurate forecast. It can be predicted that the weather will turn cold next winter, for instance, without knowing anything about the causes of seasonal temperature changes. This is a prediction based on observed facts. Thus it is with astrologers. "I can't tell you *why* a thousand people with a certain element in their horoscopes are different from a thousand people without that element," said one New York astrologer, "but when I see a horoscope with a certain element in it my experience tells me what it is going to mean about the individual concerned."

This astrologer has degrees in biology and botany. He first became interested in astrology when he decided to debunk it. He had trouble doing so. Predictions he expected to be wrong turned out, in fact, to be startlingly accurate. In the end, he left his government job and became a full-time astrologer in Manhattan, where he now serves a number of business and professional people.

Not all scientists have done as complete a turnabout. But even those who are otherwise skeptical about astrology concede that celestial forces influence our weather. RCA Communications, Inc., which operates the biggest long-distance radio communications network in the world, employs John H. Nelson, a radio-weather forecaster, to predict atmospheric disturbances. He bases his predictions on the way the planets line up in the sky: certain line-ups mean certain kinds of weather. Forecasting months in advance, Nelson is right 93 percent of the time. Nelson doesn't know what *forces* from the planets affect the Earth's weather. All he can do is point to his record of accuracy in warning of magnetic storms and disturbed radio communications.

Your record of accuracy in delineating your own (as well

as anyone else's) character, personality, talent and abilities
will be enormously increased by applying the simple rules
outlined in this book. There is nothing at all mystical or
occult about the way you will learn to recognize and utilize
the facts about celestial influence. All the usual camouflage,
mystery and gobbledegook often mixed up with astrology is
stripped away in these pages; instead, you will find a clear,
concise and direct method of setting up any horoscope—and
then interpreting it.

Although there is nothing said here about occult ways of
predicting the future, there is a kind of implicit understanding in the material that (given certain elements of exact
knowledge) you will quickly see the inevitability for certain
things to happen. For analogy, if you *know* a man has driven
his high-powered sports car to a series of wild parties, and
you *also* know he is irresponsible, inclined to drink too much
and neglect the maintenance of his car, it is not too difficult
to predict the high rate of probability that he will have a
serious accident. If you have more specific information, you
may even be able to tell *when* it will happen!

In a much broader sense, this kind of prediction is implied,
say, in your chart if you happen to have Jupiter, the planet
associated with expansion and abundance, in the second house
(personal finances) and in the Sign of Cancer, the most
tenacious of all Signs. If Jupiter is well aspected to the
Moon (associated with the public, and women) in Pisces (a
Sign known for understanding and wit), and also with the
Sun in Leo (a flamboyant showbusiness Sign), you can predict with startling accuracy that you will become enormously
rich, successful and famous in the theater, movies or TV.

The positions of other planets, such as Saturn, Venus and
Uranus, will indicate which branch of showbiz it will be.
Saturn in Capricorn could make you an executive, Venus in
Leo would indicate an actor, and so on. Each element re-
fines the interpretation (and narrows the choice of the individual). A good professional astrologer doesn't actually
deal in predictions *per se*. What he does is consider all the
"forces" at work in the natal horoscope, both conflicting and
harmonious. From this, he (or you) can render an educated
guess about the outcome of almost any situation in which
the client finds himself. Given the natal horoscope, certain
influences can be determined by calculating the (current)
transiting planets. With such a wealth of "inside" information at his disposal, the astrologer (or student) can easily
state with confidence what he thinks will happen in the fu-

ture. The result often seems "amazing" or "incredible" to the layman.

If you commit to memory the few simple rules given in this book, you will soon find yourself in a position to make the same kind of educated guesses about any horoscope. It takes a little practice and experience, but the effort is well worth the trouble. Even student astrologers find themselves constantly in demand, the center of attention at almost every gathering. People love to hear about themselves and want to know how their relationships with others will work out, or if they are coming into a good cycle.

With little variation, every astrologer begins with his own horoscope and then branches out to investigate the charts of loved ones, friends, business associates, et al. What is generally termed "prediction" in astrology applies to many fields, some of them quite scientific, as you'll discover in the closing pages of this book.

George J. McCormack of Fair Lawn, New Jersey, who has predicted overwhelming storms in the coming years, can be called plainly a "weather astrologer." A white-haired, lean, peppery old gentleman, he worked for Bell System Laboratories until his retirement, when he began to devote full time to astro-meteorology. In this field he sprang to prominence back in 1947. A full three months in advance, he forecast the very hour of a howling blizzard that buried the New York metropolitan area on December 26. His feat so impressed the nation that industries, farm groups, railroads and cities in 36 states arranged to buy his services on a contract basis. "Astro-weather will be taught in universities within ten years," McCormack states confidently.

Perhaps so. Scientific support of the idea is growing. In 1961 the late Dr. Andrew Douglass of the Lowell Observatory in Flagstaff, Arizona, reported on a long-range study of tree rings as an indication of the weather back through history. In the course of his research he had found definite relationships between weather and occurrences in outer space. "Combining what we know of tree ring growth, sunspot cycles and planetary movements," he said, "holds the key to forecasting weather conditions decades in advance."

At least in terms of weather, then, there is real evidence that goings-on in the cosmos broadly affect our lives here on Earth. But what of individual lives, specific fates? How can the positions of stars and planets have anything to do with the likelihood of a man's rise to fame and fortune, or the time of his death?

One explanation may lie in the fact that the nervous systems of all creatures on Earth, including man, work by means of electronics. Tiny electronic pulses operate the brain; they move muscles. These pulses are so small that they can't be detected singly by the most delicate instruments yet devised; they can only be identified in groups. If they are this delicate, they might conceivably be affected by electromagnetic radiation from distant stars in the heavens.

We live in an environment that hums with forces. Stars emit radiation that ranges up and down the electromagnetic spectrum: low-frequency radio waves; higher-frequency radiation that we call visible light; on past ultra-violet to X-rays and still higher frequencies. Within the solar system, the Sun and its planets maintain a complicated interplay of magnetic fields. Gravity itself is believed to be a type of electromagnetic force. All these forces bounce off and shoot through a human being in ever-shifting patterns from the day of his birth.

Do they affect him? Probably. One current theory is that they cause the gradual body deterioration we call "old age." "Nobody really knows why living things age," says biologist Dr. Clement Markert, of Johns Hopkins University. "Since the body continually replaces many of its cells with new ones throughout its life, you can't properly think of the body as 'wearing out' the way a car does. Yet for some reason the body goes into a decline after it reaches adulthood, and eventually the individual dies."

Why? Apparently something goes wrong with the information code by which new cells are built as duplicates of the old. In childhood and young adulthood this duplication process works almost perfectly. But with advancing age, new cells begin to appear which don't work right. Eventually there are so many of these poorly built cells in the body that it can't carry on its complex functions any more, and it stops. The cause of this bad copying? Many biochemists think that radiation, blasting through an individual throughout his lifetime, may damage the pattern-making machinery of his cells.

There is a great deal of other evidence that celestial forces directly influence life and death. For example, at an MIT conference on magnetism in 1961, Dr. Robert O. Becker, of the State University of New York, reported the discovery of an electromagnetic field within the human body. This in itself wasn't surprising, since a human being is in effect a kind of electronic device. What was interesting, from the astrological viewpoint, was Doctor Becker's further statement that this human electromagnetic field evidently fluctuates in tune with changes in the Earth's field. "At present," wrote Doctor Becker, "we can only suspect a general relationship of some kind between the whole of the human species and the whole of the electromagnetic phenomenon that engages the Sun, other stars and the galaxies."

Science has now begun to *demonstrate* direct linkages between celestial movements and the behavior of animals and men. Biologist Dr. Frank Brown of Northwestern University showed that oysters sense the position of the Moon and regulate their activities by it. Ordinarily, oysters open and close their shells in phase with ocean tides. Doctor Brown wanted to see what oysters would do if there were *no* tides. He hauled some out of the sea off New Haven, Connecticut, shipped them to Evanston, Illinois, and put them indoors in a tank of sea water at even temperature under a steady, dim light. For two weeks they continued to open and close their shells in phase with the tides at their old ocean home Then abruptly they changed their rhythm. Their shell-opening cycle slipped into phase with the tides that would have existed if there had been an ocean covering Illinois The hypothesis: it is not the ebb and flow of tidal water but the position of the Moon itself that governs oysters' behavior. The mystery: what is the force from the Moon that does this?

Men and women aren't oysters, but celestial forces have definitely been shown to affect human behavior The American Institute of Medical Climatology in Philadelphia, working with the police and fire departments major hospitals and the University of Pennsylvania Medical School, conducted a three-year study (1959–1961) of human reactions to the phases of the Moon. Conclusions: cases of murder, rape, aggravated assault and arson are most common during Full Moon periods.

Much of human life, if not most of it, seems to be governed by chance. But perhaps existence is *not* all chance. Perhaps a good part of it is influenced by these forces science is now beginning to detect, the forces on which astrologers base their predictions.

I began to take an interest in these predictions in 1957. I didn't believe in astrology. In fact I expected to debunk the idea that stars and planets affect human destiny.

I remember my first introduction to professional astrology on a dark, stormy September night in New York in 1957.

Hunched against the driving rain, I hunted out a building
I'd been directed to and rang the bell to an astrologer's door.
A saturnine man opened it and led me into his book lined
study. Soon our conversation turned to the 1960 Presidential
election, then three years in the future. The astrologer said,
"Evidence indicates that Senator Jack Kennedy will be
nominated and elected."

This wasn't easy to believe in 1957. Kennedy was only
one of several possible candidates being mentioned for the
Democratic nomination. It was hard to visualize him as the
next President. In fact, the majority of political pundits in
that year seemed to feel the Republican nominee, most likely
Richard Nixon, would win in 1960.

The astrologer said no. "The possibility of Nixon as President is so remote that it's almost nonexistent." Then he added,
"You see, Nixon's horoscope indicates that he will live for a
long time. Whoever is elected President in 1960 will not live
out his term."

Over the next few months I talked to other astrologers.
Many came up with the same prediction—that the President
elected in 1960 would not survive his term. They based the
prediction partly on Kennedy's personal horoscope, partly on
an odd astrological fact involving the largest planets, Jupiter
and Saturn.

Once every 20 years, the orbits of these two giants bring
them into what astrologers call "conjunction"—that is, they
move into the same segment of sky as seen from Earth. Every
time this had happened since 1840, the American President
in office or elected that year had died: (1840—William H.
Harrison; 1860—Abraham Lincoln; 1880—James A. Gar-
field; 1900—William McKinley; 1920—Warren G. Harding;
1940—Franklin D. Roosevelt). The next Jupiter-Saturn conjunction was scheduled for 1960.

As the election approached, astrologers became more specific in their forecasts. In early 1960 the president of the
Astrologers Guild of America warned that the Vice-Presi-
dential candidate "should be chosen with great care, since
he will probably ascend to the Presidency late in 1963."
Then, after Kennedy was elected, Olive A. Pryor, an astrologer, talked about a Presidential horoscope "filled with
afflictions, most of which begin in October 1963. Anything
can happen to the President in this year."

On November 22, 1963, in Dallas, Texas, an obscure young
malcontent with a rifle seems to have justified all these astrologers' warnings.

Since 1957 I have continued my search for fakery among stargazers, but all the evidence I have found has made me wonder whether astrology is not, in fact, a science rather than a fraud.

I have engineered experiments to test predictions astrologers have given me. In one, I bought a package of flower seeds and planted half of them on a day judged by astrologers to be inauspicious, the other half on a "fertile" day. Both halves grew in the same soil; both received the same care, the same water, the same sunlight.

The seeds from the first half failed miserably. Those that germinated at all produced stunted, yellowish stalks. Right alongside, the second half developed lush green plants that survived a long hot summer and bloomed profusely.

Many highly respected men share the view that astrology is no fraud. Burton Browne is a once-obscure businessman who rose to fortune as the founder of the Gaslight key club chain. Browne synchronizes his affairs with the movements of the planets; his astrologer is Katherine de Jersey, well-known among business and professional men for her acumen. "She has never been wrong in all the time I've known her," says Browne flatly.

Another famous devotee of astrology was the psychiatrist Carl Jung, who used astrology in his studies of personality. Astrologers are fond of saying, "He's a Scorpio type," or "a typical Aquarian." They believe that people born under the same zodiacal Sign have discrete personality traits in common. Doctor Jung found this to be true. Human personalities, he said, "coincide in the most remarkable way with traditional astrological expectations."

One way in which the accuracy of astrological forecasts is tested is by comparing people with like horoscopes. If there is anything to what astrologers say, such people ought to lead markedly similar lives.

A few years ago, two unrelated women met for the first time in a hospital room in Hackensack, New Jersey. It turned out that they had been born on the same date of the same year, in towns not far distant. The women's last names were Hanna and Osborne, but both had the same first name—Edna. Each had come to the hospital to give birth to a first child. The babies had been born at the same hour, had weighed the same and had been given the same name—Patricia Edna.

The women's husbands also had identical first names—

Harold. Each Harold was in the same business and owned
the same make, model and color car. The Hannas and the
Osbornes had been married three and a half years and shared
the same anniversary. Both husbands had been born in the
same year, month and day. Both women were blue-eyed
brunettes—of the same height, and weight, and they wore
the same size clothes. They had the same number of brothers
and sisters. Their husbands were of the same religion—a
different one from that of the wives, which was also the
same.

Each family owned a dog named Spot of the same mixed
breed, size and age. Both dogs were acquired under almost
identical circumstances at the same time. . . . The parallels
went on and on.

Another strange case came to light when two poultry trucks
of the same model collided in Miami in June 1961. The
drivers, presenting identification, learned that they were
identical twins separated from birth. Same business, wives of
the same first name. Same number of children—same ages,
same sexes.

Or consider this case: on July 19, 1958, a 21-year-old
laborer from New Rochelle, New York, was arraigned in
the death of a 36-year-old drifter. At the same time in Mount
Vernon, New York, his twin brother was arrested for killing
a 36-year-old junkyard operator. They had had no personal
contact for two months prior to the tragedies.

Astrologers do not believe coincidence alone explains such
cases. They argue that people paired like those are propelled
along life's trail by some external force acting equally on
each.

What force? Where does it come from? How does it
work? Astrologers don't know. They only say that the force
is directly concerned with the Earth and everything on it,
and that what we do know of the force as it existed on the
date of an individual's birth, can be interpreted accurately
to reveal what events are likely to occur in his or her life.

1

The Truth About Astrology

One of the most important reasons for the general scientific apathy toward astrology is that no one has formulated any final specific rules governing the phenomenon. Astronomers refuse to study a subject they believe to be "superstitious nonsense." Nevertheless, a group of British scientists *inadvertently* proved that mysterious exogenous forces are active in some of the strangest of all terrestrial phenomena.

In 1964, astronomers in Great Britain were completely baffled by the ruination of their photographic emulsions. Mysteriously, the gelatinous substance somehow became full of holes. In photographic plates of astronomical objects these tiny holes were disastrous; they ruined every picture.

The scientists searched frantically for the source of their trouble and discovered a totally new, completely unknown kind of bacteria that digested the gelatin of the plates. They traced the bacteria to pure rainwater they used to wash their plates. This was exceptionally good water because of its softness, and was easily drained from the rooftops of the buildings surrounding the observatory.

It soon became apparent that these bacteria appeared only at certain times—immediately following an inferior conjunction of Venus—but *only* when the conjunction was accompanied by a huge magnetic storm on the Sun! Somehow the planetary "tail" of Venus, blown by the solar wind toward the Earth, gave rise to the strange bacteria in our atmosphere, which then came down in the next rainfall.

"If this is true," one of the astronomers said, "we should have had invasions of these bacteria every time the combination happened." A close examination of their records of

every inferior conjunction of Venus *combined* with a magnetic storm on the Sun coincided perfectly with the ruination
of their photographic plates. (See *Analog*, November, 1964,
"Invasion By Washing Water.")

If *astrologers* had made this discovery, and tried to interest
astronomers in checking it out, the allegations would have
been dismissed with derisive snorts of "sheer coincidence."

Yet Webster defines coincidence as "a group of concurrent
events or circumstances, or one of them, remarkable from
lack of apparent causal connection." Another way of putting
it could be, "a 'coincidence' is sometimes an effort to avoid
reason." All things that happen *are,* after all, effects, and
every effect does have a primal cause.

And every *cause* presupposes some intelligence or purpose.
(It should be pointed out here that the existence of Pluto
was astro*logically* deduced long before it was jointly discovered by two teams of astronomers.)

Although logic is only one avenue or approach to scientific truth, it is possible to arrive at a logically inevitable
conclusion that human beings are powerfully influenced by
celestial conditions that surround us on all sides. (*a*) Sunspots and solar flares (which are colossal, roaring magnetic
storms on the Sun) have a strong effect on the Earth's
weather, particularly on the ionosphere, which lies in the high
reaches of the upper atmosphere. (*b*) Bio-climatologists have
proven that positive and negative ions in the atmosphere
affect the way we think, feel and behave. (*c*) Electrical
charges in the atmosphere, as well as geomagnetism and
electromagnetism, affect plants, animals and humans. (*d*)
The Moon has an important, direct effect on atmospheric
moisture, on climate, plants, animals and humans. (*e*) In
certain respects, oxygen itself is magnetic, therefore solar
magnetic fields and sunspots affect the Earth's atmosphere
magnetically as well as thermally. (*f*) Cosmic radiation from
the surrounding universe is known to alter DNA and RNA,
the nucleic acids found in living organisms. (*g*) Geomagnetism affects animal and human organisms; they respond to
geomagnetic changes. (*h*) The planets in their orbits are
known to trigger sunspots and solar flares; these phenomena
can be predicted by the angles formed among the planets as
seen from the Sun.

These harmonic positions of the planets affect solar magnetic field activity and the magnetic field patterns of the
Earth, consequently all living things, including humanity—
individually as well as collectively.

In the July 4, 1966, issue of *Product Engineering,* editor L. F. Tangerman said, "I've been told, at one time or another, that the greatest interference with long-distance radio transmission is not local atmospherics, but electrical effects from planets, notably Saturn. Modern meteorologists have gone so far as to guess that the planets may also affect missile electronic systems and even the human brain, giving some credence to the old astrologers' respect for the heavenly bodies.

"The brain is supposedly an electro-chemical device. We and the Russians have experimented with tiny radio receivers in damaged brain areas to stimulate nerves from external transmitters so muscles will be activated. Two doctors have just reported that strong but harmless electrical fields are generated when water splashes into a tub or basin; the positive charge goes down the drain but the negative one remains in the atmosphere and may be a greater factor in our post-wash feeling of well-being than the water itself. Joseph Molitorisz, ME, also discovered recently that it's an electrical differential that causes sap to flow and makes trees grow— and a reversal of the polarity will make the trees die (PE, Jan. 31, '66, p. 26).

"Now comes a report from Chicago that our fatigue in cars, planes, trucks and office buildings is caused by barring of the earth's electromagnetic field. It seems that our structures form "Faraday cages" (grounded metal boxes that kill the field)—so we get tired because the human body needs electrical energy.

"Who says so? Dr. Cristjo Cristofv, father of the 'Cristofv effect.' We use the 'Cristofv effect' to detect nuclear explosions anywhere in the world, but it was originally applied by the Germans to determine V-1 and V-2 rocket accuracy in World War II. Cristofv got his PhD in Berlin in 1928, was research director of the sound ranging and artillery lab for the Bulgarian Royal Ministry of Defense, as well as an expert on high explosives and teacher of physics. When the Russians entered Bulgaria, Cristofv scooted out and came to the U.S. in 1947. He has been special consultant for our armed services and for Emerson Electric, Lockheed, and Chicago Aerial Corp. He received the Air Force Exceptional Service Award in 1963.

"He says the earth's magnetic field is positively polarized and measures about 200 volts/meter. His 'anti-fatigue device' is a metal-enclosed can about the size of an orange, in which a solid-state device is connected to a battery. It is suspended on a slim probe from the ceiling and provides an 800-volt per meter field

"Tests of pilots in T-2s and of truck drivers on the St. Louis-Milwaukee haul showed greater alertness and less tiredness, according to Cristofv. He reports the 11-hour truck run cut to 8½, with drivers feeling less tired and able to sleep more restfully afterward. Similar tests in factories and buildings are reported to show similar results.

"Metal isn't the only offender, according to Cristofv. Plastics have an inherent high negative charge (as high as 50,000 volts/meter), which degrades performance even more. So plastic seat covers, draperies, bedspreads, and the like can make trouble. He exposed cats to a field of that intensity; in three or four weeks their appetites fell off, sex drive evaporated, and they ran scared from mice.

"Ford and Chrysler are reportedly interested. Dr. Cristofv points out that if 'efficiency is raised, accidents due to human error can be greatly reduced,' so long-distance auto drivers are a particularly good potential for improvement through the findings.

"Can it be that the astrologers were right? Are our depressed and non-energetic cycles a result of our efficient structures and the position of the planets or the phase of the Moon? Do we need to recharge our personal batteries? Sounds Moon-mad—but is it?"

While RCA's astronomical expert, John H. Nelson, plots the positions of the planets in order to predict ionospheric storms for the world's largest long-distance radio communications network, former science editor John J. O'Neill of the New York *Herald Tribune* successfully predicted earthquakes according to eclipses and the New and Full Moon periods.

It is well known among astrologers that eclipses precede radical changes in weather, earthquakes, volcanic eruptions, and among people who happen to have major planets (in their horoscopes) at the same degree at which the eclipse takes place.

For a still unexplained but generally—and validly—accepted reason, the Moon influences differently when it is waxing than when it is waning. There is definite correlation between human behavior and phases of the Moon. A Philadelphia Police Department report recently included an exhaustive study entitled: "Effect of Full Moon on Human Behavior." Thousands of patrolmen, precinct sergeants, sheriffs and deputies all over the nation are convinced from their own experience that the Full Moon produces an eerie influence that releases uncontrollable urges in man and beast alike.

According to the Inspector of Philadelphia's General Services Division, which prepared the report, "Crimes against the person seem to increase as the night of the Full Moon draws near. People whose antisocial behavior has psychotic roots—firebugs, kleptomaniacs and homicidal alcoholics— seem to go on a rampage as the Moon rounds. They calm down when the Moon begins to wane."

Philadelphia, New York, Chicago, Los Angeles, San Francisco and Detroit police have noted this alarming tendency for madness and mayhem to recur with the Full Moon period. Here are a few lurid headlines chosen at random from many of the same kind:

LUNAR MADMAN ON THE PROWL AGAIN. (Bath, England)

MAD HEAD HUNTER OF PLAINFIELD STRIKES AGAIN IN FULL MOON. (Plainfield, Wisconsin)

NOTTING HILL MOON SLAYER CAPTURED . . . EIGHT VICTIMS DIED. POLICE BELIEVE HE KILLED ONLY DURING FULL MOON. (London)

POLICE THINK MAD BOMBER TIMES BOMBS WITH FULL MOON. (New York)

Although few realize it, racial rioting *always* reaches a peak of frenzy during Full Moon periods.

According to Sir William Blackstone, founding father of both British and American law: "A lunatic is indeed one that hath lucid intervals . . . frequently depending on the change of the Moon."

In the early Sixties, Dr. Leonard J. Ravitz, a neuropsychiatrist, concluded studies based on the *electrodynamic* theory of life. He found that all living things, including human beings, have bio-magnetic fields. Indeed, that man is a bio-magnetic animal. The electrical rhythm in human beings coincides with the lunar phase, the positions of the large planets and even distant constellations of stars. According to the theory of Dr. Ravitz, those distant, massive celestial objects, the stars and planets, are affected by the same basic electrodynamic forces that affect human beings.

This seems to be a rather broad and sweeping conclusion, but this is how it is demonstrated as approaching the true condition of the universe—the interaction of celestial bodies and all things on them.

Considering that man's scientific prowess and ability to distinguish truth from mere superstition has increased enormously during the past few centuries, it is interesting to note that most of the latest scientific research confirms the idea of planetary influence in our lives.

Still, we have skeptics quoting the objections of people who lived a hundred or more years ago—people who were lacking in scientific knowledge and experimentation, and whose opinions were little, if any, more advanced than the "superstition" they condemned. One of the most interesting and compelling passages against the practice of astrology was written in 1840 by Charles MacKay, LL.D., in his "Memoirs of Extraordinary Popular Delusions and the Madness of Crowds."

"Many are the follies into which men have been led by their eager desire to pierce the thick darkness of futurity. God himself for his own wise purposes, has more than once undrawn the impenetrable veil which shrouds those awful secrets; and, for purposes just as wise, He has decreed that, except in those instances, ignorance shall be our lot forever. It is happy for man that he does not know what the morrow is to bring forth; but, unaware of this great blessing, he has, in all ages of the world, presumptuously endeavored to trace the events of unborn centuries, and anticipate the march of time."

This mechanistic tirade, accusing astrologers of regarding the planets as existing mainly to guide man's destiny, overlooked the basic fact that no astrologer anywhere has ever been known to claim that the planets existed (or were created) *solely* to predict individual destiny. On the face of it, this is as preposterous a statement as any you're liable to come across in the so-called occult sciences.

Anyone who has ever taken the trouble to investigate some of man's ancient beliefs, myths or so-called "superstitions" has found that germ of truth which enabled each postulate to persist through centuries or millennia. Why? Simply because the oldest of these beliefs were too valuable to discard. They *worked*, which is a lot more than some psychiatrists can claim about their own exotic practices. For centuries, aborigines in America and elsewhere had been using mold—the basic material from which the "wonder drug" penicillin was derived—as a cure for infection. Naturally, the civilized, sophisticated doctors who came upon the practice saw only a filthy superstition. Characteristically, they were *blind* to the fact that the mold *did* work, that it *cured* infections!

There is a basic analogy here to current science, which (officially) rejects the idea of astrology on one hand while quietly assimilating their own (astrological) discoveries on the other. Probably all scientists would tumble to the often fantastically obvious correlations between celestial-terrestrial phenomena if they would—just once—open their minds to the *intention* of Nature rather than bumbling along with cold, often meaningless facts and measurements. Only those who are part scientist and part poet may perceive the Grand Design, the essential drift of the mysteries of the Universe. Pierre Teilhard de Chardin was one of these. So was Johannes Kepler, who, while totally lacking the formal tools to prove his findings, demonstrated the (still unexplained) mathematical relationship between the distances of the planets and their velocities (The Law of Areas). Kepler was, of course, an *astrologer* who found in the geometrical principle of the solar system a reflection of the "Spirit of God."

Although astrology and religion cannot be combined without confusion, it is the sole responsibility of scientists to seek truth *wherever* it may be found without unfounded bias or prejudice.

Kepler once tried to fit the five regular geometric solids between the orbits of the planets. It didn't work, so he showed that the regular polygons that could be accurately drawn between concentric circles demonstrated the *astrologically* important angles between planets: the quadrature or square (90°), the trine (120°), conjunction (0°), opposition (180°), the sextile (60°) and several minor aspects, each being multiples of 15 degrees from the other. Kepler rediscovered that these angles were related to the total number of degrees in a circle—in the following proportions: 1/2, 2/3, 3/4, 4/5, 5/6, 3/5 and 5/8. It's easy to visualize this circle as being straightened into a violin string; these astrologically potent angles correspond exactly to the different divisions which yield harmonics.

Kepler was ecstatic. "The music God made during the Creation, He also taught Nature to play; indeed, she repeats what He played to her."

Johannes Kepler is regarded as a great, pioneering astronomer, one of the founders of the New Cosmology, yet the scientific moppers-up who are continually brainwashed against serious study of such phenomena merely repeat the errors of *their* teachers on this and pass it on to their students; every text on astronomy adopts a patronizing attitude toward Kepler and other great men who happened to be astrologers, but who nevertheless made amazing *astronomical* discoveries.

Despite the fact that astrology has been victimized for centuries by the accumulation of nonsensical debris, its truths are there, even though buried, for anyone who desires to approach them from the viewpoint of a purposefully created universe. For all its protestations, astronomy remains basically sterile; it is uncommitted, it has not made a decision about what it's all about. It is the body of current knowledge; astrology is the soul. Astronomy flatly refuses to search for *reason* underlying the mysteries of its technological discoveries. In this sense, astronomy is not a science at all, but simple mechanics.

Guy Murchee touched on one of the most exciting and truly "scientific" correlations in "The Realm of the Tree" in the August, 1966 issue of *Diplomat* magazine:

"One of the simplest tree forms found in maples, ashes, horse chestnuts and dogwoods is the pairing of leaves, twigs or branches, two of which grow from their mother stem exactly opposite each other, while the next pair above or below also grow opposite each other but at right angles to the first pair, giving maximum dispersion of foliage."

A somewhat more complex dispersion in many other trees is the spiral. You can demonstrate it easily with a string. Tie the string to the base of a leaf, then stretch it along the twig and branch and loop it around each leaf stem in a smooth curve. With elm and linden trees you will discover that on the average each leaf is 180 degrees around its twig from the next one. Your string will spiral rather tightly— half a turn around for each leaf. The leaves of a beech tree will give you a one-third turn per leaf because its twigs have leaves spaced at 120 degree intervals. It becomes intensely interesting (and more revealing) as you go along.

"An apple tree, oak or cypress," says Murchee, "with the common distribution of leaves at 144 degrees, averages two-fifths a turn, a holly or spruce three-eights, a larch five-thirteenths, and so on. *These fractions are not just random,* for each numerator and each denominator is the sum of the two immediately preceding it, both sequences of numbers forming the same simple and regular progression: 1, 1, 2, 3, 5, 8, 13, 21, 34, 55, 89, 144, 233, 377.

"This particular progression is called the Fibonacci series in honor of its Thirteenth Century Italian researcher and investigator. It is the basis of *tree design* and is presumably a part of the same ubiquitous Music of the Spheres that builds harmony into atoms, molecules, crystals, Suns and galaxies and makes the Universe sing—as Pythagoras taught in 500 B.C."

The line of communication is clearly open for scientists

who are willing to investigate nonmaterialistic correlations. It is at once both exciting and rewarding to perceive (without psychism, spiritual illumination or religious fervor) the sheer beauty and necessity of man's oneness with the universe.

That great doubter, Charles Fort, whom so many regarded as a "science baiter" because he dramatized the preposterousness of many scientific delusions, said he could not determine where the real differences in things lay. The idea of an essential similarity between a microbe, a star and a kangaroo was his version of the ubiquitous nature of intelligence, therefore Life. No one has ever satisfactorily explained, for example, why snowflakes *always* have six equidistant arms, yet no two have ever been found to be alike. Similarly, all varieties of bees everywhere on Earth build six-sided honeycombs. Crystals with electrical properties also reflect Nature's demand for order and conformity. Diamonds, for example, *always* have twelve sides and must be cut along the lines of their axes.

Electron photomicrography clearly shows the atoms of tungsten and other crystals to radiate along twelve equidistant arms—almost as though the Earth's passage through twelve constellations in the course of one solar orbit were somehow reflected, or symbolized, in the metals and crystals of its planetary body.

Chemistry has also recently begun to notice some rather odd "coincidences" among certain atomic and molecular structures—one of which, incidentally, mysteriously bridges the gap between trees and man. Rutherford Platt, in *The Great American Forest*, wrote, "Chemists, probing the structure of chlorophyll, stumbled on an amazing piece of information that may reveal an extraordinary relationship between trees and man: If a single atom of *magnesium* is detached from the chlorophyll molecule and an atom of *iron* is put in its place, the same numbers of atoms and their arrangements become a molecule of red blood." (!)

Whatever it is that scientists *believe* they're doing, it remains as a self-evident truth of nature that the mind of man is a pattern-seeking entity. We appear to be at the end of that period in history when the establishment of organized knowledge-gatherers are able to dictate which study is permissible and which is taboo.

Authoritarianism, whether it manifests in civil, clerical, political or scientific activities, is being challenged on every front. Rigid answers are no longer satisfactory to the new, probing, dynamic questions. Sooner or later it must occur to a majority of us that we are in fact polarizations of the same forces we have detected throughout the universe. This positive and negative magnetic polarization is an intrinsic property of electrical phenomena. All matter, organic and inorganic, participates in and depends upon the flow of these energies which, as Einstein pointed out, are actually matter in motion.

The general direction of science henceforth will be diametrically opposed to 19th Century materialism. Only then will we develop true knowledge and understanding of the immanent influence of our celestial environment, and our part in it. And my guess is that science will coincide more and more emphatically with the patterns astrologers have recorded so successfully for so long.

2

What Is a Horoscope?

At the exact moment and from the specific location of your birth, the Sun, Moon and all the planets of the solar system were in specific places. Your horoscope is a map, "picture" or diagram of the heavens for that all-important event. The electromagnetic, gravitational pattern of the solar system at the time of your birth indelibly marks your personality and character. Let's say it happened in the fall—October 15, to be exact. You may call yourself a "Libran." If in November, a "Scorpion." What you *mean* by this is that the Sun was transiting through a certain Sign of the celestial Zodiac for an entire month. Many people were born all over the world during that month, but at the same time and place of *your* birth, chances are that very few or no other babies were born.

That map of the heavens as seen from a specific location on the Earth on a certain date in a certain month—in a specific year and at a certain hour and minute—is one of the most important factors in making you unique in the world. Chances are that no one with your horoscope has existed for 25,000 years and no one will be born with your horoscope for another 25,000 years. That's how long it takes for all the planets to return to their same positions, in their same Signs and same relationships to each other.

In addition to the Sun's being in any of the twelve astrological Signs, there are almost limitless ways for horoscopes to be different. If you have the Sun in Gemini, you will learn here how this factor may be modified if the Moon was in the Sign Leo at your birth. Moreover, Jupiter might be in Sagittarius and/or Saturn might be in Capricorn. Mercury,

never straying far from the Sun, must be in the Sun's Sign
or the one before or after it. The chart of the heavens for
your birth is one of the most important and valuable documents you will ever own, and you'll learn how to calculate
it in these pages. Properly used, it can be worth more to
you than insight, understanding, vocational counseling or
money.

By learning how to set up and interpret even one horoscope, you will already have saved anywhere between five
and twenty times the price of this book!

Nearly everyone thinks he knows what a horoscope is.
Most people believe it is a prediction they read in the daily
newspaper. But these are merely limited Sun Sign readings—
interpretations based broadly on the daily position of the
fast-moving Moon with respect to any of the twelve Signs
of the Zodiac.

The same limitation applies to the monthly "guidance"
articles in those astrology magazines you see on the news-
stands. Most of them presume to reveal usually positive
secrets about your future health, wealth and love. I don't
intend these remarks as a blanket condemnation of this kind
of entertainment. In fact those "readings" are what often
attract people who then become really interested and eventually do serious research in better methods of astrological
prediction.

All mass-produced so-called "horoscopes" apply to you as
an individual only in a *general* way. They thrive as a publishing phenomenon because there are many people primarily
concerned with their personal interests, who derive some kind
of satisfaction from reading what the future might bring.
Subjectively, the whole universe performs an orbit about
each of us, and we tend to view ourselves in a most kindly
light. My point is that no one, regardless of his objectivity, is
able to see himself from the "outside." Although most books
on astrology provide this kind of insight, they, too, concentrate solely on your favorable chances.

In all likelihood this is the quality that has made astrology
such a perennially popular subject. Until the last few centuries only the horoscopes of kings, emperors and noblemen
were considered of sufficient importance to be calculated and
interpreted specifically and carefully. In time the rich and influential became astrology's foremost patrons; then came
military men and politicians. Now you can probably find a
competent professional astrologer somewhere in your own
town. According to the astrologer's reputation and the

amount of work done on a chart, the fee for a horoscope of you as an individual will vary between fifteen and one hundred dollars. The skills necessary to become a competent professional have never been fully determined, but *anyone* with average intelligence can learn to calculate a horoscope. Knowing how to *interpret* properly the myriad possibilities in a chart is another question entirely. Depending on the individual, it can take months or years. Good astrologers are forever learning something new.

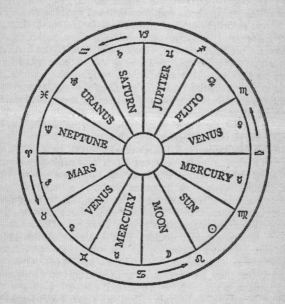

Natural order of the zodiac, beginning with Aries (♈) on the ascendant. The ruling planet of each Sign is in the Sign it rules, i.e., the influence of the Sign and planet are most nearly alike.

Generally speaking, the radix, or horoscope, is an Earth-centered wheel divided into 12 radiating segments or "houses" and Signs. The houses always remain in the same positions, but the "spokes" of the wheel, the configuration of stars from your place of birth, at its exact time, can be in any of the twelve Signs. Often they overlap. Thus those Signs and houses symbols for the planets are placed; this part of horoscopy (ideally) is done with great mathematical and astronomical exactness. When you consider that there are 360 degrees to a circle (30 degrees to a Sign), 60 minutes to a degree and 60 seconds of arc to one minute of arc, it can become very exact indeed.

And yet in spite of this wonderful exactitude, some of the most excellent *personal* astrologers simply skip the use of logarithms or precision mathematics and scribble out a chart in a few minutes—using only *proportionate* math. Let's say they have an ephemeris (table of planetary positions), traditionally set up for noon, Greenwich time. If the birth time is six P.M., they simply add *one-fourth* of each planet's 24-hour motion to arrive at what are roughly the correct positions of the celestial bodies. You need not perform intricate logarithmic calculations here. By checking the lists of dates at the end of each chapter on each of the planets, you will not only learn where each was located at your birth, but *also what each position means.*

In the last paragraph I stressed the term "personal" astrologer. There are many different kinds of astrologers—including some who practice astrology but call it something else—like "solar biology" or "astrogeophysics," sometimes "geoastrophysics." It all boils down to the fact that there are areas of specialization within astrology that almost no one hears about. Take medical astrology, for example. There are only a few dozen medical doctors in the United States able to diagnose ailments according to the rules and aphorisms of Hippocrates, the medical astrologer of classic Greek antiquity. But they are largely concentrated in two groups—one in the east, notably New York, and the other in the west, mainly Southern California. Small as these groups are, they have stimulated a good deal of scientific research into what biologists once called "biological clocks." As a result, it is becoming more fashionable now to concede that many of the mechanisms which control living things are exogenous, i.e., emanating from terrestrial and extraterrestrial sources.

Another specialization in astrology is astro-meteorology—the prediction of weather on a seasonal or yearly basis by the setting up of charts of the heavens for the exact moment the Sun crosses the equinoxes and solstices, the dates on which the seasons change—the four cardinal points of the celestial compass. This is a very ancient art and is probably the first use ever made of astrology. Chapter 16 will give you the details about how accurate this branch of the science of the stars can be when used with technical proficiency. It should also provide some insight into the workings of the Scientific Establishment. America's largest long-distance communications network times its short-wave broadcasts according to the advice of a staff astronomer who reports on favorable planetary conditions, i.e., when the angular positions of the planets cause clear weather.

Sub-specializations of astro-weather prediction include the forecasting of earthquakes, volcanic eruptions, drought and disease epidemics. Specific examples of how this is done appeared in *Astrology: The Space Age Science.*

Two founders of the American Federation of Astrologers, John Hazelrigg and G. J. McCormack, were successful in getting a fair description of astrology into the *New International Encyclopedia* in the 1940s:

> Astrology is the study of the influence of the Sun, Moon, planets, stars on all things terrestrial, including man. It is based on experience in observing that world events coincide with mathematical patterns between, and cycles of, celestial bodies. Likewise, events in the lives of people coincide with changing relationships of celestial bodies to positions they held at birth. These can be accurately predetermined mathematically. Their manifestation is modified both by environment and heredity.
>
> Originally there were two basic kinds of astrology, Natural and Mundane. Natural astrology is that branch out of which astronomy has grown. Mundane astrology is a study of planetary influences at times of earthquakes, epidemics, wars, good times, etc. As a result, natal astrology came into being, dealing with horoscopes of kings and rulers, and later, everyone.
>
> In more recent times, like other sciences, astrology has been divided into specialized fields, such as astro-psychology, -meteorology, -pathology, horary astrology, etc. Although often objected to as a pseudo-science, investigation has shown that these objections usually result from the misuse or adaptation of a few astrological principles for the purposes of attempting to tell fortunes. This is not the function of genuine astrology or sincere astrologers. Perhaps the greatest moral step forward for the proper application of astrology was through the formation of an American organization dedicated to investigation, research and education, which also established a code of moral ethics, and later an examination system with high tenets for those who profess to be astrologers.

History of Astrology. As archeological research pene-
trates over farther into antiquity, it pushes back the birthdate
of astrology. The earliest reliable records, the Chinese Tri-
grams of Fui-Hi, indicate that astrology was then well-de-
fined in China. It antedates written records in India when
Hindu astrology was first passed down by word of mouth.
Study of the Hebrew Scriptures, the Old Testament of the
Christian Bible, indicates the active use of astrology by the
Hebrews. Western astrology grew from that of the Middle
East. Isaac Newton pointed out its use by the first dynasties
of Egypt, quoting from Diodenos that the Chaldeans learned
it from the Egyptians. Akkadian celestial observations date
back to 4310 B.C.; the Tablets of Sargon I (circa 3800 B.C.)
clearly show the Chaldeans were competent astrologers.

It later moved to Greece. Hippocrates, the "Father of
Medicine," correlated the climactic periods in acute diseases to the motion of the Moon. From Greece, astrology
moved to Rome and Arabia. But it did not originate in a
single country. The earliest records of Mexico, Central and
South America, and many other people of antiquity indicate
astrological science developed proportionately to the advancement of the level of civilization of those people.

As predestination took over the philosophy of the Dark
Ages, astrologers became fatalistic. All the great minds of
ancient and modern history—from Hippocrates through
Ptolemy, from Copernicus through Newton—first became
astrologers. As man began to rid himself of the shackles of
fatalism, astrology became less and less an attempt to tell
fortunes. It was a method of interpreting celestial *influences*
affecting the life of man.

In all fields of human endeavor and knowledge there are
and have been charlatans. It would be eminently unfair to
write a history of law, medicine or religion depicting dis-
barred lawyers, medical quacks and unfrocked clergymen. It
is equally one-sided to refer to those who have misused
astrological knowledge as though they were typical. No one
knows what might have developed in place of the Copernican system, if Copernicus had not attended the great astrological school established at Craco by the King of Poland.

Terms in Astrology. Astrology has four principal terms:
Zodiac, House, Planets and Aspects. There are many more,
but these are basic. The zodiac with which the Western astrologer deals is the Sun's apparent path in the heavens
which is inclined at an angle of 23° 27' to the celestial
equator. Its twelve divisions are the signs of the Zodiac.
The Houses are twelve equal divisions of space at a given
time from a specific point on Earth. They relate to twelve
major departments of life. The planets are those of our
solar system. For the sake of convenience, however, astrologers refer to the Sun, a *fixed* star, and the Moon,

Earth's natural satellite, as "planets." Aspects are the cyclical and geometric interrelationship of the celestial bodies. Some of these angular relationships are favorable, some adverse, and others are variable. Such aspects have been shown to be highly significant in medical and psychological studies, in the transmission and receiving of radio signals and in barometric changes.

Both officially and unofficially, nations and leaders, both of the past and present, have successfully employed the talents of astrologers. Sixteen years before the Great Fire of London, astrologer William Lilly predicted the disaster. In the same year (1651) Lilly also foretold that the Great Plague would spread throughout Europe in 1665. American astrologer Louis de Wohl predicted the successful invasion of North Africa, Sicily and Italy for Army officials in the Pentagon six months before it took place during World War II. But in natal astrology no sincere astrologer predicts a specific thing will necessarily happen to an individual on a given day. Certain trends can be timed with great precision; knowing in advance that a particular influence will prevail, one is in a position to take advantage of one situation or to avoid another.

This is a conservative description of astrology, what a horoscope is and how it may be used in the business of living. Although unofficially endorsed by the American Federation of Astrologers, it lacks the philosophical impact of the following statement from *Saturday Review* by Franz Hartmann, M.D.:

"Man is the quintessence of all the elements, and a son of the universe or a copy in miniature of its soul, and everything that exists or takes place in the universe, exists and may take place in the constitution of man The congeries of forces and essences making up the constitution of what we call Man is the same as the congeries of forces and powers that on an infinitely larger scale is called the Universe, and everything in the Universe reflects itself in Man, and may come to his consciousness; and this circumstance enables a man to know himself, to know the Universe, and to perceive not only that which exists invisibly in the Universe, but to foresee and prophesy future events."

It is extremely difficult for people living in a space-age technocracy to realize that the majority of the world's greatest scientists and philosophers of the past were in fact astrologers. Only a few scientists today are studying the influence of the stars and planets on human character and destiny. Yet this field was taken very seriously by the great thinkers of the past. Astrology, "the science of the stars," and astronomy, "the order of the stars," were two slues of the same coin. With the gradual acceptance of the Copernican system (which, incidentally, was powerfully resisted by scientists and astronomers of the time), the schism between astrology and astronomy grew wider, then became complete. Despite the current popularity of astrology, it has failed to enchant most modern academic or scientific communities.

Despite Hazelrigg's and McCormack's efforts, astrology is defined in *Webster's Collegiate Dictionary* (G. & C. Merriam Co., Springfield, Mass., Fifth ed.) as:

"The pseudo or (fraudulent) science which treats of the influence of the stars upon human affairs and of foretelling terrestrial events by their positions and aspects."

It is generally (though erroneously) believed that the Copernican system dealt the death blow to astrology because astrologers still use the geocentric [Earth-centered] system of horoscopy. Even near-illiterates today know that the Sun, not the Earth, is the center of our planetary system. Some astrologers who use the heliocentric system though, have had no better luck in gaining acceptance of astrology's basic tenets than those who still use the old Earth-centered system. Moreover, the latter have a more sensible stance: "If we lived on the Sun, we'd use heliocentric charts, but the fact is that we live on the Earth. . . ."

However it may be approached, astrology is usually treated as the pariah of all sciences. Some of the hatred directed toward the idea is suprisingly irrational. Here's what the *New Modern Encyclopedia* (Published by Wm. H. Wise & Co., N.Y.C.) has to say:

Astrology—The ancient art of divining future events, especially the fate of human beings, from the position of the stars. Among the Greeks and Romans the word was synonymous with astronomy, and it was not until the 16th Century that a clear distinction began to be made. Astrology owes its origin to the ancient belief that the Earth was the center of the Universe to which all else was tributary. The Chinese, Egyptians, Chaldeans, Romans and most other ancient peoples were implicit believers in astrology. Even some of the great astronomers who must have known they were perpetrating a fraud, received large fees for "casting horoscopes." During the Middle Ages the ordinary method of casting horoscopes was to divide a planisphere or globe into twelve sections by cucles running from pole to pole like those which mark the meridians of longitude. Each of the twelve sections was called a "house of heaven"; each house symbolized an advantage or disadvantage, and each was ruled by one of the heavenly bodies. As the Sun, Moon and stars all pass once in 24 hours through the heavens represented by the twelve houses, the important matter was to ascertain what house and what star were in the ascendancy at the time of the person's birth, because *all persons born in the same part of the world at the same time were supposed to have the same future.** This idea vanished among civilized people when it was learned that the Earth itself is one of the heavenly bodies—but astrology still flourishes in Asia and Africa, and is practiced by charlatans in other parts of the world.

It is difficult to imagine how, if the idea of astrology is basically fraudulent and erroneous, it was *independently* discovered by the Incas of Peru, the Hebrews, Persians, Chinese, Indians, Europeans and Polynesian peoples. Either the whole world went insane in exactly the same way about an identical set of facts—or there is something of reality and truth in astrology.

Disregarding little gems such as the fact that Mark Twain swore by astrology all his life (he was born under Halley's comet and accurately predicted his own death by its return), it is staggering to think that the five men who are responsible for creating what is now known as the New Cosmology were all astrologers: Copernicus, Kepler, Galileo, Tycho Brahe and Sir Isaac Newton.

Even today, although officially without status, serious astrological research is under way in places as interesting as the Earth and Planetary Sciences Division of the U.S. Naval Ordinance Depot at China Lake, California. Meteorologists at the National Center for Atmospheric Research and the High Altitude Observatory in Boulder, Colorado are also checking it out. The former director of NCAR and the High Altitude Observatory once even confessed that he knew how to cast and interpret horoscopes!

Essentially, the horoscope is a map of the heavens for a given moment in time from a specific location on the Earth. The patterns made by the planets and the aspects between them at the time of birth enable almost anyone who has studied the subject to deliver some remarkable interpretations of your character, personality, individuality. In many cases an astrologer will be able to forewarn you of an accident-

* Author's Italics.

prone period, or to advise you that when, say, Jupiter enters your house of money, it will be a good financial period, one in which you could make successful investments.

The horoscope blank is a wheel divided into twelve equi-distant segments of 30° each. The lines dividing these seg-ments are called "cusps" while the segments themselves are called "houses." Each house signifies a definite sphere of life activity. The houses are counted in a counterclockwise di-rection, beginning with the first house (or Ascendant) at "9 o'clock."

Not only is the influence of a planet modified by the Sign it is in, it is further modified by the *mundane* house in which it happens to fall. If Mars, for example, falls in the first house, the Ascendant, its influence manifests itself physically, and you will probably have a prominent mark or scar on your face or head—unless there are good aspects from Venus, Jupiter, the Sun or Moon.

The twelve houses are roughly analogous to the twelve Signs, and in their chronological order. The first house equates to Aries, the second to Taurus, the third to Gemini, etc. Here are the twelve houses and the life activities with which they compare:

First house: Physical body, self-centered interests.	ARIES
Second house: Money, possessions and se-curity.	TAURUS
Third house: Communications, relationship to environment.	GEMINI
Fourth house: Home, parent, beginnings and endings.	CANCER
Fifth house: Children, amusements, recrea-tion and display.	LEO
Sixth house: Health, service, efficiency.	VIRGO
Seventh house: Partner(s), unity with other(s) on a personal level.	LIBRA
Eighth house: Sex expression, self-sacrifice.	SCORPIO
Ninth house: Travel (abroad), self projec-tion to new horizons.	SAGITTARIUS
Tenth house: Career, material responsibility, social status.	CAPRICORN
Eleventh house: Friends, hopes and wishes; identification with group objectives.	AQUARIUS
Twelfth house: Self-undoing, escapism, con-finement, self-sacrifice.	PISCES

In your horoscope, Jupiter acts as the principle of expansion, good will, good fortune, successful financial dealings and foreign affairs; you can easily anticipate the result when this great planet moves into the second (money) house of your chart.

Without giving a complete description of *all* the planetary influences at the moment: the character of Saturn is almost the opposite of Jupiter; its influence is reflected in your life when this ringed planet moves into your second house of personal finances. Over periods of thousands of years during which billions of horoscopes were examined and compared, this planet has been shown to make people serious, profound and cautious, and to inspire excellent abilities to organize and execute plans of action. When transiting your *second* (financial) house, Saturn indicates a constricting or withholding of money, and means you must work even harder for what little you are able to come by.

People who have Saturn in the fifth house (of children, pleasure and amusement) at birth tend to be deprived of these things in their life. With *Jupiter* in the fifth at birth, there tends to be an *abundance* of the things represented by that department of life. This gets to be very complicated, for example, if someone has Jupiter (abundance) in the fifth house (children) and Saturn (constriction) in the second house (finances)—or vice versa, at birth.

Yet these are merely perfunctory examples of what the horoscope is all about. Mars represents action, energy and courage; people with a well-aspected Mars in the second house (I am referring here to their *natal* horoscope) always have plenty of money earned through their own initiative. The second Sign, Taurus, represents the principles of the second (money) house and vice versa.

Without being too specific, and as mentioned before, Dr. Harlan T. Stetson of the Massachusetts Institute of Technology, while lecturing before the New York Electrical Society, touched on the subject of solar, lunar and planetary correlations with terrestrial events: "If these relationships are not pure coincidence," he said, "they may prove the beginning of two new sciences—solaristics and lunaristics—scientific versions of medieval astrology By means of these it may be possible to predict the flux of business cycles and the coming of earthquakes, as well as other phenomena."

Horoscopes are set up by astrologers for corporations, states and even whole nations. American and foreign astrologers use charts for the birth of their nations in attempting to predict prosperity, foreign policy the outcome of wars and so forth For centuries it has been a practice among Mundane or State astrologers (who predict events for nations, continents and cities) to calculate a horoscope for the exact moment a new ship is launched into the water. Using these charts, many astrologers have made remarkable predictions about the fates of certain ships A comparatively recent case in point was the launching of the nuclear submarine *Thresher*. Soon after the *Thresher* slid from the stocks, a New York astrologer set up a horoscope for the launch and predicted to her class that disaster would overtake the huge submarine, with the possible loss of all lives aboard The *Thresher* eventually broke up and sank, as predicted, with the loss of 129 men.

It seems totally and absolutely irrational to believe that cosmic forces could have anything to do with the fate or destiny of non-living things such as a ship or a space vessel. Yet astrologers seem to do this with confidence—and often with great success.

What special qualities or properties does a horoscope have?

According to the *New International Encyclopedia:* "It is well to point out that the predictions of the better class of astrologers are not haphazard guesses, as is frequently supposed, but are based upon rigid scientific determinations from observed phenomena, according to rigid rules of interpretation . . . also that astrology lays no claims to absolute prediction of future events, undertaking merely to point out the direction which affairs are likely to take, other things being equal."

When you have finished this book, and I suspect you'll want to skip mostly to the meanings of the planets in the Signs at the time and from the place of your own birth, you should know enough about yourself to make some fairly accurate predictions, especially if you relate the configurations of the stars at your birth to the upcoming (or transiting) configurations.

3

Three Power Points
in Your Chart

Writer Hal Boyle once observed: "Whenever I see a young girl or an old lady reading an astrology book on the subway, I have the feeling that 5,000 years of civilization have gone down the drain of time."

Although his is a bigoted stance, I can understand how he feels. One difference between us, to me, is that I have concrete reasons for seeing *his* viewpoint. Boyle, on the other hand, knows little of a subject he publicly condemns. Never having done any hard research in the lives of people who share identical horoscopes, he cannot possibly know whether such people lead parallel existences or not. There is far more evidence in favor of this than either science or sociology currently acknowledges openly.

It's unfortunate that some young girls and old ladies credulously accept everything they read in astrology magazines. It is equally unfortunate that Hal Boyle earnestly condemns a subject he knows nothing about. Astrology isn't some sort of cult or religion. True, it isn't really a complete science, either—at least not in the accepted sense. But as long as you can go into it without taking astrology or yourself *too* seriously, it can be a lot of fun. It can also be an eye-opening adventure into the unknown. With astrology, you *are* able to determine the personality and basic character of almost everyone you meet. You can gain insight into the way others think, feel and behave.

Essentially, this tends to make other people and life itself more interesting. And it makes you more tolerant and kindly toward characteristic and personality differences. The ancient, basic rules of astrology do indeed work—just as they are supposed to.

There are some fundamentals. The position of the Sun is the single most important element in your chart. A man born with the Sun in Gemini, for example, is not as easygoing (or stubborn) as someone with the Sun in Taurus. On the other hand, a Taurus Sun isn't usually as communicative, spontaneous or changeable as a Geminian.

Taking things in their proper order, the focal points of your horoscope are the *Sun's* Sign, the *Moon's* Sign and the Sign on the *Ascendant* of your chart. The Ascendant is covered in Chapter 6, and is determined by the exact hour and minute of your birth. If you don't have this information, it becomes more difficult to determine your correct Ascending Sign.

Keep in mind that the Earth (in fact the entire solar system) is totally surrounded by millions of stars—even whole constellations or groupings of stars. Along the belt of the ecliptic, i.e., the apparent path of the Sun through the Zodiac, are the twelve main constellations (or Signs) with which we're concerned here, from Aries through Pisces. Just as the Earth orbits the Sun once each year, making it seem as though our local star were moving through each constellation, the Earth is also turning on its axis once every 24 hours. If you were born in N.Y.C. at 6 P.M. on September 3, 1942, the sky looked very different then than it did for a person born this minute in Los Angeles.

At night when you look at the stars or Moon over a period of time they seem to be sliding across the sky from East to West. The seeming motion of the cosmos causes the 12 constellations to rise or ascend daily from below the Eastern horizon and to set about 12 hours later in the West, depending on the latitude. Thus, if you were born on April 5 at 1:30 A.M. near the 40th degree of North Latitude, the *Sign* ascending would be Capricorn. Two hours later it would be Aquarius; in another two hours it would be Pisces, etc. Twelve Signs, each requiring two hours to "rise," complete the diurnal cycle or Earth day of 24 hours.

Sooner or later you're going to hear the argument that even if those stars *could* influence human life, they're not only too distant, but *they also are no longer there!* The light from some stars takes hundreds or even thousands of years to reach the Earth. What you're seeing is the light from a star that *used to be there*, but due to cosmic motion is, at *this* moment of time, someplace else.

This is a true statement of fact.

But astrologers use *Signs*, not the actual constellations for which the Signs were originally named. Because of what is called the Precession of the Equinoxes, i.e., the slow backward movement of the Sun's apparent position with regard to the constellations, astrologers say the Sun *is* (for their purposes) in Taurus on April 29. And this method has been borne out enough times to establish it as valid. Astronomers, however, say it is in Gemini.

Astrologers who know astronomy have concluded that the stars and constellations are meant to be used as celestial *markers* for certain times of year on Earth. These positions, educated astrologers now believe, imply that a different geomagnetic condition exists at the equator than at the poles, say, and that there is variety from different longitudes and latitudes as well. (Coordinates such as right ascension and declination are extended into space in order for navigators and astronomers to locate quickly any celestial body.)

For example, the great planet Jupiter, when situated at the Vernal Equinox (the extended plane of the Earth's equator), has a completely different effect on the geomagnetic field than it has when transiting the Winter Solstice Any astrologer who has ever seriously investigated this phenomenon has deduced that the *angles* formed among the planets as they looked when we were born are the cause of varying conditions in our lives. The Signs and constellations are merely points of reference whose real influence, if any, has never been scientifically determined.

Astrological Signs are 30-degree areas of space through which the planets move as they orbit the Sun. The Signs of the Zodiac which comprise the constellations with which astrology is concerned are symbolized as follows:

1. Aries   ♈ Horns of a ram
2. Taurus   ♉ Horns and head of a bull
3. Gemini   ♊ A pair of twins, ideally Castor and Pollux
4. Cancer   ♋ Stylized claws of a crab
5. Leo   ♌ Capital lambda; first letter of Leo
6. Virgo   ♍ IIAP, first three letters of Parthenos, the Virgin, stylized
7. Libra   ♎ A pictograph of a balance or scale
8. Scorpio   ♏ A stylized scorpion
9. Sagittarius ♐ Arrow, symbol of the Centaur-archer

10. Capricornus ♑ Stylized version of a half-fish, half-goat
11. Aquarius ♒ Sumerian-Egyptian symbol for water (the water bearer)
12. Pisces ♓ Stylized drawing of two joined fishes

One result of NASA space probes is that increasing numbers of intelligent, unbiased people in all professions now realize that, basically, astrology has true merit. American Presidents Woodrow Wilson and Franklin D. Roosevelt, as well as some space scientists, have stated their conviction that man is indeed influenced by surrounding celestial forces. Photographer David Duncan, during a recent television interview, talked about his prize-winning pictures—photographs that have taken him all over the world, through several wars, and into the lives of great men.

"I was very interested in those astrologers who were guests here a few weeks ago," Duncan said. "I'm an Aquarian and I think there's a certain fate or destiny working in my life. I've always wanted to photograph beautiful things, but usually wound up taking pictures of violence and death. It seems to be inescapable."

This is the kind of clue by which any astrologer could deduce that photographer Duncan has a powerfully aspected Mars in his chart—or that the Signs of Scorpio and/or Aries are focal points in his horoscope, even though his Sun Sign is Aquarius. Scorpio and Aries are militant Signs closely associated with violence, war, and the military—and physical courage. His Sun Sign, taken by itself, is a powerful, but general indication of his character, and is strongly modified by other factors in his chart.

In your horoscope, the Sun represents the deepest part of your individuality. Wherever the Sun happened to be at your birth, that Sign is usually the most powerful, overriding factor in considering your chart. This is why people are referred to as, say, Sagittarians, Aquarians or Taureans. They might *also* have the Moon in Capricorn, Aries, Leo—or *any* of the twelve Signs. And an Ascendant elsewhere. Another example: Someone with the Sun in Virgo might have the Moon in Cancer with Pisces Ascendant, yet they are still referred to as being a "Virgo."

In casting the horoscope, Mercury, Venus, Mars, Jupiter, Saturn, Uranus, Neptune and Pluto can be scattered around the Zodiac in any number of patterns. An astrologer will often find someone with the Sun in Libra and five or six planets in

Scorpio. In cases like *this*, the relatively weak Libran Sun may easily be completely overpowered by the "stellium" of planets in the strongest of all the Signs—Scorpio. This is a rare situation, however. The norm is that those who are born when the Sun is in any of the twelve Signs are called "natives" of that Sign because of the Sun's enormously powerful influence.

This could confuse people who know a little about the Egyptian, Greek, Roman and British versions of the twelve Signs. The stated physical characteristics of these Signs in turn do not seem to apply, say, to the Chinese, yet all Oriental peoples had developed a sophisticated version of astrology and astronomy before anything of its kind appeared in Europe. This also applies to the Incas of Peru and to what we prefer to call the ancient "Central American" nations.

It boils down, we must confess, to the fact that human *physical* characteristics (despite what some astrology books claim) are *mainly* influenced by genetics—only minusculely controlled by cosmic forces. By the same token, the most powerful and influential celestial body in our scheme of things is *not*, finally, the great blazing Sun but our own planet Earth, on which we live and depend for our existence. An entirely new and probably more accurate kind of astrology will be introduced when Earth's exact influence is finally determined and included in the casting of horoscopes. This is not done today. Whether man actually originated on this planet or another world, as some scientists now propose, he has successfully adapted to *terrestrial* conditions, and is essentially a *Terran*.

(Almost all of Africa south of the Tropic of Cancer, by the way, is devoid of any original knowledge of the cosmos. In fact, no culture south of the equator has ever independently developed astronomy, mathematics *or even written a language of its own!* This is one reason why astrology addresses itself so largely to the Northern Hemisphere.)

All advanced cultures north of the equator seem to have independently discovered astrology, astronomy and mathematics, however. Every one of these nations agrees on the nature of the influence of the planets, the Sun and Moon, the Signs of the Zodiac, and the existence and meaning of the four "elements," Fire, Air, Earth and Water.

It helps to realize that each of these "elements" (i.e., psychological conditions) relates to three of the twelve Signs. The first Sign, Aries, is called a fiery Sign (indicating zeal and enthusiasm) and is harmonious (by reason of its 120° or *trine* angle) with Leo and Sagittarius, also fiery Signs.

Taurus, the second Sign, is earthy (practical and constructive) and is in harmonious angle (120°) with Virgo and Capricorn, each of which are earth Signs.

Gemini the third Sign, is airy (changeable and communicative) and is in trine aspect (or 120° from) the other Air Signs, Libra and Aquarius. (A popular misconception about Aquarius is that it is a Water Sign because its symbol is that of a Water Bearer, yet it is an *Air* Sign.)

Cancer, the fourth Sign, is watery (emotional) and harmonizes with Scorpio and Pisces, also water Signs in "trine" or 120° aspect from each other.

Not only is the trine a fortunate and happy aspect among the Signs and planets, but even 60° or half this measure operates harmoniously. As a general rule of thumb, people born two months before or *after* your birthday (i.e. 60 days apart) are harmonious for you. Three months apart are harmonious. But 4 months, or about 120 days, is ideal. It makes sense if you consider that fire and water Signs do *not* mix well and that earth and water Signs instinctively tend to understand how the others think and feel. And it also works with the fire and air Signs. In the second instance, Scorpio (water) and Virgo (earth) are likely to be harmoniously related because of the 60° or sextile aspect existing between them.

With Leo (fire) and Libra (air), there is another sextile relationship, based on mutual or complementary views.

None of the foregoing implies, however, that people born with the Sun in Scorpio (water) and those born with the Sun in Leo (fire), for example, can*not* get along harmoniously. Each horoscope (unless identical) is a different arrangement or pattern of planets, as we've said, and the Leo "native" may have a Scorpio Moon or Ascendant, thus giving an affinity for a Sign that would not otherwise attract.

Generally, this is how astrology works—the fundamentals painted in broad strokes. These rules can be quickly grasped and easily used by almost anyone. I'm going to avoid all possible technicalities here and acquaint you instead if I may with basic astrological data that you can easily check by only casual observation. It doesn't take long, and it's fun to see people thinking and acting in ways they're "supposed to"—according to their Sun Sign.

We've covered the twelve Signs and the four elements (which are repeated three times around the Zodiac). These can be further refined to constitute *Cardinal, Fixed* and *Mutable* qualities. Consider the harmoniously *trined* fiery Signs, for example: although Aries, Leo and Sagittarius share the same basic fiery temperament, each expresses it in an entirely different and interesting way.

Aries is *Cardinal*, Leo is *Fixed* and Sagittarius is *Mutable*; yet all are fire Signs. These three adjectives apply to each of the four elements, and are therefore repeated four times around the Zodiacal wheel. Cardinal Signs (Aries, Cancer, Libra and Capricorn) are fast-acting, spontaneous. The fixed

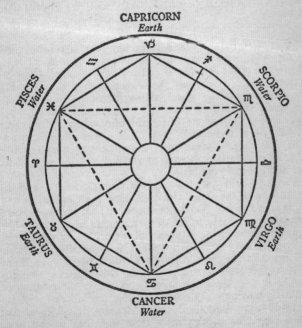

The harmonious relationship (60° or Sextile) between water and earth Signs

Signs (Taurus, Leo, Scorpio and Aquarius) are deliberate, difficult to move. Mutable Signs (Gemini, Virgo, Sagittarius and Pisces) are changeable, sometimes combine the characteristics of fixity and cardinality.

Beginning with the first Sign, Aries, you can quickly determine much of the personality and character of all twelve Sun Signs according to the following list:

1. ARIES—Cardinal (*fire*)
2. TAURUS—Fixed (*earth*)
3. GEMINI—Mutable (*air*)
4. CANCER—Cardinal (*water*)
5. LEO—Fixed (*fire*)
6. VIRGO—Mutable (*earth*)
7. LIBRA—Cardinal (*air*)
8. SCORPIO—Fixed (*water*)
9. SAGITTARIUS—Mutable (*fire*)
10. CAPRICORN—Cardinal (*earth*)
11. AQUARIUS—Fixed (*air*)
12. PISCES—Mutable (*water*)

If you were born on June 15 of any year at sunrise, then the Sun was in the first house; this then is your Ascendant, and you are what astrologers call a *double* Gemini. Born on the same date at sun*set*, the Ascendant is the *opposite* Sign, Sagittarius. The wheel of the horoscope is like a 24-hour clock. If you were born at high noon, the Sun's symbol must be at the top of the wheel, the Midheaven. At midnight it should be at the bottom (the Nadir). The skilled astrologer is thus able to visualize your horoscope generally without *exact* calculations as soon as you tell him the year, date, place and hour of your birth.

Every planet in your horoscope is characterized by and relates to one of the four "elements," and the Cardinal, Fixed and Mutable Signs. Your horoscope and all others (*except those of people born at the same time and place*) have different arrangements or patterns which can identify you almost as certainly as your fingerprints. It is physically impossible *even for twins* to share precisely *identical* horoscopes. Some twins, in fact, are born *hours* apart. This creates major differences in the Ascending Signs as well as in the position of the fastest moving of all celestial bodies, the Moon. In a comparatively short period of time, Mercury and Venus, also fast-moving planets, can orbit from one Sign to the next, either in direct or retrograde motion (about which more later).

An important thing to remember is that, fundamentally,

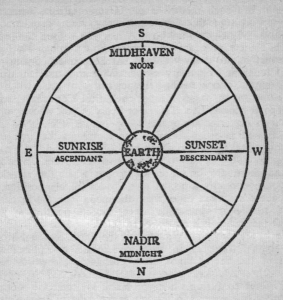

In most temperate latitudes it takes roughly two hours for each Sign to "rise" as the Earth turns. If you were born at high noon anywhere, the symbol for the Sun (☉) must be at the top of the chart. If you were born at midnight, the Sun's symbol must be at the bottom; at sunrise—in the east; at sunset—in the west. The horoscope is exactly opposite from a geographical map because you are looking upward at the heavens.

the air and fire Signs are harmoniously aspected to each other, though *adversely* aspected to the earth and water Signs— and vice versa. (This is symbolized in Solomon's seal, or the Star of David, which was composed of two equilateral triangles, an upright one imposed upon an inverted one. It still survives as the religious symbol for world Jewry, yet most people seem to have little or no knowledge of the astrological wisdom it has represented since ancient times.)

62 WRITE YOUR OWN HOROSCOPE

The Sign of the Moon at your birth triggers certain events in your life each month as our natural satellite completes another orbit of the Earth. Let's say *your* Moon was in Aquarius when you were born. When you consult the listing of the planets' positions (in chapters Four through Thirteen) for every day of every year, you can keep track of your personal lunar and planetary month. With an Aquarian Moon, for example, you are riding the peak of your cycle when the *transiting* Moon passes through Aquarius. Conversely, when the Moon transits Leo, Taurus or Scorpio, you who have the Moon in Aquarius are unable to operate as efficiently—or to feel as well as usual—because Leo represents the *opposition* of your natal Moon's position while Scorpio and Taurus are in *square* (90°, or adverse) aspect to your Aquarius Moon.

And there are times of the month when the transiting Moon is *favorably* aspected to its *radix* (natal) position. In fact, there are *more* times when the moon is in the favorable trine, sextile or semisextile aspect (to its position at your birth) than when it is adversely aspected.

There are only eight planets plus the Earth, Sun and Moon, but some astrologers, in order to associate one planet with each of the twelve Signs, have postulated the existence of two or three *additional* planets, usually called "X," "Y" or "Z." This seems confusing when you learn, say, that the Moon is the ruler of Cancer and the Sun is the ruler of Leo. Neither of these celestial bodies are "planets." The ruler of a Sign is that celestial body whose characteristics are most like the Sign. Leo (Sun) people are dramatic, bold, regal. Cancer (Moon) people are sensitive and impressionable. Still, there's some kind of harmonious vibration between each heavenly body and the Signs of the Zodiac. Every Sign has a planetary "ruler," but Mercury, Venus and Mars have traditionally been assigned as the rulers of *two* Signs each.

Mars is ascribed as the ruler of the first Sign, Aries, and also the eighth Sign, Scorpio.

Venus rules the second Sign, Taurus, and the seventh Sign, Libra.

Mercury rules the third Sign, Gemini, and the sixth Sign, Virgo.

The Moon rules the fourth Sign, Cancer.

The Sun rules the fifth Sign, Leo.

Jupiter rules the ninth Sign, Sagittarius.

Saturn rules the tenth Sign, Capricorn.

Uranus rules the eleventh Sign, Aquarius.

Neptune rules the twelfth Sign, Pisces.

The anomaly that has arisen since the discovery of Pluto in 1931 has been the assigning of this outermost planet to the Sign Scorpio, leaving Mars as the ruler only of Aries.

The Sun, Moon and Ascendant in most horoscopes are usually in three different Signs. There will be times, as we've noted, when a native will be born at sunrise, so his Sun Sign and Ascendant will be the same. If that Sign happens to be Virgo, he is called "a double Virgo." With the Sun *and Moon* in the rising Sign (or Ascendant) he's a double Virgo with the Moon on the Ascendant. Although it is rare, there are some gifted people born during a New Moon or eclipse who also have a whole stellium or grouping of planets in the ascending Sign.

A classic example of this happened on February 4th and 5th 1962. This was the date (depending on which side of the International Date Line you lived) on which the rarest astronomical phenomena in thousands of years took place. All five of the ancient planets: Mercury, Venus, Mars, Jupiter and Saturn, *plus* the Sun and Moon orbited into near-perfect alignment in the scientific-humanitarian Sign of Aquarius. Five planets in one Sign is rare enough, but this occurred at the exact time that a total solar eclipse took place.

The astrological community knew about it many years in advance, and had been predicting great scientific and sociological upheavals. Moreover, those children born at (or close to) the Great Conjunction-Eclipse, they reasoned, would eventually become the nucleus of the greatest advancement mankind has thus far achieved. The astrological press throbbed with warnings of things to come as a result of this extraordinary celestial event. Unfortunately, a mere handful of Indian zealots, who use a different system of astrology from that of the Western hemisphere, were preparing for the end of the world—and received almost all the press coverage.

(According to the most ancient Hindu predictions, whenever the Sun, Moon and planets line up in *Capricorn,* all civilization will be destroyed and a new World Age will begin. The present Hindu system of astrology is one Sign (30°) different from the Western "Tropical" Zodiac. While American and European astrologers anticipated immense social and technological changes because the conjunction-eclipse would occur in *Aquarius,* the Hindus clung to their old system, expecting it to take place in Capricorn.)

A single blood-chilling fact emerged from comparisons of the horoscopes of world leaders to the charts of the conjunction-eclipse. Saturn has always been considered a "malefic"

planet, representing serious obstacles, and eclipses indicate
radical change, often by violence and death. His months before
the great celestial event, astrologers noted that the rare
eclipse would take place at the exact degree of President John
F. Kennedy's natal Saturn, which at fourteen degrees of
Aquarius was in the house of his career. Combining this
evidence with other astrological factors, it was universally
dreaded that President Kennedy would be assassinated. One
of the most outstanding astrological predictions ever made
was that his assassin would *also* be assassinated! (*American
Astrology,* November, 1963)

The Midheaven, or President Kennedy's tenth house, was a
focal, Cardinal point in his chart. With Saturn at that point
in his horoscope, many astrologers who diligently searched
for future planetary transits foresaw that tragedy would strike
when the eclipse triggered that fatal degree of his chart.

Would anyone, knowing that such high political office
might cost his life, turn it down? It hardly seems likely, but
we'll explore the possibility of fate and free will in the final
chapter.

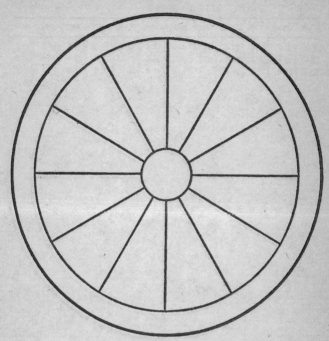

Horoscope blanks

Horoscope blank; locate your Ascendant or rising Sign on pages 152, 153 or 154, place the symbol at the "9 o'clock" position, then fill in the succeeding symbols in a *counter-clockwise* direction. At the end of each chapter outlining the influences of the planets, find the Zodiacal Sign each planet was in on your birthdate, then insert the symbol for that planet between the proper "spokes" of the horoscope wheel. Page 157 shows the symbols for the planets and Signs.

Horoscope blanks

Horoscope blanks

Horoscope blanks

Horoscope blanks

Horoscope blanks

Horoscope blanks

4

Your Sun Sign

Like everyone else on this Earth of ours, you have all twelve Zodiacal Signs and ten (solar) celestial bodies (including the Sun and Moon) in your horoscope. It is the *arrangement* of these various elements in your chart that determines your basic character and individuality.

The circle comprising the Zodiac, like any other circle, contains 360 degrees, and each *Sign* of the Zodiac contains 30 degrees of celestial arc. Due to what is called equinoctial precession, i.e., the backward motion of the equinoxes during the past two thousand years, the constellations for which the Signs were originally named are no longer in their original positions. These constellations of stars were viewed by ancient astrologers as well as modern astronomers as *markers* in the cosmos rather than actual power sources. The argument of astronomers that astrology is 2,000 years behind the times is, therefore, not true.

Astronomers also like to claim that "astrologers still think the Earth is the center of the universe, with the Sun, stars and planets all revolving around it." Astrologers do realize that the Sun is the center of our solar system, of course, but they also recognize that we live on the Earth (*not* the Sun) and are more interested in what happens to us on *this* planet.

If you were born with the Sun in the Sign of Cancer, Scorpio or Pisces (the Water Signs), the first *decanate* (ten days, or ten degrees) is different from the second and third decanates.

In addition to the *Water* Signs, there are three *Air* Signs, three *Fire* Signs and three *Earth* Signs, as I have indicated.

And their decanates vary as well. Water in astrology indicates *emotion*.

The Air *(mental)* Signs are: Gemini, Libra and Aquarius.

The Fire *(enthusiasm)* Signs are: Aries, Leo and Sagittarius.

The Earth *(practical)* Signs are: Taurus, Virgo and Capricorn.

You have *all* these Signs in your horoscope; everyone does. But there are different degrees of the various Signs on the Ascendant (the rising Sign), in the Midheaven and on other parts of the chart. In part, this is what makes each of us interesting and different.

At this point we are dealing solely with the position of the Sun—the single most important and powerful element in your horoscope. In astrological language the Sun is dry, masculine and life-giving. Our local star rules your individuality. (In the chapter on medical astrology, you will learn how the Sun rules the heart, the right eye of the male and the left eye of the female.) Its position in your chart also determines your individual success and social progress—your position in life.

The dates for the Sun's entry into each Sign are given here, but there are some years when this happens a day earlier or later than the times shown. If you were born well within the mentioned dates, you can be certain you belong to that group. If you were born at the change of Signs (called the cusp), then you are a combination of both and should read both.

Dates for the position of the Sun are given *before* each Sign is delineated. For the Moon and planets, the dates are given at the *end* of each chapter.

SUN IN ARIES: first Sign. Cardinal, fiery and masculine.
☉ ♈
(Between March 20 and April 20)

Born when the Sun is in Aries, you are pioneering, headstrong and impulsive. Full of ambition, you love new ideas and enterprises. You have tremendous enthusiasm, persistence and will power, but need to exercise discretion in personal dealings. You are inclined to go right to the point, even if it means being blunt. Indignation and anger come too easily, and your remarks can be cutting. Nobody bosses you around; you'd much rather be at the head of your own organization or at least leading the field in some new endeavor. You are self-assertive, impulsive and restless—always giving the impression of urgency. Although you probably have a fiery temper, you don't hold a grudge for long. You have a great love of justice, freedom and individual deter mination. The Aries man is usually frank and direct, a freedom-loving go-getter. The female of this interesting, zealous Sign is capable and ardent. Born between March 20 and March 30, the first decanate of Aries, you are inclined to be more pioneering and adventurous than usual. If you were born between March 30 and April 10, read the paragraph for LEO to gain further insight into your generous, proud and dramatic nature. If born in the SAGITTARIUS decanate of Aries (April 10 to April 20), read how the open, ingenious, sports-loving influence of Sagittarius affects you.

SUN IN TAURUS: second Sign. Fixed, earthy and feminine.

$$\odot \ \text{\textbgreek{8}}$$
(Between April 20 and May 21)

You like to take your time about things. You are extremely patient and probably have a pleasant, melodious voice. Your symbol is the bull—gentle and yielding when things are going smoothly, but if provoked you become angry, even furious, and difficult to appease. You are constructive, methodical and deliberate, but not very original. You'd rather follow the accepted and reliable paths worn by others. In a negative sense there are times when your natural caution and prudence degenerate into obstinacy and stubbornness. This is when you are too heavy and possibly something of a bore. The Sun in Taurus makes you stable, firm, self-reliant and persistent. You are willing and able to wait a long time for your plans to jell. You have an inordinate love of comfort and ease; the physical pleasures hold a great deal of interest for you. Venus, your ruling planet, gives you a love of peace and beauty in nature. You love amusements, good books, music and art. You have excellent powers of endurance, a sound sense of material values. Despite what is said about your love of leisure and contentment, you can be a hard, methodical worker as long as there are no sudden changes and if security is the ultimate goal. You are possessive, affectionate and sensual, completely aware of the powers of your body. If you were born between April 20 and April 30, you are more reliable, practical and steadfast than most other Taureans; you *must* have security. Born between April 30 and May 10, the VIRGO decanate of Taurus, see that Sign for its intelligent, discriminatory influence. If you were born

in the CAPRICORN decanate of Taurus, between May 10 and
May 20, you have high ambitions, are extremely practical,
secretive and reserved; see Sun in CAPRICORN.

SUN IN GEMINI: third Sign. Mutable, airy and masculine.
⊙ ♊
(Between May 21 and June 21)

You are the *communicator* of the Zodiac, easily recognizable
for your active mind, quick wit and conversational ability.
Many people born in this Sign (Mercury, "messenger of the
gods" is your planetary ruler) are found in occupations where
correspondence, writing, transmission or the exchange of
ideas play a large part. You are excitable and mentally
agile, very hard to pin down. You insist on doing things your
own way, which could be very difficult for others unless
they unquestioningly accept your duality. You are ingenious
for figuring out ways of transmitting things from one place
to another. You are ambidexterous, versatile and alert, but
can be restless, inquisitive and a waster of your own energies.
One of Gemini's chief faults is a tendency to be too changeable and unreliable. You are easily influenced by kindness.
Apt to be a good, quick reasoner, you love logic—or at least
your version of it. With the Sun in Gemini, you often seem
superficial, but like Virgo, you enjoy experimentation and
proof, or at least strong evidence. For this reason you'd make
a good investigator, with your flair for the spoken or written
word. Whatever you learn is quickly imparted to others; it is
difficult for you to be secretive. You are interested in the
sciences, you like to read and can easily undertake two or
more occupations at once. Your active imagination can work
for or against you, but you are usually able to arrive quickly
at conclusions not easily reached by others. Generally, you
have a kindhearted, sympathetic disposition but your sensitivities are myriad. You are idealistic and guided by a strong
intuitive faculty. You like being busy and almost never lose
your ambitious streak. Most of the obstacles and setbacks
you experience are caused by your love of diversity and variety. Born in the first decanate, between May 21 and May
30, you are very strongly ruled by GEMINI. Between May 30
and June 10, read LIBRA for the influence of this peace-lov-
ing Sign of artistic and musical appreciation. If you were
born between June 11 and June 21, read AQUARIUS to learn
how this idealistic, inventive, humanitarian Sign influences
the third decanate of Gemini.

SUN IN CANCER: fourth Sign. Cardinal, watery and
feminine. (☽) ♋
(Between June 21 and July 23)

The Moon, fastest moving of all celestial bodies, is the ruler
of Cancer. Born when the Sun was in Cancer, you are sensitive, versatile, and shy. Still . . . you love publicity and the
limelight. Whether you show it or not, you are inordinately
sensitive and influenced by kindness, consideration and sympathy; you fear criticism or ridicule. You are moody, sentimental, imaginative and sympathetic. While outwardly giving
the impression of self-assurance, you need security. Like your
symbol, the crab, you have a self-protective, hard outer shell
to hide your sensitive, soft interior. You are attracted to the
mysterious and occult and probably like astrology, strange adventure and the mysteries of nature, particularly on and in
the sea. Your sensitivities are not confined to people; emotional receptivity makes you vastly influenced by your surroundings. You probably have a nice comfortable home, a
womblike shelter where you can withdraw to restore your
self-confidence. One of your idiosyncrasies is having something to eat and drink nearby, whether you are at home or
traveling. Cancer rules the stomach and emotions. You are
changeable and therefore have experienced the vicissitudes of
life, with many changes in occupation. You are extremely
frugal, prudent and industrious. You are conscientious in
your work and usually manage to squirrel away a fair portion
of your earnings. Since Cancer has the most retentive memory, you never forget a cut or a kindness. You love your
country, your home and family. You revere your ancestors
and might have the family coat of arms hidden away somewhere. Some of the best patriots and founders of fortunes are
born in this defensive, protective Sign. If your birthdate is
between June 21 and June 30, you are in the CANCER decanate of this Sign. If born between July 1 and July 12, read
SCORPIO for an insight into this shrewd, powerful, secretive
decanate of your Sign. If you were born between July 13 and
July 23, read PISCES for the psychic, mediumistic qualities
of this Sign in your decanate.

SUN IN LEO: fifth Sign. Fixed, fiery and masculine. ⊙ ♌
(Between July 23 and August 23)

The blazing Sun is the ruler of Leo, whose symbol is the
kingly lion. You are frank, open hearted, generous and phil-

anthropic, with a marked dramatic flair. There is a basic conflict in your nature caused by the static quality of a *fixed* Sign with the highly active fire element. You hate being bogged down in details and prefer doing things in a big way. Leo rules the heart and affections. You are a sincere affectionate lover; you thrive on it and are sincere in your desire to bring happiness into your loved one's life. You are a natural leader who feels instinctively that your place in life is one of authority and organization. You are rarely small or mean in your desire to lead and rule, but there is a chance that your great sense of pride might seem overbearing or dominating to others. You are sincere, ardent and highly appreciative of affection freely given—and you generously return it. With your philosophical, active mind and warm disposition, you have many friends who admire your independent, determined, ambitious nature. You have a strong, forceful personality and are quick to anger; like Aries and Sagittarius, however, you are equally quick to forgive. You tend to carry yourself with a kind of regal bearing and are powerful and forthright in your expression. You like the fact that your kind of physical magnetism doesn't go unnoticed. You also love drama, a high position in life—and children. Leo is an inventive, intuitive Sign, industrious, honest and fond of sports. Your active mind, candid nature, generosity and sincerity are an enormous help up the ladder of success. You express an impressive urge for authority. Born between July 23 and August 2, you are in the LEO decanate of Leo, self-expressive, intense and spontaneous. Between August 3 and August 12, read SAGITTARIUS to learn how this outgoing, sportsmanlike Sign influences the second decanate of LEO. If you were born between August 13 and August 23, you are an impetuous, interesting combination of Leo and the ARIES decanate of this sign. Read Aries.

SUN IN VIRGO: sixth Sign. Mutable, earthy and feminine.
☉ ♍
(Between August 23 and September 23)

Although you have a mercurial disposition and may be quick to anger, you'd rather negotiate your differences than face possibly ruinous combat. Virgo, like Gemini, of which Mercury is co-ruler, is a Sign of mental activity. You are good with the written and spoken word and are a good, logical reasoner; this gives you the ability to learn quickly and you have a vast store of knowledge of which few are aware because of your naturally reticent disposition. You are serious, thoughtful, modest and hard-working. In fact, a lot of your time is spent in service to others, one way or another. Your chief desire is to acquire knowledge and attain mental refinement. Although inclined to worry too much about small details that escape most people, you are not easily discouraged. Mentally, you are a detailer, practical and cautious, with good foresight. High on your list of interests are diet and hygiene. You are critical, discriminating and practical. You seek to evaluate life by the analysis of facts and logic. You are active and interested in many things, but these interests often change. You are reserved, conscientious and precise, a lover of art, literature and orderliness in everything. You desire the material blessings of life but cannot easily acquire them. People born with the Sun in Virgo seldom show their true age; it is one of the long-lived Signs. If you were born between August 23 and September 2, the first decanate, the foregoing tendencies of VIRGO are intensified. Born between September 3 and September 13, the CAPRICORN decanate of Virgo, read CAPRICORN to learn how this ambitious, enduring, persevering Sign influences you. Read the influence of TAURUS if you were born in the third decanate of Virgo—September 13 to September 23; this gives you the constructive, beauty-loving wealth-attracting talents of TAURUS.

SUN IN LIBRA: seventh Sign. Cardinal, airy and masculine.

⊙ ♎

(Between September 23 and October 23)

You love peace, beauty and harmony in your life. Chances are you either have married—or will marry—comparatively early in life. With Venus as the planetary ruler of your Sign, you dislike drudgery or any kind of dirty work. You are modest, artistically inclined, neat and particular. You love the arts and all cultural pleasures and amusements. You make the most agreeable and pleasant sort of friend, and are a natural peacemaker. At heart you are a perfectionist and are completely unhappy when placed in an environment of conflict or discord. With the Sun in Libra, you desire peace, justice and harmony in all things. You are sensitive to the conditions of friends and associates; this is particularly so in regard to your marriage or business partner. Libra is a Sign that bestows a sure sense of equilibrium; you are usually known to be charming, kind, easy-going, courteous and agreeable. You may be artistically or musically inclined or trained.

You can usually be found wherever there are gay social activities You enjoy social success through your pleasant disposition and cheerful outlook. If you were born between September 23 and October 2, the influence of LIBRA will be more pronounced than at any other birthtime in October. If born between October 3 and October 13, read AQUARIUS to learn how you are influenced by this detached, scientific, humanitarian Sign. Born between October 13 and October 23, Libra blends with the GEMINI decanate to produce an interesting combination of changeable mental activity with the diplomatic characteristics of Libra.

SUN IN SCORPIO: eighth Sign. Fixed, watery and feminine.

☉ ♏

(Between October 23 and November 22)

Scorpio is the most occult, secretive and powerful segment of the Zodiac You who are born when the Sun was in this Sign are suspicious skeptical, critical, reserved and calculating. Unless other factors modify these basic characteristics you are forceful blunt and sarcastic. In competitive professions such as politics and law you can be extremely aggressive At best the Scorpio influence makes you courageous, creative and scientific, capable of boldness and daring Most of your success in life stems from originality and shrewdness. You tend to mind your own personal business and expect others to do the same. It may be a different story in your profession or career, however. The chances are that you cause trouble for others. There is an intensity of thinking and feeling in you, a certain inflexible strength of will, the power and passion of deep inner conviction You have tremendous reserve energy and recuperative ability No other Sign ranges so widely between good and evil Scorpio is the only Sign with three symbols: the lowly deadly scorpion; the serpent symbolizing wisdom, and the high-soaring eagle, symbolizing spiritual attainment. You have a deep love of the elemental powers of nature and are strongly conservationist. You find the sea and all activities connected with it a source of never-ending interest You are cagey and economical on one hand and fond of luxuries on the other. There is also a kind of basic Spartanism about you, a certain willingness to rough it, or to tear everything down and begin all over again You have shrewd, keen judgment and the ability to size up situations and people at a glance. Your emotions run deep and strong; few people know what you are think-

ing, except that you have strong likes and dislikes. If you
were born between October 23 and November 2, the SCORPIO
characteristics of this Sign will exhibit the strongest characteristics
of this powerful Sign. If born between November 2 and
November 12, read PISCES to learn how this psychic Sign
influences the second decanate of Scorpio. Between November
12 and November 22, read the characteristics of CANCER
to learn how this defensive, possessive Sign influences the
third decanate of Scorpio.

SUN IN SAGITTARIUS: ninth Sign. Mutable, fiery and
masculine. ⊙ ♐
(Between November 22 and December 22)

More than any other Sign you love your liberty, freedom, independence. You hate bosses and dictatorial attitudes, and
tend to view attacks on the weak or helpless as a personal
affront. You are self-reliant, candid in your opinions, frank
and outspoken in your judgments. You are ambitious, honest
and possess a great store of friendliness and good will toward
others—until they prove to be unworthy of it. Your symbol
is the archer, half man, half horse: your remarks usually fly
like arrows, directly to their mark. You have a love of outdoor sports, a respect for science, philosophy and religion.
Since you are frank, honest and outspoken, you need to
develop diplomacy; Sagittarians can be blunt, penetrating or
cutting in their remarks. Generally, however, the Sun in
Sagittarius makes you generous, bright, hopeful and jovial.
You have a charitable, ambitious and active nature, are
not easily discouraged. You are able to make fast calculations and have a great deal of foresight that verges on the
prophetic. You can often foresee the outcome of world
political movements long before they become apparent to
others; this also applies to business enterprises or personal
developments. With your earnest, generous and charitable
nature, there are times when others try to impose upon you.
Fortunately, your ability to size up an individual or a situation makes these attempts transparently clear. Few people
can fool you for very long. If you were born between November 22 and December 1, the SAGITTARIUS decanate of this
jovial Sign, the foregoing applies doubly to you. If you were
born between December 1 and December 11, the ARIES
decanate of Sagittarius, read the characteristics of this fiery,
pioneering Sign to learn how it modifies your basic nature.
Read the influence of LEO if you were born between Decem-

ber 11 and December 21, because this proud, noble Sign has left its indelible imprint on your basic character.

SUN IN CAPRICORN: tenth Sign. Cardinal, earthy and feminine. ☉ ♑
(Between December 22 and January 19)

The symbol of the tenth Sign of the Zodiac is the climbing, persevering mountain goat. Like this tough little animal, you find many obstacles in your path as you struggle toward your goals. By sheer persistence, patience and concentration you are eventually able to overcome all obstacles in the way of success. You are often disappointed but never entirely discouraged. With the Sun in Capricorn you act with dignity and a good sense of your own values. You have a good mind and solid reasoning ability. Usually thoughtful, quiet and serious, you make a natural executive. There may be a tendency to have trouble with your knees or to experience hyperacidity of the digestive tract. This is often brought about by worry or the suppression of emotions. You tend to be somewhat too conventional, too severe in your judgments, and rather cool and calculating in your affections. You are practical, economical and a good investigator. Being cautious and frugal, you make the most of opportunities that come your way. Saturn, the planet of constriction and discipline, rules Capricorn, and strongly affects those born when the Sun transits this patient, persistent Sign. With concentrated effort you can triumph over circumstances that would discourage anyone with less willpower and determination. If you were born between December 22 and January 1, the first decanate of Capricorn, you conform almost rigidly to accepted standards of disciplined behavior. If you were born between January 1 and January 10, read the section on TAURUS to learn how this fixed, earthy Sign influences you. Read VIRGO if you were born between January 10 and January 20; this third decanate makes you highly particular and discriminating.

SUN IN AQUARIUS: eleventh Sign. Fixed, airy and masculine. ☉ ♒
(Between January 20 and February 19)

The Sun in the Sign of Aquarius gives you an idealistic nature, with strong likes and dislikes. You won't be bullied or driven by anyone; you cherish your freedom and indepen-

dence almost as much as a Sagittarian. You are a progressive
thinker and a humanitarian with a good streak of originality.
You are usually determined, quiet, patient and easy to meet.
Even so, you are cautious, probably quite intelligent, thoughtful, studious and philosophical. You tend to view the world with
a detached attitude and an unconventional air. However, you
always identify yourself with any progressive movement and
firmly believe in the brotherhood of man. Although you have
excellent reasoning abilities, you are also intuitive. Others see
you as refined, pleasant and generous, with many friends
among the opposite sex. You have very advanced, sometimes
radical new ideas. In expounding some of these views you
might be looked upon as eccentric. You are inclined to be
scientific, unpredictable, and a lover of the curious and
unusual. You are honest, sincere and usually cheerful, which
makes you slow to anger but difficult to appease. You are
most influenced by kindness. As a lover, your dispassionate,
independent nature creates the appearance of complete emotional detachment from the loved one. The Sun in Aquarius
gives you fertile mental qualities that suit you best for group
work of a reformative nature rather than endeavors involving personal factors. If you were born between January 20
and January 30, the AQUARIUS characteristics are crystallized.
Between January 30 and February 9th, however, you will be
influenced by the changeable, communicative nature of the
GEMINI decanate. Between February 9th and February 19,
the LIBRA decanate makes you more sociable, artistically or
musically inclined.

SUN IN PISCES: the last Sign. Mutable, watery and
feminine. ⊙ ♓
(Between February 19 and March 20)

In many ways Pisces is the most mystical and occult Sign of
all. Compassionate to a fault, the Pisces-born cannot stand
to see others suffer. You are kind and sympathetic to animals,
children and people in distress. You tolerate much adversity
in your life and tend to suffer inwardly. You are easily
moved to tears by the sight or knowledge of someone else
suffering. You are usually modest, possibly timid and lacking
in self-confidence, but you have a certain faith in the unknown. In you there is a desire to care for the sick and
needy, to overcome the illusion of religious and social bar-
riers of conformity and to share the feelings of others. Being
born under such a sensitive water Sign, Pisceans often have a

characteristic weakness for alcohol and a love for the sea.
You are the most "unworldly" of all the twelve Signs. It is
nearly impossible to force your fluid nature into a regi-
mented pattern of behavior. You have a creative imagination,
and are intuitive, impressionable and receptive to what goes
on around you. You are intensely emotional and submissive,
just as likely to delude yourself about reality as to be fooled
by the unscrupulous. You have a tendency to become despon-
dent or over-emotional; this creates a hard-to-overcome negativism and a lack of that vital spark of life and energy.
Pisceans should try to cultivate a more positive attitude, a
less subjective emotional outlook. Chances are you may be
too gullible, temperamental and indecisive for your own good.
You are uncertain and changeable, and perhaps too reserved
or secretive. If you were born between February 19 and
March 1, the full influence of this PISCES decanate makes you
even more psychic and impressionable. If you were born in
the CANCER decanate, between March 1 and March 10, read
the characteristics of this tenacious Sign. If you were born
between March 10 and March 20, you belong to the SCORPIO
decanate of Pisces and will have some of the intensity of
thought, feeling and expression of this powerful Sign.

5

Your Moon Sign

One of the most important factors in selecting a favorable time to invest, marry, travel, etc., is the position of the transiting Moon at the time in relation to your own natal horoscope. For instance, if the Sun at your birth was located at 10 degrees of Gemini in its orbit, then, no matter in which Sign your *natal* Moon was located, you will experience events corresponding to this Sign each month when the Moon transits ten degrees of Gemini.

If you were born at the time of a New Moon (called a "lunation" in astrology), the Sun and Moon were in the same position of the heavens. Astrologers loosely call this a "conjunction," although a true conjunction of the two luminaries, strictly speaking, must result in a total solar eclipse. Not many people are born at the exact time of an eclipse, but those few are remarkable in one way or another, depending on the degree and Sign of the eclipse and its location in the horoscope.

The most important eclipse of modern times occurred on February 4, 1962. Children born during that total eclipse have not only the Sun and Moon located at 15 degrees of Aquarius (the altruistic, scientific, humanitarian Sign) they also have Mercury, Venus, Mars, Jupiter and Saturn closely aligned. This small group (which to a lesser degree includes all children born a couple of days before and after the eclipse) are destined for great new accomplishments during the next several decades.

Whenever an eclipse occurs in the present in the same Sign

and same degree as your natal Sun, Moon or any other planet in your horoscope, something of an unusual nature will take place in your life—a change that corresponds exactly with the symbolic conditions that appear in your horoscope. A valuable piece of astrological information is that the New Moon, Full Moon and eclipses invariably bring about changes (*if* they occur where planets are located in your natal horoscope). An eclipse on your *birthday* is the simplest example of this because it occurs in conjunction with your natal Sun.

The Moon is also an important arbiter in all other terrestrial events. Military commanders of both ancient and modern times have noticed the tendency for mass troop movements to follow each eclipse. Some of these troop movements actually followed the line of the eclipse's path.

Immediately following a solar eclipse in 1945, the American First Army was ordered to cross the Rhine. General Omar Bradley followed General Eisenhower's orders (which, incidentally, had been given to him by Franklin Delano Roosevelt) and withdrew his forces (behind the eclipse's path, as it happened). Russian troops were thus permitted to roll in and occupy East German territory, which is Communist-dominated to this day.

Another example of the "coincidence" of troops massing along the line of an eclipse occurred on November 2, 878 A.D. The path of this eclipse covered what is now known as Old Wapping Road, which runs from Chester to London. In 878, however, there was no such road in existence. In a most remarkable battle, King Alfred, who was fighting the invading Vikings, managed to stop the enemy dead in his tracks all along the path of that ancient eclipse. Britons occupied one side and Vikings the other. This is exactly how the nation was divided.

The Moon has been shown to be a functional factor in dozens of modern scientific studies, many of them originating from large universities and medical centers. Dr. Frank Brown of Northwestern University, Evanston, Illinois, for example, has experimented in this area. Dr. Robert O. Becker of the V.A. Hospital in Syracuse, New York's Upstate Medical Center, and Dr. Igho Kornblueh of the American Institute of Medical Climatology, have given reports of their studies that favored the idea of lunar influence in our lives.

Dr. Brown took some oysters from Long Island Sound at New Haven, Connecticut and flew them to his laboratory in

Evanston, Illinois where he kept them alive and nourished in a tank of salt water of even temperature under a steady, dim light. Oysters open and close their shells at 12 hour intervals (in exact phase with the tides which are caused by the Moon). The oysters continued this behavior as though they were still in New Haven—but only for a couple of weeks. At about the time Dr. Brown concluded that their activity was inherited, the mollusks "clammed" up tightly when they should have been open. It happened that a Full Moon was then directly overhead at Evanston, Illinois!

By the time the Moon had set below the horizon the oysters had "readjusted" their rhythm *exactly* as though they were in a tidal basin in Evanston. Yet they were completely divorced from temperature changes, night and day, or high and low tides. Dr. Brown, who has conducted myriad experiments of this nature, stated that some completely undetectable "force" from the Moon is responsible for virtually all monthly cycles on Earth.

As a result of practical, first-hand experiments and the knowledge he gained from them, Dr. Brown, who is Morrison Professor of Biology at Northwestern University, admitted to Chicago astrologer Katherine de Jersey that astrology must gradually be recognized as the basis of a true science.

Dr. Robert O. Becker and his colleagues in Syracuse, New York, mapped out the human bio-magnetic field and proved beyond doubt that it is powerfully influenced by the Earth's own magnetic-field. In turn, the geomagnetic field fluctuates in perfect phase with the positions of the Sun, Moon and planets.

In-depth studies have also revealed the further refinement of basic personality differences among people born during a waning Moon as compared to those born when the Moon was waxing. When the Moon is decreasing in light (waning), it tends to cause introversion. Conversely, extroverts are usually born after the New Moon, when the lunar crescent is increasing (waxing) in apparent light.

The late Llewellyn George, an erudite astrologer, teacher, writer and publisher, said: "Some New Moons are very important, depending on whether the luminaries at their conjunction form any important aspects in the individual's nativity. When the lunation occurs in a favorable place in the horoscope and in good aspect to some of the radical planets it betokens that the month, summed up in a general way, will be fortunate especially if no strongly malign aspects testify otherwise, but even then such lunation will tend to mitigate the evil."

(The ancient Oriental Yin-Yang symbol—reflected in the flag of the Republic of Korea—signifies an anciently known astrological principle: The Sun is ruler of the day and the Moon of the night. The Incas of ancient Peru, who mined gold and silver in prodigious amounts, were Sun and Moon worshipers, as were virtually all civilized people at one time or another in their histories. *We* call the Incas "pagans," but the entire European economy was based on the billions of dollars' worth of gold and silver plundered from their cities and temples and shipped home by the Christian Spaniards.)

The Moon is next in importance to the Earth and the Sun. Its influence has been studied for millennia and generally concluded by astrological scholars to be "cold, moist, phlegmatic and feminine. She is fruitful and convertible in nature, being fortunate or unfortunate, according to her position by house in a chart, and her aspects and location in the Zodiac (by Sign) at that time." (William Lilly, *An Introduction to Astrology*, pub. by Geo. Bell & Sons, London, 1647)

In astrology the Sun represents the positive life-giving principle, while the Moon symbolizes the receptive or passive side. So much speculation and far-out, unscientific writing has been done about the Moon that it is easy to understand how its influence corresponds to the romantic and fanciful side of human nature. Astrologically, the Moon rules the *personality*, the Sun rules the basic *individuality*, and the Ascendant governs the way we walk and talk, our gestures and outer mannerisms—generally, the physical body.

A classic example of the (often weird) kind of thinking inspired by the Moon is H. P. Blavatsky's passage in *The Secret Doctrine*. ". . . then the Moon (our satellite) pouring forth into the lowest globe of our planetary ring, our Earth . . . all its life, energy and powers; and having transformed them to a new centre becoming virtually a dead planet, in which rotation has almost ceased since the birth of our globe. . . ."

It is one of the misfortunes of astrology that this kind of negativism characterized much of what passed for the science of the stars during the 19th century.

Since the Sun correlates to the character and the Moon to the personality, it is a general rule that if the Moon is closer to the Midheaven (on top of the horoscope) at the time of your birth than the Sun, it makes the *personality* stronger than the character. This is just one of the myriad indicators astrologers use to gauge the whole man. If the Sun is more highly elevated than the Moon, the *individuality* dominates the personality. According to their horoscope, some people tend to express their Moon Sign most, even though the vast majority largely manifest their Sun Signs.

From what follows, you should be able to determine the influence of the Moon on your *personality*. This is *fairly* general, and refers only to where the Moon was at the time of your birth.

A list of the Moon's position from 1890 to 1970 will be found at the end of this chapter.

MOON IN ARIES ☽ ♈

This being the first Sign of the Zodiac, the Moon here means you're liable to be impulsive and enthusiastic. Your personality is often militantly aggressive and you may be given to periods of irritation and anger. Your self-reliance and independence are highly pronounced. You want to have your own way in almost everything and will not be ordered around by anyone. The only discipline you will permit is that which is self-imposed. You tend to be impulsive and unconventional, yet these are the traits which will bring you either great popularity or notoriety. You most like being in a position of authority, and will in all likelihood eventually wind up in an executive capacity or some position of leadership. You set your own pace and choose your own life's work, regardless of the advice of friends and relatives. There is some kind of estrangement or lack of sympathy between you and your parents. Whatever you do is usually viewed as sudden or totally unexpectedly by conservative observers. The Moon in Aries is good for original schemes, ventures, independent operations and military life. Nevertheless, you probably have an attraction for occultism or some other form of mysticism. This tendency can also manifest itself in secrecy in some of your dealings.

MOON IN TAURUS ☽ ♉

You are basically rather conservative, a person who tends to resist anything threatening the status quo. You love all that is beautiful and harmonious; unlike Aries, you are not impulsive. You have a deep desire to become successful, and to this end you will conservatively, positively and ambitiously work. Those with the Moon in Taurus attract good friends and usually acquire money, houses and/or land. Anything that is old, established, weighty and conservative is appealing to one with this position of the Moon. Regardless of what kind of work you do or what business you are engaged in, you will ultimately earn your share of financial remuneration. It may be that the kind of work you do is not considered worthy of your abilities or standing in the community. There may even be something mysterious or secretive about it. You can also make money through wholesale associations, trading societies, co-operative companies, etc. You have a generally kindly and sociable personality, and a good disposition, but you tend to be a little too materialistic and are probably quite sensual. You like a pleasant social life, and probably have a good speaking or singing voice, as well as a love for the theater, for making friends and joining groups or societies.

MOON IN GEMINI ☽ ♊

You are very active, both physically and mentally. If you are not reading, studying or communicating, you are visiting other people, walking, riding and making short trips. You may have more than one house and are likely to change your residence frequently. This position of the Moon is good for the intellect; you like books, scientific and literary subjects. You are liable to live by your wits in one way or another, and could earn your livelihood as an intellectual—a writer, teacher, journalist, salesman, designer or speaker. You probably change occupations as frequently as you change your residence, or you might have more than one profession. You are probably quite skillful with your hands, or may even be ambidextrous, able to do two things at once. All things being equal, you are inclined to be involved in some occupation involving mental ability. You may lack perseverence or be somewhat less than honest in your dealings with others. Gemini is a subtle Sign. When a chart with the Sun or Moon in Gemini is adversely aspected at birth, it often results in scheming or dishonesty. Worst of all (as far as your friends and associates are concerned), you can do this with great charm and wit.

MOON IN CANCER ☽ ♋

You are as much a lover of ease and comfort as one born
with the Moon in Taurus. Yet you lack either the stubbornness or the stability of Taurus, unless the Sun or Ascendant
is in this fixed, earthy Sign. You are changeable, versatile
and keenly emotional. Yet when you are surrounded by
home comforts, good food and drink, you are friendly,
sociable, imaginative and generous. Your environment plays
a large part in your attitude and outlook. In fact, you are
acutely sensitive to exogenous influences, and tend to adopt
a kind of protective coloring from the people and places with
which you associate. You are conservative and domestic by
nature, and love your home, family and ancestry. You may
have been strongly attached to your mother and you may
bear a strong resemblance to her. You are often luckiest when
you listen to or take the advice of other people to carry out
someone else's plans—unless the Sun was in Leo, Aries or
Sagittarius when you were born. Each of these Signs is
noted for being positive and independent. You may have an
inherent talent for expressing how other people think and feel,
and might be a good actor or mimic. There is a strong attraction for water in your psychology; you enjoy living or
vacationing by large bodies of water or traveling by ship.
You are sensitive, intuitive—perhaps able to display psychic
abilities.

MOON IN LEO ☽ ♌

You are proud, ambitious and have no hesitation about as-
suming heavy responsibility or appearing prominently in the
public eye. You have a natural affinity for roles of authority.
Your innate pride makes you rather prone to love affairs;
in fact you probably enjoy great popularity with the opposite
sex because of your susceptibility and sincerity in love. You
attract the admiration of superiors and will eventually enjoy
the favor of people in higher brackets. Where money is concerned, you are generous to a fault. You are equally generous with your affections, as well as being generally honest,
straightforward and idealistic. The Moon in Leo often tends
to be associated with high intelligence, a love of the arts and
the theater, music, painting and literature. On the other hand,

you may display an inordinate love of luxuries for their own sake—jewelry and extravagant clothing, say. You have a lively, persevering spirit, a good mind and good organizational ability.

MOON IN VIRGO ☽ ♍

You have an excellent mind and a good memory, and are best suited for work of an intellectual nature. You could easily become highly successful in the position of an agent, manager, dealer in health foods, doctor, dietitian or druggist. Your ambitions are generally minimal, but you are a good, trustworthy employee as well as a reasonable and considerate employer. You probably lead a simple, unpretentious life, quiet and easygoing. You do best while in the employ of some sort of association, company or corporation. The general tendency of those with the Moon in Virgo is to take numerous trips and to have a lot of friends, particularly if you are a woman. Even so, there could be some secret problem concerning your own marriage. You like to investigate things and, in one way or another, you'll probably earn your living through your mental abilities. You are discriminating, highly selective and judicious. Because of these traits, you are attracted to scientific and occult subjects, and could possess great intuitive abilities or, to some degree, clairvoyance.

MOON IN LIBRA ☽ ♎

You make friends easily and are attracted to refined and harmonious people and circumstances. The Moon in Libra usually inclines toward partnership in love, business or marriage. You are generally popular and well liked for your kindness, good will and affectionate nature. A great deal of your destiny in life stems from your association with other people, usually one person of a powerful persuasion. You are generally easily influenced and your judgment can be swayed by others; this is because of your love of company, friends and society in general. Your attraction for music, painting and the fine arts generally may stem from your own untapped artistic or musical abilities. You like good clothes and probably have a nice wardrobe. Your approach to life is harmonious, with a well-balanced outlook; these are key

words for you with the Moon in Libra. Partnership indeed
plays a large part in your life. Although you are not necessarily inconstant, almost everything you do in life depends
to a large extent on someone else. In fact, you accomplish
much more when you are working in association with another
person.

MOON IN SCORPIO ☽ ♏

You are a battler by nature and temperament. Every problem
you face in life is usually faced alone, with assurance, confidence in your abilities and self-reliance. You often bring
about the thing you are trying to avoid. You are outspoken,
blunt, energetic, positive and hard working. You are something of a puzzle, even to yourself. While on the surface you
might seem to be agreeable and amenable to change, the
fact is that your motivations run a lot deeper than they appear. You are basically conservative and averse to any
changes, particularly if they are forced on you by other
people or circumstances. When you do switch allegiance to
an idea, you are fully capable of supporting or engineering
great revolutionary changes. Scorpio is probably the most
misunderstood of all the Signs. With the Moon placed here,
you probably know why others don't understand you. You
are inclined to irritation, anger and revenge; there are some
people who think you lack a strong moral code or that you
drink too much. Yet you have great willpower, energy, determination, a love of pleasure and the desire to satisfy your
tastes. This position of the Moon is associated closely with
some work in connection with death; for example, you might
be an insurance claims adjustor, policeman, fireman or soldier. You have a powerful attraction toward the opposite sex,
and vice versa—a condition that can cause considerable
difficulty in your life, and may indicate more than one
marriage.

 MOON IN SAGITTARIUS ☽ ♐

You love the great outdoors, your freedom and independence.
You are jovial (derived from Jove or Jupiter, the ruling
planet of Sagittarius), active, fond of travel and sports. You
appear to be restless and unsettled, either physically or mentally. Even though your religions beliefs may be unorthodox,

you are sincere, candid and cordial toward others. There is a tendency to be blunt, to state whatever occurs to you at the moment and to think about it afterward, if at all. You say whatever you think, an admirable quality but not always a diplomatic one. You could easily have two vocations, or frequently change your job. You are generally good-natured, kind and honest, with a high-minded regard for the welfare of others; in fact, an injustice to someone else amounts almost to a personal injury to you. You are quick to anger, but have a forgiving nature and do not usually hold a grudge. You are a natural teacher, something of a minor prophet, able to foresee the outcome of events from a long distance. You have an active intuition, with accurate dreams that often come true. You dislike being tied to one place and will often change your residence.

MOON IN CAPRICORN ☽ ♑

You are a born administrator or executive, with enough generalship to achieve a certain degree of celebrity. Depending on the rest of your horoscope, this could work out either beneficially or adversely; it might mean fame or notoriety. Chances are your ambition, dedication, practicality and hard work will eventually bring you to public attention as a prominent and respected individual. Some of the drawbacks of this position of the Moon are that it tends to make you rather cold and calculating; too often you are careless of the feelings of others. If your Sun or Ascendant is in one of the Cardinal Signs: Aries, Cancer, Libra or Capricorn, your future success is almost assured. But whatever fame or influence you gain, it is almost certain that some kind of enemy will appear, either secretly or openly, to try to ruin your reputation, whether you deserve it or not. Fortunately, this enemy will probably fail. You know how to influence others, and can put on a good show when the situation seems to call for it. You share with a person whose Moon is in Scorpio a good deal of creative energy, trouble through or with the opposite sex and (in a badly aspected chart) a lack of control in certain important areas of your life. Despite all else, you are one of the prime movers who knows how to get things done and will work tirelessly toward any goal you have set.

MOON IN AQUARIUS ☽ ♒

You have great intuitive powers and imagination, and enjoy the good opinion of friends and colleagues. You are sympathetic, sociable, outgoing and yet can often display a highly unorthodox, independent and unconventional attitude. Unimaginative people might consider you to be slightly eccentric because of your off-beat interests or hobbies. Whatever is intellectually or socially stimulating, original or unusual will attract you. You may have a strong inclination for educational, political, scientific or social work. At heart you are something of a humanitarian, highly idealistic (though not always practical). Large movements supporting great causes gain your support, or you may belong to a mystical or secret society, brotherhood or association. You are inventive, original and scientifically inclined. With Moon in Aquarius, you are probably gifted with an inclination toward occult subjects; astrology or clairvoyance, say. You are extremely humane and broadly sympathetic, a true liberal in the best sense of the word. You get along famously with people who are congenial and think as you do. In all probability you may belong to a society, club, association or group who think and believe as you do.

MOON IN PISCES ☽ ♓

You are attracted to whatever appeals to your emotions and feelings—in music, literature or poetry. Emotion is a major factor in all your activities. You are generally changeable, sometimes undependable, too easily discouraged when you are confronted with trouble, opposition and obstacles. You love variety and are apt to change your mind about things frequently. Yet you are rather easygoing, somewhat shy and retiring in many contacts. The Moon in Pisces has often been cited by astrologers as an unfavorable position causing glandular disorders and overweight. Although you are probably outwardly gay and hopeful, with a seemingly good sense of humor, you are prone to become easily depressed and could even lack a common sense of humor. It has been frequently observed that this position of the Moon is likely to lead to periods of intemperance, dissipation and even dishonesty, but this must be considered with the total aspects in anyone's horoscope before any flat conclusion can be drawn. The fact is that Moon in Pisces *can* be one of the most appealing, entertaining and humorous of all the positions. At one time or another, hospitals, prisons or institutions of some kind will play an important role in your life. You may have a flair for music, composing or writing. Whatever you do, it is emotional and romantic; your creative output is fluid, prodigious and imaginative.

The following tables will enable you to locate the position of the Moon by Sign at the time of your birth. Each day given is the one on which the Moon *changed* Signs. If you were born, say, on December 7, 1941, you will see that the symbol next to the date indicates that the Moon moved into Leo, but does not indicate the exact time this took place. So (depending on the time) the Moon might still have been in the *preceding* Sign. As with the ascending Sign, you simply read the characteristics bestowed by the Moon in *both* Signs and insert the lunar crescent in the Sign that "feels" most natural to you. The Moon in Leo gives an entirely different characteristic temperament than when in its own Sign, Cancer, for example. This applies to each succeeding Sign, thus making it a simple matter of choosing one or the other. This little exercise in judgment will not only sharpen your insight, it will also strengthen your intuitive ability to determine the Sun Signs, Moon Signs and Ascendants of other people.

1890

JAN.	FEB.	MAR.	APR.	MAY	JUNE	JULY	AUG.	SEPT.	OCT.	NOV.	DEC.
2 ♊	1 ♋	2 ♌	1 ♍	1 ♎	2 ♐	1 ♑	2 ♓	2 ♉	2 ♊	1 ♋	1 ♌
4 ♋	3 ♌	5 ♍	4 ♎	3 ♏	4 ♑	3 ♒	4 ♈	5 ♊	4 ♋	3 ♌	3 ♍
7 ♌	6 ♍	7 ♎	6 ♏	6 ♐	6 ♒	5 ♓	6 ♉	7 ♋	7 ♌	6 ♍	6 ♎
9 ♍	8 ♎	10 ♏	8 ♐	8 ♑	8 ♓	7 ♈	8 ♊	10 ♌	9 ♍	8 ♎	8 ♏
12 ♎	10 ♏	12 ♐	10 ♑	10 ♒	10 ♈	10 ♉	11 ♋	12 ♍	12 ♎	11 ♏	10 ♐
14 ♏	13 ♐	14 ♑	12 ♒	12 ♓	12 ♉	12 ♊	13 ♌	15 ♎	14 ♏	13 ♐	12 ♑
16 ♐	15 ♑	16 ♒	15 ♓	14 ♈	15 ♊	14 ♋	16 ♍	17 ♏	16 ♐	15 ♑	14 ♒
18 ♑	17 ♒	18 ♓	17 ♈	16 ♉	17 ♋	17 ♌	18 ♎	19 ♐	19 ♑	17 ♒	16 ♓
20 ♒	19 ♓	20 ♈	19 ♉	19 ♊	20 ♌	20 ♍	21 ♏	22 ♑	21 ♒	19 ♓	19 ♈
22 ♓	21 ♈	23 ♉	21 ♊	21 ♋	22 ♍	22 ♎	23 ♐	24 ♒	23 ♓	21 ♈	21 ♉
24 ♈	23 ♉	25 ♊	24 ♋	23 ♌	24 ♎	25 ♏	25 ♑	26 ♓	25 ♈	24 ♉	23 ♊
27 ♉	25 ♊	27 ♋	26 ♌	26 ♍	27 ♏	27 ♐	28 ♒	27 ♓	27 ♉	26 ♊	25 ♌
29 ♊	28 ♋	30 ♌	29 ♍	28 ♎	29 ♐	29 ♑	30 ♓	29 ♓	28 ♊	28 ♋	28 ♌
				31 ♏		31 ♈					30 ♍

1891

JAN.	FEB.	MAR.	APR.	MAY	JUNE	JULY	AUG.	SEPT.	OCT.	NOV.	DEC.
2 ♎	1 ♏	2 ♐	1 ♑	2 ♓	1 ♈	2 ♊	1 ♋	2 ♍	2 ♎	1 ♏	3 ♑
4 ♏	3 ♐	5 ♑	3 ♒	4 ♈	3 ♉	5 ♋	3 ♌	4 ♎	4 ♏	3 ♐	5 ♒
7 ♐	5 ♑	7 ♒	5 ♓	7 ♈	5 ♊	7 ♌	5 ♍	7 ♏	7 ♐	5 ♑	7 ♓
9 ♑	7 ♒	9 ♓	7 ♈	9 ♉	7 ♋	9 ♍	8 ♎	9 ♐	9 ♑	7 ♒	9 ♈
11 ♒	9 ♓	11 ♈	9 ♉	11 ♊	10 ♌	12 ♎	11 ♏	12 ♑	11 ♒	10 ♓	11 ♉
13 ♓	11 ♈	13 ♉	11 ♊	14 ♋	12 ♍	14 ♏	13 ♐	14 ♒	13 ♓	12 ♈	13 ♊
15 ♈	13 ♉	15 ♊	14 ♋	16 ♌	15 ♎	17 ♐	15 ♑	16 ♓	15 ♈	14 ♉	16 ♋
17 ♉	16 ♊	17 ♋	16 ♌	18 ♍	17 ♏	19 ♑	18 ♒	18 ♈	17 ♉	16 ♊	18 ♌
19 ♊	18 ♋	20 ♌	18 ♍	21 ♏	19 ♐	21 ♒	20 ♓	20 ♉	19 ♊	18 ♋	20 ♍
22 ♋	20 ♌	22 ♍	21 ♎	23 ♐	22 ♑	23 ♓	22 ♈	22 ♊	22 ♋	20 ♌	23 ♎
24 ♌	23 ♍	25 ♎	23 ♏	25 ♑	24 ♒	25 ♈	24 ♉	24 ♋	24 ♌	23 ♍	25 ♏
27 ♍	25 ♎	27 ♏	26 ♐	28 ♒	26 ♓	27 ♉	26 ♊	27 ♌	26 ♎	25 ♍	28 ♐
29 ♎	28 ♏	30 ♐	28 ♑	30 ♓	28 ♈	30 ♊	28 ♋	29 ♎	29 ♏	28 ♎	30 ♑
			30 ♒	30 ♉			30 ♌			30 ♐	

Key: Aries   Taurus   Gemini   Cancer   Leo   Virgo
          ♈   ♉   ♊   ♋   ♌   ♍

1892

JAN.	FEB.	MAR.	APR.	MAY	JUNE	JULY	AUG.	SEPT.	OCT.	NOV.	DEC.
1 ♒	2 ♈	2 ♉	1 ♊	2 ♌	1 ♍	1 ♎	2 ♐	1 ♑	1 ♒	1 ♈	1 ♉
3 ♓	4 ♉	4 ♊	3 ♋	5 ♍	3 ♎	3 ♏	5 ♑	3 ♒	3 ♓	3 ♉	3 ♊
5 ♈	6 ♊	6 ♋	5 ♌	7 ♎	6 ♏	6 ♐	7 ♒	5 ♓	5 ♈	5 ♊	5 ♋
8 ♉	8 ♋	9 ♌	7 ♍	10 ♏	8 ♐	8 ♑	9 ♓	7 ♈	8 ♉	7 ♋	7 ♌
10 ♊	10 ♌	11 ♍	10 ♎	12 ♐	11 ♑	10 ♒	11 ♈	9 ♉	10 ♊	9 ♌	9 ♍
12 ♋	13 ♍	14 ♎	12 ♏	15 ♑	13 ♒	13 ♓	13 ♉	12 ♊	11 ♋	12 ♍	11 ♎
14 ♌	15 ♎	16 ♏	15 ♐	17 ♒	15 ♓	15 ♈	15 ♊	14 ♋	13 ♌	14 ♎	14 ♏
17 ♍	18 ♏	19 ♐	17 ♑	19 ♓	18 ♈	17 ♉	17 ♋	16 ♌	15 ♍	17 ♏	17 ♐
19 ♎	20 ♐	21 ♑	20 ♒	21 ♈	20 ♉	19 ♊	20 ♌	18 ♍	18 ♎	19 ♐	19 ♑
22 ♏	23 ♑	23 ♒	22 ♓	23 ♉	22 ♊	21 ♋	22 ♍	21 ♎	20 ♏	22 ♑	21 ♒
24 ♐	25 ♒	25 ♓	24 ♈	25 ♊	24 ♋	23 ♌	24 ♎	23 ♏	23 ♐	24 ♒	24 ♓
26 ♑	27 ♓	28 ♈	26 ♉	27 ♋	26 ♌	26 ♍	27 ♏	26 ♐	26 ♑	27 ♓	26 ♈
29 ♒	29 ♈	29 ♉	28 ♊	30 ♌	28 ♍	28 ♎	29 ♐	28 ♑	28 ♒	29 ♈	28 ♉
31 ♓			30 ♋			31 ♏			30 ♓		30 ♊

1893

JAN.	FEB.	MAR.	APR.	MAY	JUNE	JULY	AUG.	SEPT.	OCT.	NOV.	DEC.
1 ♋	2 ♍	1 ♍	2 ♏	2 ♐	1 ♑	1 ♒	2 ♈	2 ♊	1 ♋	2 ♍	2 ♎
3 ♌	4 ♎	4 ♎	5 ♐	5 ♑	3 ♒	3 ♓	4 ♉	4 ♋	4 ♌	4 ♎	4 ♏
5 ♍	7 ♏	6 ♏	7 ♑	7 ♒	6 ♓	5 ♈	6 ♊	6 ♌	6 ♍	7 ♏	6 ♐
8 ♎	9 ♐	8 ♐	10 ♒	9 ♓	8 ♈	8 ♉	8 ♋	8 ♍	8 ♎	9 ♐	9 ♑
10 ♏	12 ♑	11 ♑	12 ♓	12 ♈	10 ♉	10 ♊	10 ♌	11 ♎	10 ♏	12 ♑	11 ♒
13 ♐	14 ♒	13 ♒	14 ♈	14 ♉	12 ♊	12 ♋	13 ♍	13 ♏	13 ♐	14 ♒	14 ♓
15 ♑	16 ♓	16 ♓	16 ♉	16 ♊	14 ♋	14 ♌	16 ♎	15 ♐	16 ♑	17 ♓	16 ♈
18 ♒	18 ♈	18 ♈	18 ♊	18 ♋	16 ♌	16 ♍	18 ♏	18 ♑	18 ♒	19 ♈	19 ♉
20 ♓	21 ♉	20 ♉	20 ♋	20 ♌	18 ♍	18 ♎	21 ♐	21 ♒	20 ♓	21 ♉	21 ♊
22 ♈	23 ♊	22 ♊	22 ♌	22 ♍	21 ♎	20 ♏	23 ♑	23 ♓	23 ♈	23 ♊	23 ♋
24 ♉	25 ♋	24 ♋	25 ♍	24 ♎	23 ♏	23 ♐	25 ♒	25 ♈	25 ♉	25 ♋	25 ♌
26 ♊	27 ♌	26 ♌	27 ♎	27 ♏	26 ♐	25 ♑	27 ♓	27 ♉	27 ♊	27 ♌	27 ♍
29 ♋		29 ♍	30 ♏	29 ♐	28 ♑	28 ♒	29 ♈	29 ♊	29 ♋	29 ♍	29 ♎
31 ♌		31 ♎		31 ♑	30 ♒	30 ♓	31 ♉		31 ♌		31 ♏

Libra	Scorpio	Sagittarius	Capricorn	Aquarius	Pisces
♎	♏	♐	♑	♒	♓

1001

JAN.	FEB.	MAR.	APR.	MAY	JUNE	JULY	AUG.	SEPT.	OCT.	NOV.	DEC.
3 ♐	1 ♑	1 ♑	2 ♓	2 ♈	3 ♊	2 ♋	2 ♍	1 ♎	3 ♐	2 ♑	1 ♎
5 ♑	4 ♒	3 ♒	4 ♈	4 ♉	5 ♋	4 ♌	4 ♎	3 ♏	5 ♑	4 ♒	4 ♓
8 ♒	6 ♓	6 ♓	7 ♉	6 ♊	7 ♌	6 ♍	7 ♏	5 ♐	8 ♒	7 ♓	6 ♈
10 ♓	9 ♈	8 ♈	9 ♊	8 ♋	9 ♍	8 ♎	9 ♐	8 ♑	10 ♓	9 ♈	9 ♉
13 ♈	11 ♉	10 ♉	11 ♋	10 ♌	11 ♎	10 ♏	12 ♑	10 ♒	13 ♈	11 ♉	11 ♊
15 ♉	13 ♊	13 ♊	13 ♌	12 ♍	13 ♏	13 ♐	14 ♒	13 ♓	15 ♉	13 ♊	13 ♋
17 ♊	15 ♋	15 ♋	15 ♍	15 ♎	16 ♐	15 ♑	17 ♓	15 ♈	17 ♊	16 ♋	15 ♌
19 ♋	17 ♌	17 ♌	17 ♎	17 ♏	18 ♑	18 ♒	19 ♈	18 ♉	19 ♋	18 ♌	17 ♍
21 ♌	19 ♍	19 ♍	20 ♏	19 ♐	21 ♒	20 ♓	21 ♉	20 ♊	21 ♌	20 ♍	19 ♎
23 ♍	22 ♎	21 ♎	22 ♐	22 ♑	23 ♓	23 ♈	24 ♊	22 ♋	24 ♍	22 ♎	21 ♏
25 ♎	24 ♏	23 ♏	24 ♑	24 ♒	26 ♈	25 ♉	26 ♋	24 ♌	26 ♎	24 ♏	24 ♐
27 ♏	26 ♐	26 ♐	27 ♒	27 ♓	28 ♉	27 ♊	28 ♌	26 ♍	28 ♏	26 ♐	26 ♑
30 ♐		28 ♑	29 ♓	29 ♈	30 ♊	29 ♋	30 ♍	28 ♎	30 ♐	29 ♑	29 ♒
		31 ♒		31 ♉		31 ♌		30 ♏			31 ♓

1895

JAN.	FEB.	MAR.	APR.	MAY	JUNE	JULY	AUG.	SEPT.	OCT.	NOV.	DEC.
3 ♈	1 ♉	1 ♉	1 ♋	1 ♌	1 ♎	1 ♏	2 ♑	3 ♓	3 ♈	1 ♉	1 ♊
5 ♉	4 ♊	3 ♊	4 ♌	3 ♍	3 ♏	3 ♐	4 ♒	5 ♈	5 ♉	4 ♊	3 ♋
7 ♊	6 ♋	5 ♋	6 ♍	5 ♎	6 ♐	5 ♑	7 ♓	8 ♉	7 ♊	6 ♋	5 ♌
9 ♋	8 ♌	7 ♌	8 ♎	7 ♏	8 ♑	7 ♒	9 ♈	10 ♊	10 ♋	8 ♌	8 ♍
11 ♌	10 ♍	9 ♍	10 ♏	9 ♐	10 ♒	10 ♓	12 ♉	13 ♋	12 ♌	10 ♍	10 ♎
13 ♍	12 ♎	11 ♎	12 ♐	12 ♑	13 ♓	13 ♈	14 ♊	15 ♌	14 ♍	12 ♎	12 ♏
15 ♎	14 ♏	13 ♏	14 ♑	14 ♒	15 ♈	15 ♉	16 ♋	17 ♍	16 ♎	15 ♏	14 ♐
18 ♏	16 ♐	16 ♐	17 ♒	17 ♓	18 ♉	18 ♊	18 ♌	19 ♎	18 ♏	17 ♐	16 ♑
20 ♐	19 ♑	18 ♑	19 ♓	19 ♈	20 ♊	20 ♋	20 ♍	21 ♏	20 ♐	19 ♑	19 ♒
22 ♑	21 ♒	20 ♒	22 ♈	22 ♉	22 ♋	23 ♌	23 ♎	23 ♐	22 ♑	21 ♒	21 ♓
25 ♒	24 ♓	23 ♓	24 ♉	24 ♊	24 ♌	24 ♍	26 ♏	25 ♑	24 ♒	24 ♈	26 ♉
27 ♓	26 ♈	25 ♈	26 ♊	26 ♋	26 ♍	26 ♎	28 ♐	27 ♒	27 ♈	26 ♉	26 ♊
30 ♈		28 ♉	29 ♋	28 ♌	29 ♎	28 ♏	29 ♑	30 ♓	30 ♈	28 ♊	28 ♊
		30 ♊		30 ♍		30 ♐	31 ♒				31 ♋

Key: Aries   Taurus   Gemini   Cancer   Leo   Virgo
　　　　　♈　　　♉　　　♊　　　♋　　　♌　　　♍

1896

JAN.	FEB.	MAR.	APR.	MAY	JUNE	JULY	AUG.	SEPT.	OCT.	NOV.	DEC.
2 ♌	2 ♎	1 ♎	1 ♐	1 ♑	2 ♓	2 ♈	3 ♊	2 ♋	1 ♌	2 ♎	1 ♏
4 ♍	4 ♏	3 ♏	3 ♑	3 ♒	4 ♈	4 ♉	5 ♋	4 ♌	3 ♍	4 ♏	3 ♐
6 ♎	6 ♐	5 ♐	5 ♒	5 ♓	7 ♉	7 ♊	7 ♌	7 ♍	5 ♎	6 ♐	5 ♑
8 ♏	9 ♑	7 ♑	8 ♓	8 ♈	9 ♊	9 ♋	10 ♍	9 ♎	7 ♏	8 ♑	8 ♒
10 ♐	11 ♒	9 ♒	11 ♈	10 ♉	11 ♋	11 ♌	12 ♎	11 ♏	9 ♐	10 ♒	10 ♓
13 ♑	14 ♓	12 ♓	13 ♉	12 ♊	14 ♌	13 ♍	14 ♏	13 ♐	12 ♑	13 ♓	12 ♈
15 ♒	16 ♈	14 ♈	16 ♊	15 ♋	16 ♍	15 ♎	16 ♐	15 ♑	14 ♒	15 ♈	15 ♉
17 ♓	19 ♉	17 ♉	18 ♋	18 ♌	18 ♎	17 ♏	18 ♑	17 ♒	16 ♓	18 ♉	17 ♊
20 ♈	21 ♊	19 ♊	20 ♌	20 ♍	20 ♏	20 ♐	20 ♒	19 ♓	19 ♈	20 ♊	20 ♋
22 ♉	23 ♋	22 ♋	23 ♍	22 ♎	22 ♐	22 ♑	23 ♓	21 ♈	21 ♉	22 ♋	22 ♌
25 ♊	26 ♌	24 ♌	25 ♎	24 ♏	24 ♑	24 ♒	25 ♈	24 ♉	24 ♊	25 ♌	24 ♍
27 ♋	28 ♍	26 ♍	27 ♏	26 ♐	27 ♒	26 ♓	27 ♉	27 ♊	26 ♋	27 ♍	27 ♎
29 ♌		28 ♎	29 ♐	28 ♑	29 ♓	29 ♈	30 ♊	29 ♋	29 ♌	29 ♎	29 ♏
31 ♍		30 ♏		30 ♒		31 ♉			31 ♍		31 ♐

1897

JAN.	FEB.	MAR.	APR.	MAY	JUNE	JULY	AUG.	SEPT.	OCT.	NOV.	DEC.
2 ♑	3 ♓	2 ♓	1 ♈	3 ♊	2 ♋	1 ♌	2 ♏	1 ♐	2 ♑	3 ♈	2 ♈
4 ♒	5 ♈	4 ♈	3 ♉	5 ♋	4 ♌	4 ♍	4 ♐	3 ♑	4 ♒	5 ♉	5 ♉
6 ♓	8 ♉	7 ♉	6 ♊	8 ♌	6 ♍	6 ♎	6 ♑	5 ♒	6 ♓	7 ♊	7 ♊
9 ♈	10 ♊	9 ♊	8 ♋	10 ♍	9 ♎	8 ♏	9 ♒	7 ♓	9 ♈	10 ♋	10 ♋
11 ♉	12 ♋	11 ♋	10 ♌	12 ♎	11 ♏	10 ♐	11 ♓	9 ♈	11 ♉	12 ♌	12 ♌
14 ♊	15 ♌	14 ♌	13 ♍	14 ♏	13 ♐	12 ♑	13 ♈	12 ♉	13 ♊	15 ♍	15 ♍
16 ♋	17 ♍	16 ♍	15 ♎	16 ♐	15 ♑	14 ♒	15 ♉	14 ♊	15 ♋	17 ♎	17 ♎
18 ♌	19 ♎	18 ♎	17 ♏	18 ♑	17 ♒	16 ♓	18 ♊	16 ♋	17 ♌	20 ♏	19 ♏
21 ♍	21 ♏	20 ♏	19 ♐	20 ♒	19 ♓	19 ♈	20 ♋	19 ♌	19 ♍	22 ♐	21 ♐
23 ♎	23 ♐	23 ♐	21 ♑	23 ♓	22 ♈	21 ♉	23 ♌	21 ♍	21 ♎	24 ♑	23 ♑
25 ♏	25 ♑	25 ♑	23 ♒	25 ♈	24 ♉	23 ♊	25 ♍	24 ♎	23 ♏	26 ♒	25 ♒
27 ♐	28 ♒	27 ♒	25 ♓	28 ♉	26 ♊	25 ♋	27 ♎	26 ♏	25 ♐	28 ♓	27 ♓
29 ♑		29 ♓	28 ♈	30 ♊	29 ♋	27 ♌	29 ♏	28 ♐	27 ♑	30 ♈	30 ♈
31 ♒			30 ♉			29 ♍		30 ♑	29 ♒		
						31 ♎			31 ♓		

Libra	Scorpio	Sagittarius	Capricorn	Aquarius	Pisces
♎	♏	♐	♑	♒	♓

1898

JAN.	FEB.	MAR.	APR.	MAY	JUNE	JULY	AUG.	SEPT.	OCT.	NOV.	DEC.
1 ♉	2 ♋	1 ♋	1 ♌	3 ♎	1 ♏	1 ♐	1 ♒	2 ♈	1 ♉	2 ♋	2 ♌
3 ♊	5 ♌	4 ♌	3 ♍	5 ♏	3 ♐	3 ♑	3 ♓	4 ♉	4 ♊	5 ♌	5 ♍
6 ♋	7 ♍	7 ♍	5 ♎	7 ♐	5 ♑	5 ♒	5 ♈	6 ♊	6 ♋	7 ♍	7 ♎
9 ♌	9 ♍	9 ♍	7 ♏	9 ♑	9 ♒	7 ♓	7 ♉	9 ♋	9 ♌	10 ♎	9 ♏
11 ♍	12 ♍	11 ♍	9 ♐	11 ♒	9 ♓	9 ♈	10 ♊	11 ♌	11 ♍	12 ♍	12 ♐
13 ♎	14 ♐	13 ♐	11 ♑	13 ♓	11 ♈	11 ♉	12 ♋	14 ♍	13 ♎	14 ♐	14 ♑
15 ♏	16 ♑	15 ♑	14 ♒	15 ♈	14 ♉	14 ♊	15 ♌	16 ♎	16 ♏	16 ♑	16 ♒
18 ♐	18 ♒	17 ♒	16 ♓	18 ♉	16 ♊	16 ♋	17 ♍	18 ♏	18 ♐	18 ♒	18 ♓
20 ♑	20 ♓	20 ♓	18 ♈	20 ♊	19 ♋	19 ♌	20 ♎	20 ♐	20 ♑	20 ♓	20 ♈
22 ♒	22 ♈	22 ♈	20 ♉	23 ♋	21 ♌	21 ♍	22 ♏	23 ♑	22 ♒	23 ♈	22 ♉
24 ♓	25 ♉	24 ♉	23 ♊	25 ♌	24 ♍	24 ♎	24 ♐	25 ♒	24 ♓	25 ♉	24 ♊
26 ♈	27 ♊	26 ♊	25 ♋	28 ♍	26 ♎	26 ♏	26 ♑	27 ♓	26 ♈	27 ♊	27 ♋
28 ♉		29 ♋	28 ♌	30 ♎	29 ♏	28 ♐	28 ♒	29 ♈	28 ♉	30 ♋	29 ♌
31 ♊			30 ♍			30 ♑	30 ♓		31 ♍		

1899

JAN.	FEB.	MAR.	APR.	MAY	JUNE	JULY	AUG.	SEPT.	OCT.	NOV.	DEC.
1 ♍	2 ♍	1 ♏	2 ♑	1 ♒	2 ♈	1 ♉	2 ♋	1 ♌	1 ♍	2 ♍	2 ♐
3 ♎	4 ♐	4 ♐	4 ♒	4 ♓	4 ♉	4 ♊	5 ♌	4 ♍	3 ♎	4 ♐	4 ♑
6 ♏	6 ♑	6 ♑	6 ♓	6 ♈	6 ♊	6 ♋	7 ♍	6 ♎	6 ♏	7 ♑	6 ♒
8 ♐	8 ♒	8 ♒	8 ♈	8 ♉	9 ♋	9 ♌	10 ♎	8 ♏	8 ♐	9 ♒	8 ♓
10 ♑	10 ♓	10 ♓	10 ♉	10 ♊	11 ♌	11 ♍	12 ♏	11 ♐	10 ♑	11 ♓	10 ♈
12 ♒	12 ♈	12 ♈	13 ♊	12 ♋	14 ♍	14 ♎	15 ♐	13 ♑	13 ♒	13 ♈	12 ♉
14 ♓	15 ♉	14 ♉	15 ♋	15 ♌	16 ♎	16 ♏	17 ♑	15 ♒	15 ♓	15 ♉	15 ♊
16 ♈	17 ♊	16 ♊	17 ♌	18 ♍	19 ♏	18 ♐	19 ♒	17 ♓	17 ♈	17 ♊	17 ♋
18 ♉	19 ♋	19 ♋	20 ♍	20 ♎	21 ♐	20 ♑	21 ♓	19 ♈	19 ♉	20 ♋	19 ♌
21 ♊	22 ♌	21 ♌	23 ♎	22 ♏	23 ♑	22 ♒	23 ♈	22 ♉	21 ♊	22 ♌	22 ♍
23 ♋	25 ♍	24 ♍	25 ♏	24 ♐	25 ♒	24 ♓	25 ♉	24 ♊	23 ♋	25 ♍	24 ♎
26 ♌	27 ♎	26 ♎	27 ♐	27 ♑	27 ♓	26 ♈	27 ♊	26 ♋	26 ♌	27 ♎	27 ♏
28 ♍		28 ♏	29 ♑	29 ♒	29 ♈	29 ♉	28 ♋	28 ♌	28 ♍	29 ♏	29 ♐
31 ♎		31 ♐		31 ♓		31 ♊			31 ♎		31 ♑

1900

JAN.	FEB.	MAR.	APR.	MAY	JUNE	JULY	AUG.	SEPT.	OCT.	NOV.	DEC.
2 ♒	1 ♓	2 ♈	1 ♉	2 ♋	1 ♌	1 ♍	2 ♏	1 ♐	1 ♑	1 ♓	1 ♈
4 ♓	3 ♈	4 ♉	3 ♊	5 ♌	4 ♍	3 ♎	5 ♐	3 ♑	3 ♒	4 ♈	3 ♉
6 ♈	5 ♉	6 ♊	5 ♋	7 ♍	6 ♎	6 ♏	7 ♑	6 ♒	5 ♓	6 ♉	5 ♊
9 ♉	7 ♊	8 ♋	7 ♌	9 ♎	8 ♏	8 ♐	9 ♒	8 ♓	7 ♈	8 ♊	7 ♋
11 ♊	9 ♋	11 ♌	10 ♍	12 ♏	11 ♐	11 ♑	11 ♓	10 ♈	9 ♉	10 ♋	9 ♌
13 ♋	12 ♌	14 ♍	12 ♎	15 ♐	13 ♑	13 ♒	13 ♈	12 ♉	11 ♊	12 ♌	12 ♍
16 ♌	14 ♍	16 ♎	15 ♏	17 ♑	15 ♒	15 ♓	16 ♉	14 ♊	13 ♋	14 ♍	14 ♎
18 ♍	16 ♎	19 ♏	17 ♐	19 ♒	18 ♓	17 ♈	18 ♊	16 ♋	16 ♌	17 ♎	17 ♏
21 ♎	19 ♏	21 ♐	20 ♑	21 ♓	20 ♈	19 ♉	20 ♋	18 ♌	18 ♍	19 ♏	19 ♐
23 ♏	22 ♐	23 ♑	22 ♒	23 ♈	22 ♉	21 ♊	23 ♌	21 ♍	21 ♎	22 ♐	22 ♑
26 ♐	24 ♑	26 ♒	24 ♓	26 ♉	24 ♊	23 ♋	25 ♍	23 ♎	23 ♏	24 ♑	24 ♒
28 ♑	26 ♒	28 ♓	26 ♈	28 ♊	26 ♋	25 ♌	27 ♎	26 ♏	26 ♐	27 ♒	26 ♓
30 ♒	28 ♓	30 ♈	28 ♉	30 ♋	29 ♌	28 ♍	30 ♏	28 ♐	28 ♑	29 ♓	28 ♈
			30 ♊			30 ♎			30 ♒		30 ♉
						31 ♎					

1901

JAN.	FEB.	MAR.	APR.	MAY	JUNE	JULY	AUG.	SEPT.	OCT.	NOV.	DEC.
1 ♊	2 ♌	1 ♌	2 ♎	2 ♏	1 ♐	1 ♑	2 ♈	2 ♊	1 ♋	2 ♍	2 ♎
3 ♋	4 ♍	4 ♍	5 ♏	5 ♐	3 ♑	3 ♒	4 ♉	5 ♋	4 ♌	4 ♎	4 ♏
6 ♌	7 ♎	6 ♎	7 ♐	7 ♑	5 ♒	5 ♓	6 ♊	7 ♌	6 ♍	7 ♏	7 ♐
8 ♍	9 ♏	9 ♏	10 ♑	10 ♒	8 ♓	7 ♈	8 ♋	9 ♍	8 ♎	9 ♐	9 ♑
11 ♎	12 ♐	11 ♐	12 ♒	12 ♓	10 ♈	10 ♉	11 ♌	11 ♎	11 ♏	12 ♑	11 ♒
13 ♏	14 ♑	14 ♑	14 ♓	14 ♈	12 ♉	12 ♊	13 ♍	13 ♏	13 ♐	14 ♒	14 ♓
16 ♐	17 ♒	16 ♒	17 ♈	16 ♉	14 ♊	14 ♋	15 ♎	16 ♐	16 ♑	17 ♓	16 ♈
18 ♑	19 ♓	18 ♓	19 ♉	18 ♊	16 ♋	16 ♌	17 ♏	18 ♑	18 ♒	19 ♈	18 ♉
20 ♒	21 ♈	20 ♈	21 ♊	20 ♋	18 ♌	18 ♍	19 ♐	21 ♒	21 ♓	21 ♉	20 ♊
22 ♓	23 ♉	22 ♉	23 ♋	22 ♌	20 ♍	20 ♎	22 ♑	23 ♓	23 ♈	23 ♊	23 ♋
24 ♈	25 ♊	24 ♊	25 ♌	24 ♍	23 ♎	22 ♏	24 ♒	25 ♈	25 ♉	25 ♋	25 ♌
26 ♉	27 ♋	26 ♋	27 ♍	27 ♎	25 ♏	24 ♐	26 ♓	27 ♉	27 ♊	27 ♌	27 ♍
29 ♊		29 ♌	30 ♎	29 ♏	28 ♐	27 ♑	29 ♈	29 ♊	29 ♋	29 ♍	29 ♎
31 ♋		31 ♍				29 ♒	31 ♉		31 ♌		31 ♏
						31 ♓					

Libra	Scorpio	Sagittarius	Capricorn	Aquarius	Pisces
♎	♏	♐	♑	♒	♓

1902

JAN.	FEB.	MAR.	APR.	MAY	JUNE	JULY	AUG.	SEPT.	OCT.	NOV.	DEC.
3 ♏	2 ♐	1 ♐	2 ♒	2 ♓	1 ♈	2 ♊	1 ♌	1 ♎	1 ♏	2 ♐	2 ♑
6 ♐	4 ♑	4 ♑	5 ♓	4 ♈	3 ♉	4 ♋	3 ♍	3 ♏	3 ♐	4 ♑	4 ♒
8 ♑	7 ♒	6 ♒	7 ♈	6 ♉	5 ♊	6 ♌	5 ♎	6 ♐	5 ♑	7 ♒	7 ♓
10 ♒	9 ♓	8 ♓	9 ♉	8 ♊	7 ♋	8 ♍	6 ♏	8 ♑	8 ♒	9 ♓	9 ♈
13 ♓	11 ♈	10 ♈	11 ♊	10 ♋	9 ♌	11 ♎	8 ♐	11 ♒	10 ♓	12 ♈	11 ♉
15 ♈	13 ♉	13 ♉	13 ♋	12 ♌	11 ♍	13 ♏	11 ♑	13 ♓	12 ♈	14 ♉	13 ♊
17 ♉	15 ♊	15 ♊	15 ♌	15 ♍	13 ♎	15 ♐	13 ♒	15 ♈	15 ♉	16 ♊	15 ♋
19 ♊	18 ♋	17 ♋	17 ♍	17 ♎	16 ♏	17 ♑	15 ♓	18 ♉	17 ♊	18 ♋	17 ♌
21 ♋	20 ♌	19 ♌	20 ♎	19 ♏	18 ♐	19 ♒	18 ♈	20 ♊	19 ♋	20 ♌	19 ♍
23 ♌	22 ♍	21 ♍	22 ♏	22 ♐	21 ♑	21 ♓	20 ♉	22 ♋	21 ♌	22 ♍	21 ♎
25 ♍	24 ♎	23 ♎	25 ♐	24 ♑	23 ♒	24 ♈	22 ♊	24 ♌	23 ♍	24 ♎	24 ♏
28 ♎	27 ♏	26 ♏	27 ♑	27 ♒	26 ♓	26 ♉	24 ♋	26 ♍	26 ♎	27 ♏	26 ♐
30 ♏		28 ♐	29 ♒	29 ♓	28 ♈	28 ♊	26 ♌	28 ♎	30 ♏	29 ♐	29 ♑
		31 ♑			30 ♉	30 ♋	28 ♍				31 ♒

1903

JAN.	FEB.	MAR.	APR.	MAY	JUNE	JULY	AUG.	SEPT.	OCT.	NOV.	DEC.
3 ♓	1 ♈	1 ♈	1 ♊	1 ♋	1 ♍	1 ♎	2 ♐	3 ♒	3 ♓	2 ♈	1 ♉
5 ♈	4 ♉	3 ♉	4 ♋	3 ♌	3 ♎	3 ♏	4 ♑	5 ♓	5 ♈	4 ♉	3 ♊
8 ♉	6 ♊	5 ♊	6 ♌	5 ♍	6 ♏	5 ♐	7 ♒	8 ♈	8 ♉	6 ♊	6 ♋
10 ♊	8 ♋	7 ♋	8 ♍	7 ♎	8 ♐	7 ♑	9 ♓	10 ♉	10 ♊	8 ♋	8 ♌
12 ♋	10 ♌	9 ♌	10 ♎	10 ♏	11 ♑	9 ♒	11 ♈	12 ♊	12 ♋	10 ♌	10 ♍
14 ♌	12 ♍	11 ♍	12 ♏	12 ♐	13 ♒	12 ♓	13 ♉	14 ♋	14 ♌	12 ♍	12 ♎
16 ♍	14 ♎	14 ♎	15 ♐	14 ♑	16 ♓	14 ♈	14 ♊	16 ♌	16 ♍	15 ♎	14 ♏
18 ♎	16 ♏	16 ♏	17 ♑	16 ♒	18 ♈	16 ♉	17 ♋	18 ♍	18 ♎	17 ♏	16 ♐
20 ♏	19 ♐	18 ♐	20 ♒	19 ♓	20 ♉	18 ♊	19 ♌	21 ♎	21 ♏	19 ♐	19 ♑
23 ♐	21 ♑	21 ♑	22 ♓	21 ♈	23 ♊	21 ♋	21 ♍	23 ♏	23 ♐	21 ♑	21 ♒
25 ♑	24 ♒	23 ♒	24 ♈	23 ♉	25 ♋	23 ♌	24 ♎	25 ♐	24 ♑	24 ♒	24 ♓
28 ♒	26 ♓	26 ♓	27 ♉	25 ♊	27 ♌	26 ♍	26 ♏	28 ♑	26 ♒	26 ♓	26 ♈
30 ♓		28 ♈	29 ♊	28 ♋	29 ♍	28 ♎	28 ♐	30 ♒	29 ♓	29 ♈	29 ♉
		30 ♉		30 ♌		31 ♏	31 ♑				31 ♊

Key: Aries ♈ Taurus ♉ Gemini ♊ Cancer ♋ Leo ♌ Virgo ♍

1904

JAN.	FEB.	MAR.	APR.	MAY	JUNE	JULY	AUG.	SEPT.	OCT.	NOV.	DEC.
2 ♋	2 ♍	1 ♍	1 ♏	1 ♐	2 ♐	2 ♓	1 ♈	2 ♊	1 ♋	2 ♍	1 ♎
4 ♌	4 ♎	3 ♎	4 ♐	3 ♑	4 ♓	4 ♈	3 ♉	4 ♋	4 ♌	4 ♎	4 ♏
6 ♍	7 ♏	5 ♏	6 ♑	6 ♒	7 ♈	7 ♉	6 ♊	6 ♌	6 ♍	6 ♏	6 ♐
8 ♎	9 ♐	7 ♐	8 ♒	8 ♓	9 ♉	9 ♊	8 ♋	8 ♍	8 ♎	8 ♐	8 ♑
10 ♏	11 ♑	10 ♑	11 ♈	11 ♈	12 ♊	11 ♋	10 ♌	10 ♎	10 ♏	10 ♑	10 ♒
13 ♐	14 ♒	12 ♒	13 ♈	13 ♉	14 ♋	13 ♌	12 ♍	12 ♏	12 ♐	13 ♒	13 ♓
15 ♑	16 ♓	15 ♓	16 ♉	15 ♊	16 ♌	15 ♍	14 ♎	14 ♐	14 ♑	15 ♓	15 ♈
17 ♒	19 ♈	17 ♈	18 ♊	18 ♋	18 ♍	18 ♎	16 ♏	16 ♑	16 ♒	18 ♈	18 ♉
20 ♓	21 ♉	20 ♉	20 ♋	20 ♌	20 ♏	20 ♏	18 ♐	19 ♒	19 ♓	20 ♉	20 ♊
23 ♈	24 ♊	22 ♊	23 ♌	22 ♍	22 ♐	22 ♐	20 ♑	22 ♓	21 ♈	23 ♊	22 ♋
25 ♉	26 ♋	24 ♋	25 ♍	24 ♎	25 ♑	24 ♑	23 ♒	24 ♈	24 ♉	25 ♋	24 ♌
27 ♊	28 ♌	26 ♌	27 ♎	26 ♏	27 ♑	27 ♒	25 ♓	27 ♉	26 ♊	27 ♌	26 ♍
29 ♋		28 ♍	29 ♏	28 ♐	29 ♒	29 ♓	28 ♈	29 ♊	29 ♋	29 ♍	29 ♎
31 ♌		30 ♎		31 ♑			31 ♉		31 ♋		31 ♏

1905

JAN.	FEB.	MAR.	APR.	MAY	JUNE	JULY	AUG.	SEPT.	OCT.	NOV.	DEC.
2 ♐	3 ♒	2 ♒	1 ♓	1 ♈	2 ♊	1 ♋	2 ♍	1 ♎	2 ♐	1 ♑	2 ♓
4 ♑	5 ♓	4 ♓	3 ♈	3 ♉	4 ♋	4 ♌	4 ♎	4 ♐	4 ♑	3 ♒	5 ♈
6 ♒	8 ♈	7 ♈	6 ♉	6 ♊	6 ♌	6 ♍	5 ♏	6 ♑	6 ♒	5 ♓	7 ♉
9 ♈	10 ♉	9 ♉	8 ♊	8 ♋	8 ♍	9 ♎	7 ♑	9 ♒	9 ♓	9 ♈	10 ♊
11 ♉	13 ♊	12 ♊	11 ♋	10 ♌	10 ♎	11 ♏	9 ♒	11 ♈	11 ♈	10 ♉	12 ♋
14 ♊	15 ♋	14 ♋	13 ♌	12 ♍	12 ♏	12 ♐	11 ♓	14 ♈	13 ♉	13 ♊	15 ♌
16 ♋	17 ♌	17 ♍	15 ♍	14 ♎	14 ♐	14 ♑	13 ♈	16 ♉	15 ♊	15 ♋	17 ♍
19 ♌	19 ♍	19 ♍	17 ♎	17 ♏	16 ♑	17 ♒	15 ♉	18 ♊	17 ♋	17 ♌	19 ♎
21 ♍	21 ♎	21 ♎	19 ♏	19 ♐	19 ♒	19 ♓	18 ♊	21 ♋	19 ♌	20 ♍	21 ♏
23 ♍	23 ♏	23 ♏	21 ♐	21 ♑	22 ♓	21 ♈	20 ♋	23 ♌	21 ♍	22 ♎	23 ♐
25 ♎	25 ♐	25 ♐	23 ♑	23 ♒	24 ♈	24 ♉	23 ♌	24 ♍	24 ♎	24 ♏	25 ♑
27 ♏	28 ♑	27 ♑	26 ♒	25 ♓	27 ♉	26 ♊	26 ♍	26 ♎	26 ♏	26 ♐	28 ♒
29 ♐		29 ♒	28 ♈	29 ♊	29 ♋	29 ♌	28 ♎	28 ♐	28 ♑	28 ♓	30 ♓
31 ♑		31 ♓	30 ♉		31 ♌		30 ♏		30 ♒		

Libra	Scorpio	Sagittarius	Capricorn	Aquarius	Pisces
♎	♏	♐	♑	♒	♓

1906

JAN.	FEB.	MAR.	APR.	MAY	JUNE	JULY	AUG.	SEPT.	OCT.	NOV.	DEC.
1 ♈	3 ♊	2 ♊	1 ♋	3 ♍	1 ♎	1 ♏	1 ♑	2 ♒	1 ♈	3 ♊	2 ♋
4 ♉	5 ♋	4 ♋	3 ♌	5 ♎	3 ♏	3 ♐	3 ♒	4 ♈	4 ♉	5 ♋	5 ♌
6 ♊	7 ♌	7 ♌	5 ♍	7 ♏	5 ♐	5 ♑	5 ♓	6 ♉	6 ♊	8 ♌	7 ♍
9 ♋	10 ♍	9 ♍	8 ♎	9 ♐	7 ♑	7 ♒	8 ♈	9 ♊	9 ♋	10 ♍	10 ♎
11 ♌	12 ♎	11 ♎	10 ♏	11 ♑	9 ♒	9 ♓	10 ♉	11 ♋	11 ♌	12 ♎	12 ♏
13 ♍	14 ♏	13 ♏	13 ♐	13 ♒	11 ♓	11 ♈	13 ♊	14 ♌	14 ♍	14 ♏	14 ♐
15 ♎	16 ♐	15 ♐	14 ♑	15 ♓	12 ♈	14 ♉	15 ♋	16 ♍	16 ♎	16 ♐	16 ♑
18 ♏	18 ♑	17 ♑	16 ♒	18 ♈	14 ♉	16 ♊	18 ♌	18 ♎	18 ♏	18 ♑	18 ♒
20 ♐	20 ♒	20 ♒	18 ♓	20 ♉	16 ♊	18 ♋	20 ♍	20 ♏	20 ♐	20 ♒	20 ♓
22 ♑	23 ♓	22 ♓	20 ♈	23 ♊	19 ♋	20 ♌	23 ♎	23 ♐	23 ♑	23 ♓	22 ♈
24 ♒	25 ♈	24 ♈	23 ♉	25 ♋	21 ♌	22 ♍	26 ♏	25 ♑	24 ♒	25 ♈	25 ♉
26 ♓	27 ♉	27 ♉	25 ♊	28 ♌	24 ♍	24 ♎	28 ♐	27 ♒	26 ♓	27 ♉	27 ♊
29 ♈		29 ♊	28 ♋	30 ♍	26 ♎	26 ♏		29 ♓	29 ♈	30 ♊	30 ♋
31 ♉			30 ♌		28 ♏	28 ♐			31 ♉		
					30 ♐	30 ♑					
						31 ♒					

1907

JAN.	FEB.	MAR.	APR.	MAY	JUNE	JULY	AUG.	SEPT.	OCT.	NOV.	DEC.
1 ♌	2 ♎	1 ♎	2 ♐	1 ♑	2 ♓	1 ♈	2 ♊	1 ♋	1 ♌	2 ♎	2 ♏
4 ♍	4 ♏	4 ♏	4 ♑	3 ♒	4 ♈	4 ♉	5 ♋	4 ♌	4 ♍	5 ♏	4 ♐
6 ♎	7 ♐	6 ♐	6 ♒	6 ♓	6 ♉	6 ♊	7 ♌	6 ♍	6 ♎	7 ♐	6 ♑
8 ♏	9 ♑	8 ♑	8 ♓	8 ♈	9 ♊	9 ♋	10 ♍	8 ♎	8 ♏	9 ♑	8 ♒
10 ♐	11 ♒	10 ♒	11 ♈	10 ♉	11 ♋	11 ♌	12 ♎	11 ♏	10 ♐	11 ♒	10 ♓
12 ♑	13 ♓	12 ♓	13 ♉	13 ♊	14 ♌	14 ♍	15 ♏	13 ♐	12 ♑	13 ♓	12 ♈
14 ♒	15 ♈	14 ♈	15 ♊	15 ♋	16 ♍	16 ♎	17 ♐	15 ♑	15 ♒	15 ♈	15 ♉
16 ♓	17 ♉	16 ♉	18 ♋	18 ♌	18 ♎	18 ♏	19 ♑	17 ♒	17 ♓	17 ♉	17 ♊
18 ♈	20 ♊	19 ♊	20 ♌	20 ♍	21 ♏	21 ♐	21 ♒	19 ♓	19 ♈	20 ♊	20 ♋
21 ♉	22 ♋	22 ♋	23 ♍	23 ♎	23 ♐	23 ♑	23 ♓	22 ♈	21 ♉	22 ♋	22 ♌
23 ♊	25 ♌	24 ♌	25 ♎	25 ♏	25 ♑	25 ♒	25 ♈	24 ♉	23 ♊	25 ♌	25 ♍
26 ♋	27 ♍	26 ♍	27 ♏	27 ♐	27 ♒	27 ♓	27 ♉	26 ♊	26 ♋	27 ♍	27 ♎
28 ♌		29 ♎	29 ♐	29 ♑	29 ♓	29 ♈	30 ♊	29 ♋	28 ♌	30 ♎	29 ♏
31 ♍		31 ♏		31 ♒		31 ♉			31 ♍		

Key: Aries   Taurus   Gemini   Cancer   Leo   Virgo
        ♈   ♉   ♊   ♋   ♌   ♍

1908

JAN.	FEB.	MAR.	APR.	MAY	JUNE	JULY	AUG.	SEPT.	OCT.	NOV.	DEC.
1 ♐	1 ♒	2 ♓	2 ♉	3 ♊	3 ♌	3 ♍	1 ♎	3 ♐	2 ♑	3 ♓	2 ♈
3 ♑	3 ♓	4 ♈	4 ♊	4 ♋	5 ♍	5 ♎	4 ♏	5 ♑	4 ♒	5 ♈	4 ♉
5 ♒	5 ♈	6 ♉	7 ♋	7 ♌	8 ♎	8 ♏	6 ♐	7 ♒	6 ♓	7 ♉	6 ♊
7 ♓	7 ♉	8 ♊	9 ♌	9 ♍	10 ♏	10 ♐	8 ♑	9 ♓	8 ♈	9 ♊	9 ♋
9 ♈	10 ♊	10 ♋	13 ♍	11 ♎	13 ♐	13 ♑	10 ♒	11 ♈	10 ♉	12 ♋	11 ♌
11 ♉	12 ♋	13 ♌	16 ♎	13 ♏	15 ♑	15 ♒	12 ♓	13 ♉	12 ♊	14 ♌	13 ♍
13 ♊	15 ♌	15 ♍	16 ♏	16 ♐	17 ♒	16 ♓	14 ♈	15 ♊	15 ♋	16 ♍	16 ♎
16 ♋	17 ♍	18 ♎	19 ♐	18 ♑	19 ♓	18 ♈	16 ♉	17 ♋	17 ♌	19 ♎	18 ♏
18 ♌	20 ♎	20 ♏	21 ♑	20 ♒	21 ♈	20 ♉	19 ♊	20 ♌	20 ♍	21 ♏	21 ♐
21 ♍	22 ♏	22 ♐	23 ♒	22 ♓	23 ♉	22 ♊	21 ♋	22 ♍	22 ♎	23 ♐	23 ♑
23 ♎	24 ♐	25 ♑	25 ♓	25 ♈	25 ♊	25 ♋	24 ♌	25 ♎	25 ♏	26 ♑	25 ♒
26 ♏	26 ♑	27 ♒	27 ♈	27 ♉	28 ♋	27 ♌	26 ♍	27 ♏	27 ♐	28 ♒	27 ♓
28 ♐	29 ♒	29 ♓	29 ♉	29 ♊	30 ♌	29 ♎	29 ♎	29 ♐	29 ♑	30 ♓	29 ♈
30 ♑		31 ♈		31 ♋		31 ♏			31 ♒		31 ♉

1909

JAN.	FEB.	MAR.	APR.	MAY	JUNE	JULY	AUG.	SEPT.	OCT.	NOV.	DEC.
3 ♊	1 ♋	3 ♌	2 ♍	1 ♎	3 ♐	2 ♑	1 ♒	1 ♈	1 ♉	1 ♋	1 ♌
5 ♋	4 ♌	5 ♍	4 ♎	4 ♏	5 ♑	4 ♒	3 ♓	3 ♉	3 ♊	3 ♌	3 ♍
7 ♌	6 ♍	8 ♎	7 ♏	6 ♐	7 ♒	6 ♓	5 ♈	5 ♊	5 ♋	6 ♍	6 ♎
10 ♍	9 ♎	10 ♏	9 ♐	9 ♑	9 ♓	9 ♈	7 ♉	8 ♋	7 ♌	8 ♎	8 ♏
12 ♎	11 ♏	13 ♐	11 ♑	11 ♒	11 ♈	11 ♉	9 ♊	10 ♌	10 ♍	11 ♏	11 ♐
15 ♏	13 ♐	15 ♑	14 ♒	13 ♓	13 ♉	13 ♊	11 ♋	12 ♍	12 ♎	13 ♐	13 ♑
17 ♐	16 ♑	17 ♒	16 ♓	15 ♈	16 ♊	15 ♋	14 ♌	15 ♎	15 ♏	16 ♑	15 ♒
19 ♑	18 ♒	19 ♓	18 ♈	17 ♉	18 ♋	17 ♌	16 ♍	17 ♏	17 ♐	18 ♒	18 ♓
21 ♒	20 ♓	21 ♈	20 ♉	19 ♊	20 ♌	20 ♍	19 ♎	20 ♐	20 ♑	20 ♓	20 ♈
23 ♓	22 ♈	23 ♉	22 ♊	21 ♋	22 ♍	22 ♎	21 ♏	22 ♑	22 ♒	23 ♈	22 ♉
25 ♈	24 ♉	25 ♊	24 ♋	24 ♌	25 ♏	24 ♐	23 ♑	24 ♒	24 ♓	25 ♉	24 ♊
28 ♉	26 ♊	28 ♋	26 ♌	26 ♍	27 ♏	27 ♐	26 ♑	27 ♓	26 ♈	27 ♊	26 ♋
30 ♊	28 ♋	30 ♌	29 ♎	29 ♎	30 ♐	30 ♑	28 ♒	29 ♈	28 ♉	29 ♋	28 ♌
				31 ♏			30 ♓		30 ♊		31 ♍

Libra	Scorpio	Sagittarius	Capricorn	Aquarius	Pisces
♎	♏	♐	♑	♒	♓

1910

JAN.	FEB.	MAR.	APR.	MAY	JUNE	JULY	AUG.	SEPT.	OCT.	NOV.	DEC.
2 ♎	1 ♏	3 ♐	2 ♑	1 ♒	2 ♈	1 ♉	2 ♋	2 ♍	2 ♎	1 ♏	1 ♐
5 ♏	3 ♐	5 ♑	4 ♒	3 ♓	4 ♉	3 ♊	4 ♌	5 ♎	5 ♏	3 ♐	3 ♑
7 ♐	6 ♑	8 ♒	6 ♓	6 ♈	6 ♊	5 ♋	6 ♍	8 ♏	8 ♐	6 ♑	6 ♒
9 ♑	8 ♒	10 ♓	8 ♈	8 ♉	8 ♋	6 ♌	8 ♎	10 ♐	10 ♑	8 ♒	8 ♓
12 ♒	10 ♓	12 ♈	10 ♉	10 ♊	10 ♌	10 ♍	11 ♏	12 ♑	12 ♒	11 ♓	10 ♈
14 ♓	12 ♈	14 ♉	12 ♊	12 ♋	12 ♍	12 ♎	13 ♐	15 ♒	14 ♓	13 ♈	12 ♉
16 ♈	14 ♉	16 ♊	14 ♋	14 ♌	15 ♎	15 ♏	16 ♑	17 ♓	16 ♈	15 ♉	14 ♊
18 ♉	16 ♊	18 ♋	16 ♌	16 ♍	17 ♏	17 ♐	18 ♒	19 ♈	18 ♉	17 ♊	16 ♋
20 ♊	19 ♋	20 ♌	19 ♍	18 ♎	20 ♐	20 ♑	21 ♓	21 ♉	20 ♊	19 ♋	18 ♌
22 ♋	21 ♌	23 ♍	21 ♎	21 ♏	22 ♑	22 ♒	23 ♈	23 ♊	23 ♋	21 ♌	21 ♍
25 ♌	23 ♍	25 ♎	24 ♏	24 ♐	25 ♒	24 ♓	25 ♉	25 ♋	25 ♌	23 ♍	23 ♎
27 ♍	26 ♎	28 ♏	26 ♐	26 ♑	27 ♓	26 ♈	27 ♊	27 ♌	27 ♍	26 ♎	25 ♏
29 ♎	28 ♏	30 ♐	29 ♑	28 ♒	29 ♈	29 ♉	29 ♋	30 ♍	29 ♎	28 ♏	28 ♐
				31 ♓		31 ♊	31 ♌				30 ♑

1911

JAN.	FEB.	MAR.	APR.	MAY	JUNE	JULY	AUG.	SEPT.	OCT.	NOV.	DEC.
2 ♒	3 ♈	2 ♈	1 ♉	2 ♋	3 ♍	2 ♎	1 ♏	2 ♑	2 ♒	1 ♓	3 ♉
4 ♓	5 ♉	4 ♉	3 ♊	4 ♌	5 ♎	4 ♏	3 ♐	5 ♒	4 ♓	3 ♈	5 ♊
6 ♈	7 ♊	6 ♊	5 ♋	6 ♍	7 ♏	7 ♐	6 ♑	7 ♓	7 ♈	5 ♉	7 ♋
9 ♉	9 ♋	8 ♋	7 ♌	9 ♎	10 ♐	10 ♑	8 ♒	9 ♈	9 ♉	7 ♊	9 ♌
11 ♊	11 ♌	11 ♌	9 ♍	11 ♏	12 ♑	12 ♒	11 ♓	12 ♉	11 ♊	9 ♋	11 ♍
13 ♋	13 ♍	13 ♍	11 ♎	13 ♐	15 ♒	14 ♓	13 ♈	14 ♊	13 ♋	11 ♌	13 ♎
15 ♌	16 ♎	15 ♎	14 ♏	16 ♑	17 ♓	17 ♈	15 ♉	16 ♋	15 ♌	14 ♍	15 ♏
17 ♍	18 ♏	17 ♏	16 ♐	19 ♒	20 ♈	19 ♉	17 ♊	18 ♌	17 ♍	16 ♎	18 ♐
19 ♎	21 ♐	20 ♐	19 ♑	21 ♓	22 ♉	21 ♊	20 ♋	20 ♍	20 ♎	18 ♏	20 ♑
22 ♏	23 ♑	22 ♑	21 ♒	24 ♈	24 ♊	23 ♋	22 ♌	22 ♎	22 ♏	21 ♐	23 ♒
24 ♐	26 ♒	25 ♒	24 ♓	25 ♉	26 ♋	25 ♌	24 ♍	25 ♏	24 ♐	23 ♑	25 ♓
27 ♑	28 ♓	27 ♓	26 ♈	27 ♊	28 ♌	27 ♍	26 ♎	27 ♐	27 ♑	26 ♒	28 ♈
29 ♒		29 ♈	28 ♉	29 ♋	30 ♍	28 ♎	28 ♏	29 ♑	29 ♒	28 ♓	30 ♉
31 ♓			30 ♊	31 ♌		31 ♐	31 ♐			30 ♈	

	Key:	Aries	Taurus	Gemini	Cancer	Leo	Virgo
		♈	♉	♊	♋	♌	♍

1912

JAN.	FEB.	MAR.	APR.	MAY	JUNE	JULY	AUG.	SEPT.	OCT.	NOV.	DEC.
1 ♊	2 ♌	2 ♍	1 ♎	2 ♐	1 ♑	1 ♒	2 ♈	1 ♉	3 ♋	1 ♌	2 ♎
3 ♋	4 ♍	4 ♎	3 ♏	5 ♑	4 ♒	3 ♓	5 ♉	3 ♊	5 ♌	3 ♍	5 ♏
5 ♌	6 ♎	6 ♏	5 ♐	7 ♒	6 ♓	6 ♈	7 ♊	5 ♋	7 ♍	5 ♎	7 ♐
7 ♍	8 ♏	9 ♐	8 ♑	10 ♓	9 ♈	8 ♉	9 ♋	7 ♌	9 ♎	7 ♏	9 ♑
9 ♎	10 ♐	11 ♑	10 ♒	12 ♈	11 ♉	11 ♊	11 ♌	9 ♍	11 ♏	10 ♐	12 ♒
12 ♏	13 ♑	14 ♒	13 ♓	15 ♉	13 ♊	13 ♋	13 ♍	11 ♎	13 ♐	12 ♑	14 ♓
14 ♐	15 ♒	16 ♓	15 ♈	17 ♊	15 ♋	15 ♌	15 ♎	14 ♏	16 ♑	14 ♒	17 ♈
17 ♑	18 ♓	19 ♈	17 ♉	19 ♋	17 ♌	17 ♍	17 ♏	16 ♐	18 ♒	17 ♓	19 ♉
19 ♒	20 ♈	21 ♉	19 ♊	21 ♌	19 ♍	19 ♎	19 ♐	18 ♑	21 ♓	19 ♈	21 ♊
22 ♓	23 ♉	23 ♊	21 ♋	23 ♍	21 ♎	21 ♏	22 ♑	21 ♒	23 ♈	21 ♉	24 ♋
24 ♈	25 ♊	25 ♋	24 ♌	25 ♎	24 ♏	23 ♐	24 ♒	23 ♓	25 ♉	24 ♊	26 ♌
26 ♉	27 ♋	27 ♌	26 ♍	27 ♏	26 ♐	26 ♑	27 ♓	25 ♈	28 ♊	26 ♋	28 ♍
29 ♊	29 ♌	29 ♍	28 ♎	30 ♐	28 ♑	28 ♒	29 ♈	28 ♉	30 ♋	28 ♌	30 ♎
31 ♋			30 ♏			31 ♓		30 ♊		30 ♍	

1913

JAN.	FEB.	MAR.	APR.	MAY	JUNE	JULY	AUG.	SEPT.	OCT.	NOV.	DEC.
1 ♏	2 ♑	1 ♑	2 ♓	2 ♈	1 ♉	1 ♊	1 ♌	2 ♎	1 ♏	2 ♑	2 ♒
3 ♐	4 ♒	4 ♒	5 ♈	5 ♉	3 ♊	3 ♋	3 ♍	4 ♏	3 ♐	4 ♒	4 ♓
6 ♑	7 ♓	6 ♓	7 ♉	8 ♊	5 ♋	5 ♌	5 ♎	6 ♐	6 ♑	7 ♓	7 ♈
8 ♒	9 ♈	9 ♈	10 ♊	11 ♋	7 ♌	7 ♍	8 ♏	8 ♑	8 ♒	9 ♈	9 ♉
11 ♓	12 ♉	11 ♉	12 ♋	14 ♌	10 ♍	10 ♎	10 ♐	11 ♒	10 ♓	11 ♉	11 ♊
13 ♈	14 ♊	13 ♊	14 ♌	16 ♍	12 ♎	12 ♏	12 ♑	13 ♓	13 ♈	13 ♊	13 ♋
16 ♉	16 ♋	15 ♋	16 ♍	18 ♎	14 ♏	14 ♐	14 ♒	16 ♈	15 ♉	16 ♋	16 ♌
18 ♊	18 ♌	18 ♌	18 ♎	21 ♏	16 ♐	17 ♑	16 ♓	18 ♉	17 ♊	18 ♌	18 ♍
20 ♋	20 ♍	20 ♍	20 ♏	23 ♐	19 ♑	19 ♒	18 ♈	20 ♊	19 ♋	20 ♍	20 ♎
22 ♌	22 ♎	22 ♎	23 ♐	26 ♑	21 ♒	21 ♓	21 ♉	23 ♋	21 ♌	23 ♎	23 ♏
24 ♍	25 ♏	24 ♏	25 ♑	28 ♒	23 ♓	23 ♈	23 ♊	25 ♌	23 ♍	25 ♏	25 ♐
26 ♎	27 ♐	26 ♐	27 ♒	30 ♓	26 ♈	26 ♉	25 ♋	27 ♍	26 ♎	27 ♐	27 ♑
28 ♏		28 ♑	30 ♓		28 ♉	28 ♊	27 ♌	29 ♎	28 ♏	29 ♑	29 ♒
30 ♐		31 ♒				30 ♋	29 ♍		31 ♐		31 ♓

	Libra	Scorpio	Sagittarius	Capricorn	Aquarius	Pisces
	♎	♏	♐	♑	♒	♓

1914

JAN.	FEB.	MAR.	APR.	MAY	JUNE	JULY	AUG.	SEPT.	OCT.	NOV.	DEC.
3 ♈	2 ♉	1 ♉	2 ♋	2 ♌	2 ♎	2 ♏	2 ♑	1 ♒	3 ♈	2 ♉	1 ♊
5 ♉	4 ♊	4 ♊	5 ♌	4 ♍	5 ♏	4 ♐	5 ♒	3 ♓	5 ♉	4 ♊	4 ♋
8 ♊	7 ♋	6 ♋	7 ♍	6 ♎	7 ♐	6 ♑	7 ♓	6 ♈	8 ♊	6 ♋	6 ♌
10 ♋	9 ♌	8 ♌	9 ♎	8 ♏	9 ♑	8 ♒	9 ♈	8 ♉	11 ♋	9 ♌	9 ♍
12 ♌	11 ♍	10 ♍	11 ♏	10 ♐	11 ♒	11 ♓	12 ♉	11 ♊	13 ♌	11 ♍	11 ♎
14 ♍	13 ♎	12 ♎	13 ♐	12 ♑	13 ♓	13 ♈	14 ♊	13 ♋	15 ♍	14 ♎	13 ♏
17 ♎	15 ♏	14 ♏	15 ♑	14 ♒	16 ♈	15 ♉	16 ♋	15 ♌	17 ♎	16 ♏	15 ♐
19 ♏	17 ♐	16 ♐	17 ♒	17 ♓	18 ♉	17 ♊	18 ♌	18 ♍	19 ♏	18 ♐	17 ♑
21 ♐	19 ♑	19 ♑	20 ♓	19 ♈	21 ♊	19 ♋	20 ♍	20 ♎	21 ♐	20 ♑	19 ♒
23 ♑	22 ♒	21 ♒	22 ♈	22 ♉	23 ♋	21 ♌	22 ♎	22 ♏	23 ♑	22 ♒	21 ♓
25 ♒	24 ♓	23 ♓	25 ♉	24 ♊	25 ♌	23 ♍	24 ♏	24 ♐	25 ♒	24 ♓	24 ♈
28 ♓	27 ♈	26 ♈	27 ♊	27 ♋	28 ♍	25 ♎	27 ♐	26 ♑	28 ♓	26 ♈	26 ♉
30 ♈		28 ♉	30 ♋	29 ♌	30 ♎	28 ♏	30 ♑	28 ♒	30 ♈	29 ♉	29 ♊
		31 ♊		31 ♍		31 ♐		30 ♓			31 ♋

1915

JAN.	FEB.	MAR.	APR.	MAY	JUNE	JULY	AUG.	SEPT.	OCT.	NOV.	DEC.
3 ♌	1 ♍	1 ♍	1 ♏	1 ♐	1 ♒	1 ♓	2 ♉	3 ♋	3 ♌	2 ♍	1 ♎
5 ♍	3 ♎	3 ♎	3 ♐	3 ♑	3 ♓	3 ♈	4 ♊	5 ♌	5 ♍	4 ♎	3 ♏
7 ♎	5 ♏	5 ♏	5 ♑	5 ♒	6 ♈	5 ♉	7 ♋	7 ♍	7 ♎	6 ♏	5 ♐
9 ♏	8 ♐	7 ♐	7 ♒	7 ♓	8 ♉	8 ♊	9 ♌	9 ♎	9 ♏	8 ♐	7 ♑
11 ♐	10 ♑	9 ♑	10 ♓	9 ♈	11 ♊	10 ♋	12 ♍	12 ♏	12 ♐	10 ♑	9 ♒
13 ♑	12 ♒	11 ♒	12 ♈	12 ♉	13 ♋	13 ♌	14 ♎	14 ♐	14 ♑	12 ♒	11 ♓
16 ♒	14 ♓	13 ♓	15 ♉	14 ♊	16 ♌	15 ♍	16 ♏	16 ♑	16 ♒	14 ♓	14 ♈
18 ♓	16 ♈	16 ♈	17 ♊	17 ♋	18 ♍	17 ♎	18 ♐	18 ♒	18 ♓	16 ♈	16 ♉
20 ♈	19 ♉	18 ♉	20 ♋	19 ♌	20 ♎	20 ♏	20 ♑	21 ♓	20 ♈	19 ♉	19 ♊
23 ♉	21 ♊	21 ♊	22 ♌	22 ♍	22 ♏	22 ♐	23 ♒	23 ♈	23 ♉	21 ♊	21 ♋
25 ♊	24 ♋	23 ♋	24 ♍	24 ♎	24 ♐	24 ♑	25 ♓	25 ♉	25 ♊	24 ♋	24 ♌
28 ♋	26 ♌	26 ♌	27 ♎	26 ♏	26 ♑	26 ♒	27 ♈	28 ♊	28 ♋	26 ♌	26 ♍
30 ♌		28 ♍	29 ♏	28 ♐	28 ♒	28 ♓	29 ♉	30 ♋	30 ♌	29 ♍	29 ♎
		30 ♎		30 ♑	30 ♓	30 ♈	31 ♊				31 ♏

Key: Aries   Taurus   Gemini   Cancer   Leo   Virgo
       ♈   ♉   ♊   ♋   ♌   ♍

1916

JAN.	FEB.	MAR.	APR.	MAY	JUNE	JULY	AUG.	SEPT.	OCT.	NOV.	DEC.
2 ♐	2 ♒	1 ♒	1 ♈	1 ♉	2 ♋	2 ♌	1 ♍	2 ♏	1 ♐	2 ♒	1 ♓
4 ♑	4 ♓	3 ♓	4 ♉	3 ♊	4 ♌	4 ♍	3 ♎	4 ♐	3 ♑	4 ♓	3 ♈
6 ♒	6 ♈	5 ♈	6 ♊	5 ♋	6 ♍	7 ♎	5 ♏	6 ♑	5 ♒	6 ♈	5 ♉
8 ♓	9 ♉	7 ♉	8 ♋	8 ♌	9 ♎	9 ♏	7 ♐	8 ♒	7 ♓	8 ♉	8 ♊
10 ♈	11 ♊	10 ♊	11 ♌	11 ♍	12 ♏	11 ♐	10 ♑	10 ♓	9 ♈	10 ♊	10 ♋
12 ♉	14 ♋	12 ♋	13 ♍	13 ♎	14 ♐	13 ♑	12 ♒	12 ♈	12 ♉	13 ♋	13 ♌
15 ♊	16 ♌	15 ♌	16 ♎	15 ♏	16 ♑	15 ♒	14 ♓	14 ♉	14 ♊	15 ♌	15 ♍
17 ♋	19 ♍	17 ♍	18 ♏	17 ♐	18 ♒	17 ♓	16 ♈	16 ♊	16 ♋	18 ♍	18 ♎
20 ♌	21 ♎	19 ♎	20 ♐	19 ♑	20 ♓	19 ♈	18 ♉	19 ♋	19 ♌	20 ♎	20 ♏
22 ♍	23 ♏	22 ♏	22 ♑	21 ♒	22 ♈	22 ♉	20 ♊	21 ♌	21 ♍	22 ♏	22 ♐
25 ♎	25 ♐	24 ♐	24 ♒	24 ♓	24 ♉	24 ♊	22 ♋	24 ♍	23 ♎	24 ♐	24 ♑
27 ♏	28 ♑	26 ♑	26 ♓	26 ♈	26 ♊	26 ♋	25 ♌	26 ♎	26 ♏	27 ♑	26 ♒
29 ♐		28 ♒	29 ♈	28 ♉	29 ♋	29 ♌	28 ♍	29 ♏	28 ♐	29 ♒	28 ♓
31 ♑		30 ♓		30 ♊			30 ♎		30 ♑		30 ♈

1917

JAN.	FEB.	MAR.	APR.	MAY	JUNE	JULY	AUG.	SEPT.	OCT.	NOV.	DEC.
2 ♉	3 ♋	2 ♋	1 ♌	1 ♍	2 ♏	1 ♐	2 ♒	2 ♈	2 ♉	3 ♋	2 ♌
4 ♊	5 ♌	4 ♌	3 ♍	3 ♎	4 ♐	4 ♑	4 ♓	4 ♉	4 ♊	5 ♌	5 ♍
6 ♋	8 ♍	7 ♍	6 ♎	5 ♏	6 ♑	6 ♒	6 ♈	7 ♊	6 ♋	8 ♍	7 ♎
9 ♌	10 ♎	9 ♎	8 ♏	8 ♐	8 ♒	8 ♓	8 ♉	9 ♋	9 ♌	10 ♎	10 ♏
11 ♍	13 ♏	12 ♏	10 ♐	10 ♑	10 ♓	10 ♈	10 ♊	11 ♌	11 ♍	13 ♏	12 ♐
14 ♎	15 ♐	14 ♐	13 ♑	12 ♒	12 ♈	12 ♉	13 ♋	14 ♍	14 ♎	15 ♐	14 ♑
16 ♏	17 ♑	16 ♑	15 ♒	14 ♓	15 ♉	14 ♊	15 ♌	17 ♎	16 ♏	17 ♑	17 ♒
19 ♐	19 ♒	18 ♒	17 ♓	16 ♈	17 ♊	16 ♋	18 ♍	19 ♏	19 ♐	19 ♒	19 ♓
21 ♑	21 ♓	21 ♓	19 ♈	18 ♉	19 ♋	19 ♌	20 ♎	21 ♐	21 ♑	22 ♓	21 ♈
23 ♒	23 ♈	23 ♈	21 ♉	21 ♊	22 ♌	21 ♍	23 ♏	24 ♑	23 ♒	24 ♈	23 ♉
25 ♓	25 ♉	25 ♉	23 ♊	23 ♋	24 ♍	24 ♎	25 ♐	26 ♒	25 ♓	26 ♉	25 ♊
27 ♈	27 ♊	27 ♊	26 ♋	25 ♌	27 ♎	26 ♏	27 ♑	28 ♓	27 ♈	28 ♊	27 ♋
29 ♉		29 ♋	28 ♌	28 ♍	29 ♏	29 ♐	29 ♒	30 ♈	29 ♉	30 ♋	30 ♌
31 ♊				30 ♎		31 ♑	31 ♓		31 ♊		

Libra	Scorpio	Sagittarius	Capricorn	Aquarius	Pisces
♎	♏	♐	♑	♒	♓

1918

JAN.	FEB.	MAR.	APR.	MAY	JUNE	JULY	AUG.	SEPT.	OCT.	NOV.	DEC.
1 ♍	3 ♏	2 ♏	1 ♐	3 ♒	1 ♓	2 ♉	1 ♊	2 ♌	1 ♍	2 ♏	2 ♐
4 ♎	5 ♐	4 ♐	3 ♑	5 ♓	3 ♈	5 ♊	3 ♋	4 ♍	4 ♎	5 ♐	5 ♑
6 ♏	7 ♑	7 ♑	5 ♒	7 ♈	5 ♉	7 ♋	5 ♌	6 ♎	6 ♏	7 ♑	7 ♒
9 ♐	9 ♒	9 ♒	7 ♓	9 ♉	7 ♊	9 ♌	8 ♍	9 ♏	9 ♐	10 ♒	9 ♓
11 ♒	11 ♓	11 ♓	9 ♈	11 ♊	9 ♋	11 ♍	10 ♎	11 ♐	11 ♑	12 ♓	11 ♈
13 ♒	13 ♈	13 ♈	11 ♉	13 ♋	12 ♌	14 ♎	13 ♏	14 ♑	14 ♒	14 ♈	14 ♉
15 ♓	15 ♉	15 ♉	13 ♊	15 ♌	14 ♍	16 ♏	15 ♐	16 ♒	16 ♓	16 ♉	16 ♊
17 ♈	18 ♊	17 ♊	16 ♋	18 ♍	17 ♎	19 ♐	18 ♑	18 ♓	18 ♈	18 ♊	18 ♋
19 ♉	20 ♋	19 ♋	18 ♌	20 ♎	19 ♏	21 ♑	20 ♒	20 ♈	20 ♉	20 ♋	20 ♌
21 ♊	22 ♌	22 ♌	20 ♍	23 ♏	21 ♐	23 ♒	22 ♓	22 ♉	22 ♊	22 ♌	22 ♍
24 ♋	25 ♍	24 ♍	23 ♎	25 ♐	24 ♑	25 ♓	24 ♈	24 ♊	25 ♋	25 ♍	25 ♎
26 ♌	27 ♎	27 ♎	25 ♏	27 ♑	26 ♒	27 ♈	26 ♉	26 ♋	27 ♌	27 ♎	27 ♏
29 ♍		29 ♏	28 ♐	30 ♒	28 ♓	30 ♉	28 ♊	29 ♌	28 ♍	30 ♏	30 ♐
31 ♎			30 ♑		30 ♈		30 ♋		31 ♎		

1919

JAN.	FEB.	MAR.	APR.	MAY	JUNE	JULY	AUG.	SEPT.	OCT.	NOV.	DEC.
1 ♑	2 ♓	1 ♓	2 ♉	1 ♊	2 ♌	1 ♍	2 ♏	1 ♐	1 ♑	2 ♓	2 ♈
3 ♒	4 ♈	3 ♈	4 ♊	3 ♋	4 ♍	4 ♎	5 ♐	4 ♑	4 ♒	4 ♈	4 ♉
6 ♓	6 ♉	5 ♉	6 ♋	5 ♌	6 ♎	6 ♏	7 ♑	6 ♒	6 ♓	7 ♉	6 ♊
8 ♈	8 ♊	7 ♊	8 ♌	8 ♍	9 ♏	9 ♐	10 ♒	8 ♓	8 ♈	9 ♊	8 ♋
10 ♉	10 ♋	10 ♋	10 ♍	10 ♎	11 ♐	11 ♑	12 ♓	11 ♈	10 ♉	11 ♋	10 ♌
12 ♊	13 ♌	12 ♌	13 ♎	13 ♏	14 ♑	14 ♒	14 ♈	13 ♉	12 ♊	13 ♌	12 ♍
14 ♋	15 ♍	14 ♍	15 ♏	15 ♐	16 ♒	16 ♓	16 ♉	15 ♊	14 ♋	15 ♍	14 ♎
16 ♌	17 ♎	17 ♎	18 ♐	18 ♑	19 ♓	18 ♈	18 ♊	17 ♋	16 ♌	17 ♎	17 ♏
18 ♍	20 ♏	19 ♏	20 ♑	20 ♒	21 ♈	20 ♉	21 ♋	19 ♌	19 ♍	20 ♏	19 ♐
21 ♎	22 ♐	22 ♐	23 ♒	22 ♓	23 ♉	22 ♊	23 ♌	21 ♍	21 ♎	22 ♐	22 ♑
23 ♏	25 ♑	24 ♑	25 ♓	25 ♈	25 ♊	24 ♋	25 ♍	24 ♎	23 ♏	25 ♑	24 ♒
26 ♐	27 ♒	26 ♒	27 ♈	27 ♉	27 ♋	27 ♌	27 ♎	26 ♏	26 ♐	27 ♒	27 ♓
28 ♑		29 ♓	29 ♉	29 ♊	29 ♌	29 ♍	30 ♏	29 ♐	28 ♑	30 ♓	29 ♈
31 ♒		31 ♈		31 ♋		31 ♎			31 ♒		31 ♉

Key:	Aries	Taurus	Gemini	Cancer	Leo	Virgo
	♈	♉	♊	♋	♌	♍

1920

JAN.	FEB.	MAR.	APR.	MAY	JUNE	JULY	AUG.	SEPT.	OCT.	NOV.	DEC.
2 ♊	1 ♋	1 ♌	2 ♎	2 ♏	3 ♑	3 ♒	1 ♓	2 ♉	2 ♊	2 ♌	1 ♍
4 ♋	3 ♌	3 ♍	4 ♏	4 ♐	5 ♒	5 ♓	4 ♈	4 ♊	4 ♋	4 ♍	4 ♎
6 ♌	5 ♍	6 ♎	7 ♐	7 ♑	8 ♓	7 ♈	6 ♉	7 ♋	6 ♌	6 ♎	6 ♏
9 ♍	7 ♎	8 ♏	9 ♑	9 ♒	10 ♈	10 ♉	8 ♊	9 ♌	8 ♍	9 ♏	8 ♐
11 ♎	10 ♏	10 ♐	12 ♒	12 ♓	12 ♉	12 ♊	10 ♋	11 ♍	10 ♎	11 ♐	11 ♑
13 ♏	12 ♐	13 ♑	14 ♓	14 ♈	14 ♊	14 ♋	12 ♌	13 ♎	12 ♏	14 ♑	13 ♒
16 ♐	15 ♑	15 ♒	16 ♈	16 ♉	16 ♋	16 ♌	14 ♍	15 ♏	15 ♐	16 ♒	16 ♓
18 ♑	17 ♒	18 ♓	19 ♉	18 ♊	18 ♌	18 ♍	16 ♎	17 ♐	17 ♑	19 ♓	18 ♈
21 ♒	19 ♓	20 ♈	21 ♊	20 ♋	20 ♍	20 ♎	19 ♏	20 ♑	20 ♒	21 ♈	21 ♉
23 ♓	22 ♈	22 ♉	23 ♋	22 ♌	23 ♎	22 ♏	21 ♐	22 ♒	22 ♓	23 ♉	23 ♊
25 ♈	24 ♉	24 ♊	25 ♌	25 ♍	25 ♏	25 ♐	24 ♑	25 ♓	25 ♈	25 ♊	25 ♋
28 ♉	26 ♊	26 ♋	27 ♍	27 ♎	28 ♐	27 ♑	26 ♒	27 ♈	27 ♉	27 ♋	27 ♌
30 ♊	28 ♋	28 ♌	29 ♎	29 ♏	30 ♑	30 ♒	29 ♓	29 ♉	29 ♊	29 ♌	29 ♍
		31 ♍		31 ♐			31 ♈		31 ♋		31 ♎

1921

JAN.	FEB.	MAR.	APR.	MAY	JUNE	JULY	AUG.	SEPT.	OCT.	NOV.	DEC.
2 ♏	1 ♐	3 ♑	2 ♒	1 ♓	3 ♉	2 ♊	1 ♋	1 ♍	3 ♏	1 ♐	1 ♑
5 ♐	3 ♑	5 ♒	4 ♓	4 ♈	5 ♊	4 ♋	3 ♌	3 ♎	5 ♐	3 ♑	3 ♒
7 ♑	6 ♒	8 ♓	6 ♈	6 ♉	7 ♋	6 ♌	5 ♍	5 ♏	7 ♑	6 ♒	6 ♓
10 ♒	8 ♓	10 ♈	9 ♉	8 ♊	9 ♌	8 ♍	7 ♎	8 ♐	9 ♒	8 ♓	8 ♈
12 ♓	11 ♈	13 ♉	11 ♊	10 ♋	11 ♍	10 ♎	9 ♏	10 ♑	12 ♓	11 ♈	11 ♉
15 ♈	13 ♉	15 ♊	13 ♋	12 ♌	13 ♎	12 ♏	11 ♐	12 ♒	14 ♈	13 ♉	13 ♊
17 ♉	16 ♊	17 ♋	15 ♌	15 ♍	15 ♏	15 ♐	14 ♑	15 ♓	17 ♉	15 ♊	15 ♋
19 ♊	18 ♋	19 ♌	17 ♍	17 ♎	17 ♐	17 ♑	16 ♒	17 ♈	19 ♊	18 ♋	17 ♌
21 ♋	20 ♌	21 ♍	20 ♎	19 ♏	20 ♑	20 ♒	19 ♓	20 ♉	22 ♋	20 ♌	19 ♍
23 ♌	22 ♍	23 ♎	22 ♏	21 ♐	22 ♒	22 ♓	21 ♈	22 ♊	24 ♌	22 ♍	21 ♎
25 ♍	24 ♎	25 ♏	24 ♐	24 ♑	25 ♓	25 ♈	24 ♉	24 ♋	26 ♍	24 ♎	24 ♏
27 ♎	26 ♏	28 ♐	26 ♑	26 ♒	27 ♈	27 ♉	26 ♊	26 ♌	28 ♎	26 ♏	26 ♐
30 ♏	28 ♐	30 ♑	29 ♒	29 ♓	30 ♉	30 ♊	28 ♋	28 ♍	30 ♏	28 ♐	28 ♑
				31 ♈			30 ♌	30 ♎			31 ♒

Libra	Scorpio	Sagittarius	Capricorn	Aquarius	Pisces
♎	♏	♐	♑	♒	♓

1922

JAN.	FEB.	MAR.	APR.	MAY	JUNE	JULY	AUG.	SEPT.	OCT.	NOV.	DEC.
2 ♓	1 ♈	3 ♉	1 ♊	1 ♋	1 ♍	1 ♎	1 ♐	2 ♒	2 ♓	1 ♈	1 ♉
5 ♈	3 ♉	5 ♊	4 ♋	3 ♌	4 ♎	3 ♏	4 ♑	5 ♓	5 ♈	3 ♉	3 ♊
7 ♉	6 ♊	7 ♋	6 ♌	5 ♍	6 ♏	5 ♐	6 ♒	7 ♈	7 ♉	6 ♊	5 ♋
9 ♊	8 ♋	10 ♌	8 ♍	7 ♎	8 ♐	7 ♑	8 ♓	10 ♉	10 ♊	8 ♋	8 ♌
12 ♋	10 ♌	12 ♍	10 ♎	9 ♏	10 ♑	10 ♒	11 ♈	12 ♊	12 ♋	10 ♌	10 ♍
14 ♌	12 ♍	13 ♎	12 ♏	11 ♐	12 ♒	12 ♓	14 ♉	15 ♋	14 ♌	13 ♍	12 ♎
16 ♍	14 ♎	16 ♏	14 ♐	14 ♑	15 ♓	15 ♈	16 ♊	17 ♌	16 ♍	15 ♎	14 ♏
18 ♎	16 ♏	18 ♐	16 ♑	17 ♒	17 ♈	17 ♉	18 ♋	19 ♍	18 ♎	17 ♏	16 ♐
20 ♏	18 ♐	20 ♑	19 ♒	19 ♓	19 ♉	20 ♊	20 ♌	21 ♎	20 ♏	19 ♐	18 ♑
22 ♐	21 ♑	22 ♒	21 ♓	21 ♈	20 ♊	22 ♋	22 ♍	23 ♏	22 ♐	21 ♑	21 ♒
24 ♑	23 ♒	25 ♓	24 ♈	24 ♉	22 ♋	24 ♌	24 ♎	25 ♐	24 ♑	23 ♒	23 ♓
27 ♒	26 ♓	27 ♈	26 ♉	26 ♊	24 ♌	26 ♍	26 ♏	27 ♑	27 ♒	26 ♓	25 ♈
29 ♓	28 ♈	30 ♉	28 ♊	28 ♋	26 ♍	29 ♎	29 ♐	30 ♒	29 ♓	28 ♈	28 ♉
				30 ♌	29 ♎	31 ♏	31 ♑				30 ♊

1923

JAN.	FEB.	MAR.	APR.	MAY	JUNE	JULY	AUG.	SEPT.	OCT.	NOV.	DEC.
2 ♋	2 ♍	2 ♍	2 ♏	2 ♐	2 ♒	2 ♓	1 ♈	2 ♊	2 ♋	1 ♌	3 ♎
4 ♌	4 ♎	4 ♎	4 ♐	4 ♑	5 ♓	4 ♈	3 ♉	5 ♋	4 ♌	3 ♍	5 ♏
6 ♍	7 ♏	6 ♏	6 ♑	6 ♒	7 ♈	7 ♉	6 ♊	7 ♌	7 ♍	5 ♎	7 ♐
8 ♎	9 ♐	8 ♐	9 ♒	8 ♓	10 ♉	10 ♊	8 ♋	9 ♍	9 ♎	7 ♏	9 ♑
10 ♏	11 ♑	10 ♑	11 ♓	10 ♈	12 ♊	12 ♋	11 ♌	11 ♎	11 ♏	9 ♐	11 ♒
12 ♐	13 ♒	12 ♒	14 ♈	12 ♉	15 ♋	14 ♌	13 ♍	13 ♏	13 ♐	11 ♑	13 ♓
15 ♑	16 ♓	14 ♓	16 ♉	15 ♊	17 ♌	16 ♍	15 ♎	15 ♐	15 ♑	13 ♒	15 ♈
17 ♒	18 ♈	17 ♈	19 ♊	17 ♋	19 ♍	19 ♎	17 ♏	17 ♑	17 ♒	15 ♓	18 ♉
19 ♓	21 ♉	20 ♉	21 ♋	19 ♌	21 ♎	21 ♏	19 ♐	20 ♒	19 ♓	18 ♈	20 ♊
22 ♈	23 ♊	22 ♊	23 ♌	21 ♍	24 ♏	23 ♐	21 ♑	22 ♓	22 ♈	20 ♉	23 ♋
24 ♉	26 ♋	25 ♋	26 ♍	23 ♎	26 ♐	25 ♑	23 ♒	24 ♈	24 ♉	23 ♊	25 ♌
27 ♊	28 ♌	27 ♌	28 ♎	25 ♏	28 ♑	27 ♒	26 ♓	27 ♉	27 ♊	25 ♋	28 ♍
29 ♋		29 ♍	30 ♏	27 ♐	30 ♒	29 ♓	28 ♈	30 ♊	29 ♋	28 ♌	30 ♎
31 ♌		31 ♎		29 ♑		31 ♈	30 ♉			30 ♍	
				31 ♒							

Key:	Aries	Taurus	Gemini	Cancer	Leo	Virgo
	♈	♉	♊	♋	♌	♍

1924

JAN.	FEB.	MAR.	APR.	MAY	JUNE	JULY	AUG.	SEPT.	OCT.	NOV.	DEC.
1 ♏	1 ♑	2 ♒	3 ♈	2 ♉	1 ♊	1 ♋	2 ♍	1 ♎	2 ♐	1 ♑	2 ♓
3 ♐	3 ♒	4 ♓	5 ♉	5 ♊	4 ♋	3 ♌	4 ♎	3 ♏	4 ♑	3 ♒	4 ♈
5 ♑	6 ♓	6 ♈	8 ♊	7 ♋	6 ♌	6 ♍	7 ♏	5 ♐	6 ♒	5 ♓	7 ♉
7 ♒	8 ♈	9 ♉	10 ♋	10 ♌	9 ♍	8 ♎	9 ♐	7 ♑	9 ♓	7 ♈	9 ♊
9 ♓	10 ♉	11 ♊	13 ♌	12 ♍	11 ♎	10 ♏	11 ♑	9 ♒	11 ♈	9 ♉	12 ♋
12 ♈	13 ♊	14 ♋	15 ♍	15 ♎	13 ♏	13 ♐	13 ♒	11 ♓	13 ♉	12 ♊	14 ♌
14 ♉	15 ♋	16 ♌	17 ♎	17 ♏	15 ♐	16 ♑	15 ♓	13 ♈	16 ♊	14 ♋	17 ♍
17 ♊	18 ♌	19 ♍	19 ♏	19 ♐	17 ♑	19 ♒	17 ♈	15 ♉	18 ♋	17 ♌	19 ♎
19 ♋	20 ♍	21 ♎	21 ♐	21 ♑	19 ♒	21 ♓	19 ♉	18 ♊	21 ♌	19 ♍	21 ♏
21 ♌	22 ♎	23 ♏	23 ♑	23 ♒	21 ♓	23 ♈	22 ♊	20 ♋	23 ♍	21 ♎	23 ♐
24 ♍	24 ♏	25 ♐	25 ♒	25 ♓	23 ♈	26 ♉	24 ♋	23 ♌	25 ♎	24 ♏	25 ♑
26 ♎	27 ♐	27 ♑	28 ♓	28 ♈	26 ♉	28 ♊	27 ♌	25 ♍	27 ♏	26 ♐	27 ♒
28 ♏	29 ♑	29 ♒	30 ♈	30 ♉	28 ♊	31 ♌	29 ♍	28 ♎	30 ♐	28 ♑	29 ♓
30 ♐		31 ♓					30 ♏	30 ♐			

1925

JAN.	FEB.	MAR.	APR.	MAY	JUNE	JULY	AUG.	SEPT.	OCT.	NOV.	DEC.
1 ♈	2 ♊	1 ♊	2 ♌	2 ♍	1 ♎	1 ♏	1 ♑	2 ♓	1 ♈	2 ♊	2 ♋
3 ♉	4 ♋	4 ♋	5 ♍	5 ♎	3 ♏	3 ♐	3 ♒	4 ♈	3 ♉	4 ♋	4 ♌
5 ♊	7 ♌	6 ♌	7 ♎	7 ♏	5 ♐	5 ♑	5 ♓	6 ♉	6 ♊	7 ♌	7 ♍
8 ♋	9 ♍	9 ♍	9 ♏	9 ♐	7 ♑	7 ♒	7 ♈	8 ♊	8 ♋	9 ♍	9 ♎
11 ♌	11 ♎	11 ♎	11 ♐	12 ♑	9 ♒	9 ♓	9 ♉	10 ♋	10 ♌	12 ♎	11 ♏
13 ♍	14 ♏	13 ♏	13 ♑	14 ♒	11 ♓	11 ♈	12 ♊	13 ♌	13 ♍	14 ♏	14 ♐
15 ♎	16 ♐	15 ♐	16 ♒	16 ♓	14 ♈	13 ♉	14 ♋	15 ♍	15 ♎	16 ♐	16 ♑
18 ♏	18 ♑	17 ♑	18 ♓	18 ♈	16 ♉	16 ♊	17 ♌	18 ♎	18 ♏	18 ♑	18 ♒
20 ♐	20 ♒	20 ♒	20 ♈	20 ♉	18 ♊	18 ♋	19 ♍	20 ♏	20 ♐	20 ♒	20 ♓
22 ♑	22 ♓	22 ♓	22 ♉	23 ♊	21 ♋	21 ♌	22 ♎	23 ♐	22 ♑	23 ♓	22 ♈
24 ♒	24 ♈	24 ♈	25 ♊	25 ♋	23 ♌	23 ♍	24 ♏	25 ♑	24 ♒	25 ♈	24 ♉
26 ♓	27 ♉	26 ♉	27 ♋	27 ♌	26 ♍	26 ♎	26 ♐	27 ♒	26 ♓	27 ♉	27 ♊
28 ♈		28 ♊	30 ♌	30 ♍	28 ♎	28 ♏	29 ♑	29 ♓	28 ♈	29 ♊	29 ♋
30 ♉		31 ♋			30 ♏	30 ♐	31 ♒		31 ♉		31 ♌

Libra	Scorpio	Sagittarius	Capricorn	Aquarius	Pisces
♎	♏	♐	♑	♒	♓

1926

JAN.	FEB.	MAR.	APR.	MAY	JUNE	JULY	AUG.	SEPT.	OCT.	NOV.	DEC.
3♍	2♎	1♎	2♐	1♑	2♓	1♈	2♊	1♋	3♍	2♎	1♏
5♎	4♏	3♏	4♑	4♒	4♈	3♉	4♋	3♌	5♎	4♏	4♐
8♏	7♐	6♐	6♒	6♓	6♉	6♊	7♌	6♍	8♏	6♐	6♑
10♐	9♑	8♑	9♓	8♈	8♊	8♋	8♍	8♎	10♐	9♑	8♒
12♑	11♒	10♒	11♈	10♉	11♋	11♌	12♎	11♏	13♑	11♒	10♓
14♒	13♓	12♓	13♉	12♊	13♌	13♍	14♏	13♐	15♒	13♓	13♈
16♓	15♈	14♈	15♊	14♋	16♍	16♎	17♐	15♑	17♓	15♈	15♉
18♈	17♉	16♉	17♋	17♌	18♎	18♏	19♑	17♒	19♈	17♉	17♊
20♉	19♊	18♊	20♌	19♍	21♏	20♐	21♒	20♓	21♉	19♊	19♋
23♊	21♋	21♋	22♍	22♎	23♐	23♑	23♓	21♈	23♊	22♋	21♌
25♋	24♌	23♌	25♎	24♏	25♑	25♒	25♈	23♉	25♋	24♌	24♍
28♌	26♍	26♍	27♏	27♐	27♒	27♓	27♉	26♊	28♌	26♍	26♎
30♍		28♎	29♐	29♑	29♓	29♈	29♋	28♋	30♍	29♎	29♏
		31♏		31♒		31♉		30♌			31♐

1927

JAN.	FEB.	MAR.	APR.	MAY	JUNE	JULY	AUG.	SEPT.	OCT.	NOV.	DEC.
2♑	1♒	3♓	1♈	2♊	1♋	1♌	2♎	1♏	3♑	1♒	1♓
5♒	3♓	4♈	3♉	4♋	3♌	3♍	4♏	3♐	5♒	4♓	3♈
7♓	5♈	6♉	5♊	7♌	6♍	5♎	7♐	5♑	7♓	6♈	5♉
9♈	7♉	9♊	7♋	9♍	8♎	8♏	9♑	8♒	9♈	8♉	7♊
11♉	9♊	11♋	9♌	12♎	11♏	10♐	11♒	10♓	11♉	10♊	9♋
13♊	12♋	13♌	12♍	14♏	13♐	13♑	13♓	12♈	13♊	12♋	11♌
15♋	14♌	16♍	14♎	17♐	15♑	15♒	15♈	14♉	15♋	14♌	14♍
18♌	16♍	18♎	17♏	19♑	18♒	17♓	18♉	16♊	18♌	16♍	16♎
20♍	19♎	21♏	19♐	21♒	20♓	19♈	20♊	18♋	20♍	19♎	19♏
23♎	21♏	23♐	22♑	24♓	22♈	21♉	22♋	20♌	23♎	21♏	21♐
25♏	24♐	26♑	24♒	26♈	24♉	23 F	24♌	23♍	25♏	24♐	24♑
28♐	26♑	28♒	26♓	28♉	26♊	26♋	27♍	25♎	28♐	26♑	26♒
30♑	28♒	30♓	28♈	30♉	28♊	28♌	29♎	28♏	30♑	29♒	28♓
			30♉			30♍		30♐			30♈

Key: Aries Taurus Gemini Cancer Leo Virgo
♈   ♉   ♊   ♋   ♌   ♍

1928

JAN.	FEB.	MAR.	APR.	MAY	JUNE	JULY	AUG.	SEPT.	OCT.	NOV.	DEC.
1 ♉	2 ♋	2 ♌	1 ♍	1 ♎	2 ♐	2 ♑	3 ♓	1 ♈	1 ♉	1 ♋	1 ♌
4 ♊	4 ♌	5 ♍	3 ♎	3 ♏	4 ♑	4 ♒	5 ♈	3 ♉	3 ♊	2 ♌	3 ♍
6 ♋	6 ♍	7 ♎	6 ♏	6 ♐	7 ♒	6 ♓	7 ♉	5 ♊	5 ♋	5 ♍	5 ♎
8 ♌	9 ♎	10 ♏	8 ♐	8 ♑	9 ♓	9 ♈	9 ♊	8 ♋	7 ♌	8 ♎	7 ♏
10 ♍	11 ♏	12 ♐	11 ♑	11 ♒	11 ♈	11 ♉	11 ♋	10 ♌	9 ♍	10 ♏	10 ♐
12 ♎	14 ♐	15 ♑	13 ♒	13 ♓	14 ♉	13 ♊	13 ♌	12 ♍	12 ♎	13 ♐	13 ♑
15 ♏	16 ♑	17 ♒	16 ♓	15 ♈	16 ♊	15 ♋	16 ♍	14 ♎	14 ♏	15 ♑	15 ♒
17 ♐	19 ♒	19 ♓	18 ♈	17 ♉	18 ♋	17 ♌	18 ♎	17 ♏	16 ♐	18 ♒	17 ♓
20 ♑	21 ♓	21 ♈	20 ♉	19 ♊	20 ♌	19 ♍	20 ♏	19 ♐	19 ♑	20 ♓	20 ♈
22 ♒	23 ♈	23 ♉	22 ♊	21 ♋	22 ♍	22 ♎	23 ♐	22 ♑	22 ♒	22 ♈	22 ♉
24 ♓	25 ♉	25 ♊	24 ♋	23 ♌	24 ♎	24 ♏	25 ♑	24 ♒	24 ♓	25 ♉	24 ♊
27 ♈	27 ♊	27 ♋	26 ♌	26 ♍	27 ♏	27 ♐	28 ♒	26 ♓	26 ♈	27 ♊	26 ♋
29 ♉	29 ♋	30 ♌	28 ♍	28 ♎	29 ♐	29 ♑	30 ♓	29 ♈	28 ♉	29 ♋	28 ♌
31 ♊				30 ♏		31 ♒			30 ♊		30 ♍

1929

JAN.	FEB.	MAR.	APR.	MAY	JUNE	JULY	AUG.	SEPT.	OCT.	NOV.	DEC.
1 ♎	3 ♐	2 ♐	1 ♑	1 ♒	2 ♈	1 ♉	2 ♋	2 ♍	2 ♎	3 ♐	2 ♑
4 ♏	5 ♑	4 ♑	3 ♒	3 ♓	4 ♉	3 ♊	4 ♌	4 ♎	4 ♏	5 ♑	5 ♒
6 ♐	8 ♒	7 ♒	6 ♓	5 ♈	6 ♊	6 ♋	6 ♍	7 ♏	6 ♐	8 ♒	8 ♓
9 ♑	10 ♓	9 ♓	8 ♈	8 ♉	8 ♋	7 ♌	8 ♎	9 ♐	9 ♑	10 ♓	10 ♈
11 ♒	12 ♈	12 ♈	10 ♉	10 ♊	10 ♌	9 ♍	11 ♏	11 ♑	11 ♒	13 ♈	12 ♉
14 ♓	15 ♉	14 ♉	12 ♊	12 ♋	12 ♍	12 ♎	13 ♐	14 ♒	13 ♓	15 ♉	14 ♊
16 ♈	17 ♊	16 ♊	14 ♋	14 ♌	14 ♎	14 ♏	15 ♑	16 ♓	16 ♈	17 ♊	16 ♋
18 ♉	19 ♋	18 ♋	16 ♌	16 ♍	17 ♏	16 ♐	18 ♒	19 ♈	18 ♉	19 ♋	18 ♌
20 ♊	21 ♌	20 ♌	19 ♍	18 ♎	19 ♐	19 ♑	20 ♓	21 ♉	21 ♊	21 ♌	20 ♍
22 ♋	23 ♍	22 ♍	21 ♎	20 ♏	21 ♑	21 ♒	23 ♈	23 ♊	23 ♋	23 ♍	23 ♎
24 ♌	25 ♎	25 ♎	23 ♏	23 ♐	24 ♒	24 ♓	25 ♉	25 ♋	25 ♌	25 ♎	25 ♏
27 ♍	27 ♏	27 ♏	26 ♐	25 ♑	27 ♓	26 ♈	28 ♊	28 ♌	27 ♍	28 ♏	27 ♐
29 ♎		29 ♐	28 ♑	28 ♒	29 ♈	29 ♉	30 ♋	30 ♍	29 ♎	30 ♐	30 ♑
31 ♏				30 ♓		31 ♊	31 ♌		31 ♏		

Libra	Scorpio	Sagittarius	Capricorn	Aquarius	Pisces
♎	♏	♐	♑	♒	♓

1930

JAN.	FEB.	MAR.	APR.	MAY	JUNE	JULY	AUG.	SEPT.	OCT.	NOV.	DEC.
1 ♒	3 ♈	2 ♈	3 ♊	2 ♋	3 ♍	2 ♎	3 ♐	1 ♑	1 ♒	2 ♈	2 ♉
4 ♓	5 ♉	4 ♉	5 ♋	4 ♌	5 ♎	4 ♏	5 ♑	4 ♒	4 ♓	5 ♉	5 ♊
6 ♈	7 ♊	6 ♊	7 ♌	6 ♍	7 ♏	6 ♐	8 ♒	6 ♓	6 ♈	7 ♊	7 ♋
9 ♉	9 ♋	9 ♋	9 ♍	8 ♎	9 ♐	9 ♑	10 ♓	9 ♈	9 ♉	9 ♋	9 ♌
11 ♊	11 ♌	11 ♌	11 ♎	11 ♏	12 ♑	11 ♒	13 ♈	11 ♉	11 ♊	12 ♌	11 ♍
13 ♋	13 ♍	13 ♍	13 ♏	13 ♐	14 ♒	14 ♓	15 ♉	14 ♊	13 ♋	14 ♍	13 ♎
15 ♌	15 ♎	16 ♎	16 ♐	15 ♑	17 ♓	16 ♈	17 ♊	16 ♋	15 ♌	16 ♎	15 ♏
17 ♍	17 ♏	18 ♏	18 ♑	17 ♒	19 ♈	19 ♉	20 ♋	18 ♌	17 ♍	18 ♏	17 ♐
19 ♎	20 ♐	20 ♐	20 ♒	20 ♓	21 ♉	21 ♊	22 ♌	20 ♍	19 ♎	20 ♐	20 ♑
21 ♏	22 ♑	23 ♑	23 ♓	23 ♈	24 ♊	23 ♋	24 ♍	22 ♎	21 ♏	23 ♑	22 ♒
23 ♐	25 ♒	25 ♒	25 ♈	25 ♉	26 ♋	25 ♌	26 ♎	25 ♏	24 ♐	25 ♒	25 ♓
26 ♑	27 ♓	27 ♓	28 ♉	27 ♊	28 ♌	27 ♍	28 ♏	27 ♐	26 ♑	27 ♓	27 ♈
29 ♒		29 ♈	30 ♊	29 ♋	30 ♍	29 ♎	30 ♐	29 ♑	28 ♒	30 ♈	30 ♉
31 ♓		31 ♉		31 ♌		31 ♏			31 ♓		

1931

JAN.	FEB.	MAR.	APR.	MAY	JUNE	JULY	AUG.	SEPT.	OCT.	NOV.	DEC.
1 ♊	2 ♌	1 ♌	2 ♎	1 ♏	2 ♑	1 ♒	3 ♈	1 ♉	1 ♊	2 ♌	2 ♍
3 ♋	4 ♍	3 ♍	4 ♏	3 ♐	4 ♒	4 ♓	5 ♉	4 ♊	4 ♋	4 ♍	4 ♎
5 ♌	6 ♎	5 ♎	6 ♐	5 ♑	6 ♓	6 ♈	8 ♊	6 ♋	6 ♌	6 ♎	6 ♏
7 ♍	8 ♏	7 ♏	8 ♑	7 ♒	9 ♈	8 ♉	10 ♋	8 ♌	8 ♍	8 ♏	8 ♐
9 ♎	10 ♐	9 ♐	10 ♒	10 ♓	11 ♉	11 ♊	12 ♌	10 ♍	10 ♎	10 ♐	10 ♑
11 ♏	12 ♑	12 ♑	13 ♓	13 ♈	14 ♊	13 ♋	14 ♍	12 ♎	12 ♏	12 ♑	12 ♒
14 ♐	15 ♒	14 ♒	15 ♈	15 ♉	16 ♋	16 ♌	16 ♎	14 ♏	14 ♐	15 ♒	14 ♓
16 ♑	17 ♓	16 ♓	18 ♉	17 ♊	18 ♌	18 ♍	18 ♏	16 ♐	17 ♑	17 ♓	17 ♈
18 ♒	20 ♈	19 ♈	20 ♊	20 ♋	20 ♍	20 ♎	20 ♐	19 ♑	19 ♒	19 ♈	19 ♉
21 ♓	22 ♉	21 ♉	23 ♋	22 ♌	22 ♎	22 ♏	22 ♑	21 ♒	21 ♓	22 ♉	21 ♊
23 ♈	25 ♊	24 ♊	25 ♌	24 ♍	24 ♏	24 ♐	25 ♒	24 ♓	24 ♈	24 ♊	24 ♋
26 ♉	27 ♋	26 ♋	27 ♍	26 ♎	27 ♐	26 ♑	27 ♓	26 ♈	26 ♉	27 ♋	27 ♌
28 ♊		28 ♌	29 ♎	28 ♏	29 ♑	29 ♒	29 ♈	28 ♉	28 ♊	29 ♌	29 ♍
31 ♋		31 ♍		30 ♐		31 ♓			31 ♋		31 ♎

Key:	Aries	Taurus	Gemini	Cancer	Leo	Virgo
	♈	♉	♊	♋	♌	♍

1932

JAN.	FEB.	MAR.	APR.	MAY	JUNE	JULY	AUG.	SEPT.	OCT.	NOV.	DEC.
2 ♏	3 ♑	1 ♑	2 ♓	1 ♈	3 ♊	1 ♋	1 ♌	1 ♎	1 ♏	2 ♑	1 ♒
4 ♐	5 ♒	3 ♒	4 ♈	4 ♉	5 ♋	4 ♌	3 ♍	4 ♏	3 ♐	4 ♒	3 ♓
6 ♑	7 ♓	5 ♓	7 ♉	7 ♊	8 ♌	7 ♍	6 ♎	6 ♐	5 ♑	6 ♓	6 ♈
8 ♒	10 ♈	8 ♈	9 ♊	9 ♋	10 ♍	9 ♎	8 ♏	8 ♑	7 ♒	9 ♈	8 ♉
11 ♓	12 ♉	10 ♉	12 ♋	11 ♌	12 ♎	11 ♏	10 ♐	10 ♒	10 ♓	11 ♉	11 ♊
13 ♈	15 ♊	13 ♊	14 ♌	14 ♍	14 ♏	14 ♐	12 ♑	13 ♓	12 ♈	14 ♊	13 ♋
16 ♉	17 ♋	15 ♋	16 ♍	16 ♎	16 ♐	16 ♑	14 ♒	15 ♈	15 ♉	16 ♋	16 ♌
18 ♊	19 ♌	18 ♌	18 ♎	18 ♏	18 ♑	18 ♒	16 ♓	18 ♉	17 ♊	19 ♌	18 ♍
21 ♋	21 ♍	20 ♍	20 ♏	20 ♐	20 ♒	20 ♓	19 ♈	20 ♊	20 ♋	21 ♍	20 ♎
23 ♌	23 ♎	22 ♎	22 ♐	23 ♑	23 ♓	23 ♈	21 ♉	23 ♋	22 ♌	23 ♎	23 ♏
25 ♍	26 ♏	24 ♏	24 ♑	25 ♒	25 ♈	25 ♉	24 ♊	25 ♌	25 ♍	25 ♏	25 ♐
27 ♎	28 ♐	26 ♐	27 ♒	26 ♓	28 ♉	27 ♊	26 ♋	27 ♎	27 ♎	27 ♐	27 ♑
29 ♏		28 ♑	29 ♓	29 ♈	30 ♊	30 ♋	29 ♌	29 ♏	29 ♏	29 ♑	29 ♒
31 ♐		30 ♒		31 ♉			31 ♍		31 ♐		31 ♓

1933

JAN.	FEB.	MAR.	APR.	MAY	JUNE	JULY	AUG.	SEPT.	OCT.	NOV.	DEC.
2 ♈	1 ♉	3 ♊	2 ♋	1 ♌	2 ♎	2 ♏	2 ♑	1 ♒	2 ♈	1 ♉	1 ♊
5 ♉	3 ♊	5 ♋	4 ♌	4 ♍	5 ♏	4 ♐	4 ♒	3 ♓	5 ♉	4 ♊	3 ♋
7 ♊	6 ♋	8 ♌	6 ♍	6 ♎	7 ♐	6 ♑	7 ♓	5 ♈	7 ♊	6 ♋	6 ♌
10 ♋	8 ♌	10 ♍	9 ♎	8 ♏	9 ♑	8 ♒	9 ♈	8 ♉	10 ♋	9 ♌	8 ♍
12 ♌	11 ♍	12 ♎	11 ♏	10 ♐	11 ♒	10 ♓	11 ♉	10 ♊	12 ♌	11 ♍	11 ♎
14 ♍	13 ♎	14 ♏	13 ♐	12 ♑	13 ♓	12 ♈	13 ♊	12 ♋	15 ♍	13 ♎	13 ♏
17 ♎	15 ♏	16 ♐	15 ♑	14 ♒	15 ♈	15 ♉	16 ♋	15 ♌	17 ♎	15 ♏	15 ♐
19 ♏	17 ♐	19 ♑	17 ♒	16 ♓	17 ♉	17 ♊	18 ♌	17 ♍	19 ♏	18 ♐	17 ♑
21 ♐	19 ♑	21 ♒	19 ♓	19 ♈	20 ♊	20 ♋	21 ♍	19 ♎	21 ♐	20 ♑	19 ♒
23 ♑	21 ♒	23 ♓	22 ♈	21 ♉	22 ♋	22 ♌	23 ♎	22 ♏	23 ♑	22 ♒	21 ♓
25 ♒	24 ♓	25 ♈	24 ♉	24 ♊	25 ♌	25 ♍	26 ♏	24 ♐	25 ♒	24 ♓	23 ♈
27 ♓	26 ♈	28 ♉	26 ♊	26 ♋	27 ♍	27 ♎	28 ♐	26 ♑	27 ♓	26 ♈	26 ♉
30 ♈	28 ♉	30 ♊	29 ♋	29 ♌	29 ♎	29 ♏	30 ♑	28 ♒	30 ♈	28 ♉	28 ♊
				31 ♍		31 ♐		30 ♓			31 ♋

	Libra	Scorpio	Sagittarius	Capricorn	Aquarius	Pisces
	♎	♏	♐	♑	♒	♓

1934

JAN.	FEB.	MAR.	APR.	MAY	JUNE	JULY	AUG.	SEPT.	OCT.	NOV.	DEC.
2 ♌	1 ♍	3 ♎	1 ♏	1 ♐	1 ♒	3 ♈	1 ♉	2 ♋	2 ♌	1 ♍	1 ♎
5 ♍	3 ♎	5 ♏	3 ♐	3 ♑	3 ♓	5 ♉	3 ♊	5 ♌	5 ♍	3 ♎	3 ♏
7 ♎	6 ♏	7 ♐	5 ♑	5 ♒	5 ♈	7 ♊	6 ♋	7 ♍	7 ♎	6 ♏	5 ♐
9 ♏	8 ♐	9 ♑	7 ♒	7 ♓	8 ♉	10 ♋	8 ♌	10 ♎	9 ♏	8 ♐	7 ♑
11 ♐	10 ♑	11 ♒	9 ♓	9 ♈	10 ♊	12 ♌	11 ♍	12 ♏	12 ♐	10 ♑	9 ♒
13 ♑	12 ♒	13 ♓	12 ♈	11 ♉	12 ♋	15 ♍	13 ♎	14 ♐	14 ♑	12 ♒	11 ♓
15 ♒	14 ♓	15 ♈	14 ♉	14 ♊	15 ♌	17 ♎	16 ♏	17 ♑	16 ♒	14 ♓	14 ♈
17 ♓	16 ♈	18 ♉	16 ♊	16 ♋	17 ♍	20 ♏	18 ♐	19 ♒	18 ♓	16 ♈	16 ♉
20 ♈	18 ♉	20 ♊	19 ♋	19 ♌	20 ♎	22 ♐	20 ♑	21 ♓	20 ♈	19 ♉	18 ♊
22 ♉	21 ♊	22 ♋	21 ♌	21 ♍	23 ♏	24 ♑	22 ♒	23 ♈	22 ♉	21 ♊	21 ♋
24 ♊	23 ♋	25 ♌	24 ♍	24 ♎	24 ♐	26 ♒	24 ♓	25 ♉	24 ♊	23 ♋	23 ♌
27 ♋	26 ♌	27 ♍	26 ♎	26 ♏	26 ♑	28 ♓	26 ♈	27 ♊	27 ♋	26 ♌	26 ♍
29 ♌	28 ♍	30 ♎	28 ♏	28 ♐	28 ♒	30 ♈	28 ♉	29 ♋	29 ♌	28 ♍	28 ♎
				30 ♑	30 ♓		31 ♊				30 ♏

1935

JAN.	FEB.	MAR.	APR.	MAY	JUNE	JULY	AUG.	SEPT.	OCT.	NOV.	DEC.
2 ♐	2 ♒	2 ♒	2 ♈	2 ♉	2 ♋	2 ♌	1 ♍	2 ♏	2 ♐	3 ♒	2 ♓
4 ♑	4 ♓	4 ♓	4 ♉	4 ♊	5 ♌	5 ♍	3 ♎	5 ♐	4 ♑	5 ♓	4 ♈
6 ♒	6 ♈	6 ♈	6 ♊	6 ♋	7 ♍	7 ♎	6 ♏	7 ♑	6 ♒	7 ♈	6 ♉
8 ♓	8 ♉	8 ♉	9 ♋	8 ♌	10 ♎	10 ♏	8 ♐	9 ♒	9 ♓	9 ♉	8 ♊
10 ♈	11 ♊	10 ♊	11 ♌	10 ♍	12 ♏	12 ♐	11 ♑	11 ♓	11 ♈	11 ♊	11 ♋
12 ♉	13 ♋	12 ♋	14 ♍	13 ♎	15 ♐	14 ♑	13 ♒	13 ♈	13 ♉	13 ♋	13 ♌
14 ♊	16 ♌	15 ♌	16 ♎	15 ♏	17 ♑	16 ♒	15 ♓	15 ♉	15 ♊	15 ♌	15 ♍
17 ♋	18 ♍	17 ♍	19 ♏	18 ♐	19 ♒	18 ♓	17 ♈	17 ♊	17 ♋	18 ♍	18 ♎
19 ♌	21 ♎	20 ♎	21 ♐	20 ♑	21 ♓	20 ♈	19 ♉	19 ♋	19 ♌	20 ♎	20 ♏
22 ♍	23 ♏	22 ♏	23 ♑	23 ♒	23 ♈	22 ♉	21 ♊	22 ♌	22 ♍	23 ♏	23 ♐
24 ♎	25 ♐	25 ♐	25 ♒	25 ♓	25 ♉	25 ♊	23 ♋	24 ♍	24 ♎	25 ♐	25 ♑
27 ♏	28 ♑	27 ♑	27 ♓	27 ♈	27 ♊	27 ♋	26 ♌	27 ♎	27 ♏	28 ♑	27 ♒
29 ♐		29 ♒	30 ♈	29 ♉	30 ♋	29 ♌	28 ♍	29 ♏	29 ♐	30 ♒	29 ♓
31 ♑		31 ♓		31 ♊		31 ♍	31 ♎		31 ♑		31 ♈

Key:	Aries	Taurus	Gemini	Cancer	Leo	Virgo
	♈	♉	♊	♋	♌ ·	♍

1936

JAN.	FEB.	MAR.	APR.	MAY	JUNE	JULY	AUG.	SEPT.	OCT.	NOV.	DEC.
3 ♉	1 ♊	1 ♋	3 ♍	2 ♎	1 ♏	1 ♐	2 ♒	2 ♈	2 ♉	2 ♋	2 ♌
5 ♊	3 ♋	4 ♌	6 ♎	5 ♏	4 ♐	3 ♑	4 ♓	4 ♉	4 ♊	5 ♌	4 ♍
7 ♋	6 ♌	6 ♍	8 ♏	7 ♐	6 ♑	6 ♒	6 ♈	7 ♊	6 ♋	7 ♍	7 ♎
9 ♌	8 ♍	8 ♎	10 ♐	9 ♑	8 ♒	8 ♓	8 ♉	9 ♋	8 ♌	9 ♎	9 ♏
12 ♍	10 ♎	11 ♏	12 ♑	12 ♒	10 ♓	10 ♈	10 ♊	11 ♌	11 ♍	12 ♏	12 ♐
14 ♎	13 ♏	14 ♐	15 ♒	14 ♓	13 ♈	12 ♉	12 ♋	13 ♍	13 ♎	14 ♐	14 ♑
17 ♏	15 ♐	16 ♑	17 ♓	16 ♈	15 ♉	14 ♊	15 ♌	16 ♎	16 ♏	17 ♑	17 ♒
19 ♐	18 ♑	18 ♒	19 ♈	18 ♉	17 ♊	16 ♋	17 ♍	18 ♏	18 ♐	19 ♒	19 ♓
21 ♑	20 ♒	21 ♓	21 ♉	20 ♊	19 ♋	18 ♌	20 ♎	21 ♐	21 ♑	22 ♓	21 ♈
24 ♒	22 ♓	23 ♈	23 ♊	22 ♋	21 ♌	21 ♍	22 ♏	23 ♑	23 ♒	24 ♈	23 ♉
26 ♓	24 ♈	24 ♉	25 ♋	25 ♌	23 ♍	23 ♎	25 ♐	26 ♒	25 ♓	26 ♉	25 ♊
28 ♈	26 ♉	27 ♊	27 ♌	27 ♍	25 ♎	25 ♏	27 ♑	28 ♓	27 ♈	28 ♊	27 ♋
30 ♉	8 ♊	29 ♋	30 ♍	28 ♎	28 ♏	28 ♐	29 ♒	30 ♈	29 ♉	30 ♋	29 ♌
		31 ♌				31 ♑	31 ♓		31 ♊		

1937

JAN.	FEB.	MAR.	APR.	MAY	JUNE	JULY	AUG.	SEPT.	OCT.	NOV.	DEC.
1 ♍	2 ♏	1 ♏	3 ♑	2 ♒	1 ♓	3 ♉	1 ♊	1 ♌	1 ♍	2 ♏	2 ♐
3 ♎	4 ♐	4 ♐	5 ♒	5 ♓	3 ♈	5 ♊	3 ♋	4 ♍	3 ♎	4 ♐	4 ♑
5 ♏	7 ♑	6 ♑	7 ♓	7 ♈	5 ♉	7 ♋	5 ♌	6 ♎	6 ♏	7 ♑	7 ♒
8 ♐	9 ♒	9 ♒	9 ♈	9 ♉	7 ♊	9 ♌	7 ♍	8 ♏	8 ♐	9 ♒	9 ♓
10 ♑	11 ♓	11 ♓	11 ♉	11 ♊	9 ♋	11 ♍	9 ♎	11 ♐	11 ♑	12 ♓	11 ♈
13 ♒	14 ♈	13 ♈	13 ♊	13 ♋	11 ♌	13 ♎	12 ♏	13 ♑	13 ♒	14 ♈	14 ♉
15 ♓	16 ♉	15 ♉	15 ♋	15 ♌	13 ♍	16 ♏	14 ♐	16 ♒	15 ♓	16 ♉	16 ♊
17 ♈	18 ♊	17 ♊	18 ♌	17 ♍	16 ♎	18 ♐	17 ♑	18 ♓	18 ♈	18 ♊	18 ♋
19 ♉	22 ♌	19 ♋	20 ♍	19 ♎	18 ♏	21 ♑	19 ♒	20 ♈	20 ♉	20 ♋	20 ♌
21 ♊	22 ♌	21 ♌	22 ♎	21 ♏	21 ♐	23 ♒	22 ♓	22 ♉	22 ♊	22 ♌	22 ♍
24 ♋	24 ♍	24 ♍	25 ♏	25 ♐	23 ♑	25 ♓	24 ♈	24 ♊	24 ♋	24 ♍	24 ♎
26 ♌	27 ♎	26 ♎	27 ♐	27 ♑	26 ♒	28 ♈	26 ♉	26 ♋	26 ♌	27 ♎	26 ♏
28 ♍		28 ♏	30 ♑	30 ♒	28 ♓	30 ♉	28 ♊	29 ♌	28 ♍	29 ♏	29 ♐
30 ♎		31 ♐			30 ♈		30 ♋		30 ♎		31 ♑

Libra	Scorpio	Sagittarius	Capricorn	Aquarius	Pisces
♎	♏	♐	♑	♒	♓

1930

JAN.	FEB.	MAR.	APR.	MAY	JUNE	JULY	AUG.	SEPT.	OCT.	NOV.	DEC.
3 ♎	2 ♓	1 ♓	3 ♉	1 ♊	2 ♌	1 ♍	3 ♏	1 ♐	3 ♎	3 ♓	1 ♈
5 ♓	4 ♈	3 ♈	4 ♊	3 ♋	4 ♍	4 ♎	4 ♐	3 ♑	5 ♓	4 ♈	4 ♉
8 ♈	6 ♉	5 ♉	6 ♋	5 ♌	6 ♎	5 ♏	7 ♑	6 ♒	8 ♈	6 ♉	6 ♊
10 ♉	8 ♊	8 ♊	8 ♌	7 ♍	8 ♎	8 ♐	9 ♒	8 ♓	10 ♉	9 ♊	8 ♋
12 ♊	10 ♋	10 ♋	10 ♍	10 ♎	11 ♐	10 ♑	13 ♓	10 ♈	12 ♊	13 ♋	10 ♌
14 ♋	12 ♌	12 ♌	13 ♎	12 ♎	13 ♑	13 ♒	14 ♈	13 ♉	14 ♋	13 ♌	12 ♍
16 ♌	15 ♍	14 ♍	15 ♏	14 ♐	16 ♒	15 ♓	16 ♉	15 ♊	16 ♌	15 ♍	14 ♎
18 ♍	17 ♎	18 ♎	17 ♐	17 ♑	18 ♓	18 ♈	19 ♊	17 ♋	17 ♎	17 ♎	16 ♏
20 ♎	19 ♏	20 ♏	19 ♑	19 ♒	21 ♈	20 ♉	21 ♋	19 ♌	20 ♏	19 ♏	19 ♐
23 ♏	21 ♐	22 ♐	22 ♒	23 ♓	23 ♉	23 ♊	23 ♌	22 ♍	22 ♐	22 ♐	21 ♑
25 ♐	24 ♑	25 ♑	24 ♓	24 ♈	25 ♊	26 ♋	25 ♍	25 ♎	24 ♑	24 ♑	24 ♒
28 ♑	28 ♒	26 ♒	27 ♈	27 ♉	27 ♋	28 ♌	26 ♎	28 ♏	27 ♒	26 ♓
30 ♒		28 ♓	29 ♉	29 ♊	29 ♌	29 ♍	28 ♐	30 ♑	29 ♓	29 ♈
		31 ♈		31 ♋		31 ♎		30 ♑			31 ♉

1939

JAN.	FEB.	MAR.	APR.	MAY	JUNE	JULY	AUG.	SEPT.	OCT.	NOV.	DEC.
2 ♊	1 ♋	2 ♌	1 ♍	3 ♏	1 ♐	3 ♒	2 ♓	3 ♉	3 ♊	1 ♋	3 ♍
4 ♋	3 ♌	4 ♍	3 ♎	4 ♐	3 ♑	5 ♓	4 ♈	5 ♊	5 ♋	3 ♌	5 ♎
6 ♌	5 ♍	6 ♎	5 ♏	7 ♑	6 ♒	8 ♈	7 ♉	8 ♋	7 ♌	5 ♍	7 ♏
8 ♍	7 ♎	8 ♏	7 ♐	9 ♒	8 ♓	10 ♉	9 ♊	10 ♌	9 ♍	7 ♎	9 ♐
10 ♎	9 ♏	11 ♐	9 ♑	12 ♓	11 ♈	12 ♊	11 ♋	11 ♍	11 ♎	10 ♏	11 ♑
13 ♏	11 ♐	13 ♑	12 ♒	14 ♈	13 ♉	15 ♋	13 ♌	14 ♎	13 ♏	12 ♐	14 ♒
15 ♐	14 ♑	16 ♒	14 ♓	17 ♉	15 ♊	17 ♌	15 ♍	16 ♏	15 ♐	14 ♑	16 ♓
18 ♑	16 ♒	18 ♓	17 ♈	19 ♊	17 ♋	19 ♍	17 ♎	18 ♐	18 ♑	16 ♒	19 ♈
20 ♒	19 ♓	21 ♈	19 ♉	21 ♋	19 ♌	21 ♎	19 ♏	20 ♑	20 ♒	19 ♓	21 ♉
23 ♓	21 ♈	23 ♉	22 ♊	23 ♌	21 ♍	23 ♏	22 ♐	23 ♒	23 ♓	21 ♈	24 ♊
25 ♈	24 ♉	25 ♊	24 ♋	24 ♍	23 ♎	24 ♐	24 ♑	25 ♓	25 ♈	24 ♉	26 ♋
28 ♉	26 ♊	28 ♋	26 ♌	26 ♎	25 ♏	26 ♑	27 ♒	27 ♈	27 ♉	26 ♊	28 ♌
30 ♊	28 ♋	30 ♌	28 ♍	28 ♏	28 ♐	30 ♒	29 ♓	30 ♉	30 ♊	28 ♋	30 ♍
			30 ♎		30 ♑	31 ♈					30 ♌

Key:	Aries	Taurus	Gemini	Cancer	Leo	Virgo
	♈	♉	♊	♋	♌	♍

1940

JAN.	FEB.	MAR.	APR.	MAY	JUNE	JULY	AUG.	SEPT.	OCT.	NOV.	DEC.
1 ♎	2 ♐	2 ♑	1 ♒	1 ♓	2 ♉	2 ♊	3 ♌	1 ♍	2 ♏	1 ♐	3 ♒
3 ♏	4 ♑	5 ♒	3 ♓	3 ♈	4 ♊	4 ♋	5 ♍	3 ♎	4 ♐	3 ♑	5 ♓
5 ♐	6 ♒	7 ♓	6 ♈	6 ♉	7 ♋	6 ♌	7 ♎	5 ♏	7 ♑	5 ♒	7 ♈
8 ♑	9 ♓	10 ♈	8 ♉	8 ♊	9 ♌	9 ♍	9 ♏	7 ♐	9 ♒	8 ♓	10 ♉
10 ♒	11 ♈	12 ♉	11 ♊	10 ♋	11 ♍	11 ♎	11 ♐	9 ♑	11 ♓	10 ♈	13 ♊
13 ♓	14 ♉	15 ♊	13 ♋	13 ♌	13 ♎	13 ♏	13 ♑	12 ♒	14 ♈	13 ♉	15 ♋
15 ♈	16 ♊	17 ♋	15 ♌	15 ♍	15 ♏	15 ♐	15 ♒	14 ♓	16 ♉	15 ♊	17 ♌
18 ♉	19 ♋	19 ♌	18 ♍	17 ♎	17 ♐	17 ♑	18 ♓	17 ♈	19 ♊	18 ♋	19 ♍
20 ♊	21 ♌	21 ♍	20 ♎	19 ♏	20 ♑	19 ♒	20 ♈	19 ♉	21 ♋	20 ♌	21 ♎
22 ♋	23 ♍	23 ♎	22 ♏	21 ♐	22 ♒	22 ♓	23 ♉	22 ♊	24 ♌	22 ♍	24 ♏
24 ♌	25 ♎	25 ♏	24 ♐	23 ♑	24 ♓	24 ♈	25 ♊	24 ♋	26 ♍	24 ♎	26 ♐
26 ♍	27 ♏	27 ♐	26 ♑	25 ♒	27 ♈	26 ♉	28 ♋	26 ♌	28 ♎	26 ♏	28 ♑
28 ♎	29 ♐	29 ♑	28 ♒	28 ♓	29 ♉	29 ♊	30 ♌	28 ♍	30 ♏	28 ♐	30 ♒
30 ♏				30 ♈		31 ♋		30 ♎		30 ♑	

1941

JAN.	FEB.	MAR.	APR.	MAY	JUNE	JULY	AUG.	SEPT.	OCT.	NOV.	DEC.
1 ♓	3 ♉	2 ♉	1 ♊	1 ♋	2 ♍	1 ♎	1 ♐	2 ♒	2 ♓	3 ♉	2 ♊
4 ♈	5 ♊	5 ♊	3 ♋	3 ♌	4 ♎	3 ♏	4 ♑	4 ♓	4 ♈	5 ♊	5 ♋
6 ♉	8 ♋	7 ♋	6 ♌	5 ♍	6 ♏	5 ♐	6 ♒	7 ♈	6 ♉	8 ♋	7 ♌
9 ♊	10 ♌	9 ♌	8 ♍	7 ♎	8 ♐	7 ♑	8 ♓	9 ♉	9 ♊	10 ♌	10 ♍
11 ♋	12 ♍	11 ♍	10 ♎	9 ♏	10 ♑	9 ♒	10 ♈	12 ♊	11 ♋	13 ♍	12 ♎
13 ♌	14 ♎	13 ♎	12 ♏	11 ♐	12 ♒	12 ♓	13 ♉	14 ♋	13 ♌	15 ♎	14 ♏
16 ♍	16 ♏	16 ♏	14 ♐	13 ♑	14 ♓	14 ♈	15 ♊	16 ♌	16 ♍	17 ♏	16 ♐
18 ♎	18 ♐	18 ♐	16 ♑	16 ♒	17 ♈	16 ♉	18 ♋	19 ♍	18 ♎	19 ♐	18 ♑
20 ♏	20 ♑	20 ♑	18 ♒	18 ♓	19 ♉	19 ♊	20 ♌	21 ♎	21 ♏	21 ♑	20 ♒
22 ♐	23 ♒	22 ♒	21 ♓	20 ♈	21 ♊	21 ♋	23 ♍	23 ♏	24 ♐	23 ♒	22 ♓
24 ♑	25 ♓	24 ♓	23 ♈	22 ♉	24 ♋	23 ♌	25 ♎	25 ♐	26 ♑	25 ♓	25 ♈
26 ♒	27 ♈	27 ♈	26 ♉	25 ♊	26 ♌	26 ♍	27 ♏	27 ♑	29 ♒	27 ♈	27 ♉
29 ♓		29 ♉	28 ♊	28 ♋	29 ♍	28 ♎	29 ♐	29 ♒	31 ♓	30 ♉	30 ♊
31 ♈				30 ♌		30 ♏	31 ♑				

Libra	Scorpio	Sagittarius	Capricorn	Aquarius	Pisces
♎	♏	♐	♑	♒	♓

1942

JAN.	FEB.	MAR.	APR.	MAY	JUNE	JULY	AUG.	SEPT.	OCT.	NOV.	DEC.
1 ♋	2 ♍	2 ♍	2 ♏	2 ♐	2 ♒	2 ♓	3 ♉	1 ♊	1 ♋	3 ♍	2 ♎
4 ♌	5 ♎	4 ♎	4 ♐	4 ♑	4 ♓	4 ♈	5 ♊	4 ♋	4 ♌	5 ♎	4 ♏
6 ♍	7 ♏	6 ♏	6 ♑	6 ♒	7 ♈	6 ♉	8 ♋	6 ♌	6 ♍	7 ♏	7 ♐
8 ♎	9 ♐	8 ♐	9 ♒	8 ♓	9 ♉	9 ♊	10 ♌	9 ♍	8 ♎	9 ♐	9 ♑
11 ♏	11 ♑	10 ♑	11 ♓	10 ♈	12 ♊	11 ♋	13 ♍	11 ♎	11 ♏	11 ♑	11 ♒
13 ♐	13 ♒	12 ♒	13 ♈	13 ♉	14 ♋	14 ♌	15 ♎	13 ♏	13 ♐	13 ♒	13 ♓
15 ♑	15 ♓	15 ♓	16 ♉	15 ♊	16 ♌	16 ♍	17 ♏	15 ♐	15 ♑	15 ♓	15 ♈
17 ♒	17 ♈	17 ♈	18 ♊	18 ♋	19 ♍	19 ♎	19 ♐	18 ♑	17 ♒	18 ♈	17 ♉
19 ♓	20 ♉	19 ♉	21 ♋	20 ♌	21 ♎	21 ♏	21 ♑	20 ♒	19 ♓	20 ♉	20 ♊
21 ♈	22 ♊	22 ♊	23 ♌	23 ♍	24 ♏	23 ♐	23 ♒	22 ♓	21 ♈	22 ♊	22 ♋
23 ♉	25 ♋	24 ♋	25 ♍	26 ♎	26 ♐	25 ♑	25 ♓	24 ♈	24 ♉	25 ♋	25 ♌
26 ♊	27 ♌	27 ♌	28 ♎	27 ♏	28 ♑	27 ♒	28 ♈	26 ♉	26 ♊	27 ♌	27 ♍
29 ♋		29 ♍	30 ♏	29 ♐	30 ♒	29 ♓	30 ♉	29 ♊	29 ♋	30 ♍	30 ♎
31 ♌		31 ♎		31 ♑		31 ♈			31 ♌		

1943

JAN.	FEB.	MAR.	APR.	MAY	JUNE	JULY	AUG.	SEPT.	OCT.	NOV.	DEC.
1 ♏	1 ♑	1 ♑	1 ♓	1 ♈	2 ♊	1 ♋	3 ♍	1 ♎	1 ♏	2 ♑	1 ♒
3 ♐	3 ♒	3 ♒	3 ♈	3 ♉	4 ♋	4 ♌	5 ♎	4 ♏	3 ♐	4 ♒	3 ♓
5 ♑	5 ♓	5 ♓	6 ♉	5 ♊	6 ♌	6 ♍	7 ♏	6 ♐	5 ♑	6 ♓	5 ♈
7 ♒	8 ♈	7 ♈	8 ♊	8 ♋	9 ♍	9 ♎	10 ♐	8 ♑	6 ♒	8 ♈	7 ♉
9 ♓	10 ♉	9 ♉	10 ♋	10 ♌	11 ♏	12 ♐	10 ♒	10 ♓	10 ♓	10 ♉	10 ♊
11 ♈	12 ♊	11 ♊	13 ♌	13 ♍	14 ♏	13 ♐	14 ♒	12 ♈	12 ♈	12 ♊	12 ♋
13 ♉	15 ♋	14 ♋	15 ♍	15 ♎	16 ♐	15 ♑	16 ♓	14 ♈	14 ♉	15 ♋	15 ♌
16 ♊	17 ♌	16 ♌	18 ♎	17 ♏	18 ♑	17 ♒	18 ♈	16 ♉	16 ♊	17 ♌	17 ♍
18 ♋	20 ♍	19 ♍	20 ♏	20 ♐	20 ♒	19 ♓	20 ♉	19 ♊	18 ♋	20 ♍	20 ♎
21 ♌	22 ♎	21 ♎	22 ♐	22 ♑	22 ♓	21 ♈	22 ♊	21 ♋	21 ♌	22 ♎	22 ♏
23 ♍	24 ♏	24 ♏	24 ♑	24 ♒	24 ♈	25 ♊	24 ♋	23 ♍	25 ♏	24 ♐
26 ♎	27 ♐	26 ♐	26 ♒	26 ♓	26 ♉	26 ♊	26 ♌	26 ♎	27 ♐	26 ♑
28 ♏		28 ♑	29 ♓	28 ♈	29 ♊	28 ♋	30 ♍	29 ♎	28 ♏	29 ♑	28 ♒
30 ♐		30 ♒		30 ♉		31 ♌			30 ♐		30 ♓

Key: Aries   Taurus   Gemini   Cancer   Leo   Virgo

  ♈   ♉   ♊   ♋   ♌   ♍

1944

JAN.	FEB.	MAR.	APR.	MAY	JUNE	JULY	AUG.	SEPT.	OCT.	NOV.	DEC.
2♈	2♊	1♊	2♌	1♍	3♏	2♐	1♑	2♓	1♈	2♊	1♋
4♉	5♋	3♋	4♍	4♎	5♐	5♑	3♒	4♈	3♉	4♋	3♌
6♊	7♌	5♌	7♎	6♏	7♑	7♒	5♓	6♉	5♊	6♌	6♍
8♋	10♍	8♍	9♏	9♐	9♒	9♓	7♈	8♊	7♋	9♍	8♎
11♌	12♎	10♎	11♐	11♑	12♓	11♈	9♉	10♋	10♌	11♎	11♏
13♍	15♏	13♏	14♑	13♒	14♈	13♉	11♊	12♌	12♍	14♏	13♐
16♎	17♐	15♐	16♒	15♓	16♉	15♊	14♋	15♍	15♎	16♐	16♑
18♏	19♑	18♑	18♓	17♈	18♊	18♋	16♌	17♎	17♏	18♑	18♒
21♐	21♒	20♒	20♈	20♉	20♋	20♌	19♍	20♏	20♐	21♒	20♓
23♑	23♓	22♓	22♉	22♊	22♌	22♍	21♎	22♐	22♑	23♓	22♈
25♒	25♈	24♈	24♊	24♋	25♍	25♎	24♏	25♑	24♒	25♈	24♉
27♓	27♉	26♉	27♋	26♌	28♎	27♏	26♐	27♒	26♓	27♉	26♊
29♈		28♊	29♌	29♍	30♏	30♐	29♑	29♓	29♈	29♊	29♋
31♉		30♋		31♎			31♒		31♉		31♌

1945

JAN.	FEB.	MAR.	APR.	MAY	JUNE	JULY	AUG.	SEPT.	OCT.	NOV.	DEC.
2♍	1♎	3♏	2♐	1♑	2♓	2♈	2♊	3♌	2♍	1♎	1♏
5♎	4♏	5♐	4♑	4♒	4♈	4♉	4♋	5♍	5♎	3♏	3♐
7♏	6♐	8♑	6♒	6♓	6♉	6♊	6♌	7♎	7♏	6♐	6♑
10♐	8♑	10♒	9♓	8♈	8♊	8♋	9♍	10♏	10♐	8♑	8♒
12♑	11♒	12♓	11♈	10♉	10♋	10♌	11♎	12♐	12♑	11♒	10♓
14♒	13♓	14♈	13♉	12♊	13♌	12♍	14♏	15♑	15♒	13♓	13♈
16♓	15♈	16♉	15♊	14♋	15♍	15♎	16♐	17♒	17♓	15♈	15♉
18♈	17♉	18♊	17♋	16♌	17♎	17♏	19♑	19♓	19♈	17♉	17♊
20♉	19♊	20♋	19♌	19♍	20♏	20♐	21♒	21♈	21♉	19♊	19♋
23♊	21♋	23♌	21♍	21♎	22♐	22♑	23♓	23♉	23♊	21♋	21♌
25♋	23♌	25♍	24♎	24♏	25♑	24♒	25♈	25♊	25♋	23♌	23♍
27♌	26♍	28♎	26♏	26♐	27♒	27♓	27♉	28♋	27♌	26♍	25♎
30♍	28♎	30♏	29♐	29♑	29♓	29♈	29♊	30♌	29♍	28♎	28♏
				31♒		31♉	31♋				31♐

Libra	Scorpio	Sagittarius	Capricorn	Aquarius	Pisces
♎	♏	♐	♑	♒	♓

1946

JAN.	FEB.	MAR.	APR.	MAY	JUNE	JULY	AUG.	SEPT.	OCT.	NOV.	DEC.
2 ♑	1 ♒	2 ♓	1 ♈	2 ♊	1 ♋	2 ♍	1 ♎	2 ♐	2 ♑	1 ♒	1 ♓
4 ♒	3 ♓	4 ♈	3 ♉	4 ♋	3 ♌	5 ♎	3 ♏	5 ♑	5 ♒	3 ♓	3 ♈
7 ♓	5 ♈	7 ♉	5 ♊	6 ♌	5 ♍	7 ♏	6 ♐	7 ♒	7 ♓	6 ♈	5 ♉
9 ♈	7 ♉	9 ♊	7 ♋	9 ♍	7 ♎	10 ♐	8 ♑	10 ♓	9 ♈	8 ♉	7 ♊
11 ♉	9 ♊	11 ♋	9 ♌	11 ♎	10 ♏	12 ♑	11 ♒	12 ♈	11 ♉	10 ♊	9 ♋
13 ♊	12 ♋	13 ♌	11 ♍	14 ♏	12 ♐	15 ♒	13 ♓	14 ♉	13 ♊	12 ♋	11 ♌
15 ♋	14 ♌	15 ♍	14 ♎	16 ♐	15 ♑	17 ♓	15 ♈	16 ♊	15 ♋	14 ♌	13 ♍
17 ♌	16 ♍	18 ♎	16 ♏	19 ♑	17 ♒	19 ♈	18 ♉	18 ♋	18 ♌	16 ♍	16 ♎
20 ♍	18 ♎	20 ♏	19 ♐	21 ♒	20 ♓	21 ♉	20 ♊	20 ♌	20 ♍	18 ♎	18 ♏
22 ♎	21 ♏	23 ♐	21 ♑	23 ♓	22 ♈	24 ♊	22 ♋	23 ♍	22 ♎	21 ♏	20 ♐
24 ♏	23 ♐	25 ♑	24 ♒	26 ♈	24 ♉	26 ♋	24 ♌	25 ♎	24 ♏	23 ♐	23 ♑
27 ♐	26 ♑	27 ♒	26 ♓	28 ♉	26 ♊	28 ♌	26 ♍	27 ♏	27 ♐	26 ♑	25 ♒
29 ♑	28 ♒	30 ♓	28 ♈	30 ♊	28 ♋	31 ♍	28 ♎	29 ♐	29 ♑	28 ♒	28 ♓
			30 ♉		30 ♌						30 ♈

1947

JAN.	FEB.	MAR.	APR.	MAY	JUNE	JULY	AUG.	SEPT.	OCT.	NOV.	DEC.
2 ♉	2 ♋	1 ♋	2 ♍	1 ♎	2 ♐	2 ♑	1 ♒	2 ♈	2 ♉	2 ♋	2 ♌
4 ♊	4 ♌	3 ♌	4 ♎	4 ♏	5 ♑	5 ♒	3 ♓	4 ♉	4 ♊	4 ♌	4 ♍
6 ♋	6 ♍	6 ♍	6 ♏	6 ♐	7 ♒	7 ♓	6 ♈	7 ♊	6 ♋	6 ♍	6 ♎
8 ♌	8 ♎	8 ♎	9 ♐	8 ♑	10 ♓	10 ♈	8 ♉	9 ♋	8 ♌	9 ♎	8 ♏
10 ♍	11 ♏	10 ♏	11 ♑	11 ♒	12 ♈	12 ♉	10 ♊	11 ♌	11 ♍	11 ♏	11 ♐
12 ♎	13 ♐	12 ♐	14 ♒	13 ♓	14 ♉	14 ♊	12 ♋	13 ♍	13 ♎	13 ♐	13 ♑
14 ♏	16 ♑	15 ♑	16 ♓	16 ♈	17 ♊	16 ♋	14 ♌	15 ♎	15 ♏	16 ♑	15 ♒
17 ♐	18 ♒	17 ♒	18 ♈	18 ♉	19 ♋	18 ♌	16 ♍	17 ♏	18 ♐	19 ♒	18 ♓
19 ♑	20 ♓	20 ♓	21 ♉	20 ♊	21 ♌	21 ♍	19 ♎	19 ♐	20 ♑	21 ♓	20 ♈
22 ♒	23 ♈	22 ♈	23 ♊	22 ♋	23 ♍	23 ♎	21 ♏	22 ♑	23 ♒	23 ♈	23 ♉
24 ♓	25 ♉	24 ♉	25 ♋	24 ♌	25 ♎	26 ♏	23 ♐	24 ♒	25 ♓	25 ♉	25 ♊
27 ♈	27 ♊	26 ♊	27 ♌	26 ♍	27 ♏	28 ♐	26 ♑	27 ♓	27 ♈	27 ♊	27 ♋
29 ♉		29 ♋	29 ♍	29 ♎	30 ♐	30 ♑	28 ♒	29 ♈	29 ♉	30 ♋	29 ♌
31 ♊		31 ♌		31 ♏			31 ♓		31 ♊		31 ♍

Key: Aries   Taurus   Gemini   Cancer   Leo   Virgo

       ♈   ♉   ♊   ♋   ♌   ♍

1948

JAN.	FEB.	MAR.	APR.	MAY	JUNE	JULY	AUG.	SEPT.	OCT.	NOV.	DEC.
2 ♎	1 ♏	1 ♐	2 ♒	2 ♓	1 ♈	1 ♉	2 ♋	2 ♍	2 ♎	2 ♐	2 ♑
4 ♏	3 ♐	4 ♑	5 ♓	5 ♈	4 ♉	3 ♊	4 ♌	4 ♎	4 ♏	4 ♑	4 ♒
7 ♐	5 ♑	6 ♒	7 ♈	7 ♉	6 ♊	5 ♋	6 ♍	6 ♏	6 ♐	7 ♒	7 ♓
9 ♑	8 ♒	9 ♓	10 ♉	9 ♊	8 ♋	7 ♌	8 ♎	8 ♐	8 ♑	9 ♓	9 ♈
12 ♒	10 ♓	11 ♈	12 ♊	12 ♋	10 ♌	9 ♍	11 ♏	11 ♑	11 ♒	12 ♈	11 ♉
14 ♓	13 ♈	14 ♉	14 ♋	14 ♌	12 ♍	11 ♎	13 ♐	13 ♒	13 ♓	14 ♉	14 ♊
17 ♈	15 ♉	16 ♊	17 ♌	16 ♍	14 ♎	13 ♏	15 ♑	16 ♓	16 ♈	17 ♊	16 ♋
19 ♉	18 ♊	18 ♋	19 ♍	18 ♎	16 ♏	15 ♐	17 ♒	18 ♈	18 ♉	19 ♋	18 ♌
21 ♊	20 ♋	20 ♌	21 ♎	20 ♏	19 ♐	18 ♑	20 ♓	21 ♉	20 ♊	21 ♌	21 ♍
23 ♋	22 ♌	22 ♍	23 ♏	22 ♐	21 ♑	20 ♒	22 ♈	23 ♊	23 ♋	23 ♍	23 ♎
25 ♌	24 ♍	24 ♎	25 ♐	25 ♑	23 ♒	23 ♓	25 ♉	25 ♋	25 ♌	28 ♏	25 ♏
27 ♍	26 ♎	26 ♏	27 ♑	27 ♒	26 ♓	26 ♈	28 ♊	28 ♌	27 ♍	30 ♐	27 ♐
29 ♎	28 ♏	29 ♐	30 ♒	30 ♓	28 ♈	28 ♉	30 ♋	30 ♍	29 ♎		29 ♑
		31 ♑				31 ♊			31 ♏		

1949

JAN.	FEB.	MAR.	APR.	MAY	JUNE	JULY	AUG.	SEPT.	OCT.	NOV.	DEC.
1 ♒	2 ♈	1 ♈	2 ♊	2 ♋	1 ♌	2 ♎	3 ♐	1 ♑	1 ♒	2 ♈	2 ♉
3 ♓	4 ♉	4 ♉	5 ♋	4 ♌	4 ♏	5 ♑	5 ♑	3 ♒	3 ♓	4 ♉	4 ♊
6 ♈	7 ♊	6 ♊	7 ♌	6 ♍	6 ♐	7 ♒	6 ♓	5 ♓	5 ♈	7 ♊	6 ♋
8 ♉	9 ♋	9 ♋	9 ♍	7 ♎	9 ♑	9 ♓	8 ♈	8 ♈	8 ♉	9 ♋	9 ♌
10 ♊	11 ♌	11 ♌	11 ♎	9 ♏	11 ♒	11 ♈	11 ♉	10 ♉	11 ♊	11 ♌	11 ♍
13 ♋	13 ♍	13 ♍	13 ♏	13 ♐	13 ♓	13 ♉	14 ♊	13 ♊	13 ♋	14 ♍	13 ♎
15 ♌	15 ♎	15 ♎	15 ♐	15 ♑	16 ♈	16 ♊	17 ♋	16 ♋	15 ♌	16 ♎	15 ♏
17 ♍	17 ♏	17 ♏	17 ♑	17 ♒	18 ♉	18 ♋	19 ♌	18 ♌	17 ♍	18 ♏	17 ♐
19 ♎	19 ♐	19 ♐	20 ♒	19 ♓	21 ♊	21 ♌	22 ♍	20 ♍	20 ♎	20 ♐	19 ♑
21 ♏	22 ♑	21 ♑	22 ♓	22 ♈	21 ♋	23 ♍	24 ♎	22 ♎	22 ♏	22 ♑	22 ♒
23 ♐	24 ♒	23 ♒	25 ♈	24 ♉	23 ♌	25 ♎	26 ♏	24 ♏	24 ♐	24 ♒	24 ♓
26 ♑	27 ♓	26 ♓	27 ♉	27 ♊	26 ♍	28 ♏	28 ♐	26 ♐	26 ♑	27 ♓	26 ♈
28 ♒		28 ♈	30 ♊	29 ♋	29 ♎	30 ♐	30 ♑	28 ♑	28 ♒	29 ♈	29 ♉
30 ♓		31 ♉		30 ♌	31 ♏				30 ♓		31 ♊

Libra	Scorpio	Sagittarius	Capricorn	Aquarius	Pisces
♎	♏	♐	♑	♒	♓

1950

JAN.	FEB.	MAR.	APR.	MAY	JUNE	JULY	AUG.	SEPT	OCT.	NOV.	DEC.
3♋	1♌	1♌	2♎	1♏	1♑	1♒	2♈	1♉	3♋	2♌	1♍
5♌	4♍	3♍	4♏	3♐	3♒	3♓	4♉	3♊	5♌	4♍	4♎
7♍	6♎	5♎	6♐	5♑	6♓	5♈	7♊	6♋	8♍	6♎	6♏
9♎	8♏	7♏	8♑	7♒	8♈	8♉	9♋	8♌	10♎	8♏	8♐
12♏	10♐	9♐	10♒	9♓	11♉	10♊	12♌	10♍	12♏	10♐	10♑
14♐	12♑	11♑	12♓	12♈	13♊	13♋	14♍	12♎	14♐	12♑	12♒
16♑	14♒	14♒	15♈	14♉	16♋	15♌	16♎	15♏	16♑	14♒	14♓
18♒	17♓	16♓	17♉	17♊	18♌	18♍	18♏	17♐	18♒	17♓	16♈
20♓	19♈	18♈	20♊	19♋	20♍	20♎	20♐	19♑	20♓	19♈	19♉
23♈	22♉	21♉	22♋	22♌	22♎	22♏	22♑	21♒	23♈	21♉	21♊
25♉	24♊	23♊	24♌	25♍	24♏	24♐	25♒	23♓	25♉	24♊	24♋
28♊	27♋	26♋	27♍	27♎	26♐	26♑	27♓	25♈	28♊	27♋	26♌
30♋		28♌	29♎	29♏	28♑	28♒	29♈	28♉	30♋	29♌	29♍
		30♍		30♐	30♒	30♓		30♊			31♎

1951

JAN.	FEB.	MAR.	APR.	MAY	JUNE	JULY	AUG.	SEPT.	OCT.	NOV.	DEC.
2♏	1♐	2♑	2♓	2♈	1♉	3♋	2♌	3♎	2♏	1♐	2♒
4♐	3♑	4♒	5♈	4♉	3♊	5♌	4♍	5♏	4♐	3♑	4♓
6♑	5♒	6♓	7♉	7♊	6♋	8♍	6♎	7♐	7♑	5♒	6♈
8♒	7♓	8♈	10♊	9♋	8♌	10♎	9♏	9♑	9♒	7♓	9♉
10♓	9♈	11♉	12♋	12♌	11♍	13♏	11♐	11♒	11♓	9♈	11♊
13♈	11♉	13♊	14♌	14♍	13♎	15♐	13♑	13♓	13♈	12♉	14♋
15♉	13♊	16♋	17♍	17♎	15♏	17♑	15♒	16♈	15♉	14♊	16♌
18♊	16♋	18♌	19♎	19♏	17♐	19♒	17♓	18♉	18♊	16♋	19♍
20♋	18♌	21♍	21♏	21♐	19♑	21♓	19♈	20♊	20♋	19♌	21♎
23♌	21♍	23♎	23♐	23♑	21♒	23♈	21♉	23♋	23♌	21♍	23♏
25♍	23♎	25♏	25♑	25♒	23♓	25♉	24♊	25♌	25♍	23♎	26♐
27♎	26♏	27♐	27♒	27♓	25♈	28♊	26♋	28♍	27♎	26♏	28♑
29♏	28♐	29♑	30♓	29♈	28♉	30♋	29♌	30♎	30♏	28♐	30♒
		31♒			30♊		31♍			30♑	

Key: Aries   Taurus   Gemini   Cancer   Leo   Virgo
          ♈   ♉   ♊   ♋   ♌   ♍

1952

JAN.	FEB.	MAR.	APR.	MAY	JUNE	JULY	AUG.	SEPT.	OCT.	NOV.	DEC.
1 ♓	1 ♉	2 ♊	1 ♋	1 ♌	2 ♎	2 ♏	2 ♑	1 ♒	2 ♈	1 ♉	3 ♋
3 ♈	4 ♊	5 ♋	3 ♌	3 ♍	4 ♏	4 ♐	4 ♒	3 ♓	4 ♉	3 ♊	5 ♌
5 ♉	6 ♋	7 ♌	6 ♍	6 ♎	7 ♐	6 ♑	6 ♓	5 ♈	7 ♊	5 ♋	8 ♍
7 ♊	9 ♌	10 ♍	8 ♎	8 ♏	9 ♑	9 ♒	8 ♈	7 ♉	9 ♋	8 ♌	10 ♎
10 ♋	11 ♍	12 ♎	11 ♏	10 ♐	11 ♒	10 ♓	11 ♉	10 ♊	11 ♌	10 ♍	13 ♏
12 ♌	14 ♎	14 ♏	13 ♐	12 ♑	13 ♓	12 ♈	13 ♊	12 ♋	14 ♍	13 ♎	15 ♐
15 ♍	16 ♏	17 ♐	15 ♑	14 ♒	15 ♈	14 ♉	15 ♋	15 ♌	16 ♎	15 ♏	17 ♑
17 ♎	18 ♐	19 ♑	17 ♒	16 ♓	17 ♉	17 ♊	18 ♌	17 ♍	19 ♏	17 ♐	19 ♒
20 ♏	20 ♑	21 ♒	19 ♓	19 ♈	19 ♊	19 ♋	20 ♍	19 ♎	21 ♐	20 ♑	21 ♓
22 ♐	22 ♒	23 ♓	21 ♈	21 ♉	22 ♋	22 ♌	23 ♎	22 ♏	23 ♑	22 ♒	23 ♈
24 ♑	24 ♓	25 ♈	24 ♉	23 ♊	24 ♌	24 ♍	25 ♏	24 ♐	26 ♒	24 ♓	25 ♉
26 ♒	27 ♈	27 ♉	26 ♊	26 ♋	27 ♍	27 ♎	28 ♐	26 ♑	28 ♓	26 ♈	28 ♊
28 ♓	29 ♉	29 ♊	28 ♋	28 ♌	29 ♎	29 ♏	30 ♑	28 ♒	30 ♈	28 ♉	30 ♋
30 ♈				31 ♍		31 ♐		30 ♓		30 ♊	

1953

JAN.	FEB.	MAR.	APR.	MAY	JUNE	JULY	AUG.	SEPT.	OCT.	NOV.	DEC.
1 ♌	3 ♎	2 ♎	1 ♏	3 ♑	1 ♒	1 ♓	1 ♉	2 ♋	1 ♌	3 ♎	2 ♏
4 ♍	5 ♏	4 ♏	3 ♐	5 ♒	3 ♓	3 ♈	3 ♊	4 ♌	4 ♍	5 ♏	5 ♐
6 ♎	8 ♐	7 ♐	5 ♑	7 ♓	5 ♈	5 ♉	5 ♋	7 ♍	6 ♎	8 ♐	7 ♑
9 ♏	10 ♑	9 ♑	8 ♒	9 ♈	7 ♉	7 ♊	8 ♌	9 ♎	9 ♏	10 ♑	9 ♒
11 ♐	12 ♒	11 ♒	10 ♓	11 ♉	10 ♊	9 ♋	10 ♍	12 ♏	11 ♐	12 ♒	12 ♓
13 ♑	14 ♓	13 ♓	12 ♈	13 ♊	12 ♋	12 ♌	13 ♎	14 ♐	14 ♑	14 ♓	14 ♈
15 ♒	16 ♈	15 ♈	14 ♉	15 ♋	14 ♌	14 ♍	15 ♏	16 ♑	16 ♒	17 ♈	16 ♉
17 ♓	18 ♉	17 ♉	16 ♊	18 ♌	17 ♍	16 ♎	18 ♐	19 ♒	18 ♓	19 ♉	18 ♊
19 ♈	20 ♊	19 ♊	18 ♋	20 ♍	19 ♎	19 ♏	20 ♑	21 ♓	20 ♈	21 ♊	20 ♋
22 ♉	22 ♋	22 ♋	20 ♌	23 ♎	22 ♏	21 ♐	23 ♒	23 ♈	22 ♉	23 ♋	22 ♌
24 ♊	25 ♌	24 ♌	23 ♍	25 ♏	24 ♐	24 ♑	25 ♓	25 ♉	24 ♊	25 ♌	25 ♍
26 ♋	27 ♍	27 ♍	26 ♎	28 ♐	26 ♑	26 ♒	27 ♈	27 ♊	26 ♋	27 ♍	27 ♎
29 ♌		29 ♎	28 ♏	30 ♑	28 ♒	28 ♓	28 ♉	29 ♋	29 ♌	30 ♎	30 ♏
31 ♍			30 ♐		30 ♓	30 ♈	30 ♊		31 ♍		

Libra	Scorpio	Sagittarius	Capricorn	Aquarius	Pisces
♎	♏	♐	♑	♒	♓

1951

JAN.	FEB.	MAR.	APR.	MAY	JUNE	JULY	AUG.	SEPT.	OCT.	NOV.	DEC.
1 ♐	2 ♒	2 ♒	2 ♈	2 ♉	2 ♋	2 ♌	3 ♎	1 ♏	1 ♐	2 ♒	2 ♓
4 ♑	4 ♓	4 ♓	4 ♉	4 ♊	4 ♌	4 ♍	5 ♏	4 ♐	4 ♑	5 ♓	4 ♈
6 ♒	6 ♈	6 ♈	6 ♊	6 ♋	6 ♍	6 ♎	8 ♐	6 ♑	6 ♒	7 ♈	6 ♉
8 ♓	8 ♉	8 ♉	8 ♋	8 ♌	9 ♎	9 ♍	10 ♑	9 ♒	8 ♓	9 ♉	8 ♊
10 ♈	11 ♊	10 ♊	11 ♌	10 ♍	12 ♏	11 ♐	12 ♒	11 ♓	11 ♈	11 ♊	10 ♋
12 ♉	13 ♋	12 ♋	13 ♍	13 ♎	14 ♐	14 ♑	15 ♓	13 ♈	13 ♉	13 ♋	12 ♌
14 ♊	15 ♌	14 ♌	15 ♎	15 ♏	16 ♑	16 ♒	17 ♈	15 ♉	14 ♊	15 ♌	15 ♍
16 ♋	17 ♍	17 ♍	18 ♏	18 ♐	19 ♒	18 ♓	19 ♉	17 ♊	17 ♋	17 ♍	17 ♎
19 ♌	20 ♎	19 ♎	20 ♐	20 ♑	21 ♓	21 ♈	21 ♊	19 ♋	19 ♌	20 ♎	20 ♏
21 ♍	22 ♏	22 ♏	23 ♑	23 ♒	23 ♈	23 ♉	23 ♋	22 ♌	21 ♍	22 ♏	22 ♐
24 ♎	25 ♐	24 ♐	25 ♒	25 ♓	25 ♉	25 ♊	25 ♌	24 ♍	24 ♎	25 ♐	25 ♑
26 ♏	27 ♑	27 ♑	28 ♓	27 ♈	27 ♊	27 ♋	28 ♍	26 ♎	26 ♏	27 ♑	27 ♒
29 ♐		29 ♒	30 ♈	29 ♉	29 ♋	29 ♌	30 ♎	29 ♏	29 ♐	30 ♒	29 ♓
31 ♑		31 ♓		31 ♊		31 ♍			31 ♑		

1955

JAN.	FEB.	MAR.	APR.	MAY	JUNE	JULY	AUG.	SEPT.	OCT.	NOV.	DEC.
1 ♈	1 ♊	2 ♋	1 ♌	3 ♎	1 ♏	1 ♐	2 ♒	1 ♓	1 ♈	1 ♊	1 ♋
3 ♉	3 ♋	5 ♌	3 ♍	5 ♏	4 ♐	4 ♑	5 ♓	3 ♈	3 ♉	3 ♋	3 ♌
5 ♊	5 ♌	7 ♍	5 ♎	8 ♐	6 ♑	6 ♒	7 ♈	6 ♉	5 ♊	5 ♌	5 ♍
7 ♋	7 ♍	9 ♎	8 ♏	10 ♑	9 ♒	9 ♓	9 ♉	8 ♊	7 ♋	8 ♍	7 ♎
9 ♌	10 ♎	12 ♏	10 ♐	13 ♒	11 ♓	11 ♈	11 ♊	10 ♋	9 ♌	10 ♎	10 ♏
11 ♍	12 ♏	14 ♐	13 ♑	15 ♓	14 ♈	13 ♉	14 ♋	12 ♌	11 ♍	12 ♏	12 ♐
13 ♎	15 ♐	17 ♑	15 ♒	17 ♈	16 ♉	15 ♊	16 ♌	14 ♍	13 ♎	15 ♐	15 ♑
16 ♏	17 ♑	19 ♒	18 ♓	19 ♉	18 ♊	17 ♋	18 ♍	16 ♎	16 ♏	17 ♑	17 ♒
18 ♐	20 ♒	21 ♓	20 ♈	21 ♊	20 ♋	19 ♌	20 ♎	19 ♏	18 ♐	20 ♒	20 ♓
21 ♑	22 ♓	23 ♈	22 ♉	23 ♋	22 ♌	21 ♍	22 ♏	21 ♐	21 ♑	22 ♓	22 ♈
23 ♒	24 ♈	26 ♉	24 ♊	25 ♌	24 ♍	24 ♎	25 ♐	24 ♑	23 ♒	25 ♈	24 ♉
26 ♓	26 ♉	28 ♊	26 ♋	28 ♍	26 ♎	26 ♏	27 ♑	26 ♒	26 ♓	27 ♉	26 ♊
28 ♈	28 ♊	30 ♋	28 ♌	30 ♎	29 ♏	28 ♐	30 ♒	29 ♓	28 ♈	29 ♊	28 ♋
30 ♉			30 ♍		31 ♑				30 ♉		30 ♌

	Key:	Aries	Taurus	Gemini	Cancer	Leo	Virgo
		♈	♉	♊	♋	♌	♍

1956

JAN.	FEB.	MAR.	APR.	MAY	JUNE	JULY	AUG.	SEPT.	OCT.	NOV.	DEC.
1 ♍	2 ♏	3 ♐	2 ♑	2 ♒	3 ♈	2 ♉	1 ♊	1 ♌	1 ♍	1 ♏	1 ♐
3 ♎	5 ♐	5 ♑	4 ♒	4 ♓	5 ♉	5 ♊	3 ♋	3 ♍	3 ♎	4 ♐	3 ♑
6 ♏	7 ♑	8 ♒	7 ♓	6 ♈	7 ♊	7 ♋	5 ♌	6 ♎	6 ♏	6 ♑	6 ♒
8 ♐	10 ♒	10 ♓	9 ♈	9 ♉	9 ♋	9 ♌	7 ♍	8 ♏	7 ♐	9 ♒	8 ♓
11 ♑	12 ♓	13 ♈	11 ♉	11 ♊	11 ♌	11 ♍	9 ♎	10 ♐	10 ♑	11 ♓	11 ♈
13 ♒	14 ♈	15 ♉	13 ♊	13 ♋	13 ♍	13 ♎	11 ♏	12 ♑	12 ♒	14 ♈	13 ♉
16 ♓	17 ♉	17 ♊	16 ♋	15 ♌	15 ♎	15 ♏	14 ♐	15 ♒	15 ♓	16 ♉	16 ♊
18 ♈	19 ♊	19 ♋	18 ♌	17 ♍	18 ♏	17 ♐	16 ♑	17 ♓	17 ♈	18 ♊	18 ♋
20 ♉	21 ♋	21 ♌	20 ♍	19 ♎	20 ♐	20 ♑	19 ♒	20 ♈	20 ♉	20 ♋	20 ♌
23 ♊	23 ♌	23 ♍	22 ♎	21 ♏	23 ♑	22 ♒	21 ♓	22 ♉	22 ♊	22 ♌	22 ♍
25 ♋	25 ♍	26 ♎	24 ♏	24 ♐	25 ♒	25 ♓	24 ♈	24 ♊	24 ♋	24 ♍	24 ♎
27 ♌	27 ♎	28 ♏	27 ♐	26 ♑	28 ♓	27 ♈	26 ♉	27 ♋	26 ♌	27 ♎	26 ♏
29 ♍	29 ♏	30 ♐	29 ♑	29 ♒	30 ♈	30 ♉	28 ♊	29 ♌	28 ♍	29 ♏	28 ♐
31 ♎				31 ♓			30 ♋		30 ♎		31 ♑

1957

JAN.	FEB.	MAR.	APR.	MAY	JUNE	JULY	AUG.	SEPT.	OCT.	NOV.	DEC.
2 ♒	1 ♓	3 ♈	1 ♉	1 ♊	2 ♌	1 ♍	2 ♏	2 ♐	2 ♑	1 ♓	1 ♈
5 ♓	4 ♈	5 ♉	4 ♊	3 ♋	4 ♍	3 ♎	4 ♐	5 ♑	5 ♒	3 ♈	3 ♉
7 ♈	6 ♉	8 ♊	6 ♋	5 ♌	6 ♎	5 ♏	6 ♑	7 ♒	7 ♓	6 ♉	6 ♊
10 ♉	8 ♊	10 ♋	8 ♌	8 ♍	8 ♏	8 ♐	9 ♒	10 ♓	10 ♈	8 ♊	8 ♋
12 ♊	10 ♋	12 ♌	10 ♍	10 ♎	10 ♐	10 ♑	11 ♓	12 ♈	12 ♉	11 ♋	10 ♌
14 ♋	12 ♌	14 ♍	12 ♎	12 ♏	13 ♑	12 ♒	14 ♈	15 ♉	14 ♊	13 ♌	12 ♍
16 ♌	14 ♍	16 ♎	14 ♏	14 ♐	15 ♒	15 ♓	16 ♉	17 ♊	17 ♋	15 ♍	14 ♎
18 ♍	16 ♎	18 ♏	17 ♐	16 ♑	18 ♓	17 ♈	19 ♊	19 ♋	19 ♌	17 ♎	16 ♏
20 ♎	19 ♏	20 ♐	19 ♑	19 ♒	20 ♈	20 ♉	21 ♋	21 ♌	21 ♍	19 ♏	19 ♐
22 ♏	21 ♐	23 ♑	21 ♒	21 ♓	22 ♉	22 ♊	23 ♌	23 ♍	23 ♎	21 ♐	21 ♑
25 ♐	23 ♑	25 ♒	24 ♓	24 ♈	25 ♊	24 ♋	25 ♍	25 ♎	25 ♏	23 ♑	23 ♒
27 ♑	26 ♒	28 ♓	26 ♈	26 ♉	27 ♋	26 ♌	27 ♎	27 ♏	27 ♐	26 ♒	26 ♓
29 ♒	28 ♓	30 ♈	29 ♉	28 ♊	29 ♌	28 ♍	29 ♏	30 ♐	29 ♑	28 ♓	28 ♈
				31 ♋		30 ♎	31 ♐				31 ♉

Libra	Scorpio	Sagittarius	Capricorn	Aquarius	Pisces
♎	♏	♐	♑	♒	♓

1958

JAN.	FEB.	MAR.	APR.	MAY	JUNE	JULY	AUG.	SEPT.	OCT.	NOV.	DEC.
2 ♊	1 ♋	2 ♌	1 ♍	2 ♏	1 ♐	2 ♒	1 ♓	2 ♉	2 ♊	1 ♋	3 ♍
4 ♋	3 ♌	4 ♍	3 ♎	4 ♐	3 ♑	5 ♓	3 ♈	5 ♊	5 ♋	3 ♌	5 ♎
6 ♌	5 ♍	6 ♎	5 ♏	6 ♑	5 ♒	7 ♈	6 ♉	7 ♋	7 ♌	5 ♍	7 ♏
8 ♍	7 ♎	8 ♏	7 ♐	9 ♒	7 ♓	10 ♉	9 ♊	10 ♌	9 ♍	8 ♎	9 ♐
11 ♎	9 ♏	10 ♐	9 ♑	11 ♓	10 ♈	12 ♊	11 ♋	12 ♍	11 ♎	10 ♏	11 ♑
13 ♏	11 ♐	13 ♑	11 ♒	14 ♈	12 ♉	15 ♋	13 ♌	14 ♎	13 ♏	12 ♐	13 ♒
15 ♐	13 ♑	15 ♒	14 ♈	16 ♉	15 ♊	17 ♌	15 ♍	16 ♏	15 ♐	14 ♑	15 ♓
17 ♑	16 ♒	17 ♓	16 ♈	18 ♊	17 ♋	19 ♍	17 ♎	18 ♐	17 ♑	16 ♒	18 ♈
19 ♒	18 ♓	20 ♈	19 ♉	21 ♋	19 ♌	21 ♎	19 ♏	20 ♑	19 ♒	18 ♓	20 ♉
22 ♓	21 ♈	23 ♉	21 ♊	23 ♌	22 ♍	23 ♏	21 ♐	22 ♒	22 ♓	21 ♈	23 ♊
24 ♈	23 ♉	25 ♊	24 ♋	25 ♍	24 ♎	25 ♐	24 ♑	25 ♓	24 ♈	23 ♉	25 ♋
27 ♉	26 ♊	27 ♋	26 ♌	28 ♎	26 ♏	27 ♑	26 ♒	27 ♈	27 ♉	26 ♊	28 ♌
29 ♊	28 ♋	30 ♌	28 ♍	30 ♏	28 ♐	30 ♒	28 ♓	30 ♉	29 ♊	28 ♋	30 ♍
			30 ♎		30 ♑	31 ♈				30 ♌	

1959

JAN.	FEB.	MAR.	APR.	MAY	JUNE	JULY	AUG.	SEPT.	OCT.	NOV.	DEC.
1 ♎	2 ♐	1 ♐	1 ♒	1 ♓	2 ♉	2 ♊	1 ♋	2 ♍	1 ♎	2 ♐	1 ♑
3 ♏	4 ♑	3 ♑	4 ♓	3 ♈	5 ♊	5 ♋	3 ♌	4 ♎	3 ♏	4 ♑	3 ♒
5 ♐	6 ♒	5 ♒	6 ♈	6 ♉	7 ♋	7 ♌	6 ♍	6 ♏	6 ♐	6 ♒	6 ♓
7 ♑	8 ♓	7 ♓	9 ♉	8 ♊	10 ♌	9 ♍	8 ♎	8 ♐	8 ♑	8 ♓	8 ♈
10 ♒	11 ♈	10 ♈	11 ♊	11 ♋	12 ♍	12 ♎	10 ♏	10 ♑	10 ♒	11 ♈	11 ♉
12 ♓	13 ♉	12 ♉	14 ♋	13 ♌	14 ♎	14 ♏	12 ♐	13 ♒	12 ♓	13 ♉	13 ♊
14 ♈	16 ♊	15 ♊	16 ♌	16 ♍	16 ♏	16 ♐	14 ♑	15 ♓	14 ♈	16 ♊	15 ♋
17 ♉	18 ♋	17 ♋	18 ♍	18 ♎	18 ♐	18 ♑	16 ♒	17 ♈	17 ♉	18 ♋	18 ♌
19 ♊	20 ♌	20 ♌	21 ♎	20 ♏	20 ♑	20 ♒	18 ♓	19 ♉	19 ♊	21 ♌	20 ♍
22 ♋	23 ♍	22 ♍	23 ♏	22 ♐	22 ♒	22 ♓	21 ♈	22 ♊	22 ♋	23 ♍	23 ♎
24 ♌	25 ♎	24 ♎	25 ♐	24 ♑	25 ♓	24 ♈	23 ♉	24 ♋	24 ♌	25 ♎	25 ♏
26 ♍	27 ♏	26 ♏	27 ♑	26 ♒	27 ♈	27 ♉	26 ♊	27 ♌	27 ♍	27 ♏	27 ♐
28 ♎		28 ♐	29 ♒	28 ♓	29 ♉	29 ♊	28 ♋	29 ♍	29 ♎	29 ♐	29 ♑
31 ♏		30 ♑		31 ♈		31 ♌	31 ♌		31 ♏		31 ♒

	Key:	Aries	Taurus	Gemini	Cancer	Leo	Virgo
		♈	♉	♊	♋	♌	♍

1960

JAN.	FEB.	MAR.	APR.	MAY	JUNE	JULY	AUG.	SEPT.	OCT.	NOV.	DEC.
2 ♓	1 ♈	1 ♉	3 ♋	2 ♌	1 ♍	1 ♎	2 ♐	2 ♒	1 ♓	2 ♉	2 ♊
4 ♈	3 ♉	4 ♊	5 ♌	5 ♍	4 ♎	3 ♏	4 ♑	4 ♓	4 ♈	4 ♊	4 ♋
7 ♉	5 ♊	6 ♋	8 ♍	7 ♎	6 ♏	5 ♐	6 ♒	6 ♈	6 ♉	7 ♋	7 ♌
9 ♊	8 ♋	9 ♌	10 ♎	9 ♏	8 ♐	7 ♑	8 ♓	8 ♉	8 ♊	9 ♌	9 ♍
12 ♋	10 ♌	11 ♍	12 ♏	11 ♐	10 ♑	9 ♒	10 ♈	11 ♊	11 ♋	12 ♍	12 ♎
14 ♌	13 ♍	13 ♎	14 ♐	13 ♑	12 ♒	11 ♓	12 ♉	13 ♋	13 ♌	14 ♎	14 ♏
17 ♍	15 ♎	16 ♏	16 ♑	15 ♒	14 ♓	13 ♈	14 ♊	16 ♌	16 ♍	17 ♏	16 ♐
19 ♎	17 ♏	18 ♐	18 ♒	18 ♓	16 ♈	15 ♉	17 ♋	18 ♍	18 ♎	19 ♐	18 ♑
21 ♏	19 ♐	20 ♑	20 ♓	20 ♈	18 ♉	18 ♊	19 ♌	21 ♎	20 ♏	21 ♑	20 ♒
23 ♐	22 ♑	22 ♒	22 ♈	22 ♉	21 ♊	21 ♋	22 ♍	23 ♏	22 ♐	23 ♒	22 ♓
25 ♑	24 ♒	24 ♓	25 ♉	25 ♊	23 ♋	23 ♌	24 ♎	25 ♐	24 ♑	25 ♓	24 ♈
27 ♒	26 ♓	26 ♈	27 ♊	27 ♋	26 ♌	26 ♍	27 ♏	27 ♑	27 ♒	27 ♈	27 ♉
29 ♓	28 ♈	29 ♉	30 ♋	30 ♌	28 ♍	28 ♎	29 ♐	29 ♒	29 ♓	29 ♉	29 ♊
		31 ♊				30 ♏	31 ♑		31 ♈		

1961

JAN.	FEB.	MAR.	APR.	MAY	JUNE	JULY	AUG.	SEPT.	OCT.	NOV.	DEC.
1 ♋	2 ♍	1 ♍	2 ♏	2 ♐	2 ♒	2 ♓	2 ♉	1 ♊	3 ♌	2 ♍	2 ♎
3 ♌	4 ♎	4 ♎	4 ♐	4 ♑	4 ♓	4 ♈	4 ♊	3 ♋	5 ♍	4 ♎	4 ♏
6 ♍	7 ♏	6 ♏	7 ♑	6 ♒	6 ♈	6 ♉	7 ♋	6 ♌	8 ♎	7 ♏	6 ♐
8 ♎	9 ♐	8 ♐	9 ♒	8 ♓	9 ♉	8 ♊	9 ♌	8 ♍	10 ♏	9 ♐	9 ♑
10 ♏	11 ♑	10 ♑	11 ♓	10 ♈	11 ♊	11 ♋	12 ♍	11 ♎	13 ♐	11 ♑	11 ♒
13 ♐	13 ♒	12 ♒	13 ♈	12 ♉	13 ♋	13 ♌	14 ♎	13 ♏	15 ♑	13 ♒	13 ♓
15 ♑	15 ♓	15 ♓	15 ♉	15 ♊	16 ♌	16 ♍	17 ♏	15 ♐	17 ♒	16 ♓	15 ♈
17 ♒	17 ♈	17 ♈	17 ♊	17 ♋	18 ♍	18 ♎	19 ♐	18 ♑	19 ♓	18 ♈	17 ♉
19 ♓	19 ♉	19 ♉	20 ♋	20 ♌	21 ♎	21 ♏	21 ♑	20 ♒	21 ♈	20 ♉	19 ♊
21 ♈	22 ♊	21 ♊	22 ♌	22 ♍	23 ♏	23 ♐	23 ♒	22 ♓	23 ♉	22 ♊	22 ♋
23 ♉	24 ♋	23 ♋	25 ♍	25 ♎	26 ♐	25 ♑	25 ♓	24 ♈	26 ♊	24 ♋	24 ♌
25 ♊	27 ♌	26 ♌	27 ♎	27 ♏	28 ♑	27 ♒	27 ♈	26 ♉	28 ♋	27 ♌	26 ♍
28 ♋		28 ♍	30 ♏	29 ♐	30 ♒	29 ♓	29 ♉	28 ♊	30 ♌	29 ♍	29 ♎
30 ♌		31 ♎		31 ♑		31 ♈		30 ♋			31 ♏

Libra	Scorpio	Sagittarius	Capricorn	Aquarius	Pisces
♎	♏	♐	♑	♒	♓

1962

JAN.	FEB.	MAR.	APR.	MAY	JUNE	JULY	AUG.	SEPT.	OCT.	NOV.	DEC.
3 ♐	1 ♑	1 ♑	1 ♓	1 ♈	1 ♊	1 ♋	2 ♍	1 ♎	3 ♐	2 ♑	1 ♒
5 ♑	3 ♒	3 ♒	3 ♈	3 ♉	3 ♋	3 ♌	4 ♎	3 ♏	5 ♑	4 ♒	3 ♓
7 ♒	5 ♓	5 ♓	5 ♉	5 ♊	6 ♌	6 ♍	7 ♏	6 ♐	8 ♒	6 ♓	5 ♈
9 ♓	7 ♈	7 ♈	7 ♊	7 ♋	8 ♍	8 ♎	9 ♐	8 ♑	10 ♓	8 ♈	8 ♉
11 ♈	10 ♉	9 ♉	10 ♋	9 ♌	11 ♎	11 ♏	12 ♑	10 ♒	12 ♈	10 ♉	10 ♊
13 ♉	12 ♊	11 ♊	12 ♌	12 ♍	13 ♏	13 ♐	14 ♒	12 ♓	14 ♉	12 ♊	12 ♋
16 ♊	14 ♋	13 ♋	15 ♍	14 ♎	15 ♐	15 ♑	16 ♓	14 ♈	16 ♊	14 ♋	14 ♌
18 ♋	17 ♌	16 ♌	17 ♎	17 ♏	18 ♑	17 ♒	18 ♈	16 ♉	18 ♋	17 ♌	16 ♍
20 ♌	19 ♍	18 ♍	20 ♏	19 ♐	20 ♒	19 ♓	20 ♉	18 ♊	20 ♌	19 ♍	19 ♎
23 ♍	22 ♎	21 ♎	22 ♐	22 ♑	22 ♓	22 ♈	22 ♊	20 ♋	23 ♍	21 ♎	21 ♏
25 ♎	24 ♏	23 ♏	24 ♑	24 ♒	24 ♈	24 ♉	25 ♋	23 ♌	25 ♎	24 ♏	24 ♐
28 ♏	26 ♐	26 ♐	27 ♒	26 ♓	26 ♉	26 ♊	27 ♌	25 ♍	28 ♏	26 ♐	26 ♑
30 ♐		28 ♑	29 ♓	28 ♈	29 ♊	28 ♋	29 ♍	28 ♎	30 ♐	29 ♑	28 ♒
		30 ♒		30 ♉		30 ♌		30 ♏			31 ♓

1963

JAN.	FEB.	MAR.	APR.	MAY	JUNE	JULY	AUG.	SEPT.	OCT.	NOV.	DEC.
2 ♈	2 ♊	1 ♊	2 ♌	2 ♍	1 ♎	3 ♐	2 ♑	3 ♓	2 ♈	1 ♉	2 ♋
4 ♉	4 ♋	4 ♋	5 ♍	4 ♎	3 ♏	5 ♑	4 ♒	5 ♈	4 ♉	3 ♊	4 ♌
6 ♊	7 ♌	6 ♌	7 ♎	7 ♏	6 ♐	8 ♒	7 ♓	7 ♉	6 ♊	5 ♋	6 ♍
8 ♋	9 ♍	8 ♍	10 ♏	9 ♐	8 ♑	10 ♓	9 ♈	9 ♊	8 ♋	7 ♌	9 ♎
10 ♌	11 ♎	11 ♎	12 ♐	12 ♑	10 ♒	12 ♈	11 ♉	11 ♋	10 ♌	9 ♍	11 ♏
13 ♍	14 ♏	13 ♏	15 ♑	14 ♒	13 ♓	14 ♉	13 ♊	13 ♌	13 ♍	11 ♎	14 ♐
15 ♎	16 ♐	16 ♐	17 ♒	16 ♓	15 ♈	16 ♊	16 ♋	15 ♍	15 ♎	14 ♏	16 ♑
18 ♏	19 ♑	18 ♑	19 ♓	19 ♈	17 ♉	18 ♋	18 ♌	18 ♎	18 ♏	16 ♐	19 ♒
20 ♐	21 ♒	21 ♒	21 ♈	21 ♉	19 ♊	21 ♌	19 ♍	20 ♏	20 ♐	19 ♑	21 ♓
22 ♑	23 ♓	23 ♓	23 ♉	23 ♊	21 ♋	23 ♍	22 ♎	23 ♐	23 ♑	21 ♒	23 ♈
25 ♒	25 ♈	25 ♈	25 ♊	25 ♋	23 ♌	25 ♎	24 ♏	25 ♑	25 ♒	24 ♓	25 ♉
27 ♓	27 ♉	27 ♉	27 ♋	27 ♌	25 ♍	28 ♏	27 ♐	28 ♒	27 ♈	26 ♈	27 ♊
29 ♈		29 ♊	29 ♌	29 ♍	28 ♎	30 ♐	29 ♑	30 ♓	30 ♉	28 ♉	29 ♋
31 ♉		31 ♋			30 ♏	31 ♒	31 ♒			30 ♊	31 ♌

Key:	Aries	Taurus	Gemini	Cancer	Leo	Virgo
	♈	♉	♊	♋	♌	♍

1964

JAN.	FEB.	MAR.	APR.	MAY	JUNE	JULY	AUG.	SEPT.	OCT.	NOV.	DEC.
3 ♍	1 ♎	2 ♏	1 ♐	1 ♑	2 ♓	2 ♈	2 ♉	1 ♋	2 ♍	1 ♎	3 ♐
5 ♎	4 ♏	5 ♐	3 ♑	3 ♒	4 ♈	4 ♉	4 ♊	3 ♌	4 ♎	3 ♏	5 ♑
7 ♏	6 ♐	7 ♑	6 ♒	6 ♓	6 ♉	6 ♊	6 ♋	5 ♍	7 ♏	5 ♐	8 ♒
10 ♐	9 ♑	10 ♒	8 ♓	8 ♈	8 ♊	8 ♋	8 ♍	7 ♎	9 ♐	8 ♑	10 ♓
12 ♑	11 ♒	12 ♓	10 ♈	10 ♉	10 ♋	10 ♌	10 ♎	9 ♏	11 ♑	10 ♒	13 ♈
15 ♒	13 ♓	14 ♈	13 ♉	12 ♊	12 ♌	12 ♍	13 ♏	12 ♐	14 ♒	13 ♓	15 ♉
17 ♓	16 ♈	16 ♉	15 ♊	14 ♋	14 ♍	14 ♎	15 ♐	14 ♑	16 ♓	15 ♈	17 ♊
19 ♈	18 ♉	18 ♊	17 ♋	16 ♌	17 ♎	16 ♏	18 ♑	17 ♒	19 ♈	17 ♉	19 ♋
22 ♉	20 ♊	20 ♋	19 ♌	18 ♍	19 ♏	19 ♐	20 ♒	19 ♓	21 ♉	19 ♊	21 ♌
24 ♊	22 ♋	23 ♌	21 ♍	21 ♎	22 ♐	21 ♑	23 ♓	21 ♈	23 ♊	21 ♋	23 ♍
26 ♋	24 ♌	25 ♍	23 ♎	23 ♏	24 ♑	24 ♒	25 ♈	23 ♉	25 ♋	23 ♌	25 ♎
28 ♌	26 ♍	27 ♎	26 ♏	25 ♐	27 ♒	26 ♓	27 ♉	25 ♊	27 ♌	26 ♍	27 ♏
30 ♍	29 ♎	29 ♏	28 ♐	28 ♑	29 ♓	29 ♈	29 ♊	28 ♋	29 ♍	28 ♎	30 ♐
				30 ♒		31 ♉		30 ♌			

1965

JAN.	FEB.	MAR.	APR.	MAY	JUNE	JULY	AUG.	SEPT.	OCT.	NOV.	DEC.
1 ♑	3 ♓	2 ♓	1 ♈	2 ♊	1 ♋	2 ♍	1 ♎	2 ♐	1 ♑	3 ♓	2 ♈
4 ♒	5 ♈	4 ♈	3 ♉	4 ♋	3 ♌	4 ♎	3 ♏	4 ♑	4 ♒	5 ♈	5 ♉
6 ♓	7 ♉	7 ♉	5 ♊	7 ♌	5 ♍	7 ♏	5 ♐	6 ♒	6 ♓	7 ♉	7 ♊
9 ♈	10 ♊	9 ♊	7 ♋	9 ♍	7 ♎	9 ♐	8 ♑	9 ♓	9 ♈	10 ♊	9 ♋
11 ♉	12 ♋	11 ♋	9 ♌	11 ♎	9 ♏	11 ♑	10 ♒	11 ♈	11 ♉	12 ♋	11 ♌
13 ♊	14 ♌	13 ♌	11 ♍	13 ♏	12 ♐	14 ♒	13 ♓	14 ♉	13 ♊	14 ♌	13 ♍
15 ♋	16 ♍	15 ♍	14 ♎	15 ♐	14 ♑	16 ♓	15 ♈	16 ♊	16 ♋	16 ♍	15 ♎
17 ♌	18 ♎	17 ♎	16 ♏	18 ♑	17 ♒	19 ♈	18 ♉	18 ♋	18 ♌	18 ♎	18 ♏
19 ♍	20 ♏	19 ♏	18 ♐	20 ♒	19 ♓	21 ♉	20 ♊	20 ♌	20 ♍	20 ♏	20 ♐
21 ♎	22 ♐	22 ♐	21 ♑	23 ♓	22 ♈	24 ♊	22 ♋	22 ♍	22 ♎	23 ♐	22 ♑
24 ♏	25 ♑	24 ♑	23 ♒	25 ♈	24 ♉	26 ♋	24 ♌	25 ♎	24 ♏	25 ♑	25 ♒
26 ♐	27 ♒	27 ♒	26 ♓	28 ♉	26 ♊	28 ♌	26 ♍	27 ♏	26 ♐	27 ♒	27 ♓
29 ♑		29 ♓	28 ♈	30 ♊	28 ♋	30 ♍	28 ♎	29 ♐	29 ♑	30 ♓	30 ♈
31 ♒			30 ♉		30 ♌		30 ♏		31 ♒		

Libra	Scorpio	Sagittarius	Capricorn	Aquarius	Pisces
♎	♏	♐	♑	♒	♓

1966

JAN.	FEB.	MAR.	APR.	MAY	JUNE	JULY	AUG.	SEPT.	OCT.	NOV.	DEC.
1 ♉	2 ♋	1 ♋	2 ♍	1 ♎	2 ♐	1 ♑	3 ♓	1 ♈	1 ♉	2 ♋	2 ♌
4 ♊	4 ♌	4 ♌	4 ♎	3 ♏	4 ♑	4 ♒	5 ♈	4 ♉	4 ♊	4 ♌	4 ♍
6 ♋	6 ♍	6 ♍	6 ♏	6 ♐	7 ♒	6 ♓	8 ♉	6 ♊	6 ♋	7 ♍	6 ♎
8 ♌	8 ♎	7 ♎	8 ♐	8 ♑	9 ♓	9 ♈	10 ♊	9 ♋	8 ♌	9 ♎	8 ♏
10 ♍	10 ♏	10 ♏	10 ♑	10 ♒	12 ♈	11 ♉	12 ♋	11 ♌	10 ♍	11 ♏	10 ♐
12 ♎	12 ♐	12 ♐	13 ♒	13 ♓	14 ♉	14 ♊	14 ♌	13 ♍	12 ♎	13 ♐	12 ♑
14 ♏	15 ♑	14 ♑	15 ♓	15 ♈	16 ♊	16 ♋	16 ♍	15 ♎	14 ♏	15 ♑	15 ♒
16 ♐	17 ♒	17 ♒	18 ♈	18 ♉	19 ♋	18 ♌	18 ♎	17 ♏	16 ♐	17 ♒	17 ♓
19 ♑	20 ♓	19 ♓	20 ♉	20 ♊	21 ♌	20 ♍	20 ♏	19 ♐	19 ♑	20 ♓	20 ♈
21 ♒	22 ♈	22 ♈	22 ♊	22 ♋	23 ♍	22 ♎	23 ♐	21 ♑	21 ♒	22 ♈	22 ♉
24 ♓	25 ♉	24 ♉	25 ♋	24 ♌	25 ♎	24 ♏	25 ♑	24 ♒	23 ♓	25 ♉	25 ♊
26 ♈	27 ♊	26 ♊	27 ♌	26 ♍	27 ♏	26 ♐	27 ♒	26 ♓	26 ♈	27 ♊	27 ♋
29 ♉		29 ♋	29 ♍	29 ♎	29 ♐	29 ♑	30 ♓	29 ♈	28 ♉	29 ♋	29 ♌
31 ♊		31 ♌		31 ♏		31 ♒			31 ♊		31 ♍

1967

JAN.	FEB.	MAR.	APR.	MAY	JUNE	JULY	AUG.	SEPT.	OCT.	NOV.	DEC.
2 ♎	1 ♏	2 ♐	1 ♑	3 ♓	1 ♈	1 ♉	2 ♋	1 ♌	1 ♍	1 ♏	1 ♐
4 ♏	3 ♐	4 ♑	3 ♒	5 ♈	4 ♉	4 ♊	5 ♌	3 ♍	3 ♎	3 ♐	3 ♑
7 ♐	5 ♑	7 ♒	5 ♓	8 ♉	6 ♊	6 ♋	7 ♍	5 ♎	5 ♏	5 ♑	5 ♒
9 ♑	7 ♒	9 ♓	8 ♈	10 ♊	9 ♋	8 ♌	9 ♎	7 ♏	7 ♐	7 ♒	7 ♓
11 ♒	10 ♓	12 ♈	10 ♉	12 ♋	11 ♌	11 ♍	11 ♏	9 ♐	9 ♑	10 ♓	9 ♈
13 ♓	12 ♈	14 ♉	13 ♊	15 ♌	13 ♍	13 ♎	13 ♐	12 ♑	11 ♒	12 ♈	11 ♉
16 ♈	15 ♉	16 ♊	15 ♋	17 ♍	15 ♎	15 ♏	15 ♑	14 ♒	13 ♓	15 ♉	14 ♊
18 ♉	17 ♊	19 ♋	18 ♌	19 ♎	17 ♏	17 ♐	18 ♒	16 ♓	16 ♈	17 ♊	17 ♋
21 ♊	20 ♋	21 ♌	20 ♍	21 ♏	20 ♐	19 ♑	20 ♓	19 ♈	18 ♉	20 ♋	19 ♌
23 ♋	22 ♌	23 ♍	22 ♎	23 ♐	22 ♑	21 ♒	22 ♈	21 ♉	21 ♊	22 ♌	22 ♍
25 ♌	24 ♍	25 ♎	24 ♏	25 ♑	24 ♒	24 ♓	25 ♉	24 ♊	23 ♋	24 ♍	24 ♎
27 ♍	26 ♎	27 ♏	26 ♐	27 ♒	26 ♓	26 ♈	27 ♊	26 ♋	26 ♌	27 ♎	26 ♏
30 ♎	28 ♏	29 ♐	28 ♑	30 ♓	29 ♈	29 ♉	30 ♋	28 ♌	28 ♍	29 ♏	28 ♐
			30 ♒			31 ♊			30 ♎		30 ♑

Key:	Aries	Taurus	Gemini	Cancer	Leo	Virgo
	♈	♉	♊	♋	♌	♍

1968

JAN.	FEB.	MAR.	APR.	MAY	JUNE	JULY	AUG.	SEPT.	OCT.	NOV.	DEC.
1 ♒	2 ♈	3 ♉	2 ♊	2 ♋	3 ♍	2 ♎	1 ♏	1 ♑	3 ♓	1 ♈	1 ♉
3 ♓	5 ♉	5 ♊	4 ♋	4 ♌	5 ♎	4 ♏	3 ♐	3 ♒	5 ♈	4 ♉	3 ♊
6 ♈	7 ♊	8 ♋	7 ♌	6 ♍	7 ♏	6 ♐	5 ♑	5 ♓	7 ♉	6 ♊	6 ♋
8 ♉	10 ♋	10 ♌	9 ♍	9 ♎	9 ♐	8 ♑	7 ♒	8 ♈	10 ♊	9 ♋	8 ♌
11 ♊	12 ♌	13 ♍	11 ♎	11 ♏	11 ♑	10 ♒	9 ♓	10 ♉	12 ♋	11 ♌	11 ♍
13 ♋	14 ♍	15 ♎	13 ♏	13 ♐	13 ♒	13 ♓	11 ♈	12 ♊	15 ♌	14 ♍	13 ♎
16 ♌	16 ♎	17 ♏	15 ♐	15 ♓	15 ♓	15 ♈	14 ♉	15 ♋	17 ♍	16 ♎	15 ♏
18 ♍	18 ♏	19 ♐	17 ♑	17 ♒	18 ♈	17 ♉	16 ♊	17 ♌	19 ♎	18 ♏	17 ♐
20 ♎	21 ♐	21 ♑	19 ♒	19 ♓	20 ♉	20 ♊	19 ♋	20 ♍	22 ♏	20 ♐	19 ♑
22 ♏	23 ♑	23 ♒	22 ♓	21 ♈	23 ♊	22 ♋	21 ♌	22 ♎	24 ♐	22 ♑	21 ♒
24 ♐	25 ♒	25 ♓	24 ♈	24 ♉	25 ♋	25 ♌	24 ♍	24 ♏	26 ♑	24 ♒	23 ♓
26 ♑	27 ♓	28 ♈	27 ♉	26 ♊	28 ♌	27 ♍	26 ♎	26 ♐	28 ♒	26 ♓	26 ♈
29 ♒	29 ♈	30 ♉	29 ♊	29 ♋	30 ♍	29 ♎	28 ♏	28 ♑	30 ♓	28 ♈	28 ♉
31 ♓				31 ♌			30 ♐	30 ♒			31 ♊

1969

JAN.	FEB.	MAR.	APR.	MAY	JUNE	JULY	AUG.	SEPT.	OCT.	NOV.	DEC.
2 ♋	1 ♌	3 ♍	1 ♎	1 ♏	1 ♑	1 ♒	1 ♈	2 ♊	2 ♋	1 ♌	1 ♍
5 ♌	3 ♍	5 ♎	4 ♏	3 ♐	3 ♒	3 ♓	4 ♉	5 ♋	5 ♌	4 ♍	3 ♎
7 ♍	6 ♎	7 ♏	6 ♐	5 ♑	5 ♓	5 ♈	6 ♊	7 ♌	7 ♍	6 ♎	6 ♏
9 ♎	8 ♏	9 ♐	8 ♑	7 ♒	8 ♈	7 ♉	9 ♋	10 ♍	10 ♎	8 ♏	8 ♐
12 ♏	10 ♐	11 ♑	10 ♒	9 ♓	10 ♉	10 ♊	11 ♌	12 ♎	12 ♏	10 ♐	10 ♑
14 ♐	12 ♑	14 ♒	12 ♓	11 ♈	13 ♊	12 ♋	14 ♍	15 ♏	14 ♐	12 ♑	12 ♒
16 ♑	14 ♒	16 ♓	14 ♈	13 ♉	15 ♋	15 ♌	16 ♎	17 ♐	16 ♑	14 ♒	14 ♓
18 ♒	16 ♓	18 ♈	17 ♉	16 ♊	18 ♌	17 ♍	18 ♏	19 ♑	18 ♒	17 ♓	16 ♈
20 ♓	18 ♈	20 ♉	19 ♊	19 ♋	20 ♍	20 ♎	20 ♐	21 ♒	20 ♓	19 ♈	18 ♉
22 ♈	21 ♉	23 ♊	21 ♋	21 ♌	22 ♎	22 ♏	23 ♑	23 ♓	22 ♈	21 ♉	20 ♊
24 ♉	23 ♊	25 ♋	24 ♌	24 ♍	25 ♏	24 ♐	25 ♒	25 ♈	25 ♉	23 ♊	23 ♋
27 ♊	26 ♋	28 ♌	26 ♍	26 ♎	27 ♐	26 ♑	27 ♓	27 ♉	27 ♊	26 ♋	26 ♌
29 ♋	28 ♌	30 ♍	29 ♎	28 ♏	29 ♑	29 ♒	29 ♈	30 ♊	30 ♋	28 ♌	28 ♍
				30 ♐		30 ♓	31 ♉				31 ♎

	Libra	Scorpio	Sagittarius	Capricorn	Aquarius	Pisces
	♎	♏	♐	♑	♒	♓

1970

JAN.	FEB.	MAR.	APR.	MAY	JUNE	JULY	AUG.	SEPT.	OCT.	NOV.	DEC.
2 ♏	1 ♐	2 ♑	3 ♓	2 ♈	3 ♊	2 ♋	1 ♌	2 ♎	2 ♏	1 ♐	2 ♒
4 ♐	3 ♑	4 ♒	5 ♈	4 ♉	5 ♋	5 ♌	3 ♍	5 ♏	4 ♐	3 ♑	4 ♓
6 ♑	5 ♒	6 ♓	7 ♉	6 ♊	7 ♌	7 ♍	6 ♎	7 ♐	7 ♑	5 ♒	7 ♈
8 ♒	7 ♓	8 ♈	9 ♊	9 ♋	10 ♍	10 ♎	8 ♏	9 ♑	9 ♒	7 ♓	9 ♉
10 ♓	9 ♈	10 ♉	11 ♋	11 ♌	12 ♎	12 ♏	11 ♐	12 ♒	11 ♓	9 ♈	11 ♊
12 ♈	11 ♉	12 ♊	14 ♌	14 ♍	15 ♏	14 ♐	13 ♑	14 ♓	13 ♈	11 ♉	13 ♋
15 ♉	13 ♊	15 ♋	16 ♍	16 ♎	17 ♐	17 ♑	14 ♒	15 ♈	15 ♉	14 ♊	15 ♌
17 ♊	16 ♋	17 ♌	18 ♎	18 ♏	19 ♑	19 ♒	17 ♓	18 ♉	17 ♊	16 ♋	18 ♍
19 ♋	18 ♌	20 ♍	21 ♏	21 ♐	21 ♒	21 ♓	19 ♈	20 ♊	19 ♋	18 ♌	20 ♎
22 ♌	21 ♍	22 ♎	23 ♐	23 ♑	23 ♓	23 ♈	21 ♉	22 ♋	22 ♌	21 ♍	23 ♏
24 ♍	23 ♎	25 ♏	26 ♑	25 ♒	25 ♈	25 ♉	23 ♊	24 ♌	24 ♍	23 ♎	25 ♐
27 ♎	26 ♏	27 ♐	28 ♒	27 ♓	28 ♉	27 ♊	26 ♋	27 ♍	27 ♎	26 ♏	28 ♑
29 ♏	28 ♐	29 ♑	30 ♓	29 ♈	30 ♊	29 ♋	28 ♌	30 ♎	29 ♏	28 ♐	30 ♒
		31 ♒		31 ♉			31 ♍			30 ♑	

Key: Aries   Taurus   Gemini   Cancer   Leo   Virgo
         ♈   ♉   ♊   ♋   ♌   ♍
     Libra   Scorpio   Sagittarius   Capricorn   Aquarius   Pisces
       ♎   ♏   ♐   ♑   ♒   ♓

6

Your Ascendant
or Rising Sign

Your Ascendant is the Sign rising on the horizon at the time of your birth; it is third in importance after the Sun and Moon.

One of the most absorbing facts in astrology, next to the uncanny manner in which we tend to demonstrate our Sun Signs, is the remarkable influence our *exact hour* of birth has on us. The man or woman with a Sagittarius Ascendant, for example, loves outdoor life, travel, horses and sports in general. He or she is usually outspoken, kindhearted and candid. Scorpio rising, on the other hand, is pretty much the opposite. Usually physically strong and enduring, the person with Scorpio rising is secretive, rather suspicious and determined. These are cursory examples of the differences that can exist between people born only two hours apart, so you can see how important it is to know the hour and minute of your birth.

If you were born a half hour or 45 minutes sooner or later than you believe, it *may* mean you have an entirely different rising Sun than the one indicated. All sunrise births have the same Ascendant as the Sun Sign, as we've noted before. For instance, if you were born at dawn on June 4th you are a *double* Gemini. At the end of this chapter a table will enable you quickly to find your own Ascendant. Simply check it against the delineations based on the rising Signs:

Locate your Ascendant from Chapter 6, write the symbol of the Ascendant at the "9 o'clock" position, then simply fill in the remaining Signs on the house cusps (the spokes of the wheel) in counterclockwise fashion.

ARIES ♈

You have good executive ability, are apt to be something of a pioneer. You have strong likes and dislikes and are usually courageous and adventurous. Chances are you tend to have outbursts of anger or irritation, but you rarely hold a grudge for long. There is something of the iconoclast about you, a tendency to kick over existing practices and institutions, to crusade for newer and better ways—at least *your* version of such improvements! You are inclined to try to force your opinions on others rather than to use the gentle art of persuasion. You are enthusiastic and generally progressive in whatever idea you happen to be pursuing—as long as the idea lasts. Although you frequently change your viewpoint and opinions, you are extremely certain of whatever you happen to believe—at the moment. At some time in your life your ambition for high office or an executive position will tax all your willpower and courage. You are so passionately opinionated that many people regard your expressions as being violent.

Wherever you have legal trouble with money or property, there will almost certainly be women involved—particularly if you are a man. With Aries ascending, you may be an only child or may lose your brother or sister. People with this Sign rising often lose their fathers at an early age; this doesn't necessarily mean by death, but in one way or another the father leaves no provision for the care and welfare of his children.

You will travel a lot, either for business or else to avoid trouble. Chances are you'll change your residence frequently and may become successful in another country. You typify the cliche of marrying in haste and repenting in leisure. Probably you'll get a divorce. One way or another, you are a true pioneer, a climber of every kind of obstacle fate put in your path. There's a kind of martyr complex about Aries, however. When afflicted, people born under this Sign can cause injury or even death to themselves.

TAURUS ♉

You don't, as a rule, easily become angered; but by the same token you're difficult to appease and liable to harbor a grudge for long periods. You tend to be self-possessed, and may seem dogmatic or even stubborn. Despite your essentially egotistical attitude, you are outwardly kindly, essentially diplomatic. You are precise, patient and probably love your own ideas. Generally you are calm, somewhat obstinate and therefore strongly passionate. Taurus ascending has a deep and abiding love of physical ease and comfort—a characteristic that might be regarded as pure laziness.

This is not necessarily so. You are firm-willed and flexible, capable of making silent decisions and pursuing them with strong, steady perseverance. You hanker for recognition and are very fond of your own possessions and property. You will probably realize your ambitions. Either by your own efforts or through some unexpected good luck, you'll acquire a fair amount of wealth. Usually your father will be helpful; in all likelihood he was or is a man of some consequence in his field.

You will also realize much happiness through children, yet

you may lose your first if it happens to be a boy. You are artistic; you love peace and harmony to such a degree that you may resist change and try to avoid all obstacles. This makes you so conservative that the chief cause of your unhappiness is your own stubborn opinions.

Even though your youth may be plagued by financial insecurity, you will gain materially through your adulthood and middle age, and develop a full appreciation for the physical comforts of life.

GEMINI ♊

You are fully capable of success in radio, television, journalism, literature or motion pictures. Although you tend to be somewhat excitable and easily upset, you are just as easily assuaged. You are original, have good ideas, are clever in legal matters, inventive, a lover of logic, science, art and literature. Generally you are well-informed, humane, flexible and easy to talk to—a born communicator.

With great subtlety you express a desire for command situations or executive position. You are one of the few who can do this with neither tyranny nor excessive pride. You come from a small to moderate-sized family which is usually well versed in music or art, although some family secrets are a cause of much unhappiness.

You have such a beautifully balanced willpower and resoluteness of purpose that few people realize your potential for real achievement. Chances are you may have a brother who holds some kind of executive office or important position.

In love there are many secrets or changes, with difficulty through or loss of children. Intrigue is your stock in trade. Gemini ascending often has two or more affairs going at once . . . either that or you may marry twice—once to a foreigner or someone from another country. This most dual of all signs frequently means the holding of two jobs or positions at once and a wide variety of friends. In fact, there is such an inordinate love of variety in your life that strife occurs as a result of the jealousy or selfishness of others. Generally, Gemini ascending also realizes unhappiness and trouble through lawyers and clergymen, even though he may be a member of one of these groups himself. In this unfortunate situation he might easily bring about his own downfall. You will probably, though, inherit property or land and accrue a great deal of professional influence.

CANCER ♋

Although some notoriety goes with it, you have many changes in position throughout your life. In a quiet way your disposition is rather impatient and severe, with an abrupt temper and a reserved exterior. You have an almost fantastic ability to absorb the ideas of others, and also possess a remarkable imagination—one that delights in exotic adventures in far-away places. Your unremitting compulsion for each new love, friendship or temporary attachment often propels you into yet another place and relationship—which usually ends in disillusion. This faculty has probably developed your most dramatic capabilities. You can be capricious and clever at using the ideas of other people. In extreme cases you could become a plagiarist or copier, one who is extraordinarily sensitive in perceiving the intentions of friends and associates.

Because of the rather fluid nature of the Moon's influence in your rising Sign, you are highly sensitive, changeable and nervous. Yet because of this nervous irritability you are enormously adaptable. Cancer ascending is remarkably capable, extremely independent and discreet in most things. You love public recognition, honor and wealth.

Still, inconstancy is your name. Your moods are as changeable as the tides. You can be timid in the face of physical danger and resourceful as well as courageous in your moral or intellectual attitudes. You can also be fanciful, gay and nebulous, or suddenly revert to caution, prudence—even mistrust. You lose materially through love affairs, children, relatives and speculation. This, moreover, occurs in the early part of your life. You are bound to become more prosperous and successful later on. There's a great tendency for obstacles, even danger, to crop up during your travels. Whatever your position, it is usually achieved in spite of the difficulties you experience through the jealousy of those who stoop to slander or spread false rumors about you. Thirty-five is the median age of stabilization for you. Whatever success you achieve is a result of your own enterprising spirit.

LEO ♌

You have nothing but contempt for the small or petty things in life. Basically, your nature is a benevolent and noble one, manifesting great pride, generosity, and probably a lot of talent. Leo ascending is the Sign of one who aspires to the higher, more influential and powerful positions in life. You are dramatic and poetic, with a love of display which others could interpret as nothing more than pure egotism. Although you are a hard worker and your success comes through persistence and endurance, whatever fame and fortune you realize usually comes without your seeking it. Like those born under the other fixed Signs, you display a good deal of self-determination and may seem haughty. Like Aries, you can reveal a flaring temperament, but your anger is a straw fire that doesn't last long.

Somehow or other you are often associated with important and influential people. You love grandeur in nature as well as in the human soul; you are attracted to everything that is bright and large and noble. Your undertakings are done with courage, yet you have fixed opinions, dogmatic ideals and strong passions. You could never admit to being ruled by these passions.

Chances are there is some disaffection or estrangement from your father—or he was separated from you while you were still very young. You love children and could have many yourself, but there is much difficulty—even sorrow— over the health of your oldest. Those with Leo ascending frequently marry more than once and can have children by each marriage. Men with Leo rising at one time or another in their lives are forced to endure great hardship, often lacking in the basic necessities of existence, such as food and a place to live.

You are likely to come into an inheritance, and so will your children. Successful business or professional people are attracted to you and vice versa; you will prosper through these associations. In the final analysis, all the vicissitudes of life will have little effect on you; you are almost certain to emerge ahead of the game.

VIRGO ♍

You have a finely discriminating sense of justice, humility, a good mind and a rather attractive and diplomatic demeanor. You'll rise in life through your own merit, attention to detail and hard work . . . in short, through your own achievements. Nevertheless, there's a lack of perspective or proportion in your outlook that causes you to overemphasize the importance of small, unimportant details.

Despite your pleasant and attractive public personality, you are difficult to know well. Only those whom you feel are sincerely affectionate or trustworthy can ever become your confidantes. You are definitely not the temperamental type; as a rule you are slow to anger, but by the same token, you don't find it easy to forgive people who have wronged you.

Being a mental Sign, Virgo ascending clings to its own ideas with a tenacity and esteem that seems to counter all the other influences of this earthy, mercurial Sign. Your willpower is strong, yet you are perfectly capable of being swayed by logic, reason and finesse. Generally of a quiet nature, you are nevertheless capable of eloquence and remarkable persuasiveness—when the occasion calls for it. By vocation you are probably inclined to theoretical science, health, hygiene and the more abstract areas of human knowledge. Your avocation could easily be gardening or amateur farming.

As an infant or child you probably endured poor health — possibly poverty. Even as an adult, most of what you manage to acquire is through your own hard work and is, therefore, richly deserved. You will probably realize some financial gain through inheritance and/or the property of your business or marriage partner. This could happen some distance from your place of birth—probably in another country. Whatever else you do, avoid speculation if you want to hold onto what you have earned. Chances are your father will marry twice, and that there are some family secrets you'd rather forget.

Although there are exceptions in every instance, relatives and neighbors are frequently inimical to your personal welfare. Probably there is a coldness or lack of sympathy in your relationship with brothers or sisters. Your own family will be small and your children not as keenly interested in marriage as you'd like them to be.

Solid happiness in love comes late to the person with Virgo rising. He or she often marries twice or has an extramarital affair. Whatever difficulties you face, your achievements and ultimate success will somehow revolve around trips and voyages, possibly associated with some changes in occupation. Don't be surprised to find yourself in later years with two homes and property in two different countries.

LIBRA ♎

This is one of the most likable and harmonious Ascendants
to have. You are sensitive and strongly influenced by your
surroundings as well as existing conditions. Libra rising gives
you an innate sense of fairness, makes you honest, courteous,
compassionate and kind. You are optimistic, candid and have
a good deal of willpower but very little perseverance. One of
your chief drawbacks stems from the fact that you will weigh
first one side of a question and then the other—and then perhaps wait to see what someone else will do—before making
a decision of your own.

Your talents include constructive and inventive ability.
Probably you have untapped genius for anything harmonious
or beautiful in life: poetry, art, music or sculpture. You
learn quickly and can master almost any branch of business.
The difficulty lies in the fact that you may, while engrossed
in any avocation, suddenly change your mind and follow
an entirely different line of interest.

Social and personal pleasures are matters of great absorp-
tion for you with Libra ascending. This is the natural Sign
of partnership and harmonious relationships; unfortunately,
too many of these connections are more disruptive than
amicable. If you haven't been born into a large family,
chances are that you'll marry into one; the only trouble with
this is that some of them may be so disputatious that legal
action will be involved.

Somehow your father is a source of difficulty or loss. If
he did not leave the scene when you were very young, he
may be a source of unforeseen obstacles, argument and un-
necessary restraint, due to his loss of position in life. There's
some kind of duplicity in your parental allegiance; either you
were adopted or your father and/or mother has remarried.
On the other hand, you'll gain enormous satisfaction and
happiness from and through your children, who will be few
in number but extremely fortunate.

Your marriage partner is apt to be comfortably fixed, and
you have a good relationship with your children. Still, you
are or will be in the public eye and will probably do considerable traveling and changing of address as a result of
your occupation. You'll take some long trips, but your chief
source of profit and success will be in your own country—
probably your home town. You will discover that your best

friends are people of great professional accomplishment and standing in the world. Association with artists, writers and other creative people will eventually reveal that one of your closest friends comes from this group.

When all is said and done, and you've lived your life to the best of your abilities, your children will be your best inspiration during your waning years.

SCORPIO ♏

By nature, inclination and temperament you are an extremist. Whatever you attempt, it is usually done with the full force of all your being. Your will is so strong you stick to a fight to the bloody end, regardless of the outcome. Scorpio rising is largely misunderstood by almost every standard. Don't overlook the fact that there are other planetary arrangements in your chart to offset what is often regarded as your Scorpio harshness, bitter critical quality and acid sarcasm. You are a born executive and like very much to operate behind the scenes. It helps to realize that Scorpio is representative of sex, death and regeneration, and that these things occupy an important area of your existence.

You share a kind of iconoclasm with Aquarius, though the latter is not the extremist you are. There's an apparently unquenchable thirst in you for finding out what makes things tick, then reassembling them to make them work better. You do this with objects, people—even institutions, if given half a chance. Very little, if anything, escapes the penetrating power of your observation. If it doesn't meet with your approval, you'll tear down any façade, any theory, any belief, to get at the truth. This makes you a natural detective. In science the intensity and keenness of your curiosity can bring you rich rewards, yet there is an Aries-like kind of martyrdom or "self-destruct" button in the mind of almost everyone with strong Scorpio aspects.

Extremism again. You have strong likes and dislikes. You hate and love with a white-hot fire, yet you are able to keep things to yourself until some plan of action is mapped out. Scorpio is exceptionally resourceful and self-reliant, and frequently malicious. You have a fertile imagination. Still . . . there are several types within the Scorpio nature, and it is difficult to know in advance just how anger will be handled. The undeveloped type, symbolized by the deadly, stinging scorpion, is capable of almost any outrage. The intermediate type is symbolized by the wily serpent, representing increased wisdom. The developed type is characterized by the high-soaring eagle, aspiring to the greatest possible heights. Here you will find scientists, orators, intensely devout evangelists and fiery debaters.

Scorpio ascending is always ambitious and usually manages to gain some sort of high office or executive position. You probably admire the military and maritime professions. You may have been close to poverty, a condition that prevails in the early part of your existence. But during the second half of your life there is more material prosperity and good fortune than you would otherwise have believed. There are excellent opportunities to travel and make money in other countries—through your marriage partner, legal dealings and/or through relatives by marriage. You are something of a lone wolf and probably have many secret love affairs. More than one marriage is indicated for those with Scorpio ascending. The first could result in the premature loss of the husband or wife through illness or accident. Eventually, despite a great series of difficulties and setbacks, you will achieve the success, good position and probably the honors you have so long desired.

SAGITTARIUS ♐

You often display two entirely different facets of personality. One of these is rather reticent, sensitive and impressionable. The other is courageous, daring—even reckless. By any measure, you are not easy to know well. One of your chief drawbacks is the overemphasis you place on action rather than its consequences. You are basically sympathetic, and driven by your ambition for achievement to action of some kind or another. You can't tolerate injury or injustice to others—it seems almost a personal affront. People with Sagittarius rising are usually versatile and clever in several areas at once. You are able to master more than one specialty.

Constraint or restraint of any kind is unbearable. You are quick to anger, but just as quickly recover and do not often hold a grudge. You comprehend new ideas and ways of life with scarcely any effort, and are very progressive and clearminded. Sagittarians carry an exuberant, youthful and happy attitude—even into old age. You tend to say what you think at the moment of stimulation, but your basic nature is friendly, even gentle. About the only time you flare up is when your basic ideals are attacked. Above all else, you love and cherish your personal freedom and independence, even though you prefer a simple way of life. You suffer when trapped in a discordant environment, and will sacrifice everything rather than be tied to an unpleasant situation, person or place.

You are more complex and difficult to understand, probably, than you realize. Always on your toes, you are friendly, outgoing and gregarious, yet your watchfulness of others amounts almost to mistrust—and can result in the very deception you strive to avoid. Your courage can never be questioned, even though you may seem quiet or even timid to those who don't know you well. You are intelligent and devoted to the *spirit*—if not the practice—of religious belief. You are good at research and study—a reasonable man or woman—with foresight, whose conversational abilities amount almost to eloquence. The opinions you hold are almost always unorthodox.

There's a lukewarm attitude in you toward most family ties. Some difficulty with your father or father-in-law amounts to a kind of torment worse than actual imprisonment. There probably was an early separation from your father. Conversely, you may be separated from your own children—or one of them. Your relationship with brothers and sisters is friendly enough, but many troubles are experienced through them. Two or three marriages (or similar associations) are in store for you. One of these is bad for your position and standing in life, but you will manage to extricate yourself. While you are in another country or far from home, one of your parents may die. You will travel extensively, and could be exposed to some danger when away from your home. You can anticipate a long and valuable career. Chances are you will end your days peacefully in a distant country.

CAPRICORN ♑

Your life is based on prudence and caution, yet once embarked on a course of action, you pursue it with dogged determination and persistence. You tend to be quietly melancholy, but you are enormously ambitious whenever your course for a certain goal is set. Among friends you can be forceful and eloquent, even if not very persuasive. Among strangers, however, you seem reticent, quiet—even shy. Your ambition for power and prestige is almost boundless; you often display great courage and are capable of realizing your ambitions, yet achievement itself leaves you unhappy. You are a little different from the norm. This is characterized by a not-unpleasant peculiarity in the way you walk and talk. You may forgive someone who offends or injures you, but you'll never forget it. As an enemy, you can be malicious. As a friend, you are faithful and sincere.

Although you may have received the assistance of your family and the support of friends and business associates, your ultimate success can be attributed almost entirely to your own persistence and hard work. There is more than enough difficulty through brothers and sisters, who often cause considerable sorrow. Unfortunately, additional strife is caused by your family, especially your father, where marriage is concerned. Somehow you don't seem to agree and this causes secret trouble and rivalry in your immediate family. You travel a lot, and conceivably could easily face great danger while on some recondite mission.

Your children are few in number, but you tend to pin all your hopes and ambitions on the oldest, thereby creating for him an emotional burden. You tend to view your husband or wife as some kind of obstacle to your large ambitions. You could lose one partner in marriage, yet acquire a considerable amount of wealth from the next. The wife of a man with Capricorn ascending is usually a wonderful career booster who influences him in many correct decisions. But the marriage has more than its share of ups and downs. In virtually every case of Capricorn rising, the love affairs are subject to enormous, far-reaching changes.

Your friends will often be found connected with Mars-type occupations—doctors, soldiers, chemists, marines and sportsmen. There is a likelihood of sudden, upsetting news about them . . . often their unexpected or untimely death. Among this group of friends, one will inadvertently cause you a great deal of strife, perhaps even the temporary loss of your reputation in middle age. Yet in spite of your own groundless worry about health and position in life—and the consequent melancholy to which you are prone—you will overcome most of your setbacks and succeed through sheer persistence and your burning ambition to reach the top of the heap.

AQUARIUS ♒

This ascending Sign makes you honest and sincere, very idealistic and humanitarian in your outlook. In some ways you are naive, but in love you are exceptionally affectionate and constant. You are fond of scientific research and the liberal arts. In fact, you probably have a great deal of literary or artistic ability—and musical aptitude for all media. Though you prefer to live quietly and have a generally retiring viewpoint, your basic philosophy is heterodox. Aquarius rising is a fixed Sign. Therefore your willpower is stronger than is apparent. In fact, there is a kind of inflexibility about your outlook.

In personality and temperament you are kindly and humane. Even though your temper is brittle and forceful when angered, you cannot bear malice toward anyone or anything. As you probably realize, your association is highly valued because of your innate sense of fairness and the overall endurance of your friendship. You enjoy solitude, but this doesn't mean you are a recluse. Just the opposite. Aquarius likes to be with people. You are cordial, cheerful and high-spirited, despite some undeserved adversity or reversal of fortune. You are enormously patient and hard working, yet your efforts are seldom crowned with the success they deserve. Whatever you do is achieved through your own devotion to a cause. Even this is liable to sudden and unexpected reversals or secret enemies who create serious obstacles. Your best friends will be found among clergymen, lawyers, journalists and doctors. If you come into an inheritance, chances are it will be more trouble—in the long run—than it is worth.

Relatives—especially one brother—is a great source of annoyance, difficulty and trouble, particularly in business affairs, which can adversely affect your reputation. You'll take many long trips on business and in the administration of family interests. Something of a dual or secretive nature is involved in your work. Perhaps there are two or more sources of income, or you may be engaged in highly classified military or government work. Whichever it is, detective-like secrecy is in order. You are required to make many short trips, either for your vocation or on family business. Whatever the route, it is very familiar, even tiresome to you.

Marriage is a virtual certainty, and usually happens early in your life. You have few children and will go to any length to provide for them. There's a good chance that twins might be born, but there is some danger of illness or accident to the oldest child. Your wife or husband has talent and is profitably employed in some artistic endeavor, such as the composition or playing of music, creating new art forms, or acting—on stage, television or in motion pictures. Your marriage is blessed with constancy and longevity; the affection of your wife or husband is enduring and sincere. Although it may seem that you are financially secure, it could be money that dangles just beyond your reach through some kind of legalistic maneuvering. Your children, however, will probably come into a sizable inheritance.

You have many good friends, one of whom will come to your rescue when it seems that everything is in danger of being lost. This may happen when you are traveling or while you're in another country. Chances are you will live out your days in this foreign nation.

PISCES ♓

You are easily moved, romantic, imaginative and impressionable—all of which are attributes of your ruling planet, Neptune. Your mind is restless, constantly seeking new ideas for the expression of your creative talents. You are changeable, and can exercise whatever authority you may have with firmness—and yet pleasantly. You can succeed through your own efforts in science, literature or the arts. In fact, there is a good chance that you will achieve celebrity status in your field. Still, you are tortured by excessive worry and fanciful notions. Although generous by nature, you tend to pursue pleasure to a point where it might be injurious to others. Your chief ambition seems to be that of enjoying yourself and tasting the good things in life.

You are a good talker with a conversational ability that might rival the gift of eloquence. You are filled with good will and can easily put yourself in the other person's position; in fact, you tend to suffer for the underdog. Conversely, you can remain emotionally aloof from two opposing ideals and render a critical judgment of one or the other with neither bias nor prejudice. Anger doesn't come easily to you, but once moved to wrath you are almost impossible to appease before wreaking some kind of vengeance, however slight.

You are passionate, impressionable and, therefore, tend to seem vacillating. The pleasure of good company is very important, and you are socially successful because of your friendly outgoing nature and cordiality. You are always busy with one thing or another, and could become successful in almost anything that interests you. You are broadminded, knowledgeable in many fields and can probably pursue two occupations at once. Whatever material rewards you realize will be the result of your own hard work and effort, possibly through successful writing or in traveling. However, you will find that you also enjoy the affection and loyalty of friends and relatives, who are fortunately numerous. There is the danger of the premature loss of a brother or sister, and your parents are not able to contribute much in the way of assistance to your future or well being. Whatever is left in the family estate may be spread so thin that it is hardly worth the trouble of administration.

Your children will be much more fortunate. And there will be several children—mostly engaged in work that takes them on extensive trips with frequent changes in residence. If a man, your wife has some kind of chronic ailment or affliction. You may marry twice because the first marriage might cause difficulty with relatives and in-laws.

Paradoxically, one of your strongest enemies in life will turn out to be your staunchest friend. Pisces ascending is fully capable of gaining great public recognition, honors and considerable wealth. Most of your friends are in important positions and able to boost your career.

YOUR ASCENDING SIGN—FOR ANY YEAR OF BIRTH

These Ascendants are most accurate at 40° N. Latitude, but are valid for anyone born between 25° and 55° N. Latitude. This covers all of the United States, Southern Canada and Northern Mexico.

Pick the date closest to your birthday (June 15 if your birthdate is June 12, for example). Also pick the time closest to the actual time of your birth. If you were born on May 5 at 9:00 P.M., see May 1 at 9:35 P.M. (the closest date and time) and you'll find you have Sagittarius Ascending.

Jan 1
Approximate Time of Birth
A.M.   P.M.

12:30 Libra	1:10 Taurus	
3:05 Scorpio	2:50 Gemini	
5:35 Sagittarius	5:05 Cancer	
7:50 Capricorn	7:30 Leo	
9:25 Aquarius	10:05 Virgo	
10:45 Pisces		
11:55 Aries		

March 1
Approximate Time of Birth
A.M.   P.M.

1:35 Sagittarius	1:05 Cancer
3:50 Capricorn	3:30 Leo
5:25 Aquarius	6:05 Virgo
6:45 Pisces	8:30 Libra
7:55 Aries	11:05 Scorpio
9:10 Taurus	
10:50 Gemini	

January 15
Approximate Time of Birth
A.M.   P.M.

2:05 Scorpio	12:10 Taurus
4:35 Sagittarius	1:50 Gemini
6:50 Capricorn	4:05 Cancer
8:25 Aquarius	6:30 Leo
9:45 Pisces	9:05 Virgo
10:55 Aries	11:30 Libra

March 15
Approximate Time of Birth
A.M.   P.M.

12:35 Sagittarius	12:05 Cancer
2:50 Capricorn	2:30 Leo
4:25 Aquarius	5:05 Virgo
5:45 Pisces	7:30 Libra
6:55 Aries	10:05 Scorpio
8:10 Taurus	
9:50 Gemini	

February 1
Approximate Time of Birth
A.M.   P.M.

1:05 Scorpio	12:50 Gemini
3:35 Sagittarius	3:05 Cancer
5:50 Capricorn	5:30 Leo
7:25 Aquarius	8:05 Virgo
8:45 Pisces	10:30 Libra
9:55 Aries	
11:10 Taurus	

April 1
Approximate Time of Birth
A.M.   P.M.

1:50 Capricorn	1:30 Leo
3:25 Aquarius	4:05 Virgo
4:45 Pisces	6:30 Libra
5:55 Aries	9:05 Scorpio
7:10 Taurus	11:35 Sagittarius
8:50 Gemini	
11:05 Cancer	

February 15
Approximate Time of Birth
A.M.   P.M.

12:05 Scorpio	2:05 Cancer
2:35 Sagittarius	4:30 Leo
4:50 Capricorn	7:05 Virgo
6:25 Aquarius	9:30 Libra
7:45 Pisces	
8:55 Aries	
10:10 Taurus	
11:50 Gemini	

April 15
Approximate Time of Birth
A.M.   P.M.

12:30 Capricorn	12:30 Leo
2:55 Aquarius	3:05 Virgo
3:45 Pisces	5:30 Libra
4:55 Aries	8:05 Scorpio
6:10 Taurus	10:35 Sagittarius
7:50 Gemini	
10:05 Cancer	

May 1
Approximate Time of Birth
A.M.	P.M.
1:25 Aquarius	2:05 Virgo
2:45 Pisces	4:30 Libra
3:55 Aries	7:05 Scorpio
5:10 Taurus	9:35 Sagittarius
6:50 Gemini	11:50 Capricorn
9:05 Cancer	
11:30 Leo	

July 1
Approximate Time of Birth
A.M.	P.M.
1:10 Taurus	12:30 Libra
2:50 Gemini	3:05 Scorpio
5:05 Cancer	5:35 Sagittarius
7:30 Leo	7:50 Capricorn
10:05 Virgo	9:25 Aquarius
	10:45 Pisces
	11:55 Aries

May 15
Approximate Time of Birth
A.M.	P.M.
12:25 Aquarius	1:05 Virgo
1:45 Pisces	3:30 Libra
2:55 Aries	6:05 Scorpio
4:10 Taurus	8:35 Sagittarius
5:50 Gemini	10:50 Capricorn
8:05 Cancer	
10:30 Leo	

July 15
Approximate Time of Birth
A.M.	P.M.
12:10 Taurus	2:05 Scorpio
1:50 Gemini	4:35 Sagittarius
4:05 Cancer	6:50 Capricorn
6:30 Leo	8:25 Aquarius
9:05 Virgo	9:43 Pisces
11:30 Libra	10:55 Aries

June 1
Approximate Time of Birth
A.M.	P.M.
12:45 Pisces	12:05 Virgo
1:55 Aries	2:30 Libra
3:10 Taurus	5:05 Scorpio
4:50 Gemini	7:35 Sagittarius
7:05 Cancer	9:50 Capricorn
9:30 Leo	11:25 Aquarius

August 1
Approximate Time of Birth
A.M.	P.M.
12:50 Gemini	1:05 Scorpio
3:05 Cancer	3:35 Sagittarius
5:30 Leo	5:50 Capricorn
8:05 Virgo	7:25 Aquarius
10:30 Libra	8:45 Pisces
	9:55 Aries
	11:10 Taurus

June 15
Approximate Time of Birth
A.M.	P.M.
12:55 Aries	1:30 Libra
2:10 Taurus	4:05 Scorpio
3:50 Gemini	6:35 Sagittarius
6:05 Cancer	8:50 Capricorn
8:30 Leo	10:25 Aquarius
11:05 Virgo	11:45 Pisces

August 15
Approximate Time of Birth
A.M.	P.M.
2:05 Cancer	12:05 Scorpio
4:30 Leo	2:35 Sagittarius
7:05 Virgo	4:50 Capricorn
9:30 Libra	6:25 Aquarius
	7:45 Pisces
	8:55 Aries
	10:10 Taurus
	11:50 Gemini

September 1
Approximate Time of Birth

A.M.		P.M.	
1:05	Cancer	1:35	Sagittarius
3:30	Leo	3:50	Capricorn
6:06	Virgo	5:25	Aquarius
8:30	Libra	6:45	Pisces
11:05	Scorpio	7:55	Aries
		9:10	Taurus
		10:50	Gemini

November 1
Approximate Time of Birth

A.M.		P.M.	
2:05	Virgo	1:25	Aquarius
4:30	Libra	2:45	Pisces
7:05	Scorpio	3:55	Aries
9:35	Sagittarius	5:10	Taurus
11:50	Capricorn	6:50	Gemini
		9:05	Cancer
		11:30	Leo

September 15
Approximate Time of Birth

A.M.		P.M.	
12:05	Cancer	12:35	Sagittarius
2:30	Leo	2:50	Capricorn
5:05	Virgo	4:25	Aquarius
7:30	Libra	5:45	Pisces
10:05	Scorpio	6:55	Aries
		8:10	Taurus
		9:50	Gemini

November 15
Approximate Time of Birth

A.M.		P.M.	
1:05	Virgo	12:25	Aquarius
3:30	Libra	1:45	Pisces
6:06	Scorpio	2:55	Aries
8:35	Sagittarius	4:10	Taurus
10:50	Capricorn	5:50	Gemini
		8:05	Cancer
		10:30	Leo

October 1
Approximate Time of Birth

A.M.		P.M.	
1:30	Leo	1:50	Capricorn
4:05	Vigro	3:25	Aquarius
6:30	Libra	4:45	Pisces
9:05	Scorpio	5:55	Aries
11:35	Sagittarius	7:10	Taurus
		8:50	Gemini
		11:05	Cancer

December 1
Approximate Time of Birth

A.M.		P.M.	
12:05	Virgo	12:45	Pisces
2:30	Libra	1:55	Aries
5:05	Scorpio	3:10	Taurus
7:35	Sagittarius	4:50	Gemini
9:50	Capricorn	7:05	Cancer
11:25	Aquarius	9:30	Leo

October 15
Approximate Time of Birth

A.M.		P.M.	
12:30	Leo	12:50	Capricorn
3:05	Virgo	2:25	Aquarius
5:30	Libra	3:45	Pisces
8:05	Scorpio	4:55	Aries
10:35	Sagittarius	6:10	Taurus
		7:50	Gemini
		10:05	Cancer

December 15
Approximate Time of Birth

A.M.		P.M.	
1:30	Libra	12:55	Aries
4:05	Scorpio	2:10	Taurus
6:35	Sagittarius	3:50	Gemini
8:50	Capricorn	6:06	Cancer
10:25	Aquarius	8:30	Leo
11:45	Pisces	11:05	Virgo

7

The Influence of Mercury

In delineating the interpretations for the eight planets in each of the twelve Signs, there will (with the single exception of Mercury—for which we've devised a shortcut) be a table at the end of each chapter showing where the planets were at the time of your birth. With the faster moving planets, Venus and Mars, it may be necessary to know the time of day you were born in order to know *exactly* when the planets changed Signs. However, if you were born one day *after* or *before* the dates given in the tables, you are within the designated Sign(s).

The basic horoscope, again, is a circle divided into twelve equidistant spokes—or a dozen (roughly) equal parts.

This will not be a mathematically *precise* horoscope, but it is an easy beginning—one that will quickly teach you the basics and allow you to refine your chart later on. For purposes of illustration, we'll use the *natural* order of the Zodiac here—with Aries ♈ on the Ascendant (the Vernal or Spring Equinox—about March 21); Cancer ♋ on the Nadir (the Summer Solstice—about June 21); Libra ♎ on the (right) descendant (the Autumn Equinox—approximately September 20); Capricorn ♑ on the Midheaven (Winter Solstice—about December 21).

These are called the Cardinal points of the chart, or the "angles," whether Cardinal Signs occupy these points or not. (If you have Aries ascending, this is what your chart looks like. If Taurus is your Ascendant, begin with *that* Sign on the Eastern or *left* side of the chart, and so on.)

In the short time that it will take you to learn to cast an exact mathematical horoscope, you will include such refinements as the exact degree of the Sign on each house cusp, and the exact degree and minute of celestial arc for every planet. For the moment, the simplest way to know how 75 percent of your chart reads and looks is to put each planet in its correct position by Sign.

From our viewpoint on Earth, Mercury moves faster than any other celestial body except the Moon. Its orbit around the Sun is described once in every 88 days, which means that it would require almost an entire additional book just to list the dates Mercury changed Signs.

There is, however, a shortcut method for you to determine where Mercury was at your birth. This small planet is so close to the Sun that it can only be in one of three Signs. Each Sign is 30 degrees apart, and Mercury is *never* more than 28 degrees from Sol! It *must,* therefore, be either in your Sun Sign or the Sign preceding or following it.

By reading all three, you'll quickly get the "feel" of the one that suits you most exactly. This is good basic training in the art of astrological synthesis. Once you've decided which is right for you, place Mercury in the proper segment of the astrological "wheel."

The symbols for the planets are the same for astronomers *and* astrologers because astronomy found it convenient to continue using the ancient astrological system. This is also true for symbols of the Signs of the Zodiac.

Both series of symbols are easy to learn and should be thoroughly memorized. They are as follows:

☉	Sun	♈	Aries
☽	Moon	♉	Taurus
☿	Mercury	♊	Gemini
♀	Venus	♋	Cancer
⊕	Earth	♌	Leo
♂	Mars	♍	Virgo
♃	Jupiter	♎	Libra
♄	Saturn	♏	Scorpio
♅	Uranus	♐	Sagittarius
♆	Neptune	♑	Capricorn
♇	Pluto	♒	Aquarius
		♓	Pisces

(The *Signs* are inserted in *counterclockwise* direction around the wheel as shown on page 156.)

Although this shortcut method will give you a rudimentary approach to horoscope making, the *precision* calculation of your chart would require a series of expensive technical books: (a) A table of houses (b) At least four ephemerides —books of planetary positions from 1890 to 1975 (c) A table of proportional logarithms (d) A book of longitudes and latitudes for the U.S. (e) A book on longitudes and latitudes for the world. By sacrificing 25 percent accuracy you will herein save on all these books.

Until recently the outermost known planet, Pluto, was considered to be as small as the *innermost* known planet, Mercury. Closer observation of Pluto revealed that it is more than four times as large as Earth. Its year amounts only to 248 of our years and its average distance from the Sun is about 3,675,000,000 miles, compared to Earth's 93 million. Light, traveling at 186,000 miles a second, reaches

Mercury about two minutes after leaving the Sun. Eight minutes later this same light will illuminate the Earth. Continuing its flight outward from our local star, this light will reach Pluto in eight *hours*. (Four *years* later it reaches the nearest star.)

Speed, smallness and proximity to the Sun are Mercury's chief characteristics—physically, at any rate. The Sun is eight million times larger than Mercury. To the ancient people of the Earth, Mercury was known as Thoth, Hermes, or "The Messenger of the Gods." The symbol of this planet is a young man flying with wings on his heels. He carries a caduceus, an insignia, of olive wood, with a pair of wings at the end and two serpents entwined around the rod. Essentially this is a good representation of the influence of Mercury and of Mercurial-type people, largely Geminians and Virgoans—or those with many planets in these Signs: logic, duality, youthfulness and speed.

Generally speaking, Mercury governs understanding and sight. It rules arms, hands, lungs, the tongue and the nervous system. The influence of Mercury in each of the twelve Signs is as follows:

MERCURY IN ARIES   ☿ ♈

You love literature and literary people; you like to read and write, and will often change your mind about the same situation when seen from a different vantage point, either in time or space. You are generally restless, fiery, impulsive, argumentive and a good debater. Your expressions, either in writing, thought or speech, are fast—*mercurial*. You are eager, earnest and expressive. You are quick to demonstrate your ideas in an interesting, unique, liberal, clever and inventive manner. But you probably realize your lack of the sober, plodding, scientific way of method and order. You are too restless, and liable to skip from one thing to another, unless Mercury is close to being either in Taurus or Pisces.

MERCURY IN TAURUS   ☿ ♉

Although you tend to be somewhat obstinate, you are generally pleasant and easygoing. You possess a highly practical and determined mind, particularly in educational situations or where your interests coincide with the necessity for mental development and training. Generally you have good judgment, a sociable, friendly and affectionate disposition and respect for religion, music, poetry and art. You probably have an excellent memory and can keep plugging determinedly in any kind of mental activity. There are times when you display almost uncontrollable flashes of anger or irritation. You are fond of the opposite sex and of all recreations and pleasure. Although your likes and dislikes are strong and you may be ruled by your own views of things (which tend to remain fixed), you acquire money through an established income and will probably end up with your own good share of material possessions.

MERCURY IN GEMINI ☿ ♊

This is a "natural" Sign for Mercury. You probably travel around a lot and find yourself doing a fair amount of studying and reading. You may quickly change from one profession or occupation to another, or else find yourself doing two things at once. You'd probably make a good executive, lawyer or politician. You like to acquire knowledge of any kind. You have an inventive, ingenious, fast-on-the-trigger, clever and resourceful mentality. Generally you tend to be generous and magnanimous, full of good humor and sympathy; and you are unbiased in your attitude toward other people and places. You need to accept things as they are. This is one of the few almost totally unbiased Signs of Mercury.

MERCURY IN CANCER ☿ ♋

You have a fine sense of rhythm which expresses itself either physically or mentally. If in the former fashion, you may excel in dancing or athletics; if in the latter, in poetry or music. You are sociably disposed, quiet, good-natured and socially graceful. Your world outlook is broad and comprehensive; you understand many things that go on in the world, and this faculty by itself probably makes you rather changeable. You love to travel, especially by water, and could easily gain through this medium. You are inclined to be lucky through members of the maternal side of your family, or inherit from your mother. At any rate, you will gain financially through affairs and occupations associated with property or land. You are discreet, tactful, have a good memory and tend to be diplomatic. Because you are sensitive and impressionable, you are most easily influenced by kindness and consideration.

MERCURY IN LEO ☿ ♌

You have a flair for managing, directing or controlling others in communication, health or labor. Chances are you will achieve a responsible, prominent position in one of these areas. You love children, the theater, art and music. In any mental activity you are able to concentrate and persevere—very often to the detriment of your other duties or endeavors. You tend to be self-independent and casual, with a love of pleasure. At the same time, you are basically kind and easy-going—as well as positive and strong-willed. You have an intuitive mind and high ideals, and cannot bring yourself to compromise them. You can be quick-tempered and fiery, confident, determined and ambitious. Generally your mind and willpower are sympathetic, expansive and progressive.

MERCURY IN VIRGO ☿ ♍

You tend to be skeptical and critical, with a finely discriminating mind and outlook. Before you are convinced of anything, you must see, know and understand the subject thoroughly. This makes you a good student, writer and detailer. You like math, literature or mental activities that tax your ingenuity, planning and dexterity. You may have innate oratorical skill or ability as a linguist. Diet, hygiene and healing are high on your list of interests. You tend to be serious and quiet and have a great love of studying and memorizing. Basically, you tend to be rather intellectual, but are never showy about it; in fact, you may be known for your reticence. Whatever you learn through your studies you can put to practical everyday use, but you tend to take on too much, to have too many projects going at once. Your achievements, although solid and enduring, probably will not bring widespread publicity or fame. For example, you can master the art of successfully writing about topics that are neglected, overlooked or unpopular—and do this in a practical, utilitarian way—but for one reason or another the *sensational* type of success someone else might achieve by doing the same job somehow eludes you.

MERCURY IN LIBRA ☿ ♎

In marriage or any other partnership, you tend to have a kind of mental or intellectual comradeship rather than one of an emotional nature. Even so, you may marry someone who is related to you in some way—or who is your social and financial inferior. This position of Mercury is excellent for music, art, poetry, education and intellectual stimulation. You have a finely developed intuitive faculty, and love a good social life, friends, refined pleasures, the theater and children. Whatever sort of educational pursuit you may be engaged in, you work best—even in reading, studying and writing—with someone else. In *partnership*. Association and partnership, either through your own choice or by necessity, is an integral part of your life. You are capable of excellent reasoning and judgment, and love making delicately balanced comparisons. You have a gentle, loving nature, with a refined outlook and a liberal mind.

MERCURY IN SCORPIO ☿ ♏

You are resourceful, inventive, secretive and could have a volatile temper. You can follow any kind of pursuit with such intensity and concentration that nothing can elude you. You tend to be both sarcastic and witty, with an excellent command of the language and a highly active mind. You like to solve problems, dig beneath the surface of natural or unnatural mysteries to find the root cause of things. Yet you are obstinate, difficult to convince and exceptionally fond of your own opinions. You can be moved to intense indignation or rage by an injustice, whether it is real or whether you have only imagined it. By the same token, you will plunge into any undertaking or cause you love with tremendous zeal and enthusiasm. You think and act in reckless, forceful and sarcastic ways. You could also be too much a lover of the opposite sex. Your neighbors, relatives and often your friends are a source of friction and trouble. You enjoy pleasure and social activities, love various mystical and occult subjects. You are curious, suspicious and highly critical, yet resourceful and fond of gathering knowledge. You are proud of your shrewd mentality.

MERCURY IN SAGITTARIUS ☿ ♐

You are just as active mentally as you are physically (if not more so); you are extremely changeable, and will jump from one thing to another or undertake the study of two different subjects at once. You like science, philosophy and religion, and probably have found yourself with two jobs or occupations at once. Failing that, you tend to change jobs frequently. Even if you have received a good, solid education, the effects will not become evident during your early years, often success comes your way later in life. You will probably travel a lot and take many short trips. These travels will have something to do with your brothers and sisters, writing or education. You tend to be a little too candid, to say exactly what is on your mind. You are often rebellious, independent and impulsive, yet by nature you are sincere, ambitious and far-sighted. You love freedom of thought and freedom of speech and cannot tolerate censorship of any kind. You love nature and appreciate all that is beautiful, as well as being fond of animals and sports, generally. Although you are changeable, you want justice all around, and are philosophical, generous and like to exercise authority.

MERCURY IN CAPRICORN ☿ ♑

You are cautious, prudent and painstaking where the development of your mind is involved. You seem to be constantly on the move, industriously pursuing your interests in philosophy, business, science or chemistry. You give the impression of restlessness or discontent with the way things are going, and are likely to be suspicious about the motivations of others. You have an innate curiosity and a natural diplomacy that hides some of your worst faults—mainly a sharply critical attitude—which you are especially careful to conceal. Your penetrating intellect, however critical and changeable, is often tactfully curious about those things that involve your career and ambitions. You are basically conservative, practical and observant. Your general outlook is quite serious and often keenly discriminating toward those who oppose you. Whether you realize it or not, you have the organizational ability of a born executive.

MERCURY IN AQUARIUS ☿ ♒

You express your interest in the affairs of others and therefore probably have a long list of friends—not all of whom are as broad or humanitarian in their outlook as you. Your high idealism doesn't always influence the less developed social consciousness of others. In you there is a general attraction for study, specifically science, invention, sociology or some kind of organizational work. You have excellent powers of reason and concentration for any task at hand. You have broad humanitarian interests and are undoubtedly familiar with the great books and writers of the present and past. You enjoy profound philosophical discussions with intellectuals and people of broad experience. You are truly original as well as discriminating, and you exercise a keen judgment of human nature—particularly its frailties. Although your refined consciousness is broad and you are a deep thinker with humanitarian ideals, the chances are you may be somewhat ahead of your contemporaries and they could consider you eccentric in some way. Your weakness is that you must have friends and life conditions on your own terms. You become so involved with the activities of others that you may neglect your own ambitions, your hopes and dreams for the future. Go ahead, *be* original, but beware of seeming *too* unorthodox.

MERCURY IN PISCES ☿ ♓

You are sympathetic to and understanding of the needs of others, yet you are liable to use this sympathy as an excuse or justification for your own lack of confidence. You tend to feel unworthy, to fear challenge and to shirk responsibility. These are grave mistakes. Learn to recognize the fact that your knowledge doesn't necessarily come from books. You are exceptionally intuitive and psychic. You understand without knowing *why* you do and are therefore inclined to denigrate your own capabilities and knowledge. You are interested in hospitals or similar institutions, and have a good judgment of human nature. You absorb data quickly and have a retentive memory. You are imaginative, absorbing and impressionable. You love travel by water, and take great pleasure in studying mystical and occult subjects. Either directly or indirectly through these, you can be of far greater help to others than to yourself.

8

The Influence of Venus

The second planet out from the Sun is Earth's "sister,"
Venus. This beautiful, mysterious world was designated by
all ancient civilized people as the "goddess of fertility,"
femininity and beauty. Venus is (interchangeably) Aphrodite
or Diana. Immanuel Velikovsky, who claims that evolution
occurs amid catastrophe, and not gradually, as some believe,
claims that less than 4,000 years ago Venus was ejected from
the gaseous atmosphere of Jupiter and roamed the solar
system as a brilliant comet for several centuries before settling
into its present stable planetary orbit. In Greek mythology,
Aphrodite (Venus) was born from the head of Zeus (Jupiter).

Until Velikovsky's early predictions about the high temperature of Venus were recently proven by America's space
probes, astronomers believed our near neighbor was a cold
(probably dead) planet. Although our sister world possesses
an opaque atmosphere (and has no natural satellite), it now
appears that Life is indeed possible there.

Astrologically, Venus is akin to the Moon in that both
influence the emotions, the refined and gentler characteristics
of men and women. People born with a well-aspected Venus,
especially if it is on or in the Ascendant, as calculated in
Chapter 6 are usually graceful, refined, charming and physically attractive.

Both Libra and Taurus are associated with Venus, and her
influence is easily detected among people with the Sun, Moon
or Ascendant in these Signs. Those with Venus as their
planetary "ruler," i.e., those who have Taurus or Libra as

their Ascendant, are noticeably sociable, considerate and kindhearted.

Still . . . it is possible that the good qualities bestowed by Venus can be offset by powerfully adverse aspects. When this is the case, the native seeks selfish pleasures at the expense of higher interests. He is apt to live on a self-centered, emotional level, seeking cheap amusement, eating and drinking too much, and so on.

The general accent of Venus is on partnership, friendship, harmony and agreeableness. She expresses her influence on your personality and character in good humor, love and generosity. But most of all in harmony.

One of the most important uses of the horoscope, as you will quickly see after making chart comparisons, is the matter of harmony or discord between individuals of the same or opposite sex. Venus figures very prominently in any such comparison. Generally, Venus, Jupiter and the Sun are considered highly beneficial influences, and Saturn and Mars are usually considered as obstacles. The favorable aspects are the sextile (60 degrees or two Signs apart) and the trine (120 degrees or four Signs apart). Depending on the planets involved, the conjunction or no distance between them can be either disadvantageous or beneficial.

If, in the horoscopes of a man and woman, Venus and Mars are in conjunction, they will be strongly attracted physically to each other. This is true for almost *any* aspect between the planet of war and the planet of love—the sextile, trine, and often the opposition or 180 degrees (i.e., planets in opposite Signs). Any of the foregoing harmonious contacts, especially among the Sun, Jupiter, Venus and Mars in the charts of a man and woman are evidence of physical attraction, affection and love. Thus if a man has the Sun in Scorpio and a woman has her Venus on his Sun, a mutually harmonious resonance is automatically in operation between them.

Conversely, if Saturn (the planet of constriction and discipline) in a woman's chart is in conjunction, opposition or square to Mars in a man's chart, the opposite effect will manifest.

You will soon learn the validity of these effects by putting the rules to the ironbound test of crucial experiments. The great Swiss psychiatrist, Carl Jung, examined the horoscopes of his patients as a shortcut aid to diagnosis of root causes of mental and emotional disturbances. He could also predict unerringly either harmony or conflict between any two personalities simply by examining their horoscopes and making critical comparisons.

In order to demonstrate the reliability of astrology as a workable tool in predicting harmony or discord between individuals, a crucial test was set up wherein he examined the planetary patterns in the horoscopes of 483 married couples, 966 individuals in all. For his control group he used 966 horoscopes of people who were not married or even acquainted—a purely random selection. He did not know which was which, except that 1,932 horoscopes were stapled together and mixed so that only by the rules of astrology could he determine the married couples from those who were not married.

Dr. Jung scored an amazing 97 percent in choosing the married couples because of the harmonious contacts among Venus, Jupiter, Mars, the Sun and the Moon. The fact that he chose 6 percent of the unacquainted couples as being married was an interesting error. Two couples of the random group Jung had mistaken as lovers eventually *did* meet and were subsequently married!

At the time of the completion of the experiment, Jung wrote: *"The statistical material shows that a practically as well as a theoretically improbable chance combination occurred, which coincides in the most remarkable way with traditional astrological expectations.*

"That such a coincidence could occur at all is so improbable and so incredible that nobody could have dared predict anything like it. It really does look as if the statistical material had been manipulated and arranged to give the appearance of a positive result."

As you set up your own chart, memorize the positions of each planet (i.e. the Sign it is in) and what it means. Later, as you set up the charts of other people—using the same rules—look for the harmonious relationships between the major "benefics," in your chart and that of anyone else you know. If you have Venus in Gemini, you will generally be attracted to mercurial people—writers, speakers, anyone in communications—and especially those who have the Sun, Moon or Mercury in Gemini. Wherever Venus or the Moon are located in your chart, this is where your emotions are most strongly attracted.

You'd hardly expect a (Mars-ruled) warrior or soldier to express the finer, more *harmonious* attributes of Venus. But anyone who has ever studied the astrology of ex-President Dwight Eisenhower knows he was born with the Moon in the blunt, aggressive, militant Sign Scorpio. And yet he expressed that kindly, accommodating, unifying nature which only his Libra Sun could bestow.

Probably the finest illustration of this quality was made by that outspoken Sagittarian statesman and philosopher, Winston Churchill, when he said of Eisenhower:

"He showed the capacity for making great nations march together more truly united than they have ever been before."

This is indeed the finest expression of a Venusian nature. Peace, accommodation and harmony. In General Eisenhower's case, it was coupled with and balanced by the iron-hard discipline of his Scorpio Moon.

At the end of this chapter you will find a listing of Venus' positions from 1890 to 1970.

VENUS IN ARIES ♀ ♈

You are an interesting mixture of harmoniousness and aggressiveness. You can be alternately as meek as a lamb or as mad as a hornet. You are impulsive and ardent in love, strongly attracted to the opposite sex and generous with your affections. You probably have a great attraction for the artistic forms of physical exercise such as ballet, ice and roller skating—possibly gymnastics or even trapeze artistry. You tend to be generous in giving gifts and in the way you spend your money and tip. You are so open-hearted and charitable, your sympathies so easily touched, that you respond instantly to any appeal for help, financial or otherwise. Naturally these characteristics tend to make you very popular. Among your many friends there may be one of the opposite sex to whom you respond quickly and ardently. This could result in a too-early, too-hasty marriage—one that you may later regret because you didn't take time to study all the potential adversities and personality differences. Since you are so romantic (*"in love with love,"* so to speak), you may be blinded by your idealism and victimized by an unworthy imitation of the real thing.

VENUS IN TAURUS ♀ ♉

All things being equal, you will probably inherit money through some sort of legacy, a business partnership or by marriage, although your nuptials could be in for postponement. Like the majority of people, you have no objection to money, but *you* are fond of it because it means ease, com-

fort and pleasure for you and yours. You like to share these
things with your friends. You tend to be more emotionally
than mentally inclined. You'd rather *feel* than think, and
therefore tend to rely more on your hunches and intuitions.
There is some danger here of giving too much of yourself;
this may not be in your best interests. Your emotions and
feelings are deep and enduring. You tend to be rather fixed
and difficult to sway once your mind is made up about something or someone. You are a staunch conservative in your
social life and pleasures. No one is likely to find you among
the *avant-garde*, either creatively, socially or sexually. The
old established, accepted and proven ways seem best. Custom,
formality and correct approach are very careful points with
you. You are very precise about this. Your love nature is
deep, affectionate, faithful and lasting.

VENUS IN GEMINI   ♀ ♊

You are probably known as a gay, romantic traveler with
many friends and acquaintants. Your intellect and emotions
are refined and clear, but apt to be dualistic. You tend to
flirt, to have several love affairs going at once, thus causing
jealousy and bringing you a good deal of grief. Yet you
bounce right back and start all over again. You are an excellent conversationalist, and have a broad (but often superficial) knowledge of many different subjects. Chances are
you make your money from more than one job or occupation—or that you change jobs frequently. Music, art, writing,
teaching and drama come easy for you if you have the educational background. Even without extensive formal education, you are able to get ahead in the world because of your
original, inventive and intuitive abilities. Venus in Gemini
makes you outgoing, friendly, sociable, good-natured, refined
—and with a love of games and light mental recreation. This
brings you among many people who admire and probably
share a deep affection for you. In turn, you flirt and recipro-
cate this love, and at the same time (paradoxically) insist on
faithfulness and loyalty from each of your emotional attachments! Your inconstancy may lead you into marriage with a
distant relative, but you're liable to be married two or more
times. You derive great pleasure from teaching, writing,
speaking and traveling to do these things. If Venus is well-
aspected, there is great affection for you among neighbors,
co-workers, brothers, sisters and relatives.

VENUS IN CANCER ♀ ♋

You have a strong protective desire to shield your loved ones, yet you need the security of being loved *yourself.* Unfortunately, this does not always develop for you. Unseen obstacles are put in the way of marriage, either because of a lack of money, the wrong job or profession or the objections of parents. Still, you are strongly attracted and attached to domesticity and probably have a strong affection for your mother, your home and the feeling of comfort and security it gives you. You are sincere and sentimental, imaginative, kindhearted and responsive to the emotions of others. You have a basically loving nature, receptive and sympathetic. You will probably have several secret love affairs and at least one marriage or alliance with someone considerably older or younger than yourself. This could very likely be with someone involved in mysticism or occultism of some kind. You are basically interested in psychic research, mystical religion and anything of a mysterious nature. You may have certain *psi* talents as well. With Venus in Cancer you tend to develop alliances or friendships with those who are on a lower rung of the social ladder. You may also become involved in an unpopular, obscure or lowly job. Yet, strangely enough, you can profit from any occupation connected with liquids or liquid refreshments. There also is a good indication that you will gain through your parents or profit by dealings in land or houses.

VENUS IN LEO ♀ ♌

You are somewhat ostentatious, a natural showman. Chances are good that you will benefit through any occupation connected with the theater, pleasure and amusement—such as singing, music or acting. You tend to dramatize your emotional experiences and to respond impulsively, spontaneously, to whatever gives you positive stimulation. You enjoy basking in the Sun (sometimes the "sun" of your own personality). You will benefit through people of good social connections and through your executive superiors, and achieve much happiness through children and young people. You are able to speculate successfully and to gain through inheritance, investment, and/or royalties. You enjoy friends, entertainment, pleasure and amusements of all kinds, especially where members of the opposite sex are concerned. You are generally kind, charitable, generous and liberal. You are also sincere, sympathetic and a warm lover. Fully appreciating the physical joys of life and often indulging in them, you run the risk of becoming effete through overindulgence. This could mean, if you're not careful, the complete discharge of your emotional batteries, resulting in a jaded insensitivity and disinterest.

VENUS IN VIRGO ♀ ♍

You need the security of being loved by someone with a high regard for your emotions; you want to feel respected and have your love treated as the delicate and rare thing it is. Unfortunately, however, you are apt to become involved with someone who runs roughshod over your feelings and treats you with either coldness or outright cruelty. You have a deceptively quiet exterior and a deeply sympathetic nature. There is some secret in your love life—possibly an affair with someone who is chronically ill, a doctor, a nurse or someone who works in a subordinate position. In any event, you are likely to experience disappointment in love, or delay in marriage caused by two affairs at once. You should be extremely cautious in financial speculation, but you might profit through joint investment with your marriage or business partner. A basic weakness of Venus in Virgo is a certain lack of discretion. You are liable to become involved romantically with someone of an unsavory reputation, thereby leaving yourself open to scandal. It would be wise to form associations only with people you know to be honest, kind and reliable.

VENUS IN LIBRA ♀ ♎

You are likely to live in a private world of peace, beauty and harmony. You are susceptible to kindly overtures and will respond with refined affection to those who inspire it. You are highly sympathetic and your love nature is rich, direct and idealistic. You tend to see the good in everything, yet you are sensitive, sometimes disillusioned, and easily hurt. Always, you search for truth, justice and more harmony; you love knowledge and are especially fond of art, music and refined pleasures. All amusements and gay social gatherings are a source of attraction. You prefer associates and friends who have some reputation in the fields of art, music, journalism or who have achieved high academic standards and are socially recognized. Your personality attracts many people because of your innate desire for a well-ordered existence, for harmony and peace again. Venus in Libra is an excellent position. It promises many friends, popularity, a good marriage and children who are musically or artistically talented. Partnerships and marriage are fortunate for you, and there is an excellent chance you will gain materially through others, as well as through the application of your own talents.

VENUS IN SCORPIO ♀ ♏

Yours is an intense, possessive, often jealous love nature. You are highly demonstrative and a volatile lover. Your passions may rule you rather than vice versa. You love luxury, and delight in pleasures of a sensational nature. Although you are powerfully attracted to the opposite sex, there is the strong likelihood of interminable delays in love, courtship and marriage. And there will be enormous difficulties to overcome with your marriage partner; disagreeable fights, jealousy, vindictiveness, and the possible death of your spouse. You like to travel, to speculate, even to scheme over ways you can capitalize on marriage or alliances with members of the opposite sex. You have a tendency to make friends with those of an antisocial nature or even those who have criminal tendencies—or with those whose interests are occult or mystical. You are generally a free and lavish spender, generous with those whose company you enjoy. You are likely to earn your living (in one way or another) through those things associated with the water Signs, Cancer, Scorpio and Pisces. Although there will be great delays in your profiting through a will, legacy, marriage or partnership, you will eventually reap some sort of financial reward from the deceased. Only through control of your intense emotions can you avoid many of the unpleasant experiences in life.

VENUS IN SAGITTARIUS ♀ ♐

You love your personal freedom and independence, and want above all to travel and explore exotic places; you love the unobtainable and could cause yourself a lot of unhappiness thereby. You tend to be ambiguous in your affections—loving two or more members of the opposite sex at the same time. You are not, however, maliciously disloyal. It is simply that

you love romance in faraway places. Generally your nature
is refined, altruistic, generous, outgoing, imaginative, gay
and lighthearted. You may have an income from two different sources, possibly through writing, publishing, or traveling
as well as from religious or philosophical interests. You are
attracted to outdoor sports, long voyages, animals (especially
horses), art and natural beauty. Because of your susceptibility to the opposite sex, you could be attracted to and involved in two or more marriages. One of these will be to
someone from a foreign country or at a great distance from
your home. This will, in these times, necessitate a great deal
of long-distance telephoning and voluminous correspondence.
Your friends will be people of importance, power and/or
good social standing. Your involvements and adventures are
usually a result of blindly following the dictates of your
emotions. Venus in Sagittarius makes you impressionable, far-
sighted, generous, prophetic and loyal in your intentions if
not in actual practice. You are inclined toward literary,
philosophical, benevolent and spiritual development.

VENUS IN CAPRICORN ♀ ♑

In affairs of the heart you are very careful of appearances or
how things might affect your social status or honor. Although
you are prudent, cautious and diplomatic, you are also inclined to marry for social or business considerations rather
than to follow the dictates of your finer emotions. This is
bound to cause coldness or a lack of interest in your spouse,
who is likely to be either wealthy or from a different strata
of social life. At any rate, this partner is or will be very
discriminating, dour and serious. There may be a wide difference in your ages. Yet you are adaptable to adversities and
tend to look on them as challenges. You may have a tendency
to seem calculating, cold and indifferent yourself, yet by sheer
grit, enterprise, willpower and hard work you will manage
to gain the respect of older people and your employer or
supervisor. It is almost certain that you'll be elevated to a
position of responsibility and entrusted with authority. You
will profit by your popularity among business and social acquaintances, make many friends in important positions, and
realize many advantages, including career advancement,
through them. You are likely to travel in foreign countries
and to inherit valuable real estate.

VENUS IN AQUARIUS ♀ ♒

This position of Venus indicates that most of your hopes, dreams, wishes and aspirations will eventually be fulfilled. In love you are earnest, sincere and faithful, yet you will, at one time or another, find yourself involved in secret affairs. You may either marry or remarry in middle or later life. You will experience some bizarre, sudden, strange and unexpected changes in love affairs. One of these will be with someone of an entirely different background --one who is eccentric in the extreme. The person you marry will be of a different age. You are entirely capable of having purely platonic friendships with the opposite sex without romantic involvement, but this is not to be recommended. You enjoy refined amusements, cultural pursuits and philosophical as well as intellectual stimulation. Although your outlook tends to be candid and sincere, you are likely to keep many of your opinions to yourself. You make friends easily—even with total strangers and are able to enjoy a wide spectrum of friends, both from the top *and* the bottom of the social stratum. You have a vast capacity for the enjoyment of social life and other pleasures. You are so outgoing, broad and altruistic in your viewpoint that you attract many people who want something from you, but who refuse to give of themselves in turn.

VENUS IN PISCES ♀ ♓

You are one of those who, fortunately or otherwise, have such a sympathetic nature that you can instantly feel and understand the sufferings of others. You tend to be rather careless or even fickle in romance. As a result, you are likely to be married more than once or to form some kind of secret alliance or affair with someone who isn't quite good enough for you. If there is a square or opposition aspect to Venus from other planets, you'll have a difficult time acquiring money—or you may lose money in a swindle, fraud or deception which you might cause yourself. Yet you are basically kindhearted and deeply sympathetic, with a tendency to help the disadvantaged and downtrodden—even if it means assisting by volunteer work in some sort of institution or hospital. You are psychic, sensitive, idealistic and highly emotional. Anywhere there is suffering or injustice, you are likely to volunteer assistance. Although you may not be lucky in love, you accept your lot in life with resignation and gain what pleasure you can from secret affairs.

TO FIND THE POSITION OF VENUS AT YOUR BIRTH

1890	Date	Zodiacal Sign
Jan.	1	Sagittarius
Jan.	2 to Jan. 25	Capricorn
Jan.	26 to Feb. 18	Aquarius
Feb.	19 to Mar. 14	Pisces
Mar.	15 to Apr. 7	Aries
Apr.	8 to May 1	Taurus
May	2 to May 26	Gemini
May	27 to June 20	Cancer
June	21 to July 15	Leo
July	16 to Aug. 10	Virgo
Aug.	11 to Sept. 6	Libra
Sept.	7 to Oct. 7	Scorpio
Oct.	8 to Dec. 31	Sagittarius

1891		
Jan.	1 to Feb. 5	Sagittarius
Feb.	6 to Mar. 5	Capricorn
Mar.	6 to Apr. 1	Aquarius
Apr.	2 to Apr. 26	Pisces
Apr.	27 to May 22	Aries
May	23 to June 16	Taurus
June	17 to July 10	Gemini
July	11 to Aug. 4	Cancer
Aug.	5 to Aug. 28	Leo
Aug.	29 to Sept. 21	Virgo
Sept.	22 to Oct. 15	Libra
Oct.	16 to Nov. 8	Scorpio
Nov.	9 to Dec. 2	Sagittarius
Dec.	3 to Dec. 26	Capricorn
Dec.	27 to Dec. 31	Aquarius

1892		
Jan.	1 to Jan. 20	Aquarius
Jan.	21 to Feb. 13	Pisces
Feb.	14 to Mar. 9	Aries
Mar.	10 to Apr. 4	Taurus
Apr.	5 to May 4	Gemini
May	5 to Sept. 7	Cancer
Sept.	8 to Oct. 7	Leo
Oct.	8 to Nov. 2	Virgo
Nov.	3 to Nov. 27	Libra
Nov.	28 to Dec. 22	Scorpio
Dec.	23 to Dec. 31	Sagittarius

1893	Date	Zodiacal Sign
Jan.	1 to Jan. 15	Sagittarius
Jan.	16 to Feb. 8	Capricorn
Feb.	9 to Mar. 4	Aquarius
Mar.	5 to Mar. 28	Pisces
Mar.	29 to Apr. 22	Aries
Apr.	23 to May 16	Taurus
May	17 to June 9	Gemini
June	10 to July 4	Cancer
July	5 to July 28	Leo
July	29 to Aug. 22	Virgo
Aug.	23 to Sept. 16	Libra
Sept.	17 to Oct. 11	Scorpio
Oct.	12 to Nov. 6	Sagittarius
Nov.	7 to Dec. 4	Capricorn
Dec.	5 to Dec. 31	Aquarius

1894		
Jan.	1 to Jan. 8	Aquarius
Jan.	9 to Feb. 12	Pisces
Feb.	13 to Apr. 2	Aquarius
Apr.	3 to May 5	Pisces
May	6 to June 2	Aries
June	3 to June 29	Taurus
June	30 to July 24	Gemini
July	25 to Aug. 18	Cancer
Aug.	19 to Sept. 12	Leo
Sept.	13 to Oct. 6	Virgo
Oct.	7 to Oct. 30	Libra
Oct.	31 to Nov. 23	Scorpio
Nov.	24 to Dec. 17	Sagittarius
Dec.	18 to Dec. 31	Capricorn

1895		
Jan.	1 to Jan. 10	Capricorn
Jan.	11 to Feb. 3	Aquarius
Feb.	4 to Feb. 27	Pisces
Feb.	28 to Mar. 23	Aries
Mar.	24 to Apr. 17	Taurus
Apr.	18 to May 12	Gemini
May	13 to June 7	Cancer
June	8 to July 6	Leo
July	7 to Aug. 13	Virgo
Aug.	14 to Sept. 12	Libra

1895	Date	Zodiacal Sign
Sept. 13 to Nov. 6		Virgo
Nov. 7 to Dec. 8		Libra
Dec. 9 to Dec. 31		Scorpio

1896	Date	Zodiacal Sign
Sept. 30 to Oct. 24		Scorpio
Oct. 25 to Nov. 18		Sagittarius
Nov. 19 to Dec. 13		Capricorn
Dec. 14 to Dec. 31		Aquarius

1896

Date		Zodiacal Sign
Jan. 1 to Jan. 3		Scorpio
Jan. 4 to Jan. 29		Sagittarius
Jan. 30 to Feb. 23		Capricorn
Feb. 24 to Mar. 18		Aquarius
Mar. 19 to Apr. 12		Pisces
Apr. 13 to May 6		Aries
May 7 to May 31		Taurus
June 1 to June 24		Gemini
June 25 to July 19		Cancer
July 20 to Aug. 13		Leo
Aug. 14 to Sept. 5		Virgo
Sept. 6 to Sept. 29		Libra

1897

Date		Zodiacal Sign
Jan. 1 to Jan. 6		Aquarius
Jan. 7 to Feb. 1		Pisces
Feb. 2 to Mar. 4		Aries
Mar. 5 to July 7		Taurus
July 8 to Aug. 5		Gemini
Aug. 6 to Aug. 31		Cancer
Sept. 1 to Sept. 26		Leo
Sept. 27 to Oct. 20		Virgo
Oct. 21 to Nov. 13		Libra
Nov. 14 to Dec. 7		Scorpio
Dec. 8 to Dec. 31		Sagittarius

1898 Use table for *1890* and subtract one day from the given dates. In other words, Venus entered Capricorn on January 1 instead of January 2.
1899 Use list for *1891* and subtract one day from the given dates.
1900 Use list for *1892* and subtract one day from the given dates.
1901 Use list for *1893* and subtract one day from the given dates.
1902 Use list for *1894* and subtract one day from the given dates.
1903 Use list for *1895* and subtract one day from the given dates.
1904 Use list for *1896* and subtract one day from the given dates.
1905 Use list for *1897* and subtract one day from the given dates.
1906 Use list for *1890*.
1907 Use list for *1891*.
1908 Use list for *1892*.
1909 Use list for *1893*.
1910 Use list for *1894*.
1911 Use list for *1895*.
1912 Use list for *1896*.
1913 Use list for *1897*.
1914 Use list for *1890* and subtract one day from the given dates.
1915 Use list for *1891* and subtract one day from the given dates.
1916 Use list for *1892* and subtract one day from the given dates.
1917 Use list for *1893* and subtract one day from the given dates.
1918 Use list for *1894* and subtract one day from the given dates.
1919 Use list for *1895* and subtract one day from the given dates.
1920 Use list for *1896* and subtract one day from the given dates.
1921 Use list for *1897* and subtract one day from the given dates.
1922 Use list for *1890* and subtract one day from the given dates.
1923 Use list for *1891* and subtract one day from the given dates.
1924 Use list for *1892* and subtract one day from the given dates.
1925 Use list for *1893* and subtract one day from the given dates.
1926 Use list for *1894* and subtract one day from the given dates.
1927 Use list for *1895* and subtract one day from the given dates.

1928 Use list for *1896* and subtract one day from the given dates.
1929 Use list for *1897* and subtract one day from the given dates.
1930 Use list for *1890* and subtract two days from the given dates.
1931 Use list for *1891* and subtract two days from the given dates.
1932 Use list for *1892* and subtract two days from the given dates.
1933 Use list for *1893* and subtract two days from the given dates.
1934 Use list for *1894* and subtract two days from the given dates.
1935 Use list for *1895* and subtract two days from the given dates.
1936 Use list for *1896* and subtract two days from the given dates.
1937 Use list for *1897* and subtract two days from the given dates.
1938 Use list for *1890* and subtract three days from the given dates.
1939 Use list for *1891* and subtract three days from the given dates.
1940 Use list for *1892* and subtract three days from the given dates.
1941 Use list for *1893* and subtract three days from the given dates.
1942 Use list for *1894* and subtract three days from the given dates.
1943 Use list for *1895* and subtract three days from the given dates.
1944 Use list for *1896* and subtract three days from the given dates.
1945 Use list for *1897* and subtract three days from the given dates.
1946 Use list for *1890* and subtract three days from the given dates.
1947 Use list for *1891* and subtract three days from the given dates.
1948 Use list for *1892* and subtract three days from the given dates.
1949 Use list for *1893* and subtract three days from the given dates.
1950 Use list for *1894* and subtract three days from the given dates.
1951 Use list for *1895* and subtract three days from the given dates.
1952 Use list for *1896* and subtract three days from the given dates.
1953 Use list for *1897* and subtract three days from the given dates.
1954 Use list for *1890* and subtract four days from the given dates.
1955 Use list for *1891* and subtract four days from the given dates.
1956 Use list for *1892* and subtract four days from the given dates.
1957 Use list for *1893* and subtract four days from the given dates.
1958 Use list for *1894* and subtract four days from the given dates.
1959 Use list for *1895* and subtract four days from the given dates.
1960 Use list for *1896* and subtract four days from the given dates.
1961 Use list for *1897* and subtract four days from the given dates.
1962 Use list for *1890* and subtract four days from the given dates.
1963 Use list for *1891* and subtract four days from the given dates.
1964 Use list for *1892* and subtract four days from the given dates.
1965 Use list for *1893* and subtract four days from the given dates.
1966 Use list for *1894* and subtract four days from the given dates.
1967 Use list for *1895* and subtract four days from the given dates.
1968 Use list for *1896* and subtract four days from the given dates.
1969 Use list for *1897* and subtract four days from the given dates.
1970 Use list for *1890* and subtract five days from the given dates.

9

The Influence of Mars

The Red Planet is probably the source of more speculation among Terrestrial scientists than any other Solarian world. It is the first post-lunar body on which our Apollo spaceships are scheduled to land. Its two mysterious "moons," Phobos and Diemos, are believed by many of our finest astronomers and planetary physicists—including the greatest living cosmologist, Dr. Fred Hoyle of Cambridge, as well as Russia's illustrious planetary physicist, Dr. I. S. Shklovsky—to be artificial "space cities."* Probably the most arresting fact about these two "steeds" of Mars is that *ancient* astrologers knew of their existence, sizes, speeds and altitude from the Red Planet. In fact, modern astronomers gave them their ancient names.

In astrology, Mars symbolizes energy, action, heat, aggression and power. Its symbol, used by astronomers and astrologers alike, is a glyph (a symbolic figure) for a shield and a spear (♂). Psychologists and doctors recognize the masculinity of Mars: they use the *same* symbol to denote the male—and Venus' symbol (♀) to denote the female.

Mars is associated with and rules two Signs, Aries and Scorpio. Since the discovery of Pluto, however, some astrologers have designated "the god of the underworld," Pluto, as the sole ruler of Scorpio.

As with the remarkably accurate early predictions he made about Venus, Dr. Immanuel Velikovsky of *Worlds in Collision* fame was again vindicated by the recently telemetered pictures of the *cratered* Martian surface. In the early 1950s he predicted that Mars would be found to be "more Moon-like

* See *Astrology: The Space-Age Science.*

than Earth-like" due to a tremendous interplanetary exchange
of meteors that occurred several thousand years ago. The
facts proved him out.

The character and influence of this mysterious red world
is viewed in a universally consistent way—even among widely
divergent cultures that supposedly had no contact in ancient
days. In the astrology of the Hebrews, Egyptians, Aztecs,
Chinese, Incas, Polynesians, Indians and Icelandic peoples,
Mars was a planet of war, a fearful red god who caused
earthquakes, volcanic eruptions, rains of meteors and myriad
terrifying phenomena.

Through centuries of refinement in modern astrology,
Mars has been observed to symbolize animal strength and
energy, ambition and desire in the horoscope. He influences
for good or ill, depending on whether other aspects applying
to him are adverse or beneficial. Generally those who are
strongly under the Mars influence are bold, enterprising, positive and have a love of leadership. They are usually excellent
with mechanical devices and highly inventive. They despise
being ordered around; their fierce ambitions often drive them
to the head of any enterprise in which they are engaged.

Mars reaches its perigee (closest possible approach to
Earth) station every 15 years. At this distance of 34 million
miles, the Red Planet shines more brilliantly than Venus,
"the Morning (or Evening) Star."

Force, courage and strength are attributed to Mars; also
the color red, and the iron in our blood. Aries and Mars are
very nearly synonymous, because Mars is the "ruling" planet
of the first Sign.

*To find where Mars was at your birth, consult the table at
the end of this chapter.*

MARS IN ARIES ♂ ♈

Aries is often referred to as "the Sign of self" because it is
the natural first house of the horoscope and indicates the
Ascendant, or physical body; Mars placed here (even if
Aries is *not* your Ascendant) makes you enterprising, independent and likely to look after your own interests first and
foremost. *You* are "Number One." You are also original,
courageous and dynamic as well as egotistical. You tend to
act on the impulse of the moment, and hate any kind of
limitation, bond or restriction that ties you down or prevents
your free-wheeling, enterprising, pioneering nature from fully
expressing itself—either in action or thought. You have a hot

temper, and could often explode into violent wrath. Although you usually simmer down as quickly as you flare up, you may be accident-prone, with a high chance of injury to your head and face. You are positive, blunt, confident and sometimes combative. Yet you are also industrious, enthusiastic, idealistic and liberal. It is difficult for you to conceal your real feelings from others. Your candor can often be a source of embarrassment or trouble. You are a born adventurer with a youthful vitality that lasts into later years. You love active sports and sharply enjoy all kinds of pleasure. Your confidence is so great and your ego so pronounced that you'll carry out your plans not only without help or encouragement, but often against tremendous obstacles and discouragement.

MARS IN TAURUS ♂ ♉

You're going to acquire a substantial amount of money and worldly goods, but not without effort. You drive steadily and faithfully toward your goals, usually the acquisition of money and the physical comforts of life, to which you may add "love." If Mars is well-aspected here (i.e. if you have planets in the earth or water Signs), you'll *handle* great sums of money, and probably *inherit* a large amount of your own as well. You are persistent, tactful, diplomatic, confident and determined to achieve your personal ambitions. You have a good mind, organizational ability, and are far-sighted enough to anticipate the outcome of the forces you manage to set on a certain course. You will probably gain substantially through your job or profession, and enjoy excellent earning power; but you're just as likely to be a free spender in pursuit of the things you enjoy. You have an almost magical ability to carry your ideas and plans into actual materialization; you can create almost anything you visualize. But if there are several adverse aspects to your Mars in Taurus (i.e. if you have many planets in fire or air Signs), you are inclined to have fits of temper and depression caused by sudden losses of money and business reversals. During adverse periods you are almost literally as mad as a bull— irritable, rash and violent. No doubt you'll marry, but it may not be the bed of roses you had anticipated.

MARS IN GEMINI ♂ ♊

You are very active, mentally restless and inclined to try changing situations to suit yourself. You probably have a high degree of mechanical aptitude and inventiveness. You are both practical and ingenious, but probably like action for its own sake. If the aspects to and from Mars are good, you might become an excellent lawyer, writer, lecturer and/or teacher. This position of Mars makes you agile, both mentally and physically. You have a strong desire to excel in education, and could become a good debater because of your blunt, forceful and aggressive mental attitudes. Your keen perception and insight are a result of your sharp mind, but you need to learn the value of concentration. If badly aspected by other planets (in the water or earth Signs), Mars in Gemini can make you extremely indecisive and often accident-prone, with the likelihood of injuring or breaking your shoulder, arms or hands. Nervousness causing excessive smoking may result in pain in your lungs. Generally speaking, the adverse aspects to Mars cause fighting and ill-will or separation from your brothers, sisters and relatives, trouble with neighbors and difficulty in writing, travel and education. Otherwise you are extremely practical, incisive and quick to make proper assessment of conditions and to arrive at correct conclusions.

MARS IN CANCER ♂ ♋

Chances are you'll have to wear glasses at some time in your life—or else you may develop some kind of eye trouble. You feel it necessary to *fight* for security; you are torn between your loyalty to home and hearth, your respect for authority, on one hand, and your rebellious urge for complete freedom and independence on the other. You are too changeable, and need to develop a more solid foundation for your enterprising spirit. This probably manifested itself early in life through trouble or open clashes with your mother. You may have been separated from her, either through estrangement or her early death. You can profit greatly from your independent, original ventures which may involve physical prowess, long trips and voyages. If Mars is adversely aspected, that is, by planets in fire Signs and air Signs, you may have an unhappy home and marriage relationship, with many changes of residence. You are likely to develop stomach ulcers or other gastric disorders unless you learn to cultivate a calmer, more harmonious outlook. Developing a sense of humor can be enormously helpful for your future happiness. Be especially careful when buying a home because it may be in danger of natural catastrophe, especially by water. Generally, you are hard-working, ambitious, courageous, sometimes rash, and likely to hold grudges for a long time after someone offends you. Try not to be so irritable and touchy; above all, avoid those sudden temperamental outbursts. You have a lot going for you.

MARS IN LEO ♂ ♌

Mars here tends to enhance your love of power, sense of grandeur and ego. You are strongly attracted to dangerous or strenuous sports, and adventures in tropical climates. You are forceful, dynamic and have enormous creative energy, if directed in the right channels. No doubt you have above average muscular strength, and a strong heart. Although your vitality is high, you may often run the danger of accidents, cuts, burns and fevers. This is generally a result of your love of hazardous work or play. You are fully able to gain the trust and confidence of superiors and will probably reach a position of authority, responsibility, trust or management. You rush into romantic situations with no thought of the outcome. You let your emotions run wild in love affairs, and are usually ardent, warmhearted and passionate. Although you can be generous, reasonable, liberal and enthusiastic, with a keen sense of justice, you also like to present overwhelming arguments, and could be regarded as defiant, too aggressive and forceful for your own good. Generally speaking, you are friendly and outgoing, affectionate and sociable. Your chief gains in life will be through the good offices of high-placed executives and businessmen. Yet you are also gifted with a good sense of timing and are a keen judge of proper investment and speculation. In short, you are a born —and often lucky—gambler. Government appointments and public affairs are excellent areas for your forceful, enterprising talents. You tend to interpret all events solely in terms of yourself, or as they affect you. Although you are magnetic and attractive to some, remember that others may be put off by your inordinate force and passion.

MARS IN VIRGO ♂ ♍

Your path to basic security lies in your ability to relegate your activities to a systematized formula. You desire your fair amount of prestige, fame and power, but Mars in Virgo often places serious obstacles in your way. You may face many reversals, setbacks and failures of an unusual or peculiar nature before ultimate success crowns your efforts. No doubt you have realized or will realize many moderately successful results from your bold and original scientific innovations or inventions. This success could be amplified if your efforts were directed toward orthodox business, foreign trade or ordinary commerce. You possess excellent reserve strength and energy, and although you quietly pursue your own methods and means of accomplishment, you are strong-willed, shrewd, acquisitive, mentally active and diplomatic. If in someone else's employ, you rarely display your innate ingenuity, but always make of yourself a valuable, almost indispensible employee. You are a fast thinker, discriminating and tactful, but liable to bring about your own illnesses through overwork. You tend to be very careful in matters of diet and hygiene, but could, nevertheless, suffer occasionally from digestive troubles. You are likely to become deeply involved with workers, service employees and/or labor in general. There is some danger of quarreling with friends, and a resulting estrangement from them. This may result from violently opposing viewpoints in labor disputes. Whenever transiting Mars is badly aspected in your chart, you tend to become grouchy, irritable, stubborn, rash, grudge-holding and secretive. During these times, play it cool and avoid overworking yourself in order to avoid illness, the loss of friends, co-workers and/or subordinates.

MARS IN LIBRA ♂ ♎

You possess powerful social urges, and want to make a favorable impression on the public. Usually you do, and it could easily be one of youthful vitality and creative power. You enjoy and need people and bask in popularity and a gay social life. Members of the opposite sex are usually a source of great attraction to you and you become involved in one romance after another, often to your own detriment. You are enterprising, like to speculate, and enjoy refined pleasures and amusements. Your ability to study and observe life is highly developed. Your inner vision is clear, your intuition is keen and your nature generally gentle. Yet you often display a surprisingly brittle temper. This is one of the positions from which Mars bestows a strong tendency for passionate and impulsive love affairs. You are not only powerfully attracted to, but also influenced by, the opposite sex. You will be disappointed in love more than once, and one of these emotional adversities may delay your marriage. Even so, there is good testimony here of an early marriage, although

perhaps much strife, argument and unhappiness may surround this partnership. You are likely to have many friends
in professional fields: lawyers, clergy, scientists, businessmen, artists and musicians. You can expect strong resistance
in business from jealous competitors, but happily will survive intact from each of these clashes. Both openly and
secretly, you will encounter envy, bitter criticism and keen
competition from others to try to surpass your successes.
Either liberally or formally, you will eventually acquire a
good education—usually later in life. This increased knowledge and experience will enhance your judgment and foresight. You are almost certain to produce children with highly
advanced intellectual abilities. You have a great need for
social approbation—and will probably earn it.

MARS IN SCORPIO ♂ ♏

The motto you live by may well be: "Get results—or else!"
You are hard-driving, self-starting, vigorous, determined, positive and tough. You'll drive yourself longer and harder than
anyone who works for you, yet you are not an easy boss.
You are magnetic, rough, and you wear well once your confidence is gained, but you devote too little time to relaxation
or pleasure Whatever you do, it is done with your own peculiar brand of intensity. You possess a great deal of creative
power, but have strong passions and need to exercise self-
control and to discipline your volcanic emotions. Your attraction for dangerous jobs could result in your entrance
into hazardous conditions that cause accidents—or you may
meet an unexpectedly violent death. You love a mystery and
like to dig beneath the surface of things until you find satisfactory answers. Moreover, this intense curiosity does not
always follow orthodox lines; you are likely to become
involved in mystical religions, psychical research and kindred
subjects. You'll profit from long trips and through marriage
as well as association with the opposite sex. *Whatever* project
you undertake, it is done with purposeful action and intensity. Your immediate and direct objective is always to
obtain concrete results. No shillyshallying. You are hard-
working, practical and know exactly how to accomplish your
aims. To others you may seem to be something of a cold
fish, caring little or nothing for the feelings of people in
general—secretive, sarcastic, selfish and vengeful. Unless
other aspects in your chart such as Venus, Jupiter or the
Sun in the earth or water Signs offset this, there is probably
a lot of truth to that. You are good with tools and could

profit in any profession where cold courage is a requisite. Would make an excellent surgeon, oil driller, deep sea diver, fighter or body contact sportsman. You possess vital magnetism.

MARS IN SAGITTARIUS ♂ ♐

You have a carefree, courageous, independent and original outlook, with a daring "don't-give-a-damn" attitude for the opinions of those in powerful positions. You love all kinds of activity for its own sake—both physical and mental. You are gifted with tremendous foresight amounting almost to prophetic ability. You are fiercely independent and idealistic, and would rather fly than crawl, yet you are always being faced with the fearful attitude of the conservative-minded; that everything must be learned by ritual and rote—starting at the very bottom. You don't quite see it this way and are not afraid to say so. You love travel and high adventure, yet you want to influence the major trends of your generation (and may very well succeed!). Generally, you are impulsive; you tend to act rashly or say whatever pops into your mind. Because you're able to see through pomp and phoniness, and are usually correct in your judgments, this makes your quarry uneasy and angry. You are, however, candid, liberal, ambitious and generous. You are also inventive, ingenious and fond of outdoor sports, all forms of athletics and strenuous exercise. You probably have a keen admiration for military and naval tactics as well as for the spartan life of the professional warrior. Your active, inventive mentality keenly enjoys good-natured debates and arguments among friends. You'll profit through inheritance, friends and/or marriage. But the indications are that more than one marriage is in store for you. Under adverse influences such as Saturn in Pisces, Cancer, Scorpio or any of the three earth Signs, Mars in Sagittarius brings trouble through orthodox religious leaders and groups, unhappy relationships with brothers, sisters, neighbors and relatives and danger in your method of livelihood. Learn to curb your tendency for candid, skeptical, unorthodox or iconoclastic appraisals of established values.

MARS IN CAPRICORN ♂ ♑

You work long and hard, often shoulder responsibilities which do not rightfully belong to you, yet you assume these burdens with patience, ambition and good will. You are a slow but intuitive learner and retain whatever knowledge you gain. You are destined to achieve recognition and honors for your faithful devotion and hard work. Early in your life you probably had some kind of affair with someone considerably older or of an inferior position or station in life—or both. Basically, you are very courageous, and highly stimulated by bold adventure. You are confident and self-reliant, perhaps too much so. Scorning proper precautions may result in accidents or injury, particularly to your knees or lower legs. You are best suited for success in public life due to your organizing, executive ability; you want plenty of space for the breadth of the plans you have in mind. You are hard-working, acquisitive, enterprising and so ambitious that you're bound to succeed in whatever you undertake. Naturally, these characteristics will attract influential and powerful people who will give you a boost. You'll probably travel a lot, deal in foreign trade and profit through science and commerce. In order to acquire the wealth you desire, you do not hesitate to risk your capital in speculation. Whether you engineer it or not, one of the most important turning points in your life will be your marriage. It will have a profound effect on your social standing and future stability. Mars in Capricorn is not especially auspicious for your relationship with one parent—probably your father. This could mean disagreement and separation—or the divorce of your parents, or the early death of one of them. If Mars is really heavily afflicted by adverse aspects from other planets at your birth, you may experience pretty much the opposite of most of the foregoing promises. In any event, your courage, persistence and ambition *are* capable of overcoming great obstacles.

MARS IN AQUARIUS ♂ ♒

Although unorthodox, you seek justice for all and will battle courageously for the rights of minorities. You are a fearless debater and an excellent reasoner. Invariably, you are able to find one rather obscure, unique peg from which to hang your arguments. Although you are altruistic and seek only the betterment of others in the public domain, you have an abrupt, often rash and impulsive way of presenting your ideas. This is because you are sensitive, idealistic and highly impatient with the inability of most people to see things as clearly as you do. You are a scientific, fast-thinking intellectual, often too far ahead of your contemporaries. You are a truly independent and original thinker and planner—enterprising and ambitious. Rarely do you change your attitude

or position, but once this does happen it is a radical, complete and irreversible switch. You are a good lecturer and
debater, convincing and powerful. You are able to marshall
your facts, present crystal-clear arguments and quickly arrive
at your conclusions. Privately you are refined and sincere, a
person who attracts friends through your interest in them
and your solid abilities. Projects for the public good and
welfare constitute areas where you can achieve recognition
and financial success. You are interested in electronics or
electrical machinery (computers and such), and are probably
very original, inventive and intrigued by space programs. You
are attracted to literature, philosophy, science and borderline
sciences. Your able, responsible character makes you a natural executive for a city, state or federal office. Mars in
Aquarius also suits you, as has been indicated, for philan-
thropies and welfare work as well as for a medical or surgical
vocation.

MARS IN PISCES   ♂ ♓

Although you are strongly influenced by others, and often
indecisive, easily depressed and indolent, you are fully capable of much achievement when working quietly and alone.
You've probably experienced an extra share of misfortune
and trouble, which you strive courageously to overcome.
While you will fight valiantly for the rights of others, you
tend to neglect your own right to be free and strong. The
tendency here is to allow yourself to be ruled by your sympathies and emotions. You are often frustrated in your need
for approval and desire for popularity. In ordinary jobs,
particularly those connected with private or public institutions, you can achieve a great deal of success. Mars in Pisces
is an indication of delays in marriage, disappointment in love
affairs and a duality in your affections. You tend to display
excessive emotion or passion while at the same time striving
to achieve harmony and avoid open conflicts. Some dissipation is indicated here, possibly through excessive use of alcohol or super-stimulated emotions. You are bound to
develop friendships with powerful or influential people at
some time in your life, and will (temporarily, at least) receive their help and gain financially from them. You need to
exercise extreme caution in dealing with liquids of any kind;
also with opiates, gas and anesthetics. Water is a potential
danger, either through scalding or drowning. You tend to
waste your time with fruitless dreams and should cultivate
the ability to act on your keen intuition in order to bring

these dreams into reality. You are almost determined to avoid concentrating on one thing at a time. This alone prevents the solid achievement of which you are capable. You are probably plagued by your constantly shifting views, emotions, plans for the future and occupation.

To find where Mars was (by Sign) at the time of your birth, consult the following table, then insert this symbol (♂) in its proper place in the horoscope blank.

TO FIND THE POSITION OF MARS AT YOUR BIRTH

1890	Date	Zodiacal Sign
Jan.	1 to Feb. 28	Scorpio
Feb.	29 to June 16	Sagittarius
June	17 to July 21	Scorpio
July	22 to Sept. 23	Sagittarius
Sept.	24 to Nov. 4	Capricorn
Nov.	5 to Dec. 16	Aquarius
Dec.	17 to Dec. 31	Pisces

1891		
Jan.	1 to Jan. 25	Pisces
Jan.	26 to Mar. 7	Aries
Mar.	8 to Apr. 19	Taurus
Apr.	20 to June 3	Gemini
June	4 to July 19	Cancer
July	20 to Sept. 4	Leo
Sept.	5 to Oct. 21	Virgo
Oct.	22 to Dec. 7	Libra
Dec.	8 to Dec. 31	Scorpio

1892		
Jan.	1 to Feb. 24	Scorpio
Feb.	25 to Mar. 13	Sagittarius
Mar.	14 to May 6	Capricorn
May	7 to Nov. 8	Aquarius
Nov.	9 to Dec. 27	Pisces
Dec.	28 to Dec. 31	Aries

1893		
Jan.	1 to Feb.10	Aries
Feb.	11 to Mar. 28	Taurus
Mar.	29 to May 13	Gemini
May	14 to June 29	Cancer
June	30 to Aug. 15	Leo
Aug.	16 to Oct. 1	Virgo
Oct.	2 to Nov. 16	Libra
Nov.	17 to Dec. 31	Scorpio

1894	Date	Zodiacal Sign
Jan.	1 to Feb. 13	Sagittarius
Feb.	14 to Mar. 27	Capricorn
Mar.	28 to May 9	Aquarius
May	10 to June 22	Pisces
June	23 to Aug. 18	Aries
Aug.	19 to Oct.12	Taurus
Oct.	13 to Dec. 30,	Aries
Dec.	31	Taurus

1895		
Jan.	1 to Mar. 1	Taurus
Mar.	2 to Apr. 21	Gemini
Apr.	22 to June 10	Cancer
June	11 to July 28	Leo
July	29 to Sept. 13	Virgo
Sept.	14 to Oct. 30	Libra
Oct.	31 to Dec. 11	Scorpio
Dec.	12 to Dec. 31	Sagittarius

1896		
Jan.	1 to Jan. 22	Sagittarius
Jan.	23 to Mar. 2	Capricorn
Mar.	3 to Apr. 11	Aquarius
Apr.	12 to May 21	Pisces
May	22 to July 1	Aries
July	2 to Aug. 15	Taurus
Aug.	16 to Dec. 31	Gemini

1897		
Jan.	1 to Mar. 21	Gemini
Mar.	22 to May 17	Cancer
May	18 to July 8	Leo
July	9 to Aug. 25	Virgo
Aug.	26 to Oct. 9	Libra
Oct.	10 to Nov. 21	Scorpio
Nov.	22 to Dec. 31	Sagittarius

1898	Date	Zodiacal Sign
Jan.	1	Sagittarius
Jan.	2 to Feb. 10	Capricorn
Feb.	11 to Mar. 20	Aquarius
Mar.	21 to Apr. 28	Pisces
Apr.	29 to June 6	Aries
June	7 to July 18	Taurus
July	19 to Sept. 2	Gemini
Sept.	3 to Oct. 30	Cancer
Oct.	31 to Dec. 31	Leo

1899		
Jan.	1 to Jan. 15	Leo
Jan.	16 to Apr. 14	Cancer
Apr.	15 to June 15	Leo
June	16 to Aug. 5	Virgo
Aug.	6 to Sept. 20	Libra
Sept.	21 to Nov. 2	Scorpio
Nov.	3 to Dec. 13	Sagittarius
Dec.	14 to Dec. 31	Capricorn

1900		
Jan.	1 to Feb. 28	Aquarius
Mar.	1 to Apr. 7	Pisces
Apr.	8 to May 16	Aries
May	17 to June 26	Taurus
June	27 to Aug. 9	Gemini
Aug.	10 to Sept. 26	Cancer
Sept.	27 to Nov. 22	Leo
Nov.	23 to Dec. 31	Virgo

1901		
Jan.	1 to Mar. 1	Virgo
Mar.	2 to May 10	Leo
May	11 to July 13	Virgo
July	14 to Aug. 31	Libra
Sept.	1 to Oct. 14	Scorpio
Oct.	15 to Nov. 23	Sagittarius
Nov.	24 to Dec. 31	Capricorn

1902		
Jan.	1	Capricorn
Jan.	2 to Feb. 8	Aquarius

1902	Date	Zodiacal Sign
Feb.	9 to Mar. 17	Pisces
Mar.	18 to Apr. 26	Aries
Apr.	27 to June 6	Taurus
June	7 to July 20	Gemini
July	21 to Sept. 4	Cancer
Sept.	5 to Oct. 23	Leo
Oct.	24 to Dec. 19	Virgo
Dec.	20 to Dec. 31	Libra

1903		
Jan.	1 to Apr. 19	Libra
Apr.	20 to May 30	Virgo
May	31 to Aug. 6	Libra
Aug.	7 to Sept. 22	Scorpio
Sept.	23 to Nov. 2	Sagittarius
Nov.	3 to Dec. 11	Capricorn
Dec.	12 to Dec. 31	Aquarius

1904		
Jan.	1 to Jan. 19	Aquarius
Jan.	20 to Feb. 26	Pisces
Feb.	27 to Apr. 6	Aries
Apr.	7 to May 17	Taurus
May	18 to June 30	Gemini
July	1 to Aug. 14	Cancer
Aug.	15 to Oct. 1	Leo
Oct.	2 to Nov. 19	Virgo
Nov.	20 to Dec. 31	Libra

1905		
Jan.	1 to Jan. 13	Libra
Jan.	14 to Aug. 21	Scorpio
Aug.	22 to Oct. 7	Sagittarius
Oct.	8 to Nov. 17	Capricorn
Nov.	18 to Dec. 27	Aquarius
Dec.	28 to Dec. 31	Pisces

1906		
Jan.	1 to Feb. 4	Pisces
Feb.	5 to Mar. 16	Aries
Mar.	17 to Apr. 28	Taurus
Apr.	29 to June 11	Gemini

1906	Date	Zodiacal Sign
June	12 to July 27	Cancer
July	28 to Sept. 12	Leo
Sept.	13 to Oct.29	Virgo
Oct.	30 to Dec. 16	Libra
Dec.	17 to Dec. 31	Scorpio

1907		
Jan.	1 to Feb. 4	Scorpio
Feb.	5 to Apr. 1	Sagittarius
Apr.	2 to Oct. 13	Capricorn
Oct.	14 to Nov. 28	Aquarius
Nov.	29 to Dec. 31	Pisces

1908		
Jan.	1 to Jan. 10	Pisces
Jan.	11 to Feb. 22	Aries
Feb.	23 to Apr. 6	Taurus
Apr.	7 to May 22	Gemini
May	23 to July 7	Cancer
July	8 to Aug. 23	Leo
Aug.	24 to Oct. 9	Virgo
Oct.	10 to Nov. 25	Libra
Nov.	26 to Dec. 31	Scorpio

1909		
Jan.	1 to Jan. 9	Scorpio
Jan.	10 to Feb. 23	Sagittarius
Feb.	24 to Apr. 9	Capricorn
Apr.	10 to May 25	Aquarius
May	26 to July 20	Pisces
July	21 to Sept. 26	Aries
Sept.	27 to Nov. 20	Pisces
Nov.	21 to Dec. 31	Aries

1910		
Jan.	1 to Feb. 22	Aries
Feb.	23 to Mar. 13	Taurus
Mar.	14 to May 1	Gemini
May	2 to June 18	Cancer
June	19 to Aug. 5	Leo
Aug.	6 to Sept. 21	Virgo
Sept.	22 to Nov. 6	Libra

1910	Date	Zodiacal Sign
Nov.	7 to Dec. 19	Scorpio
Dec.	20 to Dec. 31	Sagittarius

1911		
Jan.	1 to Jan. 31	Sagittarius
Feb.	1 to Mar. 13	Capricorn
Mar.	14 to Apr. 22	Aquarius
Apr.	23 to June 2	Pisces
June	3 to July 15	Aries
July	16 to Sept. 5	Taurus
Sept.	6 to Nov. 29	Gemini
Nov.	30 to Dec. 31	Taurus

1912		
Jan.	1 to Jan. 30	Taurus
Jan.	31 to Apr. 4	Gemini
Apr.	5 to May 27	Cancer
May	28 to July 16	Leo
July	17 to Sept. 2	Virgo
Sept.	3 to Oct. 17	Libra
Oct.	18 to Nov. 29	Scorpio
Nov.	30 to Dec. 31	Sagittarius

1913		
Jan.	1 to Jan. 10	Sagittarius
Jan.	11 to Feb. 18	Capricorn
Feb.	19 to Mar. 29	Aquarius
Mar.	30 to May 7	Pisces
May	8 to June 16	Aries
June	17 to July 28	Taurus
July	29 to Sept. 15	Gemini
Sept.	16 to Dec. 31	Cancer

1914		
Jan.	1 to May 1	Cancer
May	2 to June 25	Leo
June	26 to Aug. 14	Virgo
Aug.	15 to Sept. 28.	Libra
Sept.	29 to Nov. 10	Scorpio
Nov.	11 to Dec. 21	Sagittarius
Dec.	22 to Dec. 31	Capricorn

1915	Date	Zodiacal Sign
Jan.	1 to Jan. 29	Capricorn
Jan.	30 to Mar. 9	Aquarius
Mar.	10 to Apr. 16	Pisces
Apr.	17 to May 25	Aries
May	26 to July 5	Taurus
July	6 to Aug. 18	Gemini
Aug.	19 to Oct. 7	Cancer
Oct.	8 to Dec. 31	Leo

1916

Jan.	1 to May 28	Leo
May	29 to July 22	Virgo
July	23 to Sept. 8	Libra
Sept.	9 to Oct. 21	Scorpio
Oct.	22 to Dec. 1	Sagittarius
Dec.	2 to Dec. 31	Capricorn

1917

Jan.	1 to Jan. 9	Capricorn
Jan.	10 to Feb. 16	Aquarius
Feb.	17 to Mar. 26	Pisces
Mar.	27 to May 4	Aries
May	5 to June 14	Taurus
June	15 to July 27	Gemini
July	28 to Sept. 11	Cancer
Sept.	12 to Nov. 1	Leo
Nov.	2 to Dec. 31	Virgo

1918

Jan.	1 to Jan. 10	Virgo
Jan.	11 to Feb. 25	Libra
Feb.	26 to June 23	Virgo
June	24 to Aug. 16	Libra
Aug.	17 to Sept. 30	Scorpio
Oct.	1 to Nov. 10	Sagittarius
Nov.	11 to Dec. 19	Capricorn
Dec.	20 to Dec. 31	Aquarius

1919

Jan.	1 to Jan. 26	Aquarius
Jan.	27 to Mar. 6	Pisces
Mar.	7 to Apr. 14	Aries

1919	Date	Zodiacal Sign
Apr.	15 to May 25	Taurus
May	26 to July 8	Gemini
July	9 to Aug. 22	Cancer
Aug.	23 to Oct. 9	Leo
Oct.	10 to Nov. 29	Virgo
Nov.	30 to Dec. 31	Libra

1920

Jan.	1 to Jan. 31	Libra
Feb.	1 to Apr. 23	Scorpio
Apr.	24 to July 10	Libra
July	11 to Sept. 4	Scorpio
Sept.	5 to Oct. 18	Sagittarius
Oct.	19 to Nov. 27	Capricorn
Nov.	28 to Dec. 31	Aquarius

1921

Jan.	1 to Jan. 4	Aquarius
Jan.	5 to Feb. 12	Pisces
Feb.	13 to Mar. 24	Aries
Mar.	25 to May 5	Taurus
May	6 to June 10	Gemini
June	20 to Aug. 2	Cancer
Aug.	3 to Sept. 18	Leo
Sept.	19 to Nov. 6	Virgo
Nov.	7 to Dec. 25	Libra
Dec.	26 to Dec. 31	Scorpio

1922

Jan.	1 to Feb. 18	Scorpio
Feb.	19 to Sept. 13	Sagittarius
Sept.	14 to Oct. 30	Capricorn
Oct.	31 to Dec. 11	Aquarius
Dec.	12 to Dec. 31	Pisces

1923

Jan.	1 to Jan. 20	Pisces
Jan.	21 to Mar. 3	Aries
Mar.	4 to Apr. 15	Taurus
Apr.	16 to May 30	Gemini
May	31 to July 15	Cancer
July	16 to Aug. 31	Leo

1923	Date	Zodiacal Sign
Sept.	1 to Oct. 17	Virgo
Oct.	18 to Dec. 3	Libra
Dec.	4 to Dec. 31	Scorpio

1924

Jan.	1 to Feb. 19	Scorpio
Feb.	20 to Mar. 6	Sagittarius
Mar.	7 to Apr. 24	Capricorn
Apr.	25 to June 24	Aquarius
June	25 to Aug. 24	Pisces
Aug.	25 to Oct. 19	Aquarius
Oct.	20 to Dec. 18	Pisces
Dec.	19 to Dec. 31	Aries

1925

Jan.	1 to Feb. 4	Aries
Feb.	5 to Mar. 23	Taurus
Mar.	24 to May 9	Gemini
May	10 to June 25	Cancer
June	26 to Aug. 12	Leo
Aug.	13 to Sept. 28	Virgo
Sept.	29 to Nov. 13	Libra
Nov.	14 to Dec. 27	Scorpio
Dec.	28 to Dec. 31	Sagittarius

1926

Jan.	1 to Feb. 8	Sagittarius
Feb.	9 to Mar. 22	Capricorn
Mar.	23 to May 3	Aquarius
May	4 to June 14	Pisces
June	15 to July 31	Aries
Aug.	1 to Dec. 31	Taurus

1927

Jan.	1 to Feb. 21	Taurus
Feb.	22 to Apr. 16	Gemini
Apr.	17 to June 5	Cancer
June	6 to July 24	Leo
July	25 to Sept. 10	Virgo
Sept.	11 to Oct. 25	Libra
Oct.	26 to Dec. 7	Scorpio
Dec.	8 to Dec. 31	Sagittarius

1928	Date	Zodiacal Sign
Jan.	1 to Jan. 18	Sagittarius
Jan.	19 to Feb. 27	Capricorn
Feb.	28 to Apr. 7	Aquarius
Apr.	8 to May 16	Pisces
May	17 to June 25	Aries
June	26 to Aug. 8	Taurus
Aug.	9 to Oct. 2	Gemini
Oct.	3 to Dec. 19	Cancer
Dec.	20 to Dec. 31	Gemini

1929

Jan.	1 to Mar. 10	Gemini
Mar.	11 to May 12	Cancer
May	13 to July 3	Leo
July	4 to Aug. 21	Virgo
Aug.	22 to Oct. 5	Libra
Oct.	6 to Nov. 18	Scorpio
Nov.	19 to Dec. 28	Sagittarius
Dec.	29 to Dec. 31	Capricorn

1930

Jan.	1 to Feb. 6	Capricorn
Feb.	7 to Mar. 16	Aquarius
Mar.	17 to Apr. 24	Pisces
Apr.	25 to June 2	Aries
June	3 to July 14	Taurus
July	15 to Aug. 27	Gemini
Aug.	28 to Oct. 20	Cancer
Oct.	21 to Dec. 31	Leo

1931

Jan.	1 to Feb. 15	Leo
Feb.	16 to Mar. 29	Cancer
Mar.	30 to June 9	Leo
June	10 to July 31	Virgo
Aug.	1 to Sept. 16	Libra
Sept.	17 to Oct. 29	Scorpio
Oct.	30 to Dec. 9	Sagittarius
Dec.	10 to Dec. 31	Capricorn

1932

Jan.	1 to Jan. 17	Capricorn
Jan.	18 to Feb. 24	Aquarius

1932	*Date*	*Zodiacal Sign*
Feb.	25 to Apr. 2	Pisces
Apr.	3 to May 11	Aries
May	12 to June 21	Taurus
June	22 to Aug. 3	Gemini
Aug.	4 to Sept. 19	Cancer
Sept.	20 to Nov. 12	Leo
Nov.	13 to Dec. 31	Virgo

1933

Jan.	1 to July 5	Virgo
July	6 to Aug. 25	Libra
Aug.	26 to Oct. 8	Scorpio
Oct.	9 to Nov. 18	Sagittarius
Nov.	19 to Dec. 27	Capricorn
Dec.	28 to Dec. 31	Aquarius

1934

Jan.	1 to Feb. 3	Aquarius
Feb.	4 to Mar. 13	Pisces
Mar.	14 to Apr. 21	Aries
Apr.	22 to June 1	Taurus
June	2 to July 14	Gemini
July	15 to Aug. 29	Cancer
Aug.	30 to Oct. 17	Leo
Oct.	18 to Dec. 10	Virgo
Dec.	11 to Dec. 31	Libra

1935

Jan.	1 to July 28	Libra
July	29 to Sept. 15	Scorpio
Sept.	16 to Oct. 27	Sagittarius
Oct.	28 to Dec. 6	Capricorn
Dec.	7 to Dec. 31	Aquarius

1936

Jan.	1 to Jan. 13	Aquarius
Jan.	14 to Feb. 21	Pisces
Feb.	22 to Mar. 31	Aries
Apr.	1 to May 12	Taurus
May	13 to June 24	Gemini
June	25 to Aug. 9	Cancer
Aug.	10 to Sept. 25	Leo

1936	*Date*	*Zodiacal Sign*
Sept.	26 to Nov. 13	Virgo
Nov.	14 to Dec. 31	Libra

1937

Jan.	1 to Mar. 12	Scorpio
Mar.	13 to May 13	Sagittarius
May	14 to Aug. 7	Scorpio
Aug.	8 to Sept. 29	Sagittarius
Sept.	30 to Nov. 10	Capricorn
Nov.	11 to Dec. 20	Aquarius
Dec.	21 to Dec. 31	Pisces

1938

Jan.	1 to Jan. 29	Pisces
Jan.	30 to Mar. 11	Aries
Mar.	12 to Apr. 22	Taurus
Apr.	23 to June 6	Gemini
June	7 to July 21	Cancer
July	22 to Sept. 6	Leo
Sept.	7 to Oct. 24	Virgo
Oct.	25 to Dec. 10	Libra
Dec.	11 to Dec. 31	Scorpio

1939

Jan.	1 to Jan. 28	Scorpio
Jan.	29 to Mar. 20	Sagittarius
Mar.	21 to May 23	Capricorn
May	24 to July 20	Aquarius
July	21 to Sept. 23	Capricorn
Sept.	24 to Nov. 18	Aquarius
Nov.	19 to Dec. 31	Pisces

1940

Jan.	1 to Jan. 2	Pisces
Jan.	3 to Feb. 16	Aries
Feb.	17 to Mar. 31	Taurus
Apr.	1 to May 16	Gemini
May	17 to July 2	Cancer
July	3 to Aug. 18	Leo
Aug.	19 to Oct. 4	Virgo
Oct.	5 to Nov. 19	Libra
Nov.	20 to Dec. 31	Scorpio

1941   Date   Zodiacal Sign

Jan. 1 to Jan. 3	Scorpio
Jan. 4 to Feb. 16	Sagittarius
Feb. 17 to Apr. 1	Capricorn
Apr. 2 to May 15	Aquarius
May 16 to July 1	Pisces
July 2 to Dec. 31	Aries

1942

Jan. 1 to Jan. 10	Aries
Jan. 11 to Mar. 6	Taurus
Mar. 7 to Apr. 25	Gemini
Apr. 26 to June 13	Cancer
June 14 to July 31	Leo
Aug. 1 to Sept. 16	Virgo
Sept. 17 to Oct. 31	Libra
Nov. 1 to Dec. 14	Scorpio
Dec. 14 to Dec. 31	Sagittarius

1943

Jan. 1 to Jan. 25	Sagittarius
Jan. 26 to Mar. 7	Capricorn
Mar. 8 to Apr. 16	Aquarius
Apr. 17 to May 26	Pisces
May 27 to June 6	Aries
June 7 to Aug. 22	Taurus
Aug. 23 to Dec. 31	Gemini

1944

Jan. 1 to Mar. 27	Gemini
Mar. 28 to May 21	Cancer
May 22 to July 11	Leo
July 12 to Aug. 28	Virgo
Aug. 29 to Oct. 12	Libra
Oct. 13 to Nov. 24	Scorpio
Nov. 25 to Dec. 31	Sagittarius

1945

Jan. 1 to Jan. 4	Sagittarius
Jan. 5 to Feb. 13	Capricorn
Feb. 14 to Mar. 24	Aquarius
Mar. 25 to May 1	Pisces
May 2 to June 10	Aries

1945   Date   Zodiacal Sign

June 11 to July 22	Taurus
July 23 to Sept. 6	Gemini
Sept. 7 to Nov. 10	Cancer
Nov. 11 to Dec. 25	Leo
Dec. 26 to Dec. 31	Cancer

1946

Jan. 1 to Apr. 21	Cancer
Apr. 22 to June 19	Leo
June 20 to Aug. 8	Virgo
Aug. 9 to Sept. 23	Libra
Sept. 24 to Nov. 5	Scorpio
Nov. 6 to Dec. 16	Sagittarius
Dec. 17 to Dec. 31	Capricorn

1947

Jan. 1 to Jan. 24	Capricorn
Jan. 25 to Mar. 3	Aquarius
Mar. 4 to Apr. 10	Pisces
Apr. 11 to May 20	Aries
May 21 to June 30	Taurus
July 1 to Aug. 12	Gemini
Aug. 13 to Sept. 30	Cancer
Oct. 1 to Nov. 30	Leo
Dec. 1 to Dec. 31	Virgo

1948

Jan. 1 to Feb. 11	Virgo
Feb. 12 to May 17	Leo
May 18 to July 16	Virgo
July 17 to Sept. 2	Libra
Sept. 3 to Oct. 16	Scorpio
Oct. 17 to Nov. 25	Sagittarius
Nov. 26 to Dec. 31	Capricorn

1949

Jan. 1 to Jan. 3	Capricorn
Jan. 4 to Feb. 10	Aquarius
Feb. 11 to Mar. 20	Pisces
Mar. 21 to Apr. 29	Aries
Apr. 30 to June 9	Taurus
June 10 to July 22	Gemini
July 23 to Sept. 6	Cancer

1949	Date	Zodiacal Sign
Sept.	7 to Oct. 26	Leo
Oct.	27 to Dec. 25	Virgo
Dec.	26 to Dec. 31	Libra

1950

Jan.	1 to Mar. 27	Libra
Mar.	28 to June 10	Virgo
June	11 to Aug. 9	Libra
Aug.	10 to Sept. 24	Scorpio
Sept.	25 to Nov. 5	Sagittarius
Nov.	6 to Dec. 14	Capricorn
Dec.	15 to Dec. 31	Aquarius

1951

Jan.	1 to Jan. 21	Aquarius
Jan.	22 to Feb. 28	Pisces
Mar.	1 to Apr. 9	Aries
Apr.	10 to May 20	Taurus
May	21 to July 2	Gemini
July	3 to Aug. 17	Cancer
Aug.	18 to Oct. 3	Leo
Oct.	4 to Nov. 23	Virgo
Nov.	24 to Dec. 31	Libra

1952

Jan.	1 to Jan. 19	Libra
Jan.	20 to Aug. 26	Scorpio
Aug.	27 to Oct. 11	Sagittarius
Oct.	12 to Nov. 20	Capricorn
Nov.	21 to Dec. 29	Aquarius
Dec.	30 to Dec. 31	Pisces

1953

Jan.	1 to Feb. 7	Pisces
Feb.	8 to Mar. 19	Aries
Mar.	20 to Apr. 30	Taurus
May	1 to June 13	Gemini
June	14 to July 28	Cancer
July	29 to Sept. 13	Leo
Sept.	14 to Oct. 31	Virgo
Nov.	1 to Dec. 19	Libra
Dec.	20 to Dec. 31	Scorpio

1954	Date	Zodiacal Sign
Jan.	1 to Feb. 8	Scorpio
Feb.	9 to Apr. 11	Sagittarius
Apr.	12 to July 2	Capricorn
July	3 to Aug. 23	Sagittarius
Aug.	24 to Oct. 20	Capricorn
Oct.	21 to Dec. 3	Aquarius
Dec.	4 to Dec. 31	Pisces

1955

Jan.	1 to Jan. 14	Pisces
Jan.	15 to Feb. 25	Aries
Feb.	26 to Apr. 9	Taurus
Apr.	10 to May 25	Gemini
May	26 to July 10	Cancer
July	11 to Aug. 26	Leo
Aug.	27 to Oct. 12	Virgo
Oct.	13 to Nov. 28	Libra
Nov.	29 to Dec. 31	Scorpio

1956

Jan.	1 to Jan. 13	Scorpio
Jan.	14 to Feb. 27	Sagittarius
Feb.	28 to Apr. 13	Capricorn
Apr.	14 to June 2	Aquarius
June	3 to Dec. 5	Pisces
Dec.	6 to Dec. 31	Aries

1957

Jan.	1 to Feb. 27	Aries
Feb.	28 to Mar. 16	Taurus
Mar.	17 to May 3	Gemini
May	4 to June 20	Cancer
June	21 to Aug. 7	Leo
Aug.	8 to Sept. 23	Virgo
Sept.	24 to Nov. 7	Libra
Nov.	8 to Dec. 22	Scorpio
Dec.	23 to Dec. 31	Sagittarius

1958

Jan.	1 to Feb. 2	Sagittarius
Feb.	3 to Mar. 16	Capricorn
Mar.	17 to Apr. 26	Aquarius

1958 Date	Zodiacal Sign
Apr. 27 to June 6	Pisces
June 7 to July 20	Aries
July 21 to Sept. 20	Taurus
Sept. 21 to Oct. 28	Gemini
Oct. 29 to Dec. 31	Taurus

1959

Jan. 1 to Feb. 9	Taurus
Feb. 10 to Apr. 9	Gemini
Apr. 10 to May 31	Cancer
June 1 to July 19	Leo
July 20 to Sept. 4	Virgo
Sept. 5 to Oct. 20	Libra
Oct. 21 to Dec. 2	Scorpio
Dec. 3 to Dec. 31	Sagittarius

1960

Jan. 1 to Jan. 13	Sagittarius
Jan. 14 to Feb. 22	Capricorn
Feb. 23 to Apr. 1	Aquarius
Apr. 2 to May 10	Pisces
May 11 to June 19	Aries
June 20 to Aug. 1	Taurus
Aug. 2 to Sept. 20	Gemini
Sept. 21 to Dec. 31	Cancer

1961

Jan. 1 to May 5	Cancer
May 6 to June 27	Leo
June 28 to Aug. 16	Virgo
Aug. 17 to Sept. 30	Libra
Oct. 1 to Nov. 12	Scorpio
Nov. 13 to Dec. 23	Sagittarius
Dec. 24 to Dec. 31	Capricorn

1962

Jan. 1 to Jan. 31	Capricorn
Feb. 1 to Mar. 11	Aquarius
Mar. 12 to Apr. 18	Pisces
Apr. 19 to May 27	Aries
May 28 to July 8	Taurus
July 9 to Aug. 21	Gemini

1962 Date	Zodiacal Sign
Aug. 22 to Oct. 10	Cancer
Oct. 11 to Dec. 31	Leo

1963

Jan. 1 to June 2	Leo
June 3 to July 26	Virgo
July 27 to Sept. 11	Libra
Sept. 12 to Oct. 24	Scorpio
Oct. 25 to Dec. 4	Sagittarius
Dec. 5 to Dec. 31	Capricorn

1964

Jan. 1 to Jan. 12	Capricorn
Jan. 13 to Feb. 19	Aquarius
Feb. 20 to Mar. 28	Pisces
Mar. 29 to May 6	Aries
May 7 to June 16	Taurus
June 17 to July 29	Gemini
July 30 to Sept. 14	Cancer
Sept. 15 to Nov. 5	Leo
Nov. 6 to Dec. 31	Virgo

1965

Jan. 1 to June 28	Virgo
June 29 to Aug. 19	Libra
Aug. 20 to Oct. 3	Scorpio
Oct. 4 to Nov. 13	Sagittarius
Nov. 14 to Dec. 22	Capricorn
Dec. 23 to Dec. 31	Aquarius

1966

Jan. 1 to Jan. 29	Aquarius
Jan. 30 to Mar. 8	Pisces
Mar. 9 to Apr. 16	Aries
Apr. 17 to May 27	Taurus
May 28 to July 10	Gemini
July 11 to Aug. 24	Cancer
Aug. 25 to Oct. 11	Leo
Oct. 12 to Dec. 3	Virgo
Dec. 4 to Dec. 31	Libra

1967   Date   Zodiacal Sign

Jan.	1 to Feb. 11	Libra
Feb.	12 to Mar. 31	Scorpio
Apr.	1 to July 18	Libra
July	19 to Sept. 9	Scorpio
Sept.	10 to Oct. 22	Sagittarius
Oct.	23 to Nov. 30	Capricorn
Dec.	1 to Dec. 31	Aquarius

1968

Jan.	1 to Jan. 8	Aquarius
Jan.	9 to Feb. 16	Pisces
Feb.	17 to Mar. 26	Aries
Mar.	27 to May 7	Taurus
May	8 to June 20	Gemini
June	21 to Aug. 4	Cancer
Aug.	5 to Sept. 20	Leo
Sept.	21 to Oct. 8	Virgo
Oct.	9 to Dec. 28	Libra
Dec.	29 to Dec. 31	Scorpio

1969   Date   Zodiacal Sign

Jan.	1 to Feb. 24	Scorpio
Feb.	25 to Sept. 20	Sagittarius
Sept.	21 to Nov. 3	Capricorn
Nov.	4 to Dec. 13	Aquarius
Dec.	14 to Dec. 31	Pisces

1970

Jan.	1 to Jan. 23	Pisces
Jan.	24 to Mar. 6	Aries
Mar.	7 to Apr. 17	Taurus
Apr.	18 to June 1	Gemini
June	2 to July 17	Cancer
July	18 to Sept. 2	Leo
Sept.	3 to Oct. 19	Virgo
Oct.	20 to Dec. 5	Libra
Dec.	6 to Dec. 31	Scorpio

10

The Influence of Jupiter

Jupiter is the fifth planet out from the Sun. It is a colossal-sized world about which little is known by astronomers. Formerly, it was believed that beneath its great banded gaseous atmosphere, an 18,000-mile-thick layer of ice encrusted its surface. It has *recently* been discovered that Jupiter (larger by far than all other planets and moons in the solar system combined!) actually *radiates* about three times as much heat as it *receives* from the Sun. This has raised the question of whether or not Jupiter is a small, cool star rather than a large, hot planet. While the average distance of Mars to the Sun is 141 million miles, Jupiter's mean distance from our star (the Sun) is about 483 million miles . . . a huge empty space exists between Mars and Jupiter. This gap is filled with cosmic rubble and meteoric debris (the asteroid belt) where in all likelihood another planet once orbited. Ancient mythology believed that that planet's name was "Vulcan," a world associated with such explosive violence that its very name has come down to us through the ages, and applies to *volcanoes.*

Jupiter is 120 times larger than the Earth, with an equatorial diameter of 89,329 miles compared to Earth's 8,000. This giant planet orbits the Sun once in about 12 Earth years (11.80 years, to be exact). In spite of its tremendous size, Jupiter makes one complete spin around its axis in 9 hours and 55 minutes compared to Earth's 24 hours. The giant of the solar system may well be the parent of most of the "inner" planets—Mars, "Vulcan" (the asteroid belt), Earth, Venus and Mercury. Jupiter has 12 moons, four of which Galileo discovered, in 1610, when he first trained his telescope on them. The two largest moons, Ganymede and Callisto each are larger than Mercury! Jupiter's atmospheric envelope is multicolored and streaked parallel to its equator. This is caused by the tremendous velocity of its axial spin.

Many large oval spots of various colors (probably gases of different densities in the atmosphere) have been observed from time to time. The most noteworthy is the Great Red Spot which is 8,000 miles wide and 30,000 miles long. It does not follow Jupiter's rotation, but tends to drift irregularly. Astronomers cannot explain it. But if Dr. Immanuel Velikovsky's cataclysmic theories continue to be vindicated at their present rate, the Great Red Spot may well be proved to be the remaining scar resulting from the "comet" Venus being torn from the Jovian atmosphere!

In astrology, Jupiter is called "the greater fortune," and Venus "the lesser fortune." Both planets seem to generate good luck in whatever Sign or house of the horoscope they are found. With only a little practice and experience, you'll notice that you tend to like people whose Sun Sign is the same as the Sign your Jupiter occupies—and vice versa. (By the same token, if Venus in a man's chart is in the same Sign as Mars in a woman's chart, a strong mutual attraction is evident. This is also true for Mars-Moon conjunctions, Venus-Ascendant conjunctions and Sun-Venus conjunctions. The charts at the end of each chapter will generally enable you to determine these harmonious contacts.) "Jovial" is the word to describe Jupiterians (also those with Sagittarius ascending). People with a strong Jupiter influence are compassionate, sociable, optimistic, honest and straightforward. They are dignified, liberal, logical, confident and determined. It is well to remember that you have Jupiter (and every other planet) placed *somewhere* in your chart. Wherever it is, it will usually bring you good luck in those areas governed by that Sign.

Check the end of this chapter for the position of Jupiter at your birth.

JUPITER IN ARIES ♃ ♈

One way or another, you are something of a pioneer, and love to travel and broaden your mind. You tend to be overly confident, brave, and a lover of sports, but *not* usually as a spectator. You are ambitious, but once success is within your grasp you are liable to switch your goal to some other pursuit. You are likely to hold down two jobs or engage in two occupations at once. This position of Jupiter encourages expansiveness and extravagance, which attributes are likely to make you very attractive to others. You are easy to reason with, a generous, honest, idealistic and philosophical person with many influential friends and sincere admirers. You are generally respected and usually fortunate in all your dealings. Anything that heightens your mental powers, or takes you traveling, has a strong appeal for you. You have a natural inclination for philosophy (unorthodox religion), literature and science. You are ambitious, optimistic, progressive and reasonable, fully capable of holding down the most responsible positions, particularly in relation to military matters or those wherein you are able to exercise authority and gain prestige. Insurance, investment and speculation are generally fortunate unless Jupiter is adversely affected by planets in the water and earth Signs. You are also lucky through children, young people, religious associates, law, travel and exporting. Virtually all your success is a result of your own efforts and qualifications—also of your marriage, domestic conditions and social standing.

JUPITER IN TAURUS ♃ ♉

Inasmuch as Jupiter signifies abundance and expansion, and Taurus is the natural house of money, your financial condition could be easy for you—too easy. You enjoy the pleasures of life so much you are apt to spend freely and engage in extravagances beyond your means. Your general tendency is to go overboard in whatever you do: spending money, eating, drinking, partying, etc. The opposite sex is good for you and you may meet many friends therein at church or religious social gatherings. You tend to be philosophical and generous, but your views on religion are fixed and dogmatic. You are generally reserved, peaceful, firm, affectionate and faithful. Although you are something of a bibliophile, and may have a good collection of books on religion, philosophy and travel, you prefer to stay close to home, except when you are forced to travel for education, business or health reasons. You love your home environment for the comfort and ease it affords and do not see any percentage in changing things or moving around a great deal. You tend to overemphasize your ability to provide for others, and may promise a lot more than you're actually able to deliver. You make some good starts, but tend to be rather lackadaisical, easy-

going, without the drive or ability to tie things up as you had
originally planned. Still, you are a great believer in justice
and equality, with a harmonious, affectionate disposition.

JUPITER IN GEMINI ♃ ♊

Although somewhat impractical, you are blessed with a good
sense of humor, a generally gay outlook and a ready flow of
conversation, correspondence and exchange of ideas. You are
compelled to keep in touch with other people, but are likely
to be rather disorganized and to scatter your mental and
nervous energies. You need to develop the power of concentration and learn to stick to one thing at a time. You are
idealistic and inspirational, but often too changeable, restless
and uncertain. Two marriages are indicated here; one of them
may be with a close associate, a neighbor or someone related
to you. However it turns out, you're bound to run into trouble
through your travels (which may be extensive), writing and
relatives—all of which affect your marriage. Jupiter in
Gemini is a born philosopher-communicator; you may graduate from writing to publishing, especially of far-sighted religious subjects, science and invention. If Jupiter is badly
afflicted in your chart (i.e. if Mars or Saturn are in earth or
water Signs), difficulties with your publisher, or publishing,
may result from unpopular or unprofitable ventures. Nevertheless, you are one of the most interesting, sincere and
voluble friends anyone could want.

JUPITER IN CANCER ♃ ♋

You have an interesting, seemingly paradoxical view of life
—one that combines an admixture of intellectual and emotional good will toward all. You are fiercely patriotic and
have a strong attachment to your own home (and home
town) and the love of your mother. Even so, you thoroughly
enjoy long travels, for education and just plain pleasure—
especially near large bodies of water. Yet you always return
to your home base. You like to eat and drink and may have
a tendency to put on extra weight. You enjoy making money
—as well as spending it on those you love. Your generosity,
expansiveness and good will are well known. You are creative, imaginative and curious about the psychic, the occult
and mysterious fields. You enjoy fine culture, art, music and
the standard forms of creative excellence established by the
old masters rather than the *avant-garde*. You enjoy a good

social life, and are known to be kindly, sympathetic, humane and charitable—whether or not your friends happen to be on the same social and economic scale. Jupiter in Cancer indicates a peaceful, happy and honorable demise, either in a distant country or far from where you were born. You are benevolent, good-humored, and likely to acquire a large share of the world's material blessings, which you generously share with your family, whether they deserve it or not. You are proud of your ancestry and loyal to your loved ones.

JUPITER IN LEO   ♃ ♌

You admire power, prestige and grandeur. You are a sincere and ardent lover, high-minded, loyal, courageous and generous. You have little trouble in gaining popularity, and are likely to fall in love with and marry someone who is highly influential—perhaps a celebrity, or someone who leads you into extravagance. You are lucky in love, speculation, and through children. You enjoy a healthy vitality, a strong constitution and the willpower and determination to hold positions of trust and responsibility. You are generally compassionate, good-natured, courteous, broad-minded and noble. You can profit greatly from long trips in association with diplomatic, educational or religious affairs. All forms of finer culture appeal to you; art, music, religion, philosophy and science. You thoroughly enjoy reaping the rewards (and honors) for your efforts. You like being the center of attention and achieving positions of social and professional prominence. You will profit financially from wise investments as well as from speculation. Fortunately, you are blessed with willpower, excellent judgment, foresight and wisdom. With your keen intuition and sense of diplomacy, you could rise in public esteem and hold a prominent government position. Your biggest drawback may be a tendency to "hold court" or expect people to treat you as "visiting royalty." But in love matters your affections are sincere and deep. You will probably be blessed with children, and those who know you will realize that you are not at all pompous in reality.

JUPITER IN VIRGO   ♃ ♍

You have an almost uncanny knack for turning small interests into profitable hobbies. This ability may be a substitute for a normal emotional give-and-take, which your discriminating nature tends to throttle. You *want* to let yourself go—to enjoy the pleasure of children, amusement and speculation, but you prudently tend to look for nonexistent troubles. You tend, too, toward the study of natural laws, particularly where they apply to diet and hygiene. You are probably pro-labor, but employees find it difficult to impose on you. You exercise great care in your choice of friends and acquaintances. Jupiter in the mental Sign of Virgo increases your powers of discrimination, practicality, prudence and discretion. You tend to be intellectually materialistic, with an innate talent for philosophical studies and scientific investigations. You are generally honest, smart, analytical and strongly critical. You need to let down your hair a little, loosen up and become less stiff and formal. Speculation, however, is not your forte. You may be able to dope out the market and invest wisely and moderately, but should avoid any sudden plunge or you're bound to come a cropper. You are lucky with co-workers and employees, fortunate in long-term investments, literature and commercial ventures—and in business generally. You will undoubtedly be promoted into higher economic and social strata than you ever anticipated earlier in life. Your business activities will take you to foreign countries where you may meet your spouse-to-be. This person is somewhat eccentric, possibly not as successful as you, or not your intellectual equal.

JUPITER IN LIBRA ♃ ♎

When well aspected—that is, by other planets in fire and air Signs, Jupiter in Libra is excellent evidence for extremely happy and profitable partnerships; this means an exceptionally good marriage blessed with fine, talented children who will bring you great credit and joy. You possess an extraordinary ability for making friends and for creating peace and harmony from anger and chaos. You have a generous, pleasing personality, one that is obviously sincere, mild, moderate, obliging, and so sociable that you try to please everyone at once. You probably have musical or artistic talent and like all sorts of cultural and intellectual stimulation. You love travel, are highly liberal and understanding, compassionate and charitable. You will enjoy and profit from the theater, places of amusement and speculation in various forms of art and entertainment. You have a hidden "hunger" for public approbation and praise. Your biggest gains will accrue through marriage, partnership, associations and undertakings that hinge on broad popular appeal. Above all else, you are dedicated to the proposition that justice, mercy, peace and harmony should prevail everywhere. (Would that there were millions more like you!)

JUPITER IN SCORPIO ♃ ♏

You like all sorts of secrets, and close association with those you believe to be in a position of power or strong influence. You are a defender of the underdog and liable to cultivate the friendship of highly eccentric occultists—even those who have criminal connections. You are not always aware of this at the outset, but you eventually manage to ferret out professional and personal secrets and are not always above using your information to the detriment of someone else's good name. You can justify or rationalize any of your actions and have enormous pride in facing down challenges and overcoming minor disasters—many of which you create yourself. You are exceptionally fortunate (or intuitive) in choosing the right investments, and you demonstrate your faith by backing small stocks or enterprises that eventually bloom into gigantic corporations which pay large dividends. You manage to take many trips, some of them under the auspices of higher executives, with some of whom you may be involved in secret dealings. You manage to acquire considerable prestige in your field, and among your colleagues, which could lead to a position of power. This serves to strengthen your ambition, perseverance, generosity and ability to undergo considerable hardship and deprivation—if you feel the aim is worthwhile. You have a paradoxical compulsion to range between constructive and destructive acts and thoughts. Generally, you have an active, confident, discriminating and shrewd mind, a love of mystery, mysticism, occultism and weird experiences during your travels. When Jupiter is adversely aspected (i.e. by planets in the air and fire Signs), beware of false friends, unwise speculation and the envy of those in powerful positions. You possess inordinate pride and should be careful about confiding the secrets of others or spending too lavishly the money received from legacies or dividends.

JUPITER IN SAGITTARIUS ♃ ♐

Sagittarius is "ruled" by Jupiter, so this is his natural Sign, wherein Jupiter tends to bestow good fortune and success in most of your undertakings. You have a sharp, intuitive mind, a generally happy and expansive spirit and a love of higher education, although your own may be somewhat less formal owing to your dislike of hidebound, formalized procedures. Somehow you feel that sitting in a classroom interferes drastically with your education. You will benefit most from broad travels, particularly voyages overseas. You are philosophical, far-sighted, candid in your opinions, generous, kindly and high-minded. You tend to be the leader in your circle of friends and associates, and will often come into great honors and praise. Jupiter in Sagittarius is an excellent position for harmonious association with educational institutions, travel agencies, religious organizations, philosophical bodies and publishing houses. You are tolerant, sympathetic, broadminded, somewhat prophetic, eminently fair and sportsmanlike, with an excellent sense of humor. You have a general liking for outdoor sports and entertainment. Your overall expansiveness gives you a love of speculation, and unbounding faith in your ultimate good luck, which usually works the way you had expected. Regardless of the difficulties you encounter, you always manage to land on your feet. You are idealistic and well-nigh incorruptible; once you've decided on the morally right thing to do, you will fight to the bitter end to defend your ideal.

JUPITER IN CAPRICORN ♃ ♑

You are something of a paradox in that you are pulled by your desire for absolute independence on one hand and for security on the other. You are apt to plunge courageously into a situation, fully intending to fight to the bitter end, but when obstacles arise and you realize the dangers involved, your initial resolution will dissolve as though it had never been. You tend to be serious, deliberate, inventive and capable of solid, practical achievements. Your education is likely to be liberal and practical, not necessarily orthodox. You have your own way of gaining knowledge, and might easily participate in the practical advancement of political, scientific, religious or philosophical knowledge. Although quietly intelligent, you are often too cautious to come out and give your views, which probably tend to range between conservative and liberal. (You seem to have one foot in each camp.)

Jupiter in Capricorn is good testimony for an executive position at some time or other in your life. You are almost certain to achieve success in a position of authority or com-

mand. You possess a fine capacity for leadership, but need
to overcome a too-cautious attitude and a tendency to care
too much about what others are liable to think of you. You
have the ambition (if not the complete confidence) and organizational ability to reach the top in almost any govern-
mental or other public career. Anything connected with
foreign affairs or international commerce is a fertile field for
your constructive, practical abilities. You'd *like* to pioneer
in new fields and be different, but your respect for tradition
and the status quo, by contrast, generates a deep sense of
insecurity. This same principle applies to your many impulses
to be generous or to shake off your fears and to travel.
Loosen up and disregard the opinions of those in authority.
They have problems of their own. Be yourself!

JUPITER IN AQUARIUS ♃ ♒

You possess a great deal of charm, combined with a broadly
liberal viewpoint. In the best, most mature and creative sense
of the word, you are a true, jovial humanitarian. You sincerely want everyone else to be happy and to enjoy the best
there is in life. Yet you are often cold or indifferent to the
normal, everyday matters that are a necessary part of living.
This is because you are supremely idealistic, with an unusual
progressive and independent outlook. Your personality has an
enormous influence on friends and associates. You are open,
friendly, easy to meet and truly interested in other people—
the more you know the better. Your friends are faithful and
sincerely affectionate. You are probably a living example of
the adage: *"If you want to have a friend, BE one."*
You are keenly interested in and gain great pleasure from
all kinds of public work, whether it involves institutions,
political movements, labor or charitable activity. You are
generally refined, far-sighted, at times even visionary. Your
congenial attitude and your sympathetic and compassionate
nature is jarred by strife, discord or lowly antagonism. You
probably have a reputation for being helpful, optimistic,
genteel and urbane. Whatever good you desire for the majority of people, you will work hard to bring it about. You
will lend or donate your money and time, join organizations
that share your broad, liberal philosophic and humanitarian
aims and views. You are inclined to follow unusual, sometimes eccentric, lines of thought and study. You like to study
the classic and ancient arts, mysticism, science, music and literature from all the ages. You often undergo strange expe-

riences through certain off-beat friends and associates. You will profit well in your profession, particularly if it is connected with congressional or government activity or some form of work for the public good.

JUPITER IN PISCES ♃ ♓

You are strongly idealistic and tend to suffer personally at the injustices you see experienced by others. Although you are charitable, kind and sympathetic, you often overlook your *own* misfortunes. You are generally sociable, and possess many outstanding talents which you are apt to play down or overlook. You are unassuming, hospitable, fond of (and kind to) animals. You are most likely to profit from friends and associates who recognize your willingness to extend sympathy and help to the poor, the ill and those who otherwise suffer misfortune. You are likely to achieve a great deal of recognition, praise and honor for your work with sanitariums, laboratories, hospitals and similar institutions. You can also achieve success with the earthy and watery elements—in land, houses, mining or shipping.

You are strongly spiritual, highly idealistic, emotional, sensitive and imaginative in a positive way. You have probably experienced many precognitive dreams and similar evidences of your *psi* talents. This may have stimulated your curiosity and interest in psychic and occult phenomena. It is a good bet that you belong to one or more organizations for research into the investigation of psychic, mystical, occult or arcane phenomena. There is some danger that you will attract a member of the opposite sex whose sole aim is to take advantage of your kind and sympathetic nature. You may do considerable traveling by water in the course of your life's work. Learn to confide your secret ambitions, dreams, visions and feelings in someone you can trust and respect. You have a tendency to suffer inwardly while wearing a smile and allowing the world to believe you are supremely happy and contented.

To find where Jupiter was (by Sign) at the time of your birth, consult the following table, then insert this symbol (♃) in its proper place in the horoscope blank.

TO FIND THE POSITION OF JUPITER AT YOUR BIRTH

Date	Zodiacal Sign
Jan. 1, 1890 to Feb. 24, 1890	Capricorn
Feb. 25, 1890 to Mar. 7, 1891	Aquarius
Mar. 8, 1891 to Màr. 16, 1892	Pisces
Mar. 17, 1892 to Mar. 24, 1893	Aries
Mar. 25, 1893 to Aug. 20, 1893	Taurus
Aug. 21, 1893 to Oct. 19, 1893	Gemini
Oct. 20, 1893 to Apr. 1, 1894	Taurus
Apr. 2, 1894 to Aug. 18, 1894	Gemini
Aug. 19, 1894 to Jan. 1, 1895	Cancer
Jan. 2, 1895 to Apr. 10, 1895	Gemini
Apr. 11, 1895 to Sept. 4, 1895	Cancer
Sept. 5, 1895 to Feb. 29, 1896	Leo
Mar. 1, 1896 to Apr. 17, 1896	Cancer
Apr. 18, 1896 to Sept. 27, 1896	Leo
Sept. 28, 1896 to Oct. 27, 1897	Virgo
Oct. 28, 1897 to Nov. 26, 1898	Libra
Nov. 27, 1898 to Dec. 25, 1899	Scorpio
Dec. 26, 1899 to Jan. 18, 1901	Sagittarius
Jan. 19, 1901 to Feb. 6, 1902	Capricorn
Feb. 7, 1902 to Feb. 19, 1903	Aquarius
Feb. 20, 1903 to Feb. 29, 1904	Pisces
Mar. 1, 1904 to Aug. 8, 1904	Aries
Aug. 9, 1904 to Aug. 31, 1904	Taurus
Sept. 1, 1904 to Mar. 7, 1905	Aries
Mar. 8, 1905 to July 20, 1905	Taurus
July 21, 1905 to Dec. 4, 1905	Gemini
Dec. 5, 1905 to Mar. 9, 1906	Taurus
Mar. 10, 1906 to July 30, 1906	Gemini
July 31, 1906 to Aug. 18, 1907	Cancer
Aug. 19, 1907 to Sept. 11, 1908	Leo
Sept. 12, 1908 to Oct. 11, 1909	Virgo
Oct. 12, 1909 to Nov. 11, 1910	Libra
Nov. 12, 1910 to Dec. 9, 1911	Scorpio
Dec. 10, 1911 to Jan. 2, 1913	Sagittarius
Jan. 3, 1913 to Jan. 21, 1914	Capricorn
Jan. 22, 1914 to Feb. 3, 1915	Aquarius
Feb. 4, 1915 to Feb. 11, 1916	Pisces
Feb. 12, 1916 to June 25, 1916	Aries
June 26, 1916 to Oct. 26, 1916	Taurus
Oct. 27, 1916 to Feb. 12, 1917	Aries

Date	Zodiacal Sign
Feb. 13, 1917 to June 29, 1917	Taurus
June 30, 1917 to July 12, 1918	Gemini
July 13, 1918 to Aug. 1, 1919	Cancer
Aug. 2, 1919 to Aug. 26, 1920	Leo
Aug. 27, 1920 to Sept. 25, 1921	Virgo
Sept. 26, 1921 to Oct. 26, 1922	Libra
Oct. 27, 1922 to Nov. 24, 1923	Scorpio
Nov. 25, 1923 to Dec. 17, 1924	Sagittarius
Dec. 18, 1924 to Jan. 5, 1926	Capricorn
Jan. 6, 1926 to Jan. 17, 1927	Aquarius
Jan. 18, 1927 to June 5, 1927	Pisces
June 6, 1927 to Sept. 10, 1927	Aries
Sept. 11, 1927 to Jan. 22, 1928	Pisces
Jan. 23, 1928 to June 3, 1928	Aries
June 4, 1928 to June 11, 1929	Taurus
June 12, 1929 to June 26, 1930	Gemini
June 27, 1930 to July 16, 1931	Cancer
July 17, 1931 to Aug. 10, 1932	Leo
Aug. 11, 1932 to Sept. 9, 1933	Virgo
Sept. 10, 1933 to Oct. 10, 1934	Libra
Oct. 11, 1934 to Nov. 8, 1935	Scorpio
Nov. 9, 1935 to Dec. 1, 1936	Sagittarius
Dec. 2, 1936 to Dec. 19, 1937	Capricorn
Dec. 20, 1937 to May 13, 1938	Aquarius
May 14, 1938 to July 29, 1938	Pisces
July 30, 1938 to Dec. 28, 1938	Aquarius
Dec. 29, 1938 to May 10, 1939	Pisces
May 11, 1939 to Oct. 29, 1939	Aries
Oct. 30, 1939 to Dec. 19, 1939	Pisces
Dec. 20, 1939 to May 15, 1940	Aries
May 16, 1940 to May 25, 1941	Taurus
May 26, 1941 to June 9, 1942	Gemini
June 10, 1942 to June 29, 1943	Cancer
June 30, 1943 to July 25, 1944	Leo
July 26, 1944 to Aug. 24, 1945	Virgo
Aug. 25, 1945 to Sept. 24, 1946	Libra
Sept. 25, 1946 to Oct. 23, 1947	Scorpio
Oct. 24, 1947 to Nov. 14, 1948	Sagittarius
Nov. 15, 1948 to Apr. 11, 1949	Capricorn
Apr. 12, 1949 to June 26, 1949	Aquarius

Date	Zodiacal Sign
June 27, 1949 to Nov. 29, 1949	Capricorn
Nov. 30, 1949 to Apr. 14, 1950	Aquarius
Apr. 15, 1950 to Sept. 14, 1950	Pisces
Sept. 15, 1950 to Dec. 1, 1950	Aquarius
Dec. 2, 1950 to Apr. 20, 1951	Pisces
Apr. 21, 1951 to Apr. 27, 1952	Aries
Apr. 28, 1952 to May 8, 1953	Taurus
May 9, 1953 to May 23, 1954	Gemini
May 24, 1954 to June 11, 1955	Cancer
June 12, 1955 to Nov. 16, 1955	Leo
Nov. 17, 1955 to Jan. 17, 1956	Virgo
Jan. 18, 1956 to July 6, 1956	Leo
July 7, 1956 to Dec. 11, 1956	Virgo
Dec. 12, 1956 to Feb. 18, 1957	Libra
Feb. 19, 1957 to Aug. 5, 1957	Virgo
Aug. 6, 1957 to Jan. 12, 1958	Libra
Jan. 13, 1958 to Mar. 19, 1958	Scorpio
Mar. 20, 1958 to Sept. 6, 1958	Libra
Sept. 7, 1958 to Feb. 9, 1959	Scorpio
Feb. 10, 1959 to Apr. 23, 1959	Sagittarius
Apr. 24, 1959 to Oct. 4, 1959	Scorpio
Oct. 5, 1959 to Feb. 29, 1960	Sagittarius
Mar. 1, 1960 to June 9, 1960	Capricorn
June 10, 1960 to Oct. 24, 1960	Sagittarius
Oct. 25, 1960 to Mar. 14, 1961	Capricorn
Mar. 15, 1961 to Aug. 11, 1961	Aquarius
Aug. 12, 1961 to Nov. 3, 1961	Capricorn
Nov. 4, 1961 to Mar. 24, 1962	Aquarius
Mar. 25, 1962 to Apr. 3, 1963	Pisces
Apr. 4, 1963 to Apr. 11, 1964	Aries
Apr. 12, 1964 to Apr. 21, 1965	Taurus
Apr. 22, 1965 to Sept. 20, 1965	Gemini
Sept. 21, 1965 to Nov. 16, 1965	Cancer
Nov. 17, 1965 to May 4, 1966	Gemini
May 5, 1966 to Sept. 26, 1966	Cancer
Sept. 27, 1966 to Jan. 15, 1967	Leo
Jan. 16, 1967 to May 22, 1967	Cancer
May 23, 1967 to Oct. 18, 1967	Leo
Oct. 19, 1967 to Feb. 26, 1968	Virgo
Feb. 27, 1968 to June 14, 1968	Leo
June 15, 1968 to Nov. 14, 1968	Virgo

Date	Zodiacal Sign
Nov. 15, 1968 to Mar. 29, 1969	Libra
Mar. 30, 1969 to July 14, 1969	Virgo
July 15, 1969 to Dec. 15, 1969	Libra
Dec. 16, 1969 to Apr. 29, 1970	Scorpio
Apr. 30, 1970 to Aug. 14, 1970	Libra
Aug. 15, 1970 to Dec. 31, 1970	Scorpio

11

The Influence of Saturn

Because of its halo of rings, Saturn is generally considered the most beautiful planet in the solar system. To this day, astronomers cannot agree on what these beautiful discs are composed of or how thick they are; estimtaes range from ten miles to eight inches. When seen edge-on, the rings flatten out and become entirely invisible. There has been recent speculation that Saturn is not the only Solarian planet surrounded by rings. Earth may also have its retinue of gossamer rings, some astronomers theorize, but they supposedly are not visible from the surface. On the face of it, this seems unlikely.

Saturn is the second largest of all the planets; slightly flattened, its equatorial diameter is 75,021 miles. From pole to pole, however, it measures 67,805 miles. Not counting the Asteroid Belt between Jupiter and Mars, Saturn is the sixth planet out from the Sun, at a mean distance of 887,-200,000 miles from its parent star. Saturn's orbital period around the Sun is 29½ Earth years—and like Jupiter's 12-year period this increment corresponds with many terrestrial cycles, indicating that there may indeed be a possible connection (between Saturn and our Earth). Also like Jupiter, gigantic Saturn spins on its axis at a tremendous velocity for so massive a body—10 hours and 38 minutes is the length of the Saturnian day. Undecipherable, but seemingly artificial, radio waves have been received from both Jupiter and Saturn, and recorded at most of the world's radio observatories. Until 1967 Saturn was believed to have only nine moons, but now a tenth—called Themis—has been discovered

and verified. The combined width of Saturn's three rings is
11,500 miles across. The outer or first ring is a little over
10,000 miles wide. After that there is Cassini's Division, a
dark band in which there is little or none of the material
which makes up the rings; this is probably about 3,000 miles
wide. The second ring is about 16,000 miles across. The innermost "crepe" ring (because it looks like dress material) is
11,500 miles wide.

The innermost edge of the rings arcs about 7,000 miles
above the surface of Saturn, which is also a multicolored,
banded giant like Jupiter. If they could be seen from the
surface, Saturn's rings would be a spectacular sight . . .
perhaps even more spectacular if viewed from one of its
moons—Titan, Hyperion, Phoebe or Themis. Titan, the
largest of Saturn's moons, is also one of the largest satellites
in the solar system, with a possible diameter of almost 4,000
miles.

Since the earliest known records of ancient astrologers,
Saturn has been equated to adversity and relegated to the
status of a *malefic* planet. Saturn's principle (its general
influence) is the exact opposite of Jupiterian expansion and
joviality. Saturn represents cold, contraction, seriousness, stability, discipline and practicality. No nonsense here. The
typical Saturn-*ruled* individual (one with Capricorn rising),
however, doesn't lack a sense of humor at all. He is inclined
to make wry, witty, cryptic observations that to the discerning
mind are incisive, apropos and often hilarious. Saturn sometimes causes temporary denial of the things promised in the
horoscope by Jupiter or Venus. Yet in retrospect (a Saturnian
condition) you often discover that your greatest obstacles
present challenges that, when overcome, give you lasting
strength and character that an easy path would not have
offered. With good aspects in your chart, Saturn will incline
you toward prudence, caution, diplomacy, seriousness, stability, conservatism, practicality, intellectual depth and good
managerial or organizational ability. Physically, Saturn governs the knees, teeth, bones and inner ear.

*Find the position of Saturn at your birth by checking the
list at the end of this chapter.*

SATURN IN ARIES ♄ ♈

As you already know, the early part of your life is the most
difficult. From this base of obstacles and adversity you can
build the strength of character to surmount anything that

may confront you for the remainder of your life. You are ambitious and determined to succeed; you desire responsibility, authority, dignity and respect, but often lack the confidence necessary to grasp the opportunity firmly when it presents itself. Yet your perseverence and hard work will ultimately be crowned with success. It does not come easily, however. Sometimes it may seem as though you fall two steps behind for every forward stride. But Saturn, often symbolized as the bearded, scythe-carrying "Father Time" will work *for* you over the years. Just as you may have felt you were deliberately "jinxed" in your youth, each year now brings you greater wisdom, less struggle and the increased prestige you've always wanted. One of your chief difficulties may be marital trouble caused by a jealous or insecure mate. On the other hand, you're not exactly easy to live with; you have a tendency to flare into anger when you are opposed, and you can be highly argumentative and cantankerous. Left to your own devices, however, you tend to reason things out and see the light of logic through quiet contemplation. Although it is possible that you may lack the depth of mind you assume, you're eventually going to win the admiration and respect of those in a position to do you the most good.

SATURN IN TAURUS ♄ ♉

You tend to be rather too stolid, and to develop great fears about losing money, love, and the comfort and security they bring. With discipline, economy and wise investment, combined with a certain amount of frugality, you will manage, though, to acquire enough material goods in the form of houses, land and securities to satisfy yourself. You tend to nurse grudges, have a quick and brittle temper and can be stubborn and resentful. Face the fact that you're going to have money trouble with relatives and could lose some of your hard-earned gains. This is a touchy situation; you're liable to place your trust in people who are unscrupulous and blame those who hold your best interests foremost. Before you're able to straighten out the resulting unhappy domestic scene, there will be losses and trouble caused by these relatives. You can gain a great deal of satisfaction and relaxation from working in or with the earthy things: raising or breeding stock, studying botany, gardening or farming. You tend to keep your personal troubles bottled up and can be reserved, diplomatic and prudent in your relationships. Generally, you are of a kindly, quiet and considerate disposition, thoughtful, determined and able to function well under emotional pressure and other adverse conditions.

SATURN IN GEMINI ♄ ♊

You have an ingenious, practical interest in all that goes on around you—in the present as well as with regard to prospects for the future. You have a built-in talent for deep intellectual achievements in writing, publishing, mathematics or science. You may have a tendency to skip from one thing to another—being equally serious about each subject, topic or study—then just dropping and forgetting about them. You are liable to experience difficulty and much sorrow in your dealings with relatives, and many obstacles, or misfortune, in short trips and traveling. You are clever and observant, resourceful, adaptable and serious-minded. Neighbors, relatives (and friends at one time or another) will succeed in placing the yoke of restraint or heavy responsibility on you, severely limiting your personal freedom and independence. You may tend to delude yourself by seeing things as you'd *like* them to be. This can cause you to become easily depressed because you are usually motivated by the finest ideals and may experience disillusionment through others. You can overcome many such setbacks by studying and applying positive philosophical attitudes. Emerson is a good example of Saturn in Gemini.

SATURN IN CANCER ♄ ♋

You are inclined to be ultrasensitive, fearful because you lack the security (either now or in the past) of the love of your parents. There is some difficulty, sorrow or anxiety indicated in your home life, through children and parent-image attachments you form—either consciously or unconsciously. You are rather changeable and lack the confidence to stand independently and break away from a stultifying past. You revere experience, age and authority because it represents the anchor and stability whose lack you feel so keenly. You want assurance, guidance—almost as a child who is overindulged and made to feel that his parents don't love him enough to care what he does. You have a powerful drive to appease those in authority or who are older, in the vain hope that these people will extend the love and security of which you feel deprived. You often tend to be discontented, dissatisfied, jealous, anxiety-ridden and changeable.

You may change your residence, your job, your interests and moods, but it always stems from the same problem— insecurity—the early denial of parental love and affection. You may marry someone older, a serious hard-working person who stimulates your active interest in helping to operate a good economical household. You will derive much satisfaction and happiness through psychic studies and occultism, but are liable to be emotionally affected by discordant conditions created by other people.

SATURN IN LEO ♄ ♌

This position of Saturn can affect the heart and cause you some sorrow in love affairs and through children. You seek to compensate by hard work for an apparent inability to derive pleasure from amusements. But this merely serves to create the additional dangers of overwork, overtaxing your heart and impairing your general health. (Psychologists could learn a good deal simply from observing how people with Saturn in Leo develop complex emotional difficulties when it comes to expressing the love they must eventually feel for someone.) There is a powerful blockage here, and you may seek an outlet for your thwarted feelings in an illicit alliance with someone unworthy of you. This is almost certain to create trouble with those who are inferior in some way. You are ambitious, determined, have a hair-trigger temper and strong spiritual inclinations. You are an odd combination of courageousness and prudence. You are generous, have a strong will, but may be a victim of too severe and limiting religious discipline as a child. Try to loosen up and reveal your true feelings; you're liable to be happily surprised at the response.

SATURN IN VIRGO ♄ ♍

Good, careful investment in real estate will almost assuredly pay off for you, but the first half of your life is liable to be plagued by obstacles, sorrow, ill health, and difficulties that could bring you to the brink of a nervous breakdown. Although you may tend to exaggerate the slight ailments with which you are plagued, you probably experience severe headaches and possible constipation. You are generally reserved, rather humble and self-effacing, discreet, extra careful and so anxious and cautious that you cause a general rundown and tired feeling in yourself through your negative thinking.

You are very serious, prudent, reserved and quiet. You also tend to be watchful ready for quick flight, mistrustful of others, doubting, anxious, gloomy, worried and easily depressed. This is an unfortunate combination for a happy marriage, and unless you make a determined effort to see the bright side of every situation, you are certain to cause troubles, misfortune and general unhappiness in any partnership or marriage. You have a good mind, and could easily excel in scientific studies of health, hygiene or literature.

SATURN IN LIBRA   ♄ ♎

If you happen to be a woman you are likely to be quite attractive, but Saturn, the celestial taskmaster, will take his good old time in finding the right marriage partner for you. Somehow, there is disappointment here—a lack of warmth, love or enthusiasm in your marriage. More than one marriage is indicated for you. Business partnerships also cause difficulty. Much as you desire and work for harmony, peace and good public relations, you develop enemies, some of whom are likely to be women rather than men.

You have refined tendencies, a liking for the better things of life—music, art, the theater and socializing—but you often become involved in controversial subjects and heated arguments. Your relations with other people are not at all what you want them to be. You seek order, harmony and justice, but run into emotional turmoil instead. The deepest love affair in your life may have ended in loss and heartbreak. There is some trouble in your employment, and there are separations from some people you love. Still, this Sign is excellent evidence of fine mental machinery in a person well-equipped for a career in law or science. The image you project to that part of the world you want most to impress is entirely too serious. Be careful of broken contracts and protect any documents pertaining to your home or land.

SATURN IN SCORPIO   ♄ ♏

When you apply your somewhat simmering volcanic nature toward achievement in the sciences, geology, archeology or researching new knowledge, you may overcome your willful, passionate, jealous nature. You are forever searching out better avenues for expressing your hidden talents. With proper training and self-discipline, you can easily develop great intellectual depth. Ordinarily you proceed with shrewdness and caution, yet you are resourceful, extremely independent and passionate. You are inclined to make sudden decisions that often surprise even yourself, but once embarked on a course of action you *will* doggedly pursue your plan to the bitter end—even when you can clearly see your own destruction looming at that end. It is as though you are unable to help yourself; but the obsessions can just as easily be checked and rechanneled, because you possess great willpower.

You are acquisitive, cautious, resourceful and calculating. You are able to overcome enormous obstacles, and, through sheer persistence, attention to detail, cleverness and patience, you can reach great pinnacles of success. One of your chief drawbacks is trouble with the opposite sex; you tend to take on secret love affairs and the burden of knowing the innermost secrets of people who confide in you. You often act in haste, drive yourself into troubled waters and live to regret your impulsiveness. Learn to accept that what is done is done and that no amount of mental or emotional rehashing will change the past. The trick is to learn from your mistakes— not to repeat them. You are fascinated by mysteries, secrets and occult studies and may have such a powerful intuitive faculty that it borders on *psi* ability.

SATURN IN SAGITTARIUS ♄ ♐

You are gifted with powerful hunches, strong intuition and accurate prophetic talents. You are therefore far-sighted, visionary, and able to foresee the logical outcome of long-range scientific and social developments. You carry yourself with dignity, and gain the esteem of others through your talents and mental abilities. Although you enjoy approbation, *self*-respect comes even higher on your list of priorities. You are deeply philosophical and sincerely religious, perhaps in a rather paradoxical "liberal-orthodox" sense. You are very serious about how the game of life is played; the stress, however, is not so much on material success, and recognition, as on the moral issues involved—one might almost say the "sportsmanship" of adhering to certain rules of discipline.

Those who stand in your way do not realize how sensitive you are or how deeply hurt you can become by the slings and arrows, the cutting antagonism and severe criticism of harsh opposition. By allowing yourself the luxury of resentment against these censures, you delay the promotion and ultimate recognition you rightfully deserve. It is almost certain that you will experience the tarnishing of your reputation at some

time in life. Your honor and ethics will be unjustly questioned
and aired in public. You will be unable to combat these setbacks with abstract philosophy or "tried and true" methods of
communicating your real stands and objectives. They're
bound to be misinterpreted. You are generally kind and
considerate, broad and humanitarian in your views and absolutely fearless and outspoken when you are involved with
the politics of economy or the promotion of sound govern-
mental fiscal policy. You need the firm feeling of conviction
that your undertakings are essentially ethical and morally
right as well as practical. You want to inspire others, but
may wind up simply insisting that everyone practice out-
dated "virtues" that have little relevance to modern society,
unless you broaden your outlook.

SATURN IN CAPRICORN ♄ ♑

Your chief characteristic is your ability to achieve in spite
of great odds. You are constantly aware of your keen desire
to lift yourself to great heights. Your ambition knows no
bounds, and you will persist in hard work, the cultivation of
those who can help, and diplomacy and tact until you
achieve the success you have set out to win. You work so
hard and play so seldom that you are liable to chronic illnesses and may even come close to a nervous breakdown
through overwork, worry and anxiety. Try not to repress your
emotions or stifle your occasional desire for fun and relaxation. Know that despite all adversity your failures are actually
minor victories because you learn from every mistake and
will succeed in the long pull.

You have a reserved, serious exterior, excellent reasoning
abilities and a determinedly stubborn faith in yourself. This
is an unbeatable combination, yet your acquisitiveness and
rather materialistic outlook make you suspicious, fearful,
melancholy, overly cautious and often deeply dissatisfied with
your progress. You tend to form attachments with those who
are your intellectual inferiors, and often members of the opposite sex. Unless Saturn is well-aspected in your horoscope,
i.e., with the Sun, Venus or Jupiter either four Signs away
(in trine) or two Signs (sextile), you may be plagued with
unfaithful or unreliable friends. Marriage could bring unexpected trouble and sorrow in your home life. You possess
good managerial and executive abilities, are well qualified to
handle responsibility and could easily operate your own business (which you'd much rather do than take orders or work
for someone else).

SATURN IN AQUARIUS ♄ ♒

You have many friends and acquaintances who will last a
lifetime. Among these people, there is someone with whom
you'll form a lasting romantic attachment. You enjoy being
attractive to the opposite sex and are serious, friendly, sociable and quite good natured generally. You tend to be cour-
teously reserved, thoughtful, considerate and (outwardly)
tractable. Whenever you become involved in anything that
attracts your interest, you take straightforward action and
are able to express yourself knowledgeably and impressively.
Like Saturn in the other fixed Signs, Scorpio, Leo and
Taurus, Saturn in Aquarius leads you to far more fortunate
circumstances in later life than during your early years. You
learn rapidly and will further refine your thinking processes
through experience, observation and study. The longer you
practice broadly progressive policies, the more profound your
mind will become and the more clearly your insight and intuition will be developed.

You are especially adept in the arts and in science, but are
likely to adopt the orthodox path to learning *and* development. However, this does not prevent your seeing things in
their broadest context and often in an entirely original and
inventive manner. With quiet, steady determination and
faithful application of the wisdom you acquire, you will reap
high financial rewards, either professionally or through employment in a large company or corporation. Your sincerity,
reasonableness and intelligence will win you the recognition
and loyal friends you value so highly.

SATURN IN PISCES ♄ ♓

You are fortunate if Saturn in Pisces is beneficially aspected
—i.e., by the Sun, Jupiter or Venus in any of the earth or
water Signs—and well placed in your horoscope. If so, you
are able to help yourself by study, meditation, volunteer work
in hospitals, prisons and mental institutions and welfare work
for the poor. Do not simply accept what you consider to
be your lot in life—many obstacles and difficulties if Saturn
happens to be adversely aspected (usually by Mars in a fire
or air Sign) in your chart. Events may occur, though, that
are completely beyond your ability to deal effectively with
them. You are often faced by and forced to deal with the
totally unexpected and completely undesirable in life. Even
when you manage to work your way into a position of dig-

nity, esteem or prestige, it takes all the willpower and determination you can muster not to hold your own there. You are often the cause of your own unhappiness and bad luck, however. You are highly emotional, strongly sympathetic and likely to feel as though others are in worse condition. You have a strong, desiring nature, but need to encourage within yourself the ability to see things optimistically, with a continuously firm attitude. Of course you have suffered mishaps, sadness, loss of love, sorrow and tragedy that may deeply affect you emotionally. Only *you* can help yourself, however—by developing *ambition:*

"All competent men should have some ambition, for ambition is like the temper in steel. If there's too much the product is brittle, if there's too little the steel is soft; and without a certain amount of hardness a man cannot achieve what he sets out to do."—Dwight D. Eisenhower

TO FIND THE POSITION OF SATURN AT YOUR BIRTH

Date	Zodiacal Sign
Jan. 1, 1890 to Jan. 23, 1890	Virgo
Jan. 24, 1890 to June 27, 1890	Leo
June 28, 1890 to Dec. 26, 1891	Virgo
Dec. 27, 1891 to Jan. 22, 1892	Libra
Jan. 23, 1892 to Aug. 28, 1892	Virgo
Aug. 29, 1892 to Nov. 6, 1894	Libra
Nov. 7, 1894 to Feb. 6, 1897	Scorpio
Feb. 7, 1897 to Apr. 9, 1897	Sagittarius
Apr. 10, 1897 to Oct. 26, 1897	Scorpio
Oct. 27, 1897 to Jan. 20, 1900	Sagittarius
Jan. 21, 1900 to July 18, 1900	Capricorn
July 19, 1900 to Oct. 16, 1900	Sagittarius
Oct. 17, 1900 to Jan. 19, 1903	Capricorn
Jan. 20, 1903 to Apr. 12, 1905	Aquarius
Apr. 13, 1905 to Aug. 16, 1905	Pisces
Aug. 17, 1905 to Jan. 7, 1906	Aquarius
Jan. 8, 1906 to Mar. 18, 1908	Pisces
Mar. 19, 1908 to May 16, 1910	Aries
May 17, 1910 to Dec. 14, 1910	Taurus
Dec. 15, 1910 to Jan. 19, 1911	Aries
Jan. 20, 1911 to July 6, 1912	Taurus
July 7, 1912 to Nov. 30, 1912	Gemini
Dec. 1, 1912 to Mar. 25, 1913	Taurus
Mar. 26, 1913 to Aug. 24, 1914	Gemini
Aug. 25, 1914 to Dec. 6, 1914	Cancer

Date	Zodiacal Sign
Dec. 7, 1914 to May 11, 1915	Gemini
May 12, 1915 to Oct. 16, 1916	Cancer
Oct. 17, 1916 to Dec. 7, 1916	Leo
Dec. 8, 1916 to June 23, 1917	Cancer
June 24, 1917 to Aug. 11, 1919	Leo
Aug. 12, 1919 to Oct. 7, 1921	Virgo
Oct. 8, 1921 to Dec. 19, 1923	Libra
Dec. 20, 1923 to Apr. 5, 1924	Scorpio
Apr. 6, 1924 to Sept. 13, 1924	Libra
Sept. 14, 1924 to Dec. 2, 1926	Scorpio
Dec. 3, 1926 to Mar. 29, 1929	Sagittarius
Mar. 30, 1929 to May 4, 1929	Capricorn
May 5, 1929 to Nov. 29, 1929	Sagittarius
Nov. 30, 1929 to Feb. 22, 1932	Capricorn
Feb. 23, 1932 to Aug. 12, 1932	Aquarius
Aug. 13, 1932 to Nov. 18, 1932	Capricorn
Nov. 19, 1932 to Feb. 13, 1935	Aquarius
Feb. 14, 1935 to Apr. 24, 1937	Pisces
Apr. 25, 1937 to Oct. 17, 1937	Aries
Oct. 18, 1937 to Jan. 13, 1938	Pisces
Jan. 14, 1938 to July 5, 1939	Aries
July 6, 1939 to Sept. 21, 1939	Taurus
Sept. 22, 1939 to Mar. 19, 1940	Aries
Mar. 20, 1940 to May 7, 1942	Taurus
May 8, 1942 to June 19, 1944	Gemini
June 20, 1944 to Aug. 1, 1946	Cancer
Aug. 2, 1946 to Sept. 18, 1948	Leo
Sept. 19, 1948 to Apr. 2, 1949	Virgo
Apr. 3, 1949 to May 28, 1949	Leo
May 29, 1949 to Nov. 19, 1950	Virgo
Nov. 20, 1950 to Mar. 6, 1951	Libra
Mar. 7, 1951 to Aug. 12, 1951	Virgo
Aug. 13, 1951 to Oct. 21, 1953	Libra
Oct. 22, 1953 to Jan. 11, 1956	Scorpio
Jan. 12, 1956 to May 13, 1956	Sagittarius
May 14, 1956 to Oct. 9, 1956	Scorpio
Oct. 10, 1956 to Jan. 4, 1959	Sagittarius
Jan. 5, 1959 to Jan. 9, 1962	Capricorn
Jan. 10, 1962 to Dec. 16, 1964	Aquarius
Dec. 17, 1964 to Mar. 2, 1967	Pisces
Mar. 3, 1967 to Apr. 28, 1969	Aries
Apr. 29, 1969 thru 1970	Taurus

12

The Influence of Uranus

Uranus, the seventh planet out from the Sun, is an eccentric banded giant with a diameter of 33,219 miles—more than four times as large as Earth. Discovered in 1781 by Sir William Herschel, Uranus' mean distance from the Sun is one billion, seven hundred and eighty-four million, eight hundred thousand (1,784,800,000) miles. Although Herschel is officially credited for discovering the plant that once briefly bore his name, it was first seen and recorded by an *astrologer* on five different occasions almost a century before. John Flamstead, the first Astronomer Royal of England (and builder of the Observatory at Greenwich), was actually a first-rate astrologer who timed the laying of the observatory cornerstone by horoscopy and recorded five notations of Uranus before the year 1690—long before its "official" discovery.

Uranus is unique in the solar system in that its axis is inclined at the peculiar angle of 98 degrees from the plane of its orbit. In effect, it lies somewhat on its side. Uranus rotates on its axis in 10 hours and 48 minutes, and takes 84 years and four days to complete one orbit around the Sun. Due to its extreme axial tilt, however, the Sun seems to stand directly above each pole at the opposite ends of its orbit. During the period when the Sun is "above" its South pole, the entire Northern hemisphere of Uranus lies in total darkness for almost 20 Earth years at a time—and vice versa.

Uranus has five known satellites, all of which orbit in the plane of the planet's equator. Their names are taken from the writings of Shakespeare and Alexander Pope: "Miranda," from *The Tempest;* "Oberon" and "Titania," from *A Midsummer Night's Dream;* "Umbriel," from *The Rape of the Lock;* and "Ariel," also from *The Tempest.*

Since the discovery of Uranus, it has been observed by astrologers to correlate with science, astrology, electricity, broad humanitarian movements, the production of earthquakes and events that occur with unexpected swiftness. Since Uranus takes 84 Earth years to complete one solar orbit, it spends about seven years in each Sign of the Zodiac. At this writing (and until September 1968), Uranus is in the Sign of Virgo. It retrogrades back into Virgo on May 22nd, 1969, and is causing many unexpected changes in the lives of those who have the Sun, Moon, or any planets in this discriminating Sign.

People born with Uranus strongly placed in their horoscope, particularly the Ascendant (First House) or Midheaven (Tenth House), or powerfully aspected in any way, are usually inventive and attracted to what seems odd or peculiar to most other people; they may appear eccentric in some ways, often curious and are actually far ahead of their time. These people are so intuitive, imaginative and farsighted that they can perceive ways and means to improve on almost anything that crosses their path. They are gifted with an uncanny imagination and a strong, constructive social consciousness. Uranus type people usually practice equality, liberty and democracy.

Paradoxically, Uranus is considered "strange," "cold," "airy," "magnetic," "positive," "malefic," "dry," and "occult," yet it "rules" science in general and astrology in particular; it is considered to be "electric," and often prompts us to act without rhyme or reason. Uranus represents the unexpected, the unpremeditated, and all things futuristic, revolutionary and visionary.

Find the position of Uranus at your birth in the listing at the end of this chapter.

URANUS IN ARIES ♅ ♈

Although you may not intentionally be so, you are apt to be blunt, rude, brusque or radically untactful in your relations with others. You have the feeling that *you know* all that is necessary to know and are too impatient to consider the dull, plodding (often actually erroneous) theories of others. You frequently find yourself involved in heated arguments which result in the loss of your friends. You have certain rather cold, scientific ideas about stimulating the in tellectual or mental qualities of young children before they are exposed to the myriad superstitions and myths of a "disorganized" society. You have a well-developed, pioneering, inventive ability, originality and resourcefulness. Coupled with a practical knowledge of business and finance, you could be a one-person unbeatable team. You tend to be rash, impulsive and forceful, extremely positive that you are in the right. You are bubbling with enthusiasm, intellectual vigor and often repressed physical activity. Nothing can dampen your great love for freedom and independence. You like to move around, travel, change your residence and *possibly* to work out totally new electronic and fluidic technological ideas or the most advanced and novel methods of accomplishing anything new or original in the age of space. Regardless of your age, it is an excellent idea to pursue additional education, be it formal or liberal.

URANUS IN TAURUS   ♅ ♉

You are apt to gain financially through original real estate and land enterprises. You are probably quite fortunate in partnership transactions and associations with progressive practical organizations that encourage innovation, ingenuity and invention, at which you are clever. If beneficially aspected, that is, if the Sun, Moon, Jupiter or Venus are in the earth or water Signs, Uranus in Taurus is a good indication for a happy and prosperous marriage, although this position *usually* brings about strife, arguments and the jealousy of your marriage partner. You are inclined to be somewhat intuitive, psychic or far-sighted. Your natural ingenuity, originality and resourcefulness are capable of meeting and overcoming almost all obstacles that fate or circumstance place in your path. You are headstrong, fully determined to achieve your goals despite any opposition, and likely to be tractable, broadminded and easygoing at one time, then switch unexpectedly to a rigidly stubborn and intractable attitude. It is best to use your innate originality during quiet times to find ways of working at an even pace with cool deliberation most of the time, rather than ploughing ahead in fits and starts. Give your sense of what is practical an opportunity to influence your decisions.

URANUS IN GEMINI ♅ ♊

You are naturally endowed with a good, logical, inventive mind, a love of study and a strong attraction for advanced thinking in all the sciences. You could become an excellent logician, an electronics expert with new, original and extremely advanced ideas, or a space age writer or communicator—or an engineer in any of these new areas. All the sciences, anything original, novel or new in concept immediately gains your favorable attention. Your ingenuity, hair-trigger responses and unusual methods of expression may cause you to be branded as something of an eccentric. You are versatile, have a facility with languages and attract unusual friends in the arts and sciences. You enjoy people and also making new friends and traveling among or with literary and advanced scientific thinkers. There may have been some difficulty with your education; you are not likely to have successfully concluded orthodox examinations for your degree(s), despite your strong interest in the sciences—or perhaps because of it. This could result in unfair, unfavorable criticism of your work later in life. You are probably talented with ESP, *psi* and clairvoyant abilities. There may have been sudden separations from your brothers, sisters and relatives —or difficulty through neighbors when you were younger. You will continue to be attracted to off-beat subjects, unusual phenomena, new ideas and scientific as well as literary reforms.

URANUS IN CANCER ♅ ♋

Even though you may love your home and children and want to enjoy the security and comfort of a good life, you encounter many difficulties on the domestic scene that will eventually bring sorrow and estrangement. You have novel and original ideas as well as unique methods of expressing your views, particularly in regard to civic activities, congressional, legislative or municipal affairs. You are intensely and actively patriotic and probably belong to one or more organizations fervently supporting the government. Yet you like to travel and probably have a strong preference for ocean voyages.

The difficulties you are likely to encounter during emotionally charged litigations concerning your home, property or land can result in financial loss and physical illness, notably some kind of stomach trouble such as ulcers. You are emotionally high-strung and very sensitive; events that others might simply shrug off as unimportant cause you a great deal of sorrow. You are too easily moved by apparent injustices to yourself or others. You have some *psi* ability and much of the sensitivity that the water Sign Cancer bestows, but your sensitivities are so close to the surface that you may appear touchy, cranky, impatient with others, restless and suddenly changeable—or liable to some form of radical behavior that seems peculiar and eccentric to your friends and associates. Make it a habit to get off by yourself occasionally to refresh and recharge these emotionally sensitive batteries.

URANUS IN LEO ♅ ♌

You hanker for (and will probably achieve) a distinguished professional career, one that is unique or exceptional in some way. You *are* more than normally progressive, and have a strong desire to display your leadership and ingenuity in an executive position controlling advances in scientific programs. You experience sudden, strange eventualities in love affairs and often suffer unexpected sorrow, loss and estrangement in conditions involving your affections. There are abrupt endings to your relationships, many of which were caused by some of your rather odd attractions and prejudices. Although you may practice physical moderation, your mind is never still, always churning up new, original schemes.

You plunge headlong into the most dangerous, exhilarating adventures and excitement you can find. There are times when you almost deliberately seem to court the wrath of friends and business associates with your complete disregard for conventional behavior, your arrogance and rebelliousness. It is virtually impossible to reason with you during such periods because you become fiery tempered, passionately fixed in your opinions and impossibly eccentric. Your force is soon abated, however, and, like a straw fire, it is often subdued as abruptly as it began. Try to anticipate these outbursts and plan in advance to keep them under tight control. Working on another new idea or invention is one good way to accomplish this. Otherwise, you have great leadership abilities.

URANUS IN VIRGO ♅ ♍

Your chief source of professional satisfaction and profit may be derived from a public career in government or in local civic groups. You also have a keen interest in the newer developments in world health, hygiene and antipollution measures. You have hidden talent in the manufacturing or production of devices to purify air, water and soil. You will gain recognition by following these and allied occupations. You have a built-in talent for mechanistic problems and could easily become a teacher or be naturally successful as an employment guidance expert or actual employer of others— particularly in the fields of biochemistry, electronics or the medical sciences. You are attracted to scientific curiosities, archeological "imponderables" and "erratic" artifacts from ancient history.

You tend to be rather fixed in your outlook, but impress people with a quiet exterior. Inwardly, you are seething with intellectual curiosity; your mind is set on being original, unencumbered and subtle. Although you are independent and eccentric, Uranus in Virgo accentuates your adept intellectual abilities and your devotion to the cause of greater health and comfort for everyone.

URANUS IN LIBRA ♅ ♎

Although you are drawn to artistic, musical, literary and scientific pursuits, you are liable to generate the animosity of open enemies who may formerly have been good friends. If Uranus is well-aspected, that is, if you have the Sun, Moon, Mercury, Venus or Jupiter in fire or air Signs, you will gravitate toward friendship with intellectually stimulating and scientifically inclined people. You are generally far-sighted and intuitive. You have an excellent imagination and a vaulting ambition. Your mental chemistry is good; you reason well and think clearly, but may be somewhat eccentric or unusual in your choice of friends and associates. You are rather restless, have a brittle temper and dislike the intervention of associates or partners in your pet projects, which might very well be in aerospace or advanced electronics.

You are inventive and ingenious, and possess a great deal of personal magnetism, all of which brings you into strange and often unexpected relationships with the opposite sex. Through at least one of these, you are likely to stun everyone with a completely unannounced or unusual kind of marriage. This may prove to be a most unfortunate decision in your life, inasmuch as it could lead to insurmountable marital difficulties, quarrels, separation, estrangement or divorce. In an extreme case, you are liable to lose your spouse through death. This is *not* a favorable position for harmonious marriage or partnership unless you devote all your efforts toward making it so.

URANUS IN SCORPIO ♅ ♏

In this position, if Uranus is very badly aspected—with Mars or Saturn, say, in Aries, Leo or Sagittarius, you are susceptible to sudden accidents, danger on or in water, or the threat of physical damage by electrical devices. When well-aspected by planets in earth and water Signs however, Uranus in Scorpio bestows great concentrative powers, strength of mind, determination and willpower. Generally with Uranus in Scorpio, your sheer persistence and spirit are exceptionally resistant, unbreakable by most exterior forces. You have a deeply ingrained love of innovation, and of new and original methods of mechanical and electronic invention.

You drive toward personal advancement in sudden, long bursts of sheer creative energy and will defy any and all who oppose your methods or suggest that you stick to standardized procedures and orthodox methods. You are nearly always at odds with people who live by "accepted" teachings. You are outspoken, sharp, stubborn, secretive, rebellious, blunt, aggressive, courageous, audacious and shrewd. Fortunately, some of our greatest inventions and long-range achievements have come from those with the courage, vision and ability of Uranus in Scorpio. Your relationship with the opposite sex is often volatile and uncontrollable. You tend to change suddenly from a platonic friendship to a passionate physical affair without quite knowing how or why. It also works the other way around. Your greatest asset is the depth and originality of your mind. Use it.

URANUS IN SAGITTARIUS ♅ ♐

You may run into difficulty occasionally with those who are scientifically or religiously orthodox, and may even experience trouble through foreign travels and business abroad. But you have a deep love of true science and possess a broad, humanitarian philosophy that may make organized religion and its practitioners seem very plodding and dull. You are strongly inclined to keep abreast of scientific and technological developments, such as supersonic jets and space voyages —any new method of long-distance travel, for that matter.

You avoid the orthodox, the conventional, and strike out in new directions to pioneer the unknown. You seek philosophical and rational understanding of the cosmos, and don't care whether or not you are personally or physically secure from danger in the process. Above all, you insist on absolute liberty—freedom of speech and movement.

You are open-hearted, generous, adventurous, daring and progressive. Although you may have been uncomfortable in academic surroundings and the discipline required by rigid studies, you instinctively understand that this is the road to broader knowledge, and affords the scope that only higher education can give—cultivation of the higher intellectual and spiritual side of your candid, spontaneous nature. You may be given to precognitive dreams; you have powerful intuition and could possess a strongly visionary, far-sighted imagination. You often have sharp premonitions of coming events that work out in the most uncanny way. It would serve you well to develop this faculty.

URANUS IN CAPRICORN ♅ ♑

During those times when Uranus in your basic horoscope is perturbed by adverse (temporary) transits of Saturn, Mars or Mercury, you tend to become uneasy, restless and impulsive. At these times, you tend to act without thinking; you become stubborn, erratic, radical and eccentric. Generally, however, Uranus in Capricorn is an excellent antidote to the dourness, conservatism, reserve and overserious attitude of this Cardinal earthy Sign. You delight in creating new methods and progressive innovations in business. You have a good, balanced sense of independence, ambition, intensified perseverance and good executive abilities. You refuse to shrink from newer, bolder enterprises. You tend to treat all people alike, regardless of their station in life, the job they hold or what their intellectual or educational qualifications may be. Your attitude is generally equitable and democratic, both to your employees and to your superiors. You can and probably will handle positions of responsibility, authority and/or power.

This position of Uranus is excellent testimony for ultimate success in positions of public trust, particularly in the operation or management of huge power or electrical generating plants, on a television station or network, with an electronics firm or in the manufacturing of new and unusual forms of transportation. You are able to anticipate and foresee the

necessities of the coming years, the conditions of people generally and their needs long in advance. You are not afraid
to make radical departures from established procedures in
order to achieve a desired goal. You possess a well-balanced,
penetrating and profound mind with excellent logic and vision.

URANUS IN AQUARIUS ♅ ♒

This is the natural position of Uranus because this eccentric
planet rules Aquarius and they are mutually compatible. Your
many and varied friends are often regarded as engaged in
unusual or off-beat occupations or somewhat extraordinary
jobs. You have a naturally obliging, friendly, pleasing personality and usually attract refined, humanitarian, sociable,
freedom-loving people such as you are yourself. Some of your
most dearly cherished beliefs, however, at least *tend* to be
peculiar or eccentric. By some kind of strange mental chemistry, you are actually able to equate your great love of freedom and independence with your work—and ultimate success
—in electronics, space technology, anything of a mechanical,
logistic computer or scientific nature. You enjoy the association of others in your field and are generally attracted to
large organizations, humanitarian social movements, advanced kinds of communications networks, government offices
and business or fraternal societies.

You can achieve great satisfaction and success through
association with other people. You just like to be "where
the people are," particularly those who are prominent in public life. You are a born innovator, highly inventive, with a
strong dash of the visionary. You quickly comprehend the
most complex social problems, grasp ideas and convey them
in terms others can understand. You are resourceful, ingenious, original, and powerfully intuitive—you have a good,
active mentality.

URANUS IN PISCES ♅ ♓

This is one of the most difficult and yet strongly psychic
positions of Uranus. You have a tendency to become involved in all sorts of occult activity, and to associate with
unusual, psychic or eccentric people. You experience strange
phenomena, and though you are not by any means unbal-
anced, you may often be subject to visions or other strange
impressions and even experiences. This frequently results in
dreams of a prophetic nature. You have the knack for sensing

things before they occur—for seeing things that are about to happen. Unfortunately, this usually manifests rather negatively—in the most dire, dismal and foreboding sort of expectations imaginable. Try to see things from the bright side rather than anticipating doom and disaster, or fearing the death of loved ones.

You have excellent ability to invent new methods of treatment for old and often "incurable" ills. Develop your latent powers of healing, study and advance your knowledge of biochemistry in order to employ your talents in a positive and helpful way. Don't be discouraged at times of sudden, unexpected misfortune or reversals. This is par for the course for an adversely aspected Uranus—particularly with Mars or Saturn in one of the fire Signs—and *always* works to your advantage in the long run if you are willing to learn.

To find the Sign Uranus occupied at the time of your birth, consult the following table:

TO FIND THE POSITION OF URANUS AT YOUR BIRTH

Date	Zodiacal Sign
Jan. 1, 1890 to Dec. 9, 1890	Libra
Dec. 10, 1890 to Apr. 4, 1891	Scorpio
Apr. 5, 1891 to Sept. 25, 1891	Libra
Sept. 26, 1891 to Dec. 1, 1897	Scorpio
Dec. 2, 1897 to July 3, 1898	Sagittarius
July 4, 1898 to Sept. 10, 1898	Scorpio
Sept. 11, 1898 to Dec. 19, 1904	Sagittarius
Dec. 20, 1904 to Jan. 30, 1912	Capricorn
Jan. 31, 1912 to Sept. 4, 1912	Aquarius
Sept. 5, 1912 to Nov. 11, 1912	Capricorn
Nov. 12, 1912 to Mar. 31, 1919	Aquarius
Apr. 1, 1919 to Aug. 16, 1919	Pisces
Aug. 17, 1919 to Jan. 21, 1920	Aquarius
Jan. 22, 1920 to Mar. 30, 1927	Pisces
Mar. 31, 1927 to Nov. 4, 1927	Aries
Nov. 5, 1927 to Jan. 12, 1928	Pisces
Jan. 13, 1928 to June 6, 1934	Aries
June 7, 1934 to Oct. 9, 1934	Taurus
Oct. 10, 1934 to Mar. 28, 1935	Aries
Mar. 29, 1935 to Aug. 6, 1941	Taurus

Date	Zodiacal Sign
Aug. 7, 1941 to Oct. 4, 1941	Gemini
Oct. 5, 1941 to May 13, 1942	Taurus
May 14, 1942 to Aug. 29, 1948	Gemini
Aug. 30, 1948 to Nov. 11, 1948	Cancer
Nov. 12, 1948 to June 9, 1949	Gemini
June 10, 1949 to Aug. 23, 1955	Cancer
Aug. 24, 1955 to Jan. 27, 1956	Leo
Jan. 28, 1956 to June 8, 1956	Cancer
June 9, 1956 to Oct. 31, 1961	Leo
Nov. 1, 1961 to Jan. 11, 1962	Virgo
Jan. 12, 1962 to Aug. 8, 1962	Leo
Aug. 9, 1962 to Sept. 27, 1968	Virgo
Sept. 28, 1968 to May 20, 1969	Libra
May 21, 1969 to June 23, 1969	Virgo
June 24, 1969 to Dec. 15, 1974	Libra

13

The Influence of Neptune

Moving outward from the Sun, the eighth world one encounters is the nebulous, most perfectly spherical of all the planets, Neptune. Discovered mathematically through the joint efforts of English, French and German astronomers, named Adams, Leverrier and Galle, on September 23, 1846, Neptune exhibited its influence by perturbing the orbit of its planetary neighbor, Uranus. Neptune is about four times the size of the Earth—27,700 miles in diameter—and is very slightly oblate. Like the other giant outer planets, Neptune rotates quite rapidly on its axis; its day is 15 hours and 48 minutes long and its year equals 164.79 Earth years; in other words it takes about 165 years to orbit the Sun. Its distance from the Sun is 2,796,700,000 miles, on the average.

Neptune possesses two satellites. Triton, discovered in 1846, is the largest known moon in the entire solar system. Larger than the planets Mars or Venus, it is nearly 5,000 miles in diameter, and at 219,000 miles from Neptune is considerably closer than our own Moon is to the Earth. The second satellite, Nereid, was discovered by Gerard Kuiper in 1949, and ranges between three to five million miles from its mother planet. As one proceeds outward from the Sun, the planets in their orbits move progressively more slowly. Neptune takes more than 13 years to pass through each Sign of the Zodiac. At a distance of almost three billion miles Neptune cannot be resolved by astronomers to more than a disc with no visible markings, even by the finest Earthbound telescopes.

Pluto has recently been discovered to be almost exactly the same size as Neptune. Consequently, instead of being regarded as an escaped moon of Neptune, Pluto is thought more likely to have been a stray comet or planet captured by the solar system in fairly recent cosmological times. The eccentricity of its orbit is greater than any other planet in the solar system. Its closest passage to the Sun (its perihelion) is almost three billion miles; its longest distance (its aphelion) is nearly five billion miles. Yet there are certain times when Pluto, the "outermost" planet, approaches almost 50 million miles *closer* to the Sun than does Neptune. Ever since it was discovered in 1930, astrologers have been equating Pluto with atomic energy, large group movements, the underworld, "rulership" of the Sign Scorpio, etc. Because of the comparatively brief period in which Pluto has been observed and studied, and because of its great distance from the earth, it seems unlikely at this point that one can confidently make reliable correlations between terrestrial events and Pluto's influence. At least we can't accurately do so until a far longer period of study has been devoted to it. For this reason, and because Pluto takes more than 20 years to pass through just one Sign of the Zodiac (retrograding in motion much of this time) it will require considerable study before astrologers can state with authority what Pluto's influence will be, say, in Aquarius, Capricorn or Pisces, between 120 and 140 years from now, or in any individual horoscope.

The astrological influence of Neptune, the eighth planet, is ephemeral, nebulous, inspirational, emotional (as a "higher octave of Venus") and almost entirely dependent on the aspects of other planets *to* Neptune and its position by Sign (and house). There is considerable doubt about the exact time of birth among a large number of people, of course, and because therefore the *house* positions of the planets are dependent on information that may be erroneous, we shall deal here with planets by Sign only. It will simplify your ability to understand the essentials of horoscope-making to learn the symbols and meanings of the planets and the symbols and meanings of the signs.

In the horoscope blanks printed at the beginning of this section you can insert the planetary symbols in their proper places beginning with the Sign on the First House cusp—the Ascendant (for you or anyone else), then read the interpretations for each planet in each sign in order to learn what makes you the way you are, why you like, love or dislike the personality of someone else. Through this kind of understanding you can learn to appreciate or at least tolerate the subtle differences that exist among all of us. From this foundation you are well on the way to developing higher skills and the facility for erecting a precision chart.

Neptune—our final planet here—is the ruling planet of Pisces, and therefore governs the feet, as you will learn in the next chapter. Neptunian-type people are usually found to be deeply involved in mystical religion, psychism, dream interpretation, spiritualism, mediumship or telepathy. When under adverse aspects, Neptunians are inclined to pretend (and believe) that something is true when in fact it is visionary or dreamlike. They make good promoters, advertising people and (when under powerfully adverse conditions) confidence men and women. When positively aspected, Neptunians psychically reach the highest essence of understanding and sympathy; they gain and possess sure knowledge of events and people—not as they may seem to be, but as they actually are. Neptune represents inner perception, extrasensory ability, ethereal feeling and almost spiritlike sensitivity. This planet is related to liquids and gases, alcohol, drugs, anesthetics and chemicals. When born strongly under Neptune (i.e., with many planets either harmoniously or adversely aspecting it), people have an affinity for liquid refreshments, love to be by the ocean, to work with chemicals or in some capacity be connected with the petroleum industry.

Find the position of Neptune at your birth in the list at the end of this chapter.

NEPTUNE IN ARIES ♆ ♈

You are impelled in the direction of reforming the existing establishment, through a politically active career or public life on the national level. You have some novel ideas concerning the medical profession or spiritual or religious matters, and often receive flashes of inspiration on ways and means of alleviating human suffering and the conditions of the poor or disadvantaged. You possess intuition, understanding, sympathy and a generally affectionate and benevolent nature. You have highly original ideas, probably prompted by your psychic or spiritual experiences. Your sensory apparatus is acute and your emotions and feelings intense. You are attracted to psychic research and secret or mystical societies. You are bound to achieve a great deal of acclaim or popularity in at least one of the various fields of occultism, and will eventually accept a leading role in some popular form of mystical religion—one that takes you traveling. You may have to be wary of a tendency for habituation simply to gratify your physical senses of sensational desires. This includes such plebian pleasures as excessive smoking or the more dangerous indiscriminate use of various forms of stimulants.

NEPTUNE IN TAURUS ♆ ♉

You have a strong leaning toward luxury, ease and mysticism. Although you can be quite sensual, you are usually easy-going, good-hearted and patient. You are generally friendly, but fiery and enthusiastic about the things you believe. In fact this position of Neptune is likely to make you short-tempered when others disagree about your rigid belief in psychic and similar phenomena. You have a good chance of achieving business success and profiting through private or secret organizations and speculation.

You are fortunate in your friendships and affections and in marriage. Although you gain by investment, you have a keen insight into the emptiness of sheer material wealth, and are likely to preach a doctrine of mental and spiritual advancement. You have a certain knack for simplifying complex scientific data, and for making basic truths interesting to the majority. Yet you tend to lack confidence in conventional ways, and often disregard or flaunt orthodox methods of carrying on a successful business. You are something of a visionary, able to foresee the outcome of human progress and achievement many years in advance. You are attracted to the artistic, beautiful and spiritual aspects of life, and have a highly developed aesthetic sense, a tendency, again, toward mysticism and the occult, and a love for what is unusual, curious, odd or antique.

NEPTUNE IN GEMINI ♆ ♊

You have a natural flair for science, mechanics, writing or anything requiring manual dexterity. You are able to express yourself with ingenuity and resourcefulness, particularly through mechanical or electrical devices and in language or mathematics. You are highly imaginative and possess a sensitive, creative mentality. You have a keen interest in mystical studies, unusual forms of liberal education, poetry and dramatic theater. You often have precognitive dreams and *déjà vu* experiences. You are impressionable, and an excellent conversationalist with a profound understanding of symbolism and good facility with languages. You are congenial, sociable, generally friendly and sympathetic.

During periods when Neptune is under adverse aspects—either natally or by transit (particularly where transiting Neptune is in conjunction with or opposition to your natal Mars or Saturn), you are liable to be confused and in a generally muddled state of mind. You're liable then to believe wild rumors and to misunderstand honest reports. When afflicted, Neptune in Gemini results in mental diffusion and the misunderstanding of promises, or deceit with contracts or in agreements. These are periods when you are mentally restless, hypersensitive and impressionable; you become involved with odd or strange friends and caught up in unconventional romances. This leads to difficulty with your family, your friends, and neighbors—and often with a brother or sister. Otherwise you have a good, prophetic mind and varied mental talents.

NEPTUNE IN CANCER ♆ ♋

You have a great love of travel, particularly of ocean cruises. In a rather dual sense, you also crave the comforts of domesticity and love your home and family. At one time or another some very unusual and weird circumstances and experiences will develop mysteriously in your home—events so strange that they will force an important change in your residence.

You possess highly developed spiritual faculties combined with an idealistic, refined and delicate personality. Your emotions are intense; you are impressionable and have a strong imagination. You either have (or have had) great understanding and sympathy for your mother, who may have taught you to love and respect Nature and science, and helped you develop along lines of spiritual communication.

Under adverse aspects, (i.e., planets in fire and air Signs) Neptune in Cancer makes you discontented, restless, changeable, excessively sensitive and impressionable. You may become involved in deception in the home. Strange or peculiar conditions in your domestic life could cause excessive anxiety, pessimism and a highly agitated physical condition—usually resulting in stomach troubles or related illness. One way or another, you'll experience a powerful drive for radical change.

NEPTUNE IN LEO ♆ ♌

If in your natal chart you have the misfortune of Neptune adversely aspected in Leo (i.e., with many planets in water or earth Signs) you tend to express yourself rashly and impulsively; you're likely to squander your money and physical energies, and to allow your feelings and emotions to override your sense of reason. This gives you an inordinate love of pleasure, which results in difficulty controlling your physical desires.

When Neptune is well-aspected (i.e., by the Sun, Moon, Mercury, Venus or Jupiter in fire Signs or air Signs), however, your mind and emotions are keen, intense and convey impressions of human emotions that are sharp and clear. You are considerate, conscientious and spiritually inclined; also generous, visionary and intuitive, with a charitable, sympathetic nature. You tend to be dignified, ambitious, benevolent, warm-hearted and reserved.

This position of Neptune is likely to cause disappointment or deception in love, or heartache through the loss of someone you love deeply and the crushing of your affections. You experience exceptional, highly unconventional conditions in your love life. You are often exposed to mysterious, almost indescribably peculiar sensations and feelings. You are deeply attached to your children and enjoy the theater, refined outdoor sports, swimming, socializing and the fine arts.

NEPTUNE IN VIRGO ♆ ♍

Your disposition is generally kind, patient, gentle and reliable. You tend to be shy and reserved in dealing with strangers, but when it comes to the rather paradoxical mixture of practicality and subjectivity, you shine like a beacon. You are probably good at math and have a strongly spiritual or mystical streak, with a deep understanding of occult phenomena and a strong intellectual bent toward mystical or spiritual matters.

You have an unusual approach to medical problems, diet and hygiene. You often express an odd or peculiar set of theories concerning employment, labor and/or medicine. You have a deep and abiding love for all small living creatures, whether they are fish, fowl, plant or animal. You may often be found nursing sick shrubs or flowers, feeding birds or fish or taking care of cats and dogs. You can excel in positions where trust, reliability and attention to detail are important requirements.

NEPTUNE IN LIBRA ♆ ♎

When Neptune in Libra is under adverse (transiting) influences by other (malefic) planets, you develop an enormous, invariably unwarranted attraction for the opposite sex. During these times you are apt to cry too easily—for little or no discernible reason. You develop too powerful emotions of sympathy and intensity of feeling. Any association or affair you may have will trigger some mysterious or peculiar reactions.

When under favorable aspects by other planets in fire or air Signs (either natal or transiting), however, Neptune brings you admiration, a good social life, love, partnership, popularity and a good marriage. You are keenly poetic, artistic and musically inclined, with an excellent imagination and a deeply compassionate and tender nature. You love peace, harmony, economic and social equality and justice. You like the theater, are fascinated by magic and mystical traditions, and have a general admiration for science and the arts or motion pictures and television. You are strongly attached to a partner, and hardly ever consider doing anything unless it is with someone you are attracted to, or with a sociable group.

NEPTUNE IN SCORPIO ♆ ♏

You have a deep and abiding love of the occult sciences. You have a quick, flaring temper and a strong attraction for what you consider to be secret or recondite arts. You are reticent, extremely secretive at times; you are reserved, and possess a persistent, determined nature. Your feelings and judgments are broad, deep and intense.

You have an excellent capacity for invention and innovation and for devising quicker and better methods of accomplishing things. Your scope of interests is broad, and you probably have a keen attraction for biochemistry, practical psychometry and the meaning of the many strange dreams you've experienced most of your life, particularly during your youth. This is an excellent position for Neptune in regard to financial gain through legacy, but you should be aware that some kind of treachery or deceit will accompany your windfall. Be careful of a tendency you may have for

overindulgence in food and drink, and try to exercise some
control over your rather excessive love of luxury and sensa-
tionalism.

NEPTUNE IN SAGITTARIUS ♆ ♐

You have an almost insatiable desire to travel—everywhere—
and as often as possible. Neptune in Sagittarius endows you
with long-range prophetic ability, and a highly developed
talent for insight into the motivations of other people. You
are liable to have sudden inspirations, or vivid dreams in
which you actually perceive visions that eventually prove to
be true. You possess superb creative ability along the lines of
editorial work and journalism; you like literature, foreign
travel and the improvement of conditions in other countries
which are often either Latin or Spanish-speaking.

You have advanced, peculiar notions about religion, the
human soul, recondite philosophy—and the "new" world of
psi talents as well as a liking for research into ephemeral,
spiritual realms of knowledge. This may be true even though
you are actively engaged in making your living in science,
art or the business world. You may at times experience
trouble during your travels in or through other countries as
a result of your sometimes offbeat ideas or different religious
views. There are times when you become restless and get an
urge to travel—for no discernible reason whatsoever. Try to
curb a slight tendency you develop at times to be emotionally
oversensitive, as a result of strange, indefinite feelings brought
on by bad dreams. Concentrate on your positive mental and
emotional talents.

NEPTUNE IN CAPRICORN ♆ ♑

You are generally cautious and careful; you possess the kind
of mind that considers all the possible repercussions before
taking final action. This results in business acumen. You have
insight that could well bring you success from stock or bond
investments in liquids such as oil, chemicals, beverages, etc.
Your reasoning is sound and your faith is strong; once you
arrive at a decision and become convinced that your pro-
jected path to a certain goal is *the* correct one, you follow it
with remarkable courage, and a lack of fear that seems to
those who know you well to indicate that you've completely
changed character and tossed all caution to the winds. Big
business and large financial transactions appeal to you. You

are also able to manage or direct private and public institutions.

You have a keen interest in psychic and clairvoyant phenomena, and, if other favorable planetary aspects in your chart agree (i.e., planets in earth and water Signs), you tend to profit through music and art rather than to appreciate it aesthetically. You are often quite serious, and can become morose and depressed, or go through severe periods of melancholy. This could have its basis in your younger years, and might be connected in some way with early difficulty and sorrow in your home—especially through some peculiar events related to your father. By confiding in a friend who proves to be unreliable and deceptive, some of your secret business activities might easily blossom into trouble and scandal. When adversely aspected, either natally or by current transits of planets in fire and air Signs, Neptune in Capricorn is liable to make you hazy, indefinite, indecisive and unable to cope with the strange conditions that arise in your family life. It is entirely possible to overcome this by consciously practicing clear, objective thinking in all your affairs until it becomes natural to be decisive and factual.

NEPTUNE IN AQUARIUS ♆ ♒

You are both spiritually and emotionally impressionable—and yet scientifically oriented—with a generally humanitarian, deeply sympathetic and understanding disposition. You are apt to hold some rather eccentric, different or odd views in regard to religion, and to be a completely original and independent scientific thinker, frequently with visionary concepts that are decades (or even *centuries*) ahead of your time! You probably belong to some kind of civic club or a public welfare organization. You tend to be active in community affairs on a broad scale. You enjoy a good social life, are open hearted, congenial and have good friends, many of whom share your love of Nature, the outdoors and conservation.

In love affairs, however, you are liable to become involved in an unusual kind of extramarital relationship that threatens an open scandal and the loss of some of your more conventional friends. Result: disappointment and denial of love; but you are not likely to become bitter or resentful about it. Instead, this may strengthen your extreme desire for independence and may cause you to become even more eccentric or unusual than is ordinarily the case with Neptune in Aquarius. If other aspects in your chart are favorable (many

planets in fire and air Signs), this could tip the scales toward
very superior intelligence.

NEPTUNE IN PISCES ♆ ♓

This is likely to be the most fortunate possible position for
Neptune, because it is the ruling planet of Pisces. You are a
good member of the family and home, with understanding
and sympathy for others. You are kindhearted, charitable and
broadminded—and just as likely to receive the same kind of
charity and sympathy from others as you dispense so freely
yourself.

However, when under transitory adverse influences, Neptune weakens your psychic powers and intuitive ability, and
creates a generally depressing condition. During temporarily
adverse transits of other planets, particularly Mercury, Mars
or Saturn, to Neptune, you experience losses and bad luck
through many odd or extraordinary coincidences that set your
plans back and deny the success of your most cherished projects—through no fault of your own.

You tend to be quiet, dignified, thoughtful, philosophical
and inspirational. Neptune intensifies your *psi* talents and
clairvoyant abilities; it gives you a keen curiosity about mysticism, spiritualism, astrology and all occult studies. You are
contemplative, too, and have a profound mind, are deeply
concerned with the mysteries of Creation, which you probe
through any avenue of knowledge available to you. You love
traveling and exploring, either on, in or under the water.

NEPTUNE'S SIGN FOR THE YEAR YOU WERE BORN

Date	Zodiacal Sign
Jan. 1, 1890 to July 19, 1901	Gemini
July 20, 1901 to Dec. 25, 1901	Cancer
Dec. 26, 1901 to May 19, 1902	Gemini
May 20, 1902 to Sept. 22, 1914	Cancer
Sept. 23, 1914 to Dec. 14, 1914	Leo
Dec. 15, 1914 to July 18, 1915	Cancer
July 19, 1915 to Mar. 19, 1916	Leo
Mar. 20, 1916 to May 1, 1916	Cancer
May 2, 1916 to Sept. 20, 1928	Leo
Sept. 21, 1928 to Feb. 19, 1929	Virgo
Feb. 20, 1929 to July 23, 1929	Leo

Date	Zodiacal Sign
July 24, 1929 to Oct. 3, 1942	Virgo
Oct. 4, 1942 to Apr. 18, 1943	Libra
Apr. 19, 1943 to Aug. 2, 1943	Virgo
Aug. 3, 1943 to Dec. 22, 1955	Libra
Dec. 23, 1955 to Mar. 10, 1956	Scorpio
Mar. 11, 1956 to Oct. 18, 1956	Libra
Oct. 19, 1956 to June 15, 1957	Scorpio
June 16, 1957 to Aug. 4, 1957	Libra
Aug. 5, 1957 to Mar. 4, 1970	Scorpio
Mar. 5, 1970 to Aug. 10, 1970	Sagittarius
Aug. 11, 1970 to Nov. 6, 1970	Scorpio

14

How the Stars Influence
Your Health

Some of the latest discoveries by space-age medics have upset the notion of "biological clocks"—a belief that the cycles and rhythms of all living things are somehow "built into" all organisms. That old belief is no longer taken as true. Space-age studies have shown that extraterrestrial forces regulate almost all natural rhythms.

Thanks to an entirely new kind of research, we know now that these rhythms correlate to and are caused by extraterrestrial forces, much of it in the form of magnetism. This force is so powerful that it is used to twist, cut and form huge chunks of cold steel; industrially it is called *magnaforming*. If magnetism (an invisible force, remember) can do this to cold steel weighing tons, it must have an effect on living tissue. Kenneth S. MacLean, M.D., a New York gynecologist and cytologist (cell expert), has been healing everything from stiff muscles to crippling arthritis with a powerful electromagnetic field.

Professor Robert J. Uffen of the University of Western Ontario has gone even further. He is convinced that "magnetism is the key to Life's origin on Earth."

When Dr. Robert O. Becker, an orthopedic surgeon at State University in New York, applied this theory to individuals in hard testing, he discovered the human biomagnetic field. With his colleagues he mapped out this field in great detail. "Celestial force fields," he said, "can and do exert an influence upon human beings and are responsible for behavioral changes."

Dr. Becker is reluctant to use the word "astrology" to

define his findings. Yet because there are direct and indirect connections between solar, lunar and planetary positions and the way we feel, think and behave, it is only logical to consider seriously what some of our remote ancestors said about astrology and health.

Among other things, astrology does concern itself with planetary influences on our physiology. Each celestial body, including the Sun and Moon, has an effect on weather, mass and individual psychology *and health*—medical astrology being the least understood in spite of its prominent role in what is currently the greatest popular renaissance of the study of the stars in modern times.

In medicine there is a rapidly growing awareness that the human body, like all matter, is a mass of electrical energy "pressed" into what we consider solid matter. It sounds highly exotic to think of all solid material as concentrations of electromagnetic light waves, but the fact is that everything is part of the electromagnetic spectrum. Oddly enough, this view is helpful in explaining how, for example, Jupiter's position and its relationship to other planets in your horoscope can be the reason you might be putting on more weight than usual.

Hippocrates, the Father of Rational Medicine, Aristotle, Galen and Al-Zahrawi (the Father of Arabic Surgery) were primarily good astrologers. During the time of classic Greek antiquity, Hippocrates, in his book, *Airs, Waters and Places,* wrote: "Astronomy contributes not the least but truly the most to medicine. For if anyone comprehends the changes of times and the rise and decline of the stars, he will foresee and prognosticate what kind of year it will be." It thus follows, he added, that individual illness can be predicted—as well as plagues and epidemics. It is entirely possible, he believed, that some may be prevented. Certain kinds of surgery (to specific points of the body) and certain drugs were to be performed and/or administered only at specific times, according to his teaching and writing.

Supporting evidence for this came about five years ago when a Florida doctor announced that hemorrhaging was more prevalent at the time of the Full Moon than during any other period of the month. This was followed by several independent studies by astrologers, which bolstered the claim that neck or throat surgery was actually dangerous on days when the Moon transited Taurus, the Sign of the Bull (which rules the neck and shoulders).

Everyone has the twelve Signs and ten (known) celestial bodies of the solar system located somewhere in his or her

natal horoscope. The exact degree of each Sign, planet, and
house cusp and several other critical factors are important,
but here are the general influences of the Sun, Moon and
the five most important planets:

THE SUN, ruler of Leo, fifth Sign of the Zodiac, also
rules the heart, the basic constitution and deep-seated, general
vitality. The Sun in your chart symbolizes the Life Force or
"Prana"—the universal substance of Life. Our blazing star
rules the entire local planetary system as well as your innermost hereditary tendencies. It appears to affect the basic "stuff
of Life," deoxyribonucleic acid—or DNA. Look to transiting
adverse aspects of the Sun for the chronic or deep-rooted
causes of sickness. Adverse aspects to this dynamic, central
focal point of the horoscope may lead to excess in food
and/or drink, or to exhaustion, or any form of dissipation.
In addition to your heart, the Sun rules your spinal column,
a man's right eye and a woman's left eye, the arteries and the
spleen. An abundance of energy from the Sun can cause
eruptive, inflammatory diseases such as measles and smallpox.
These facts are recognized by many leading authorities in
the new medical study of biomagnetics.

Many highly effective and liberal-minded doctors and psychiatrists in America and Europe consult a patient's horoscope for diagnostic clues. For obvious reasons, not all will
admit it, but Eugene J. Scheimann, a Chicago medical doctor,
has found horoscopy to be almost miraculous as a shortcut
tool for diagnosis and prognosis in otherwise baffling illnesses.
Josephine Favini, M.D., Ph.D. of Scranton, Pennsylvania,
uses the medical horoscope of patients to detect the basis for
most ailments, and she is a favored lecturer at medical groups
and conventions. Dr. Fred Sims Pounds, a brilliant osteo-
pathic physician and surgeon, is a dedicated astrologer and
medical researcher with enormous prestige in Tempe, Arizona. He is also an officer of the American Federation of
Astrologers and has lectured to the faculty and medical students of Ivy League universities.

The urgent need to know more and more about the influence of the cosmic environment on human beings has
prompted heretofore undreamed-of studies of space medicine
by the National Aeronautics and Space Administration.

The Hebrew Medical Journal *Harofé Haivri* (Volume One,
1963) was instrumental in attracting thousands of modern
doctors to consider at least a partial reevaluation of astrology
on human health conditions. In an article by Benjamin L.

Gordon, M.D. of Atlantic City, New Jersey, titled "The Impact of Astrology on Medicine," ancient Babylonian, Hebrew, Greek, Egyptian and Chaldean medical knowledge was impartially reviewed, and cited as a major source of modern clinical studies relating the Sun, Moon, and planets to human health and disease conditions.

THE MOON, ruler of Cancer, fourth Sign of the Zodiac, affects the breasts, stomach (also the emotions) and functions of the body. It is probably no accident or coincidence that the most advanced ancient civilizations independently agreed on the nature and influence of each celestial body. Unlike the blazing golden Sun, the cold silvery Moon was believed to rule the left eye of a man and the right eye of a woman. Luna seems to affect the hereditary chain of molecules called RNA (ribonucleic acid). RNA has been scientifically shown to affect the memory. It has long been known to astrologers that people born in the Sign of Cancer or otherwise strongly under the lunar influence have exceptionally good memories. Now we find that RNA is the stuff from which memory is made. Here is additional justification for the repeated claim that emotional and mental imbalance or derangement is connected with the Moon's influence (the term "lunatic" is related here). Diseases under the Lunar influence are asthma (disorders in the body's mucous membranes), ulcers and other stomach illnesses, abscesses and tumors.

MERCURY, ruler of Gemini and Virgo, governs the nervous system, physical sense perception, respiration and the bioelectrical field (synapses and dendrites at the nerve endings). This ancient "messenger of the gods" is the fast-moving planet associated with nervous disorders: over-excitement, neurasthenia, indecision and restlessness. Those who are born with the Sun, Ascendant or several planets in Gemini or Virgo are strongly affected by Mercury's retrograde periods, when it *appears* to move backward—a phenomenon relative to the Earth's and Mercury's orbits.

VENUS, ruler of Taurus and Libra, governs the neck, throat, larynx, esophagus, kidneys and the internal reproductive system. Being the planet of balance, it rules the inner ear and affects emotional responses to musical harmony, equilibrium and artistic sensibilities (again depending on its position by Sign and house and the aspects to and from

other planets). Look to the position of Venus and her aspects
to the Sun, Moon or Ascendant for clues to inflammation of
the throat such as tonsilitis as well as kidney disease, goiter
and other lymphatic ailments.

MARS is the ruler of Aries and the co-ruler, or lower
octave of Scorpio. The adverse position and/or relationship
of Mars to the Sun, Saturn or Jupiter in a horoscope indicates debilitation, lack of muscular coordination and weakness. When computer studies are made of the relationship
between muscular dystrophy and the adverse influence of
Mars in the horoscopes of the stricken, science may well
have leapfrogged all *cures* and discovered a method of *pre-
vention*. The best current method is to *time* a child's birth
in order to benefit from the good aspects to and from
Mars. Mercury has a great deal to do with muscular coordination; both palsy and muscular dystrophy result from adverse aspects between the Sun, Mars and Mercury at birth.
Mars rules your strength, vigor, courage and animal vitality.
When adversely aspected by transiting planets superimposed
against the natal chart, the Red Planet produces a *concentrated* biomagnetic field in the body, inducing fever as well
as the transformation of calories and carbohydrates into heat
and energy. Mars is intimately associated with the red blood
corpuscles, with hemorrhaging from injuries, with accidents
and operations. All wounds, all genital and muscular disorders, are under the nominal signature of Mars. This also
applies to all contagious and infectious diseases.

JUPITER is the ruler of Sagittarius and the lower octave
of Pisces. This banded giant of the solar system is now recognized by planetary physicists as a small sun rather than a
huge planet. During the past few years scientists have been
compiling evidence indicating that the known comets (as
well as the outer planets: Neptune, Uranus and Pluto) may
actually have originated from the immense body of this
"planet of abundance," as the Romans and Greeks called it.
Jupiter is larger than all other Solarian planets combined.
Due to some totally unexplained paradox, as I've mentioned
before, Jupiter radiates more than two and a half times more
energy than he receives from the Sun. According to the observations of medical astrologers, many centuries before the
time of Hippocrates, Jupiter's designation as the planet of
abundance was determined by his position in the charts of
millions of human beings. Jupiter rules the liver and cellular

nutrition, and therefore the building of new flesh and blood.

It has been demonstrated countless times that those who have Jupiter on the Ascendant (the Eastern horizon) at birth, usually have some difficulty with weight control; this part of the horoscope represents the physical body—and Jupiter symbolizes abundance. Psychologically, Sagittarians and Jupiter-ruled people are usually of the "jovial" type (this is a purely astrological term)—expansive and gregarious. Their diseases are usually high blood pressure, diabetes and illnesses caused by congestion—a general overrichness of the physical system. Interestingly enough, this can also include liver trouble, gout or even high cholesterol count.

SATURN is the beautiful ringed ruler of Capricorn. Its principle is contraction, precisely opposing Jupiterian expansion. Saturn is the perfect symbol for what Dr. Lloyd Graham of Grant's Pass, Oregon, calls a negative biomagnetic field— (the human body's electrical charge) at its most intense. "Whatever Jupiter promises, Saturn denies," is a good rule of thumb, when both planets are equally or heavily aspected in a health horoscope. Generally, however, if Jupiter is more favorably aspected by Venus or the Sun, the health of the native is excellent.

In spite of its concentric rings and beautiful colors, Saturn, when under transiting adverse aspects, causes a *decentrated* (cold) energy field in the human body. Saturn is also responsible for impediments to inner physical functions, causing obstructions, sluggishness and poor circulation. According to Saturn's position by house, Sign, and aspects to other planets, either natally or by transit, the slowing down of any physiological process may be determined. Saturn is a major cause of constipation, rheumatism and similar complaints. Because of the physiologically and mentally constricting influence of this planetary ruler of Capricorn, Saturn often produces melancholy, emotional depression and the kind of fear that weighs heavily on a person. The result is a wholly negative attitude —one that might easily thwart all attempts at a fast cure. Psychological depression *can*, usually, be traced to a *temporary* (transiting) bad aspect made by Saturn. Even amateur astrologers can easily predict when it will be over by noting how long it takes Saturn to move several degrees "out of orb" of a bad aspect. It is important to remember that our bad periods and cycles are largely caused by adverse transits of the planets to sensitive points *in* our horoscopes. Just remember that 90 degrees (square) and 180 degrees (opposi-

tion) are adverse, while 60 degrees (sextile) and 120 degrees
(trine) are beneficial. Everything passes.

It's no accident that we consider the serious, dour, sad or
melancholy person or mood as "saturnine." This is another
purely astrological term—and one that has been with us from
the most ancient times.

The late Dr. William Davidson of Chicago wrote that
"Medical astrology, as astro-diagnosis, is *of* the profoundest
use to nearly everyone. It is the key to the idiosyncrasies of
the body . . . you'll find that your horoscope can be a greater
contribution to your health than you suspect. It shows you
not only know how to keep well, how to prevent disease, but
also what approach for the cure of it. For the professional,
it is priceless."

15

Interview with
an Astro-Economist

Astrology is in big business more than most people suspect, or than big business will admit, and it looks as though it's there to stay. One of America's largest tobacco companies provides a personal astrological service for some of its customers. RCA Communications studies the angular positions of the planets and predicts radio weather with 93 percent accuracy. Consolidated Edison, one of America's giant power utilities, revamped its entire underground cable system as a result of astrological discoveries.

Lieutenant Commander David Williams, who was primarily responsible for this development, was for years the manager of cable purchases for Con Ed. His record in the U.S. military forces dates back to service during the Mexican Border Campaign; he also served during World Wars I and II. He was born in Leeds, England, and came to the United States at the age of seven. He received his degree in electrical engineering from Cooper Union in New York, and has been a lifelong student of science and economic cycles—and ultimately, of astrology. While serving as vice president of the New York chapter of the Foundation for the Study of Cycles (now the Foundation for the Study of Recurring Events), he was also a member of the New York Academy of Sciences and the Astrologers Guild of America (of which he served several terms as president).

He travels extensively, lectures on economic cycles and writes a regular feature for an astrological magazine in his spare time. Although he practices what he preaches, and uses his planetary system to net good profits in the market, he declines to offer advice for two reasons: "First, I'm retired. And second, I have no license to act as a broker or adviser." Still, he has been known to give valuable tips to close associates and friends. His reluctance to become deeply involved in stock market counseling stems from the certain knowledge that he'd be inundated with requests.

During his Navy career, and while he managed cable purchases for Con Ed, his championing of astrology was often challenged. In early August 1960, for example, he was a guest, with several fellow executives, aboard a yacht called the *Inspiration*, owned by Henry Fried, the president of Mackay Construction Corporation. Someone suggested that if astrology were so accurate and helpful, Williams should be able to choose accurately the winner of November's Presidential election.

He went them one better—he had already cast the horoscopes of Kennedy and Nixon. The triple predictions he made then were considered so incredible that he was asked to write them down and have them signed by six witnesses. Here's the terse note Williams scribbled:

"Aug. 4/60 Abd. Inspiration. Prediction by D. Williams: 'Kennedy will be elected and will die in office and will be succeeded by Johnson.'"

His friends were impressed when Kennedy won the election by a slim margin. But when the young chief executive was shot and killed on November 22, 1963, many questions concerning the nature of fate or free will followed the shocked silence of those who remembered David Williams' written prediction. Of course, Johnson's Vice Presidency had been scarcely in the wind at the time.

Williams claims that magnetic disturbances on the Sun are caused by certain angular relationships among the planets; these same relationships also have a disturbing effect on man, whose biomagnetic field is profoundly affected by resultant changes in the Earth's magnetism.

"Is it any wonder then," he inquires, "that the habits, nature, even the destiny pattern of a newborn baby should be affected by the planetary dispositions at his birth? With its first breath the newborn child takes in billions of electrons, inducing an electronic pattern which is influenced all his life by the magnetic field formed by the planets."

Those astrologers who did charts preceding the blackout of the Northeastern U.S. on November 9, 1965, *knew* what would happen, though they couldn't say exactly why.

Six years before that near-disaster, Consolidated Edison's

underground cables failed, and half a million New Yorkers were deprived of electrical services. Both David Williams and John H. Nelson, the man who predicts radio weather for RCA, belonged to the Foundation for the Study of Cycles. Williams recalls that Nelson had charted the positions of the planets for August 17, 1959, and predicted a severe magnetic storm for that date.

While a large segment of New York struggled along with a power blackout, Williams learned from RCA's Nelson that short-wave radio communications were also blanked out in the entire Northeastern area. The ex-Navy man figured it was more than a coincidence that the blackout and iono-spheric-geomagnetic disturbances occurred at the same time. Since cables were his specialty, he wondered if *they* could have been affected by the adverse planetary setup Nelson had predicted more than a month before.

Rather than ponder and do nothing, he risked the ridicule of Con Ed's engineers by presenting his astrological theories for their study. No one poked fun at his suspicions. Instead, he was asked to predict the time of the next disturbance if he could.

"That's the difference between the theoretical scientist and the practical engineer," Williams observed later. "The scientist is usually happy enough to try and figure things out in a lab, but the engineer wants to know 'does it work'? and isn't too concerned about theory."

He went along with the engineers, and chose August 30, a Sunday, as the date of the next bad cable trouble. Sure enough, there were twelve cable failures on that date—three times the normal amount.

Encouraged, he studied cable failures from 1954 to 1959 and discovered a strong correlation with geomagnetic disturbances, but he wanted to check this out with his foreign colleagues. He went to his native England and held consultations with British engineers. When he returned he presented what he thought might be a geomagnetic activity-proof cable to Consolidated Edison. This involved wrapping all cables with polyethylene over lead shielding. Con Ed went ahead. Considering Con Ed's fantastic 8,460-mile network of underground cable, this was an extremely costly undertaking. But the reduction of power breakdowns during the following years more than compensated for the ten percent increase in cable costs.

This is just one example, according to David Williams, of how important economic changes have resulted from astro-

logical studies. There are others, and apparently there will be
many more in the years to come. I interviewed Mr. Williams
at his home in Queens, New York early in 1967. Here are
some of his views regarding questions almost anyone might
want to ask a solid, scientifically oriented astrologer—especially an expert in this area who employs his skills to
predict business cycles and make substantial profits on the
stock market:

Question: Basically, what is the rationale of your conviction that the stars and the planets affect life on Earth?

Williams: After forty years of observing the correlation
between planetary patterns and events here on Earth, such as
the correlation with business cycles, the correlation with stock
market cycles, the correlation with historical events, I'm perfectly satisfied that it is a valid technique of predicting things
that will happen in the future.

Question: You've written a book called *Astro-Economics*
—*A Study of Astrology and the Business Cycle* (put out by
Llewellyn Pub. Co. in 1958). What's the reaction from brok-
ers and market investors?

Williams: The reaction has been uniformly gratifying.
While not all the people who've read the book are fully convinced of its validity, they are open minded and are willing
to believe in the *possibility* of there being a valid correlation
between planetary patterns and the business cycle.

Question: Since there's an element of chance in investment,
what part do you think superstition plays among people who
dabble in the market?

Williams: Well . . . the word "superstition" is, in the light
of many new discoveries, a relic of ancient days. What we
do not understand we call "superstition." Once an explanation
for something is given, it is no longer considered a superstition to believe in it. All investing involves an element of
chance. Whatever is claimed by anybody, there's just no such
thing as an infallible system for success in the stock market
any more than there is an infallible system for success in
any other activity or human endeavor. On the other hand,
the use of a technique that has been shown to have a reasonable or high degree of accuracy is far better than chance.
This would be something that most people can profit by.

Question: Articles about you and your astrological system
have appeared in various magazines, even on the front page
of *The Wall Street Journal.* Jess Stearn documented your prediction of President Kennedy's election and assassination.
How could you have known of this in 1960?

Williams: At that time I was thoroughly familiar with the twenty-year death cycle of our presidents, and so, when I was asked on August 4, 1960 by a group of my associates who I thought would be elected to the Presidency according to my interpretation of the planetary patterns, I was able to choose Kennedy unhesitatingly. His chart was more in line with the prevailing planetary patterns as well as the national horoscope than was Nixon's.

Question: And from this you deduced that he would also be assassinated?

Williams: Not that he would be assassinated, but that he would die while still in office.

Question: If economic cycles can be predicted with confidence, why is it that more people do not use astrology before buying or selling stock?

Williams: Simply because they don't know about it. Financial astrology is a relatively new branch of mundane astrology. Really very little is known about it by the general public.

Question: What would happen if the majority of counselors and stockbrokers suddenly began using the system you describe?

Williams: Well then it would be self-defeating. The proof of that is that there are other systems of predicting stock market activity that are used by professionals, such as the Dow theory. The historic evidence shows that when the majority of traders or investors in the market act upon the Dow theory's signal, they bring to pass what the signal is supposed to indicate.

Question: With your military, naval, industrial and scientific background and interests, what really prompted you to study astrology and develop the idea of Astro-Economics?

Williams: Oh, when I transferred from the engineering department to the purchasing department of the Edison Company in 1927 . . . well, naturally I became interested in what caused prices to go up and down, and my studies of economics revealed that there was a theory going back to Professor Jevons in 1875 that the business cycle was caused by the Sunspot cycle . . . or, occurred synchronously with the Sunspot cycle. When I studied the literature on the Sunspot cycle I learned that a great many of the astronomers believed that the Sunspot cycle was caused by planetary configurations. That, in turn, led me to the study of astrology, which I continue to the present.

Question: In the graphs of American business activity in your book, you've drawn some remarkable parallels between angular planetary positions and the condition of the market. Can you explain roughly how this works?

Williams: It has been observed over periods of many centuries that when planets are in approximately the same position of the heavens . . . that is, when they are zero degrees apart, or when they are ninety degrees apart—or when they are 180 degrees apart—that discordant conditions arise here on Earth. When the planets are sixty degrees apart or 120 degrees apart, it has been found that harmonious conditions prevail. Now, these conditions are not only physical, insofar as they are observable in physical phenomena such as radio transmission, magnetic disturbances and disturbances with power lines but they are also manifested in the relationships between human beings—the reactions of human beings.

Question: How are Sunspots linked to the position of the planets?

Williams: Well, there were two very prominent schools of thought in the middle and latter part of the 19th Century which had opposing ideas as to the origin of Sunspots. One group felt that Sunspots originated from disturbances within the Sun, and the other, equally prominent, group of astronomers felt that Sunspots were caused by the planetary positions. As of today the controversy has not been resolved.*

Question: The bibliography of your book is extensive, and you've probably made newer studies since it was published. Have you discovered anything you hadn't known before?

Williams: Yes. After the book, Astro-Economics, was published, many of the readers asked me if the same theory could be applied to the stock markets. Well, that entailed additional research, and since the stock market fluctuates more rapidly and frequently than the business cycle, I found that these more frequent variations were due to planetary cycles of a shorter duration than those covered in the book Astro-Economics.

Question: Astronomers since Copernicus and Galileo have known that the Sun is the center of the solar system. Why do astrologers insist on using the Earth as a central point of reference?

Williams: That isn't unique with astrologers; all navigators use the geocentric system; all surveyors use the geocentric system—because they are concerned with measuring something with relation to the Earth on which they are located . . . and

_____

* Since this writing, it is almost universally accepted that planets cause Sunspots and solar flares. J.F.G.

similarly the astrologer is concerned with effects of planetary movements on an individual located at a specific point on the Earth, not on the Sun.

Question: Your book was published in 1958. In it you have a graph relating business to planetary positions that stretches from 1949 to 1968. How accurate has it been?

Williams: I recently made a checkup on that and other graphs in *Astro-Economics,* and I found that the degree of accuracy was of the same order of magnitude as other charts shown in the book, namely about 68 percent.

Question: What advice do you have for investors in 1968?

Williams: I've predicted that 1968 will see a rising market . . . but again—it will be subject to reactions from time to time. Now, a word about reactions—there is a peculiarity in our Internal Revenue laws which permits investors to claim long-term capital gains after holding a stock for six months or more. Such gains are taxed at only half the rate of short-term gains; therefore, if people buy at the bottom of a break it is more than likely that a great many of them will hold the stock for more than six months before they sell so as to get the advantage of a lower tax rate. We can therefore expect market "reactions" from time to time—and usually at six-month intervals.

Question: You say that two adverse aspects will nullify a good one or vice versa. Can't this be construed as an excuse for a bad prediction?

Williams: You can't have it both ways. In my book I show how there are numerous instances where the different planetary cycles will peak—or bottom out—sometimes at different periods and sometimes at almost the same span of time. Thus, if one cycle is *topping* out on a given day and another cycle is *bottoming* out on a given day, they cannot *both* be right; one is right and one is wrong, and that's what accounts for the relatively low *general* average of these predictions. On the other hand, when I take an individual planetary cycle and relate it to the market or the business cycle, it is often as high as 85 percent accurate.

Question: Is it possible for an astrologer to make predictions about specific stocks? Can you set up a chart, let's say, for a corporation?

Williams: Yes, you can set up a corporation's chart. But I don't think it has been too successful, because the only thing that you can go by, in most cases, is the date of incorporation, and that doesn't necessarily mean the *idea* for that particular corporation originated at—or near—that date. I know of some people who have made a great deal of money in the market by buying stocks whose chart and date of incorporation had aspects that were favorable to their own natal chart . . . their horoscope.

Question: Isn't it rather an exotic notion that the *time* someone got the idea to form a corporation could be a determining factor in that corporation's future?

Williams: It's the only idea, so far, that possibly explains how or why charts for incorporation dates do not always seem to work. I'd like to see several new companies incorporate under ideal astrological conditions.

Question: Do we have any truly ideal situations to look forward to in the near future?

Williams: Well, there's no time when there aren't some discordant elements present, but one has to take, really, the weighted average of all the influences present. Naturally, a 120-degree beneficial aspect between Jupiter and Venus would be far more powerful than an adverse aspect, say of 90 degrees between Mercury and Mars. It has been observed that the more favorable planets, such as Jupiter and Venus, have a stronger influence . . . perhaps because of their size and nearness to the Earth or Sun. Whatever the reason, this is the observed experience.

Question: You seem to dominate the field of Astro-Economics. Are there others who do the same kind of work and research?

Williams: There undoubtedly are, but so far as I know there are only two who actually have advertised that they predict from planetary patterns. Most professional security advisors who use astrology do it on the Q.T.

Question: Do you always find planetary reasons for depressions, wars, periods of inflation and bull markets?

Williams: Yes. They are very closely related. The most accurate indication of depression is when a pair of outer planets, such as Jupiter and Uranus, are in the same degree of longitude--or, as we say, in conjunction. The conjunctions of the major planets have had the highest degree of correlation with periods of panic of any of the planetary patterns that I have studied.

Question: In your estimation, what is the future for your kind of astrological-economic study and practice?

Williams: I think that more and more reputable security advisors will use it as a tool to supplement the various other technical tools that they use, primarily because of its accuracy for exactly timing changes in the market.

Question: Are there other important areas of human interest and involvement to which astrology can honestly address itself?

Williams: Yes. One of the more important phases of application for astrological knowledge is in the field of international relationships. For example, I have predicted that, beginning with the entrance of Saturn into Aries on March 3, 1967, the probability of a truce in Vietnam will be far greater than it has been heretofore. The United States will be in a far more favorable position to negotiate a truce with everyone concerned.*

Question: Why is it that a nation like India, which is so astrology-conscious, is also so economically poor and financially unstable?

Williams: Well, India is cursed with the superstitions inherent in their polytheistic religious beliefs, and so they are, in a sense, the slaves of superstition. Particularly with respect to cow worship. The so-called "sacred cows" eat enormous quantities of food which could be far better used to feed India's starving masses. The cows themselves are a great potential food source, but the superstitious Hindu population won't touch them. The fault doesn't lie with the minority who believe in astrology but with the majority who refuse to shed ancient superstitions.

Question: Apparently there are some eminent scientists now engaged in research into astrology. What sort of developments can explain this new attitude?

Williams: The developments of the space age have made it imperative that physical scientists learn more and more about what goes on in outer space. And so they have developed far more sensitive instruments, to learn more about our celestial environment than has ever been possible before. The result is that we are now in a position to plot the orbit of a projectile in such a way as to avoid inharmonious regions of interplanetary space.

Question: Is there some way that magnetic angles between planets can affect whole populations, perhaps all men on Earth at the same time?

Williams: Well, to a certain degree everyone is affected by a given planetary configuration. But the extent of the in-

---

* The opportunity for a Vietnam truce did seem imminent early in March, 1967, but neither side extended itself quite far enough, and it was lost. Williams was close to being right.—J.F.G.

fluence varies from place to place, because the angular relationship to a particular spot on Earth varies with the location
of the Earth and its position in relation to the other planets,

Question: If humans are told to buy or sell according to
celestial influence, and if the economic barometer actually
reflects planetary conditions, how much free will do we have?

Williams: The individual is never really *compelled* to act.
The influences are there, whether those influences are favorable or unfavorable. Some individuals will be immune to
those influences. Some would *like* to act according to celestial
stimuli, but do not have the wherewithal to act on them.

Question: What would you advise someone who wanted to
investigate and use the astrological system on the market?

Williams: Unfortunately, there really isn't any up-to-date
textbook on stock market forecasting. I hope in the next year
or so to bring out such a textbook, and then people could
try it out before actually investing, to determine for themselves if the system works well enough to use it.

Question: What is the future of astrology? Do you think it
will ever become a science?

Williams: No. Astrology will never become a science. It's
an art, and a great deal of its success depends upon the skill
of the practitioner. If the practitioner doesn't have sufficient
experience and knowledge, then that practitioner's interpretation of planetary positions will not be very good. It's just
as in medicine; an unskilled practitioner of medicine can
make a wrong diagnosis which is not very helpful to his
patient. *Medicine* is not a science; it's an art.

Question: You buy stocks according to your own astrological calculations?

Williams: Oh, yes. Yes indeed I do. And I've been, I'm
happy to say, very successful at it.

16

Astrological Organizations and Practicing Astrologers

ASTROLOGICAL ORGANIZATIONS

Modern astrology is undergoing a phenomenal growth and increase in interest. This attention is not confined to laymen who want to know more about themselves and their friends, neighbors, relatives or business associates. It has spread into several high academic and scientific areas. From time to time government and other officials, too, approach the subject, usually under the guise of normal, personal curiosity. The sweeping revolution in our concept of man's relationship with his environment—both terrestrial and celestial—is at last prompting research and discovery of astrological facts that would have been generally jeered at before Sputnik I was orbited in 1957.

There are more serious students of astrology today than ever before in the history of modern physical science. In some areas it has actually made inroads into scientific areas that no one could have foreseen—excepting, perhaps, a handful of the better astrologers of a few decades ago.

The headquarters of the American Federation of Astrologers is located on Capitol Hill, at 6 Library Court, S.E., Washington, D.C. 20003. And there are branches, as well as other astrological organizations, throughout the country (and the rest of the world).

Despite the renaissance of astrology in America and other countries there is a definite scarcity of qualified teachers and practitioners. Most would-be clients or students are usually exposed to one of two extremes in astrological material: (a)

the light entertainment you find in newspapers and magazines
or (b) difficult, often complex books of rules, laws and
aphorisms intended solely for the most advanced students.

Key words and clues frequently do more to increase understanding of astrology than stacks of dusty old textbooks,
or than the rules laid down in Ptolemy's *Tetrabiblos*. In a
recent issue of the *Bulletin of the American Federation of
Astrologers*, the following list was reprinted:

SIGN	KEY WORDS	EXPRESSION
Aries	I am	Aspiration
Taurus	I have	Integration
Gemini	I think	Reason
Cancer	I feel	Expansion
Leo	I will	Assurance
Virgo	I analyze	Assimilation
Libra	I balance	Equivalence
Scorpio	I desire	Creativity
Sagittarius	I see	Illumination
Capricorn	I use	Organization
Aquarius	I know	Originality
Pisces	I believe	Sacrifice

By following the general, rather loose rules previously
outlined for the layout of your horoscope, you will have
saved yourself lengthy study and the necessity of buying
long lists of expensive, technical books (although it is entirely
possible that you might want to pursue the study and learn
its many technicalities).

Although it is not necessary to be an astrologer to belong
to the American Federation of Astrologers, its Code of
Ethics must be signed and abided by. In addition, each member is usually recommended by two others.

The code reads as follows:

I, the undersigned, subscribe to the following Code of
Ethics:

I recognize that a precise astrological opinion cannot honestly be rendered with reference to the life of an individual
unless it is based upon a horoscope cast for the year, month,
day and time of day plus correct geographical location of
the place of birth of that individual, and I agree not to render
such an opinion without this detailed information, unless the
horoscope of the individual has been rectified by accepted
astrological methods, or unless I positively state to the inter-

ested party that such conclusions are reached by alternative methods.

I agree not to interpolate or introduce into any astrological deduction, verbally or otherwise, any interpretation which my conclusions appear to warrant that are irrelevant to the Science of Astrology, without first stating definitely that such deductions are neither based upon the life chart nor identified with the science.

I agree to honor and respect all confidences which may be reposed in me by consultation and to hold such confidences inviolable excepting wherein they may involve an act of felony or treason.

I agree not to use my identification with the American Federation of Astrologers, Inc., as a signature of publicity in any unethical manner. I agree to assist in any way I can in the elimination of the charlatan who may be masquerading under any form of title that can be construed to mean a connection with Astrology designed to mislead the public or trade upon their credulity in any way; and I hereby subscribe to this Code of Ethics as a condition of my membership in the American Federation of Astrologers, Inc.

The Federation reserves the right to terminate membership at the discretion of the Board of Directors.

The officers and board of directors of the AFA and their addresses are:

President: Dorothy B. Hughes, 1833 Queen Anne Avenue, North, Seattle, Washington 98109

First Vice President: Dr. Bertrand R. Adams, 1013 Adams St., Prairie Ark, Ames, Iowa 50010

Second Vice President: Dr. F. Sims Pounds, Jr., 16-D Danelle Plaza, 3300 South Mill Ave., Tempe, Arizona 85281

Third Vice President: Oscar Weber, 58 Birchcroft Road, Canton, Massachusetts 02021

Treasurer: Muriel Thomas, P.O. Box 1080, Pueblo, Colorado 81002

Corresponding Secretary: Mildred Johnson, 1947 S. Bedford St., Los Angeles, California 90034

Recording Secretary: Howard Hammitt, Jr., P.O. Box 1825, San Francisco, California 94101

Executive Secretary: Paul R. Grell, 412 Fifth Street, S.E., Washington, D.C. 20003

Directors: Cordelia E. Coull, 5014 8th Avenue, South, Gulfport, Florida 33707

Clara M. Darr, 2527 Broadway, Toledo, Ohio 43609

Stella Ann Morgan, 241 Sixth Ave., Apt. 7-H,
New York, N.Y. 10011

Oscar Weber, the former president, was preceded by
Howard Duff. The current President, Dorothy B. Hughes, began studying astrology in 1946. She is a graduate of St.
Helen's Hall College, and a former teacher of philosophical
astrology at the Rosicrucian Fellowship in Seattle. Mrs.
Hughes is an excellent practical astrologer, having been a
member of the AFA for 15 years, as well as of her local
group, the Seattle Astrological Association. An honorary Life
Member in the AFA, she's listed in *Who's Who of American
Women 1966*, teaches advanced astrology classes (to many
scientifically and technically oriented university students), and
owns one of the most complete astrological bookshops in the
nation.

The American Federation of Astrologers has affiliates in
various parts of the nation. Listed alphabetically (by states)
they are:

The Church of Light, Inc., Main office 3974 West 6th,
Los Angeles, California 90005. Mail address: P.O. Box 1525,
Los Angeles, Calif. 90053.

Educational Astrology, Inc., Mildred Johnson, Secretary,
1947 South Bedford Street, Los Angeles 34, California.

First Temple of Astrology, 733 South Burlington Street,
Los Angeles, California (57).

Colorado Astrological Association, Inc., Laura F. Rom-
strom, Executive Secretary, P.O. Box 4111, South Denver
Station, Denver, Colorado.

Washington Astrological Association, 631 East Capitol
Street, S.E., Washington, D.C. 20003.

Astrology Club of St. Petersburg, Florida, Anna Andersen,
Secretary-Treasurer, 4227 36th Avenue North, St. Petersburg 13, Florida.

Winter Haven Astrological Association, R. 2, Box 350,
Winter Haven, Florida.

Friends of Astrology, Gloria Barrett, President, 5329 North
Spaulding Avenue, Chicago 25, Illinois.

New Orleans Astrological Society, Evna Edmundson, President, 1021 Royal Street, New Orleans 16, Louisiana.

New England Astrological Association, Frances Aldred
Sakoian, President, One Monadnock Road, Arlington 74,
Massachusetts.

Astrological Club of Greater St. Louis, Alma Blum, Presi-
den, 3022 Longfellow Blvd., St. Louis 4, Missouri.

Astro-Research Society, Mrs. Lily Krome, Corresponding Secretary, 9155 Edna Street, St. Louis 37, Missouri.

Research Astrologers, Nora Morrison, Secretary-Treasurer, 4986-A Oletha Avenue, St. Louis 9, Missouri.

Astrologers' Guild of America, Inc., 520 Fifth Avenue, New York, N.Y. 10036.

The Church of Light, Inc., of New York, 1472 Broadway, New York, N.Y. 10036.

Astrological Study Group of Columbus Theosophical Lodge, 827 West Broad Street, Columbus, Ohio.

Ohio Astrological Association, Nora M. Forrest, President, 1330 Giel Avenue, Lakewood 7, Ohio.

The Planetheirs, Mary C. Barton, President, 1926 Woodbridge Street, Toledo 15, Ohio.

The Starlighters, Charline Shipman, Secretary-Treasurer, 2477 Broadway, Toledo 9, Ohio.

Pittsburgh Astrology Association, Harriet Friedlander, President, P.O. Box 8241, Pittsburgh 17, Pennsylvania.

Cellar School of Astrology, Dorothy B. Hughes, President, 1412 Fifth Avenue West, Seattle 99, Washington.

North Star Astrological Group, Elaine Birkes, Secretary-Treasurer, 3105 North 32nd Street, Tacoma 7, Washington.

Wisconsin Starlighters, Inc., Miss Louise S. Ivey, President, 7010 West North Avenue, Milwaukee 13, Wisconsin.

The Astrological Association of England is a staid, scientifically oriented organization boasting the names of prominent writers and scientists as members. Unlike the American Federation of Astrologers, whose *Bulletin* is mailed free each month to its entire membership, *The Astrological Journal,* the official organ of the British Astrological Association, is priced at three shillings and sixpence (forty-nine cents in American money) and is issued quarterly. Its quality is objective and scholarly, on about the same level as general orthodox scientific and technical journals here in America. The Association's President is John M. Addey, 85 Cheam Road, Sutton, Surrey, England. General Secretary: Jim Stephenson, 30 Eardley Crescent, London, S.W. 5. Members' Secretary & Treasurer: Miss A. L. Phillips, 57 Woodside, London, S.W. 19, England.

An astrological outfit called The Rising Star puts out a monthly semi-technical prediction of coming world events and shows (with horoscopes) the planetary conditions that accompany political and scientific progress, wars, economic cycles and the general psychological conditions which cause these changes. You can receive a sample copy of this interesting little pamphlet called *The Calendar of Mundane Cycle Chart, Progressed Aspects*, from The Rising Star at 3004 E. 13th St., Wichita, Kansas 67214, and form your own judgment about its accuracy or value.

There are numerous other quasi-astrological groups and small organizations purporting to deal seriously with astrology. In most cases, however, they also include other weird —and possibly "wonderful"—areas of speculation that are far beyond the fringes of the aim of this book—to demonstrate as simply as possible that a rational and logical case exists for the theorem that each of us is a discrete entity whose psychology may be accurately determined, as Carl Jung demonstrated, by our individual horoscopes.

—AND PRACTICING ASTROLOGERS

Just about anyone interested enough to read a book on astrology eventually wants to consult a practicing professional astrologer. Your satisfaction from such a visit depends entirely on the astrologer's capability, experience and attitude—and your motivation. There *is* something of scientific value to astrology, despite all the drivel and charlatanism with which it is surrounded, as you've probably concluded by now, so pick a *good* astrologer.

A recent case for astrology was found in the marriage of a pair of Time Twins or Astro-Twins (this phenomenon was covered in detail in my book, *Astrology: The Space Age Science,* Chapter One) in Seoul, Korea. This Oriental couple were born in the same town at the same minute, 11 P.M., May 23, 1934, and have lived virtually identical lives, doing the same things at the same times, and having accidents and illnesses and the same or similar experiences at the same time. (All investigated cases of Time Twins do, and there have been many.) Each astro-twin became a lecturer at the same university at the same time and eventually they married each other and produced a child. This is where the phenomenon turned into a scientific "oddity." The child, Ungyong Kim, at the age of three was known as the "Einstein of Seoul," a youngster with an habitually grave expression and a brain that profoundly amazes psychologists and other experts. This prodigy is now so mentally advanced that he reads, writes and solves the most difficult mathematical problems almost in the

wink of an eye. The Intelligence Quotient for genius is a
figure of 160. Kim took three I.Q. tests which resulted in
scores of 173, 200 and 210.

Orthodox experts regard the fact that some believe this
little mental giant to be a direct result of the mating of two
people with identical horoscopes as sheer nonsense.

There are, however, serious radio and television shows
coming out now all over the nation that deal with astrology,
without actually endorsing belief in the subject. *Your Daily
Horoscope* is one, *Starscope* is another. Each is a syndicated
TV show.

Until early in 1967, astrological columnist and ex-newsman
Sydney Omarr had a show on KNX in Los Angeles. WCAU
in Philadelphia ran a similar show, on a regular basis, with
Ed Harvey and Jack McKinney as hosts. They ran out of
astrologers. And CBS station WEEI had an astrology show
in Boston.

Former President of the American Federation of Astrologers Oscar Weber currently is host to an ambitious astrological radio show on WRYT in Boston on Saturdays and Sun-
days at 1:30 and Monday through Friday at 12:15 P.M.

In Montgomery, Alabama, Erie Clay Watts, a member of
the AFA, has a daily radio program of WFMI.

The television show on astrology you're most likely to
see, on a syndicated basis, is Metromedia's *Panorama,* originating on WTTG-TV in Washington, D.C. The hostess for
the astrological segment of *Panorama* is typical of the new
breed of knowledgeable, educated astrologers. Margot Mason
is an attractive author of several substantial books, and the
owner of the entire astrological library of world-famed Evan-
geline Adams, who won astrology's case in a New York
courtroom in the early 1930's by accurately interpreting (in
great detail) the chart of an unknown person who turned
out to be the judge's son. Born in Denver, Colorado, Miss
Mason has traveled extensively throughout the world, studied
at several universities and researched astrology, its history
and origins, in many countries. Her insight and philosophy
have resulted in one of the most popular television presenta-
tions of astrology in the nation.

A husky astrological intellectual, and confidant of world-
famous personalities, is Sydney Omarr, author, magazine
editor, and former CBS news editor in Los Angeles. With astrologers such as Omarr, Margot Mason, Oscar Weber and
Chicago's Katherine de Jersey continually presenting a rational picture of the ancient scientific art, the National Asso-

ciation of Broadcasters may well withdraw their overall line against programs encouraging interest in astrology.

It would be impossible to give a complete list of all the contributors to *astrologia sana* in one book. The best service I can perform here is to list (a minority) of the teachers and practitioners of astrology who have allowed their names to be listed in the *Bulletin* of the AFA. This list is compiled alphabetically by states and countries. Each astrologer listed has subscribed to the Code of Ethics of the American Federation of Astrologers. The AFA has not, however, conducted tests as to the teaching ability or astrological knowledge of each individual. "Because of their adherence to the high ethical standards of the Federation, it is believed each person listed is qualified as outlined," the AFA states, though, adding that, "Any violation of ethical standards should be brought to the attention of the Executive Secretary, AFA, 6, Library Court, S.E., Washington, D.C. 20003."

ARIZONA

Carl Payne Tobey, Route 2, Box 770, Tucson, Arizona 85715 (Natal astrology) (Practitioner—one who practices astrology—*future* transits of planets and the general conditions of the life, not specific events.)

ARKANSAS

Caryl Holmes (Miss), 1116 Stage Coach Road, Little Rock, Arkansas (Practitioner).

Gussie H. Moore, 1305 Greenwood Ave., Hot Springs (Solar astrology, personal instruction, practitioner).

CALIFORNIA

Lucille L. Adams, 2019 Keates St., San Diego, Calif. 92106 (Natal astrology taught. Practitioner).

Fritzi Armstrong, 435 Powell St., San Francisco 2, Calif. (Teaches all branches. Practitioner).

Grace Clements DeLuce, Box 32005, El Sereno Station, Los Angeles, Calif. 90032 (Practitioner).

Angela Diamond, 13939 Victory Blvd., Van Nuys, Calif. 91401 (Teacher, natal astrology, personal instruction. Practitioner).

Doris Chase Doane, 2337 Coral St., Los Angeles, Calif. 90031 (Teaches all branches. Courses by class, private or mail).

Daisy M. Duvall (Miss), 1290 Wynn Road, Pasadena, Calif. P1107 (Teaches natal astrology, rectification, calculation, progressions and primary arcs. Personal and class instruction).

Alyse Forrey (Miss), 16114 Marlinton Drive, Whittier, Calif. 90604 (Teaches all branches. Research. Practitioner).

Patricia Franklin, 480 Larch Lane, Santa Cruz, Calif. (Teaches natal astrology. Personal instruction. Practitioner).

Dr. I. J. Gibson (Miss), 5025 7th Ave., Sacramento, Calif. (Teaches natal astrology. Practitioner).

Norma Hammond, 4767 Reinhardt Drive, Oakland, Calif. (Teaches all branches. Personal, class instruction. Practitioner).

Henry Robert Hazell, 106 Sanchez St., Apt. 11, San Francisco, Calif. 94114 (Teaches all branches. Personal instruction. Practitioner).

Ivy M. Jacobson, 6374 N. Encinita Ave., Temple City, Calif. 91780 (Teaches natal astrology. Personal, class and mail instruction. Practitioner).

Pauline Jordan, 5132 Lincoln Ave., Los Angeles, Calif. 90042 (Practitioner. Natal and progressed horoscopes).

Frances Cleveland Karle, 760 Cambridge Ave., Menlo Park, Calif. (Practitioner. Natal and progressed horoscopes).

Lota Kempster, 807-A East Pedregosa St., Santa Barbara, Calif. (Teaches natal and mundane astrology. Personal and class instruction. Practitioner).

Mayne Kenny, 2915 West 67th St., Los Angeles, Calif. 90043 (Teaches natal astrology, progressions. Personal instruction).

Margaret Latvala, 4437 Alpha St., Los Angeles, Calif. 90032 (Teaches natal astrology. Personal instruction).

Mabel Lytton, 2511 Kent St., Los Angeles, Calif. 90026 (Teaches natal astrology. Personal instruction).

Franka Moore (Miss), 8254 Oakdale, Canoga Park, Calif. (Teaches natal astrology. Practitioner).

Burton W. Morse, 2141 Seville Ave., Balboa, Calif. (Teaches natal astrology. Personal instruction. Practitioner).

Lois O. Navarre, 1127 Harding St., Long Beach 5, Calif. (Practitioner).

Dale Richardson, 4664 Lilycrest Ave., Los Angeles, Calif. 90029 (Practitioner).

Dane Rudhyar, P.O. Box 636, San Jacinto, Calif. 92383 (Teaches natal and mundane or State astrology. Practitioner).

Mabel Schultz, 18409 Citrus Edge St., Azusa, Calif. 91702 (Practitioner).

Phyllis E. Stanick, 748 Orange St., Long Beach, Calif. 90813 (Teaches natal astrology).

W. O. Sucher, 5410 Agnes Ave., North Hollywood, Calif. 91607 (Teaches heliocentric, combination of heliocentric and geocentric astrology).

Joseph R. Viracola, P.O. Box 1853, Beverly Hills, Calif. (Teaches natal astrology. Practitioner).

COLORADO

Dr. Howard W. Polk, D.C., 30 West Nevada Place, Denver 23, Colorado (Teaches natal, medical astrology. Personal instruction).

Muriel Thomas (Miss), P.O. Box 1080, Pueblo, Colorado 81002 (Teaches natal astrology. Class instruction).

CONNECTICUT

Ruth Gerry, R.F.D. #1, Box 183, North Windham, Conn. 06256 (Teaches natal astrology. Personal instruction. Practitioner).

DISTRICT OF COLUMBIA

Catharine T. Grant and Ernest A. Grant, 631 East Capitol St., Washington, D.C. 20003 (Teaches all branches. Class, private and mail. Instruction. No horoscope delineation by mail).

FLORIDA

Irene T. Beale, Route 2, Box 360, Winter Haven, Florida 33882 (Teaches natal and progressed astrology. Personal instruction only).

Margaret Gilbert, 3220 Empedrado, Tampa, Florida 32935 (Practitioner).

Phyllis D. Harrison, 1935 Tyler Ave., Eau Gallie, Fla. 32935 (Teaches natal astrology. Practitioner. Child guidance according to astrology).

Pearl I. Markowitz, 7411 S.W. 63rd Court, Miami, Fla. 33143 (Teaches natal astrology. Class instruction only).

M. Dean Schumaker, 709 8th Ave., Palmetto, Fla. 33561 (Teaches natal, vocational guidance according to natal chart. Personal instruction).

ILLINOIS

Charles E. Goldsmith, Box 7383, Main Post Office, Chicago, Ill. 60680 (Practitioner).

Hortense H. M. Gottschall (Miss), 3508 N. Pine Grove Ave., Chicago 13, Ill. (Teaches natal, heliocentric, geocentric astrology. Personal and class instruction. Practitioner).

INDIANA

Carol V. Wilson, 3456 Winthrop Ave., Indianapolis, Indiana 46205 (Teaches natal astrology. Class and private instruction only).

KANSAS

Mildred Schuler (Miss), 3004 East 13th St., Wichita, Kansas 67214 (Teaches mundane and natal astrology. Class instruction).

LOUISIANA

Evna Edmundson, 1021 Royal St., New Orleans 16, Louisiana (Teaches natal astrology as a philosophy. Class and private instruction).

Edna G. Rowland, 2150 Beech St., Baton Rouge, Louisiana (Practitioner).

MARYLAND

John A. Csepely, 2825 Hollins Ferry Road, Baltimore, Maryland 21230 (Practitioner. Natal astrology).

MASSACHUSETTS

Clara V. Cotta, 30 Canterbury Road, Newton Highlands 61, Mass. (Teaches natal astrology. Personal instruction. Practitioner).

Joan Harmon, 6 James St., Holbrook, Mass. 02343 (Practitioner).

Isabel M. Hickey, 95 St. Botolph St. 2nd Floor, Boston 15, Mass. (Teaches natal, esoteric astrology. Personal instruction. Practitioner).

Muriel D. Jay, 11 Bates Road, Lexington, Mass. 02173 (Teaches natal astrology. Personal and mail instruction. Practitioner).

Leonora K. Luxton, 39 Pembroke Road, Weston, Mass. 02193 (Teaches natal, mundane astrology. Personal, class and mail instruction. Practitioner).

Dorothea Lynde, 51 Belle Ave., West Roxbury, Mass. 02132 (Teaches natal astrology. Private and class instruction. Practitioner).

Oscar Weber, 58 Birchcroft Road, Canton, Mass. 02121 (Teaches natal astrology. Private and class instruction. Practitioner).

MICHIGAN

Betty Jean Barron, 3200 Raynell, Lansing, Mich. 48910 (Teaches natal astrology. Practitioner).

Velma S. Benham, 5237 Commonwealth, Detroit 8, Mich. (Teaches all branches. Personal, class instruction. Practitioner).

Rosyl Savage, 153 N. Prairie Road, Comstock, Michigan (Teaches natal astrology. Personal and class instruction only).

MISSOURI

Pauline S. Johnson, 6632 Prospect Ave., Kansas City, Missouri 64132 (Teaches natal astrology. Class and private instruction).

Faye Kershaw, 4970 Eichelberger, St. Louis 9, Missouri (Teaches all branches of natal astrology. Practitioner).

NEBRASKA

Elizabeth Marie Glackin, 2218 S. 43rd St., Omaha, Nebraska 68105 (Practitioner).

NEW HAMPSHIRE

Clifford W. Cheasley, 400 D. Gage Hill Road, Pelham, New Hampshire 03076 (Teaches natal astrology, also astrology-numerology. Personal, class and mail instruction. Practitioner).

NEW JERSEY

Dorothy Allison, 118 Raymond Ave., Nutley, New Jersey 07116 (Teaches natal astrology. Class and private instruction. Practitioner).

George J. McCormack, 39-25 Wenonah Drive, Fair Lawn, N.J. 07411 (Subject taught: astro-meteorology only, a specialization. Practitioner: astro-meteorology only).

Stella Voorhees, 26 Woodcrest Ave., Short Hills, N.J. (Teaches astro-psychology, philosophy. Personal and class instruction).

NEW MEXICO

Wanda J. Schenck, 263 Gene St. N.W., Albuquerque, N.M. 87107 (Teaches natal astrology. Personal and class instruction. Practitioner).

NEW YORK

Virginia Anderson, 166 Hawthorne Ave., Yonkers, N.Y. 10705 (Teaches natal astrology. Personal, class instruction. Practitioner).

Celestine M. Biddle, 6925 Maple Dr., North Tonawanda, N.Y. 14120 (Teaches natal astrology. Private instruction).

Doris Kaye MacAlduff (Miss), 22 East 38th St., New York, N.Y. 10016 (Practitioner).

Lynne Palmer (Miss), 500 E. 77th St., Apt. 315, New York, N.Y. 10021 (Teaches natal astrology. Personal instruction. Practitioner).

NORTH CAROLINA

Bertha A. Burger, P.O. Box 20375, Charlotte, North Carolina 28202 (Teaches natal astrology, rectification of birth time. Practitioner).

OHIO

Clara M. Darr, 2527 Broadway, Toledo 9, Ohio (Teaches natal astrology. Class and personal instruction. Practitioner).

Catherine G. Hill, 442 Liberty St., Painesville, Ohio 44077 (Teaches natal astrology. Class and personal instruction).

Dr. Regina E. Lorr, D.C., 14940 Euclid Avenue, East Cleveland, Ohio (Teaches natal astrology. Personal and class instruction. Practitioner).

Robert O. Wonder, Route 3, Box 93, Tiffin, Ohio (Teaches general astrology, conventional system).

OREGON

Helen H. McFarland, 405 New Fliedner Building, 1017 S.W. Washington St., Portland, Oregon 97205 (Teaches natal astrology. Personal instruction. Practitioner).

PENNSYLVANIA

Wilma H. Baird, 1824 72nd Ave., Philadelphia, Pa. 19126 (Teaches natal astrology. Class, personal instruction).

Martha E. Knotts, 619 Allegheny Ave., Pittsburgh 33, Pa. (Teaches all branches. Class and private instruction).

TEXAS

Beatrice J. Jameson (Miss), P.O. Box 595, San Antonio, Texas 78206 (Teaches natal astrology. Private, class, mail instruction. Practitioner).

UTAH

Elsbeth Weidemann, 474 L St., Salt Lake City 3, Utah (Teaches natal and mundane astrology. Personal, class or mail instruction. Practitioner).

WASHINGTON

Helene S. Birondo (Miss), P.O. Box 82, Anacortes, Washington 98221 (Teaches elementary astrology. Personal, mail instruction. Practitioner).

WISCONSIN

Florence F. Linn, 1812 College Ave., Racine, Wisconsin (Teaches natal and esoteric astrology. Personal, class instruction).

FOREIGN

(There are many more foreign astrologers; only those who are members of the American Federation of Astrologers are listed here.)

CANADA

Florence L. Fraser, 4987 Earles Street, Vancouver 16, British Columbia, Canada (Teaches natal astrology, class and mail instruction. Practitioner).

H. S. D. Starnaman, 337 Bain Ave., Toronto 6, Ontario, Canada (Teaches all branches. Personal and class instruction. Correspondence courses).

Ida White, P.O. Box 77, Mont-Rolland, Terrebonne, Quebec, Canada (Teaches natal astrology. Personal instruction).

ENGLAND

Timothy J. Nichol, 46 Fernshaw Road, London, S.W. 10, England (Teaches general astrology).

PARIS—BRUSSELS—SWITZERLAND

Germaine Holley, 127 rue du Ranelagh, Paris 16, France (Teaches natal astrology. Personal and class instruction. She conducts classes in Paris, Brussels and Switzerland).

HUNGARY

Dr. Alexander Barna, 21 Attila St., Budapest, Hungary (Teaches natal astrology. Instruction by mail).

INDIA

G. Sri Rama Murthi, Director, Bharat Astrology Institute, Tekkali P.O., Eastern Railway, Srikakulam District, Andhra Pradesh, India (Teaches Hindu, predictive astrology, Parasara, Jaimini and Tajick systems. Class, private, mail instruction. Practitioner).

JAPAN

Toshitake Hifumi, 400 Hiyoshicho Kohoku-ku, Yokahama, Japan (Teaches natal and mundane astrology. Personal and mail instruction. Practitioner).

NEW ZEALAND

Reginald Howan, G.P.O. Box No. 904, Aukland, New Zealand (Teaches all branches of astrology. Personal and class instruction. Practitioner).

These then, are a fair sampling of the astrologers available to the general public. Among the more prominent astrologers who teach and lecture on a regular basis is Marc Edmund Jones, Ph.D., Route 1, Box 629, Stanwood, Washington. Dr. Jones was a pioneer motion picture writer, a successful writer of magazine stories, and subsequently a scholar who is considered among the few top cerebral American astrologers. Dr. Jones is responsible for a long list of rather weighty astrological and philosophical books that form the basis of much of American astrology.

"I'm afraid," said the erudite Dr. Jones, when I talked to him about this book, "that astrology is still 90 percent fortune-telling." This is the general opinion of the handful of *intellectuals* who also happen to be astrologers, including Sydney Omarr, Carl Payne Tobey, George J. McCormack, Virginia R. Anderson, Dane H. Rudhyar and several others.

In one of his letters to me, Dr. Jones suggested, "Perhaps you can be an effective figure in changing the picture, and so again all strength to your good right arm! I find myself very lonely in my own attempts in that direction."

I'm not really certain I understand what *"fortune-telling"* is. In fact there is much about astrology that dazzles and baffles me, even after years of study. Though I lay no claim to being the best student of astrology, I do confidently perceive, however dimly, that almost diminished ray of wisdom which persists in shining from astrology, despite all orthodox resistance to the idea—and, even more importantly, despite the fads, fallacies, superstitions and often Godawful notions of those who merely fancy themselves astrologers.

In the final analysis the astrologer you can depend on is the one who consistently comes up with accurate charts and analyses. It need not be 100 percent of the time, but he should certainly produce a far higher percentage of "hits" than you could expect from purely random guessing. It may seem that I've downgraded some ideas in these pages that simply did not appeal to me. Not so. I'm all for using anything that *works*. It makes not a whit of difference to me what anyone thinks, regardless of his "authority" or "expertise," and despite his academic qualifications, if a system proves effective.

What really matters is: does astrology work? This question implies, of course, that we must evaluate the beyond-chance hits made by those studying certain recurring conditions in the surrounding universe.

It has been my experience, despite all "reliable" and "authoritative" orthodox experts, that what is generally referred to as astrology does indeed work—and with an amazingly high incidence of accuracy! And this despite all the fraud, fakery and charlatanism that unscrupulous characters have heaped on the study.

Try it and see. You've nothing to lose; you may gain enormous insight into human nature, not to mention an expanded philosophy.

Some of my best friends are astrologers who recognize our Oneness with the planet on which we live. We have much more in common than we have begun to realize.

17

Fate vs. Free Will

Using the rule of Occam's Razor (i.e., the simplest explanation is usually the most accurate), the reason for the general academic reluctance to adopt serious studies of astrology is not generated by a lack of acceptable evidence, but largely because the majority of us suspect that there is something fatalistic about it. In a sense, the idea of complete freedom is a fetish in this country, and at this time in history. We refuse, many of us, to think about any limitations on our freedom.

In the memory banks of the world's most sophisticated computers, and in all of us (scientist and layman alike) there seems to be a powerful aversion to anything that could change our accepted view of Life—particularly human consciousness and its essential meaning. *Any* kind of change is uncomfortable, but when it affects our basic concepts we tend to regard it as a revolutionary threat.

To refuse to consider the evidence for cosmic influence on our world is against all the stated principles of science. This stance is irrational, perhaps neurotic. But so is the fear that generates the irrationality. Most laymen tend to overlook the fact that scientists are human beings cursed (or blessed) with the same kind of prejudices, and bias, as any other cross-section of humanity.

One powerful argument in favor of the astrological thesis that we are strongly influenced by celestial forces, is that human events tend to occur in various kinds of cycles. Accordingly, we can therefore expect a reversal of present scientific attitudes to the idea that humanity's destiny hinges on *exogenous forces*. This would simply be the conclusion of one cycle and the beginning of another.

Suppose that at an indeterminate future date, when a network of the largest computer memory banks in the world exists, someone decides to ask a central input station a crucial question about human subjective consciousness and free will. I submit that, given all the data, a computer will respond that human beings have only a fractional control over their destiny.

To discipline the mind so that thinking is channeled in a desired direction indicates a certain amount of freedom of choice. Left to its own "free and normal" functioning, the brain (or mind) operates somewhat like ordinary light, i.e., a seemingly indiscriminate rambling off in all directions. An ordinary electric light, for example, radiates on many wavelengths at once. Technically this kind of light is called "incoherent."

A laser beam, on the other hand, is a fine example of disciplined or "coherent" light. Trillions of photons from a laser are traveling on the same wavelength—"in step," so to speak—like a battalion of soldiers in precision march across a bridge. Long before Roman legions conquered the Mediterranean world, military men knew what happened when troops marched across a bridge in synchronized motion. Ultimately this regular pounding either weakened or demolished the bridge. To avoid this, soldiers were ordered to break step and walk in a kind of random, chaotic fashion, thus neutralizing the effect of a regular beat.

Whenever any purposeful efforts, be they marching troops, beams of intensely coherent light, or concentrated human thought, are used for a clearly defined ultimate purpose, we have excellent examples of the kind of discipline that strongly supports the case for free will. Randomness and chaos, on the other hand, characterize a *lack* of free choice, either in science, social psychology or in our personal lives.

Even a cursory study of human history makes our cherished belief in free will an elusive matter at best. The fact that a chemist can unfailingly predict the result of combining two parts hydrogen to one part oxygen to produce water is perfect proof of the existence of a natural law which unfailingly *permits* it. It has never been even loosely determined to what degree humans are governed by exogenous forces. The entire idea of outside influence is usually shrugged off as violently contradictory to the beliefs we so dearly cherish. The great majority of people throughout known history seem to have blindly accepted the dogma that each man is a free agent, entirely capable of exercising, if not willing to exercise, his freedom of choice.

This belief has never been scientifically challenged. All authority, both secular and clerical, promotes and supports it. Orthodox science, which, like logic, is only one of the avenues approaching reality, aids and abets the universally accepted notion that all human beings have a God-given free will, and that animals function solely by instinct (whatever that is).

The mere mention of the credibility of the opposite idea triggers all the time-worn clichés (and often brings down the wrath) of the sizable majority. It seems to be in the vested interest of leaders in every age of history to support the belief that man has a divine free choice in all his affairs, and that what he makes of his life is entirely his own responsibility.

There's a certain "necessity" about this. World leaders, law enforcement officials, the clergy and most people seem to distrust human nature and fear the consequences if it should ever be proved that we are *not* entirely self-determining creatures. It's a paradoxical situation, an irrational stance.

We should have *some* faith in our institutions! That which we call civilization seems to work—more or less. But on the other hand, so do, for example, those colonies of industrious insects: ants, bees and termites, which operate by "instinct." They don't engage in self-destructive wars, a fact that may explain our relative dominance over them, because conflict, struggle and strife have resulted in most of mankind's greatest advances.

Egyptian astrologers were familiar with the cycles of civilization. (The phoenix was their symbol of death—and resurrection from the ashes of the old.) They weren't such believers in divinely given free will.

Item: Whenever this concept of free will is closely examined, some rather unnerving facts emerge. Certainly the freedom of a young soldier drafted into service during wartime is sharply curtailed. What are the chances of a child born blind to become a brain surgeon, for example? What chance has a low-grade moron of becoming a business executive—or for that matter, of leading a well-ordered life? It may be symbolic that, aside from the death penalty, the worst punishment our society metes out to its law offenders is imprisonment—the curtailing of physical freedom. In all of us there is a distinct dread of having our freedom taken away. This is reflected in the constitutions of the world's democracies. It is as though all humans instinctively, subconsciously recognize the flimsiness of the idea of personal independence. To lose what little we have is a tragic event.

Even "unreasoning" animals will fight to avoid being caged or trapped. On the other hand, there are times when we willingly trade some of our freedom for a seemingly greater long-range benefit.

As far as we know, no one has ever been known to request his or her existence. Life is thrust on us. Each comes into a world not of his making and (to a greater or lesser degree) is impelled along a life path by forces both tangible and intangible. With magnificent hindsight we understand the inevitability of someone else's life—given a certain set of circumstances to begin with. We can't, however, be objective about ourselves. The question is, what are the known, visible or tangible forces? I submit that it is rather like Newton's Third Law of Motion—applied to human events. (For every action there is an opposite and equal reaction.)

Most of us have only the faintest idea that this law could exist. Each decision we make is boobytrapped with conditions over which we have no control. Thus the man who is weary of commuting to his office, but hates to live in the city, and still has to make a living, obviously cannot get off the treadmill. The skeins are wound even tighter if he hates his job or happens to be frustrated in some other area of his life.

"But there are escape mechanisms," the old argument states: "There are any number of 'outs' for anyone who wants to use them. He can play golf—or take a vacation. He can quit his job and go into another field—or simply do some hard drinking."

Choose any solution. Theoretically, the alternatives are almost infinite. The trick of fate is that he can "choose" no more than one at a time—and usually brings about certain other *inevitable* conditions as a result of his choice.

There is simply no way of knowing with certainy whether our choices are truly free or if they are the inevitable, predictable outcome of everything that has happened before. If there is one thing most astrologers, astronomers, chemists, politicians and clergymen unilaterally agree on it is the theorem: "Man possesses a free will." Yet some of the most learned men of all ages were essentially astrologers who could cast the horoscopes of infants and accurately foretell

the kind of human beings those babies would become. Not
in vague, general terms, but in specific detail, such as personality, intelligence, talents, accomplishment, ailments and
(most important) the motivating force of the deeper individuality.

Consider evolution and the statement, "Man is a free
agent endowed with high intelligence and conscience—and
is therefore accountable for all his acts." In essence, this
has been the attitude of orthodox authority of every age in
every land. It seems to be a crucial necessity. If *any* Establishment (itself buffeted by invisible forces it neither recognizes nor understands) were to concede that intangible
forces *might* be shaping man's destiny, the fear is that the
status quo would be forced to make changes that might lead
to its downfall.

Again, evolution. The residue of 19th Century materialism
and Victorianism has sullied the world outlook of several
generations. These views, originally the "Divine Right" of
kings, and now the very idea of authority itself, are mutually
exclusive alternatives, currently being questioned by the new
generation.

It is relevant that this particular world cycle was predicted
by many sages, seers and astrologers. History possesses a
certain inevitability. To those who understand it, the occurrences we call great world events do *not* come as a shock.
The assassination which led to World War I (and ultimately
to World War II and the Cold War) was predictable. In fact,
it *was* prophesied. To some it is a horrible thought that the
future might be a foregone conclusion. Yet there are many
clear predictions about coming events in the world.

We reject them because they imply that we have little or
nothing to say about the future. If he'd known about it in
advance, how could President Franklin D. Roosevelt have
prepared America for a space race or a manned voyage to
Mars? How serious was this prospect to anyone in authority
before or during World War II? Yet these are modern
realities, the existence of which was curtained by a couple of
decades of time.

And yet we can see the historic necessity of one great
event triggering another, of Soviet Russia's launching of
Sputnik I and the subsequent technological contest. There's
a certain *inevitability* about all sequences of events; they
occur in a certain order due to ironclad necessity. America
couldn't have been defeated by Japan or Germany, just as

it was impossible for Hitler to have successfully invaded Russia. The tides of history were against him.

You don't have to be an astrologer to foresee the radical changes wrought by the present questioning of all institutions. Fewer and fewer people believe there are matters that should *not* be questioned. There are few sanctuaries left for the True Believer; the bulwarks of materialism and Victorianism are disintegrating. In the next ten years the world will change more than it has during the past two hundred. Predictably so.

Consider Teilhard de Chardin: "It is an extraordinary thing. Scientists for the last hundred years have been examining, with unheard of subtlety and daring, the mysteries of material atoms and the living cell. They have weighed the electron and the stars. They have dissected hundreds of thousands of specimens of the vegetable and animal world. They are striving with infinite patience to link the human form anatomically to that of the other vertebrates. They endeavor to examine the springs of human psychology, or to isolate the laws governing the exchanges of products and services in the growing complexity of our society. Now in the midst of these great labours, almost nobody has yet decided to put the main question: 'But what exactly is the phenomenon of man?' That is to say in rather more precise terms: 'What is the place and purpose of this extraordinary power of thought in the development of the world of experience?' " (Pierre Teilhard de Chardin's *The Vision of the Past*.)

More evolution: the materialistic scientific establishment would have us believe that certain molecular ingredients were formed by some mysterious process in the backwaters of Earth's primordial seas—and that, as a result of natural forces, Life simply evolved into ever more complex living organisms—*without* teleological direction—*without* intelligence or purpose. Such a stance makes Life a monstrous accident. Man is peculiarly adapted to the electromagnetic-gravitational field in the Earth, Sun, Moon and planets. There is no certainty that he can exist with the alien astrology of a different planet.

This evolution is a tricky thing. Did some of those ancient amino acid and carbon molecules possess the free choice necessary for them to "decide" to evolve into what is currently the most sophisticated form of vertebrate life on Earth? No one is prepared to state what the bees or ants might "think," but it is obvious that they *are* industrious, that they *are* social and tend to group together. Instinct, or free will?

No answer has yet been found. Man also seeks the compan-
ionship of his own kind.

Each spring teeming throngs of young people at Fort
Lauderdale, Florida, gather along a narrow stretch of beach
about one hundred yards long. An empty beach stretches for
miles on either side of this mass of humanity.

Fish travel in schools, wolves in packs, cattle in herds and
lions in prides. Considering the law of self-preservation, it is
probably safe to assume that every living creature possesses
a faculty somewhat like the human ego. Seals, walruses and
sea elephants battle each other over possession of a harem.
Business executives cling to precarious positions while the
younger men try to stake out their own precarious claim in
the corporate structure. Humanity probably has more in
common with other species than it suspects.

If those primordial molecules did *not* decide to evolve, then
Life as we know and understand it is eternally *acted upon*
by invisible, as yet unknown forces which shape its destiny, create its myriad forms, and once pushed Homo
Sapiens into his present precarious position of world dominance.

According to the ever-changing cycle or style of this age,
man is a self-determining creature, capable of bringing order
out of the simmering cauldron of history. Communists in
Russia and China really believe they have pulled it off. Like
a good novel, history has the characteristic of inevitability.
Officially America has thrown off the yoke of colonialism and
proclaims itself a model of democracy for the rest of the
world. This is entirely relative. We consider ourselves lib-
erators; many countries believe we are oppressors and that
the Reds point toward ordered freedom. The odd thing about
these basically humanitarian revolutions are (a) that each
has subsequently inflicted on weaker nations the same conditions they fought to overthrow and (b) that long before
they occurred, all revolutions were predicted by someone,
somewhere. Any predictable event is charged with the aura
of inevitability. Neither a nation nor its leaders and people
have any choice in a truly unavoidable situation; a sky diver
might just as well try to "fall" upward!

When science states that if you do thus and so, *this* condition must inevitably follow, and then it works out as predicted, you are dealing with an inflexible natural law. If astrologers through the ages have noted a tendency for wars to
follow eclipses where "malefic" planets were in evil aspect to
the eclipse—and then those wars happened on schedule—

our *collective* free will probably adds up to not much above zero.

Yet these are the actual conditions with which we are faced and under which we are forced to live. We're able to accept an obvious fact if it is not too troublesome or painful. But all of us *are* swept along by the tides of history. No one is immune to the peculiar influence of his own age.

One interesting corollary in astrology is the tendency for each generation to typify the influence of positions of the outer (more ponderous) planets. Neptune is a huge, banded-atmosphere planet four times the size of Earth and takes nearly 165 years to perform one orbit of the Sun. In terrestrial nature there are many cycles of 165 years to correlate with Neptune's orbit. By the same token, Uranus, another banded giant of a planet, exerts its influence on several generations. Uranus takes 84 years and four days to complete one cycle of the Sun. Saturn's 29½-year solar orbit coincides with hundreds of terrestrial cycles. And Jupiter, the giant of the solar system, larger than all other planets combined, has the clearest relationship to Earthly cycles. Its 11.80-year orbital period also conforms to the major Sunspot cycle, which is widely known to influence barometric changes, ionospheric disturbances and the commodity and stock market.

The fact that many of these planetary cycles are interlaced has created some difficulty for astro-economists like Lt. Cmdr. David Williams in sorting out the correlations for impatient skeptics. It took mankind long eons to trace the connection between planetary orbits and the things influenced by each body. Since the discovery of Pluto in 1931, many interesting studies are being made of its influence. By far the most intriguing was made by Spengler in his *Cycles of Civilization*. Pluto's orbit of the Sun takes about 250 years. Tracing this increment far back into ancient Chinese civilization, Spengler found that the overthrow of one dynasty took place when Pluto was at its perigee (closest approach to the Sun) *station* every 125 years. A century and a quarter later, when Pluto was at its aphelion station, conditions began changing for yet another dynastic change, when Pluto once more came to its closest solar approach.

Moreover, the capital of China was continually reestablished every 250 years (right on the "click" of the planetary dial, so to speak), first in northern China, and then in southern China, for as far back as Chinese records of civilization are available.

Astrologers since ancient times have known what Dr.

Richard Head of the National Aeronautics and Space Administration's Electronics Research Center is just discovering that Jupiter's colossal moon is largely responsible for great solar magnetic storms, especially every 12 years when the giant planet comes closest to the Sun. Solar flares and magnetic storms cause enormous changes in our ionosphere. In 1965 the National Engineering Science Co. reported that ionospheric disturbances also affected the troposphere, and thus *all* lower atmospheric conditions (as astro-meteorologists since Hipparchus have claimed).

Furthermore, the cavity between the Earth's surface and the ionosphere is regarded by scientists these days as a completely resonant system: its characteristic resonance is about one-eighth of a second, the exact time it takes for light to speed once around the Earth.

As electronics science editor Rex Pay pointed out in the May 15, 1967, issue of *Technology Week*, this resonant frequency is thus 8 cps (eight cycles per second), which is congruent with that of the Alpha rhythm of the human brain. The geomagnetic field, therefore, provides the "fine tuning mechanism for this characteristic frequency."

Dr. Robert O. Becker, orthopedic surgeon at Syracuse Veterans Administration Hospital and New York's Upstate Medical Center, has discovered that human behavior is predictably affected by changes in this frequency, by fluctuations in the geomagnetic field (which subtly but powerfully affects the human biomagnetic field), and by the angular positions of the planets in their orbits.

Dr. Becker regards ancient astrological theories concerning unseen celestial and terrestrial forces not simply as superstitious nonsense, but as the basis for a new super-science of the future. As *Technology Week* stated: "The positions of the planets probably plays a much larger part in human affairs than anyone previously supposed. From this point of view, one of the most important reasons for sending man to the Moon is to see what happens to his behavior after chronic exposure to a very low magnetic field."

As long ago as 1962, Dr. Becker warned an international space symposium of grave dangers to astronauts when they invaded the interplanetary environment with its wildly fluctuating electromagnetic fields.

One of the most important aspects of science is the fact that increased knowledge seems to give us proportionate control over the forces of Nature. Relatively speaking, we have not even begun to ask the correct questions. We cling to outmoded, obviously superstitious beliefs, one of which is that man is solely responsible for all that happens in history. Both Toynbee's and Spengler's studies have shown the real extent of man's control of history. As long as we accept an ego-centric view of life, our control of Nature will remain minimal, at best.

If humanity actually did control such forces, history would *never* be changed by droughts, earthquakes, ice ages, floods or widespread disease. If we cannot perceive a cause-effect mechanism to the limitations on our freedom, we are unwilling to accept life as it is.

A hurricane stops a sailing we had planned; we accept the necessity of that. The Cold War prevents us from visiting China or Cuba; we accept that. Earth's deadly radiation belts thwart the efforts of astronauts to travel to the planets. We accept these limitations because they are tangible—and so huge that we cannot possibly control them.

And yet, humanity is enclosed by many more invisible cages—intangible prisons. With hard realism, most of us must eventually reconcile ambitions and goals with personal abilities. Men are *not* all created equal, however much we may want to hold this truth to be evident. Many potential financiers are forced by conditions beyond their control to make a living as clerks. Millions of us are frozen at various rungs on what we call the ladder of success. The style of this materialistic age is such that almost everyone wants to reach the top. The harsh reality is that only a relative few manage to achieve "success" (which means many things to many people).

No one has ever explained, fairly and fully, to the talented boy who wants to become a fine writer, artist, or musician why he winds up as a hack—or worse yet, apparently destroys his own talent. Charles E. Luntz' book, *Vocational Guidance by Astrology* gives a good picture of the life potential in every horoscope. Each chart has, by definition, a great deal of inevitability and a comparatively slim margin for error. Acceptance of a relative kind of predestination is not as unwholesome as we may have come to believe. Knowing the truth about ourselves and where we can go from *there* is far more important than the blind belief that we are the lords of creation.

To sum up: there are some areas of free choice; this varies among individuals and in different departments of life. Properly calculated and accurately interpreted, the horoscope will reveal the areas of your greatest freedom of choice,

as well as the most constricted, or compulsive, territory in
your natal chart—and therefore your life.

Predictably, the next important breakthrough in human
knowledge, after the *psi* faculty has been explored and
charted, will be a universal study of the impinging forces of
the universe—and how much control we really have over
our destiny.

This is bound to result in increased freedom and greater
control over our lives, but the fact will probably remain
that a large number of aspects in our lives are simply waiting
there to be experienced. This could be for good or ill; it all
depends on how much of the free will you were born with
you'll decide to use.

Once you've set up the rudimentary chart this book de-
scribes, see how many planets are sextile (two Signs apart)
or trine (four Signs apart); how many are in square (three
Signs apart) or opposition (six Signs apart). Of course, you
won't know the exact *degree* of each planet, or the degrees
of the Signs on the house cusps, but with many trine and
sextiles (as well as conjunctions, i.e., planets together), you
will find you have a greater freedom of choice, and go
through life much more easily, than those with many planets
in opposition or square aspect; the latter are known by astrologers to create obstacles and conflict.

However, it is an observable (albeit paradoxical) fact that
obstacles are regarded by people with strong willpower as
challenges to be overcome. Historically, the greatest achievers
were people with many squares and oppositions in their horoscopes. The secret seems to be that they had many planets
in the fixed Signs, Taurus, Leo, Scorpio and Aquarius. And
since these Signs are in *all* horoscopes, the chances are that
you have one or more planets in these stabilizing Signs.